T0419047

Dispersals and Diversification

Brill's Studies in Indo-European Languages & Linguistics

VOLUME 19

The titles published in this series are listed at *brill.com/bsiel*

Dispersals and Diversification

Linguistic and Archaeological Perspectives on the Early Stages of Indo-European

Edited by

Matilde Serangeli
Thomas Olander

BRILL

LEIDEN | BOSTON

Cover illustration: Female (sister) and male (brother) skeletons from Khvalynsk II. Photo by Igor Borisovich Vasiliev. Copyright Sergey Alexandrovich Agapov (reproduced with permission)

The Library of Congress Cataloging-in-Publication Data is available online at http://catalog.loc.gov
LC record available at http://lccn.loc.gov/2019954948

Typeface for the Latin, Greek, and Cyrillic scripts: "Brill". See and download: brill.com/brill-typeface.

ISSN 1875-6328
ISBN 978-90-04-41450-1 (hardback)
ISBN 978-90-04-41619-2 (e-book)

This book is printed on acid-free paper and produced in a sustainable manner.

Printed by Printforce, the Netherlands

Contents

Preface and Acknowledgements

On 13–15 September 2017 an international interdisciplinary conference, "The Split: Reconstructing early Indo-European language and culture", was organized at the University of Copenhagen by the prospective editors of this book. The speakers were specialists in historical linguistics, comparative mythology and prehistoric archaeology, and the overarching topic of the conference comprised the linguistic stages before and after the dissolution of Proto-Indo-European, as well as the beliefs and cultures of the speakers. By combining the evidence from the disciplines just mentioned and from ancient genetics we aimed at highlighting a formative process in Eurasian prehistory, namely the spread of Indo-European languages.

We are excited that we are now able to present to a broader public the results of the conference. The book contains several of the contributions to the conference as well as further articles focussing on the same questions, and a general introduction to the theoretical and methodological problems of connecting historical linguistics, comparative mythology, prehistoric archaeology and ancient genetics.

We are extremely grateful to the publisher's anonymous peer reviewer, who meticulously and critically read and commented all the submitted articles, which not only cover early Indo-European language and culture from the perspectives of different disciplines, but also present material from a wide array of Indo-European and non-Indo-European languages, from Abkhaz to Zenaga. Without the reviewer's enormous efforts, this book would have been significantly less error-free.

We also wish to wholeheartedy thank H. Craig Melchert, series editor of *Brill's Studies in Indo-European Languages & Linguistics*, for accepting the volume in the series, for his help and support in the editorial process and for his constructive and well-informed comments on all the contributions.

We are furthermore indebted to Benedicte Nielsen Whitehead, who did a critical reading of the contributions and improved the book significantly with her keen editorial eye, and to the Department of Nordic Studies and Linguistics, University of Copenhagen, for financially supporting Benedicte's work with the book.

The conference and this book are among the outcomes of two research projects which were both located at the Roots of Europe Center in the Department of Nordic Studies and Linguistics, University of Copenhagen: Matilde Serangeli's "The Linguistic Origins of Europe: Word-formation and Lexicon in Anatolian and Core Indo-European" (2016–2018, funded by the European

Union's Horizon 2020 Programme under the Marie Skłodowska-Curie grant agreement No 705090) and Thomas Olander's "The Homeland: In the Footprints of the Early Indo-Europeans" (2015–2018, funded by the Carlsberg Foundation). We are very grateful to these foundations for supporting research in the topics treated in this book and for making it possible to disseminate up-to-date knowledge of our intriguing prehistoric past to a broader audience.

Matilde Serangeli
Thomas Olander

Notes on Contributors

David W. Anthony
is an Emeritus Professor at Hartwick College. He specializes in the Eneolithic and Bronze Age societies of the Eurasian steppes, emphasizing Indo-European linguistics and links between archaeology and language, the evolution of Eurasian steppe pastoralism, modeling human migration, and the study of ancient DNA in Eurasian steppe populations.

Rasmus Gudmundsen Bjørn
is a PhD student at the Max Planck Institute for the Science of Human History (Jena). He holds a BA and an MA degree in Indo-European Studies from the University of Copenhagen (2017) with a minor in Norse Philology. His research areas include the formative stages of Proto-Indo-European and the methodology in discerning cognates and loanwords from chance phenomena in prehistory.

José L. García Ramón
is Senior Fellow in Linguistics at the Center for Hellenic Studies (Washington / Harvard University) since 2015, Docente a Contratto at the Università Cattolica del Sacro Cuore (Milan), and corresponding member of the Académie des Inscriptions et des Belles Lettres (Paris). Formerly he served as Professor of Historical–Comparative Linguistics at the University of Cologne (until 2015) and of Greek Philology at the Universidad Autónoma de Madrid. His research centers on morphosyntax, lexicon and onomastics, poetic language and Indo-European reconstruction, with a special interest in Greek (also Mycenaean), Latin and Italic, Indo-Iranian and Anatolian.

Riccardo Ginevra
is a 2019–2020 Fellow at Harvard University's Center for Hellenic Studies. He received his PhD in Historical Linguistics in 2018 from the Università per Stranieri di Siena in joint supervision with the University of Cologne, where he has since been lecturing on Comparative Indo-European Poetics and Mythology.

Adam Hyllested
is a comparative–historical linguist specialized in the prehistory of Eurasian languages, focusing on etymology, language relationship and contacts. He holds an advanced research degree (*magisterkonferens*) in Indo-European

Studies, Uralic Linguistics and Balkanistics, and a PhD in Comparative Linguistics, both from the University of Copenhagen. He is a founding member of the interdisciplinary Roots of Europe Centre at the University of Copenhagen, established 2008.

James A. Johnson
is currently Lecturer in Anthropology at the University of Wyoming. He is Project Director of the Uy River Valley Communities of Practice project in Russia and Lead Director of the Bel'sk Project in Ukraine. His work focuses on exploring the materialized socio-political connections between mobile peoples and place / time, including a comparative examination of how those connections impact local ecologies through time.

Kristian Kristiansen
is Professor of Archaeology at the Department of Historical Studies, University of Gothenburg. His books include *Europe before history* and *The rise of Bronze Age society* (with Thomas B. Larsson), and most recently the co-edited books *Organizing Bronze Age societies* (with Timothy Earle), *Trade and civilization* (with J. Myrdal and T. Lindkvist) and *Warfare in Bronze Age society* (with Christian Horn), all at Cambridge University Press. He is co-editor of the *Critical Heritage Studies Element Series* at Cambridge University Press.

H. Craig Melchert
is Distinguished Professor of Linguistics and A. Richard Diebold Professor of Indo-European Studies Emeritus, University of California, Los Angeles. He previously taught at the University of North Carolina, Chapel Hill, for twenty-nine years. His research centers on historical linguistics, with special emphasis on the Anatolian sub-family of Indo-European. His interests include the modeling of language change, reconstruction of the culture and society of the Proto-Indo-European speech community, and the application of modern linguistic formal theories to ancient Indo-European languages and their prehistory.

Matthew Scarborough
studied Classical Philology and Linguistics at the Universities of Alberta (BA 2009, MA 2011) and Cambridge (PhD 2017). Since 2015 he has been Research Associate in Comparative Indo-European Linguistics in the Department of Linguistic and Cultural Evolution of the Max Planck Institute for the Science for Human History (Jena). His research interests include Ancient Greek dialectology and the application of phylogenetic and quantitative methods to linguistic data for the investigation of cladistic hypotheses.

Peter Schrijver
is Professor of Celtic Languages and Culture at Utrecht University. He specializes in the historical grammar of western Indo-European languages and of Northeast-Caucasian. He is the author of several books, including *Studies in British Celtic historical phonology* and *Language contact and the origins of the Germanic languages*.

Matilde Serangeli
is Research Associate in Comparative Indo-European Linguistics at the Department for Indo-European Studies, Friedrich-Schiller University Jena. Formerly she was a Marie-Curie Postdoc Fellow at the research centre Roots of Europe, University of Copenhagen, and Research Associate at the University of Cologne, where she earned her PhD (2015). Her research focuses on language change in the Indo-European languages, with special attention to the morphology and semantics of Anatolian and Ancient Greek.

Zsolt Simon
holds a PhD degree from the Eötvös Loránd University, Budapest (2013). He is a research associate at the Institut für Assyriologie und Hethitologie, Ludwig-Maximilians-Universität München, and formerly a research fellow at the Research Institute for Linguistics of the Hungarian Academy of Sciences, Budapest, and at Koç University, Istanbul. He is co-author of the Digital Philological–Etymological Dictionary of the Minor Ancient Anatolian Corpus Languages.

Rasmus Thorsø
is a PhD student at the *EUROLITHIC* project (Leiden University), specializing in the history of the Armenian language. He studied Indo-European linguistics at the University of Copenhagen, where he received his MA degree in 2016.

Michael Weiss
is a professor in the Department of Linguistics at Cornell University in Ithaca, N.Y. He is the author of *Language and ritual in Sabellic Italy* (2010) and *Outline of the historical and comparative grammar of Latin* (2nd ed. expected 2019). He has been co-editor of three Festschrifts and has written articles about Latin, Oscan, Umbrian, Greek, Celtic, Indo-Iranian, Slavic, Tocharian, Anatolian, and Proto-Indo-European.

Introduction: Dispersals and Diversification of the Indo-European Languages

Matilde Serangeli

1 Preliminaries

In these years we are witnessing noticeable progress in the understanding of the processes that, by the end of the Neolithic Era, introduced Early Indo-European-speaking communities into Europe and Asia, causing a major shift in the linguistic and cultural landscape. A significant new approach to the Indo-European (IE) question has emerged in the last two decades which analyses the massive migration waves that brought the IE-speaking peoples to Europe and Asia in the light of a series of migration phenomena characterising historical events of the same kind (Anthony 2007). This perfectly matches the diverse and complex linguistic profile of the early IE-speaking communities as suggested by the results from comparative linguistics, and it is, of course, more representative of the reality of interactions between locals and newcomers as known from attested historical events. In the last few years, studies on ancient DNA (aDNA) have validated this approach: the diverse and complex genetic heritage of human remains from the Neolithic and Bronze Age confirms that Eurasian communities moved from one place to another, to some extent mixing with the locals. Thus, it has become increasingly clear that such a complex story cannot be told by a single discipline, as was already pointed out in the pioneering works of Mallory (1997, 1989), Mallory & Adams (2006), and Anthony (2007). The work of these scholars has inspired more systematic collaboration and cooperation between linguistics, archaeology, and genetics that enable scholars to proceed towards more significant results. The next step for IE studies, then, will be to overcome the cultural, genetic, and linguistic boundaries in prehistory and to emphasize the crucial nodes connecting these previously isolated fields.

Dispersals and diversification has been conceived with this purpose in mind. The contributions it contains offer new insights into the processes by which the IE branches separated from the protolanguage, with the common aim to shed light on the multifaceted prehistory of Eurasia and the role that the speakers of early IE played in it. The bulk of the contributions deals with what we call Proto-Indo-European (PIE), the proto-language of all Indo-European languages. Thus, besides two archaeological chapters focussing on the recon-

 | DOI:10.1163/9789004416192_002

struction of the genetic and cultural traits of the early IE-speaking peoples (Anthony, Kristiansen), six chapters focus on the linguistic peculiarities of the Anatolian branch in comparison with non-Anatolian PIE (Simon, Melchert, García Ramón, Ginevra, Hyllested, Bjørn). Three chapters focus on later stages of IE (or PIE *tout court*, see below): two of these are devoted to the Italo-Celtic debate (Schrijver, Weiss), and one to the question of the Balkanic unity (Thorsø). Finally, two chapters consider methodological issues (Johnson, Scarborough).

2 The Archaeological and Genetic Contribution: The Arrival and Settlement of Indo-European Speakers in Europe and Asia

The 5th to 3rd millennia BCE witnessed impressive material and cultural changes that led to a reshaping of Eurasia. Language must have accompanied these changes. Two mutually exclusive prehistorical events are commonly considered to have fostered the arrival and diffusion of IE languages and cultures in Europe and Asia: the Neolithization process, during which agriculture was introduced (Renfrew 1987), and migration waves from the Pontic–Caspian steppes (Gimbutas 1956, 1970, 1977, Anthony 2007). Despite the results of recent studies from phylogenetic linguistics (Bouckaert et al. 2012, Heggarty 2014, 2015, and below § 4), the hypothesis that the IE languages spread in Europe together with the introduction of agriculture from the Fertile Crescent through Anatolia during the Neolithic seems less plausible. The introduction of agriculture was certainly a crucial prehistoric event, but it most probably occurred several millennia earlier than the spread of the IE-speaking peoples. Agricultural techniques developed between the 10th and the 7th millennia BCE in the Fertile Crescent and expanded westwards into Europe, until then occupied by hunters and gatherers, through the immigration of farming populations from Anatolia during the early phase of the Neolithization process. The reconstructed vocabulary of PIE supports neither a leading nor a participative role of the IE-speaking peoples in this process. It rather suggests that early IE-speaking peoples were associated with a pastoral-nomadic culture. In other words, the paucity of PIE words for crops and land cultivation, in stark contrast to the numerous terms for several technological innovations like the wheel, dairy and wool production, speaks against the arrival of the IE-speaking peoples through the introduction of agriculture in Europe (Anthony 2007: 321–322, 440). In addition, most of the scanty agricultural vocabulary does not seem to have an IE origin, which easily suggests that the first European farmers spoke non-IE languages (Iversen & Kroonen 2018: 516 ff.).

By contrast, the expansion of the Yamnaya pastoral–nomadic steppe population about 3300–2700 BCE from the Pontic–Caspian steppes in Eurasia currently represents the best archaeological option for the dispersals and diversification of the IE-speaking populations and their dialects that may have started to expand slightly after 4000 BCE (Gimbutas 1977, Mallory 1989: 183, Anthony 2007, Chang et al. 2015, Kristiansen et al. 2017). As is well known, the hypothesis of the spread of the IE languages with the Yamnaya expansions does not account for the Anatolian branch, which shows linguistic features that allow us to distinguish a so-called early PIE that includes Anatolian (a.k.a. Proto-Indo-Hittite or Proto-Indo-Anatolian) from a late (post-Anatolian) PIE (a.k.a. PIE *tout court*) that does not include it.[1] In particular, the absence of a terminology for wagons in Anatolian on the one hand, and the finding of wooden parts of wagons from Yamnaya sites from the late 4th millennium BCE as well as the wide attestation of a shared terminology for wagons in the non-Anatolian branches of IE on the other, support an earlier separation of the Anatolian branch from the mother language. It would follow that the Yamnaya expansion must have occurred *after* both the Anatolian split and the invention and diffusion of wheeled vehicles—that is, possibly after 3500 BCE. This expansion may have ended earlier than the end of the 3rd millennium BCE, since Anatolian (Hittite) and Indo-Iranic (Old Indic from Mitanni) are already formed branches with documentary attestations by 2500 and 2000 BCE (Kroonen et al. 2018).

As briefly anticipated above, ancient genetics supports this scenario. Two massive migration waves in prehistoric Europe have been confirmed by aDNA analysis: the first one, around 7000 BCE, from Anatolia and the second one, around 3000 BCE, from the Pontic–Caspian steppes (Haak et al. 2015, Allentoft et al. 2015). All samples from IE-speaking populations that have been genetically analysed so far have ancestry from steppe populations. The only exception is Anatolia, which instead shows Caucasian ancestry attested from the Chalcolithic until the Bronze Age (Damgaard et al. 2018, Wang et al. 2018). Interestingly, aDNA reveals a quite unexpected distribution of the genetic components of the Yamnaya populations: those from the Volga-Caspian steppes have about 50% ancestry from Caucasus Hunter-Gatherers (CHG/Iran), indicating a hunter-gatherer population that arrived from the south during the Upper Paleolithic and occupied both the Caucasus Mountains and western Iran, without mixing with Eastern Hunter-Gatherers (EHG) nor with Western Hunter-Gatherers (WHG). The other 50% of Yamnaya ancestry comes from EHG, who repre-

1 For a critical overview of the nomenclature devoted to these two groups see Olander 2019.

sent a variant of the Ancient North Eurasian (ANE) genetic type that was prominently present among hunters and fishers from a region extending from the Eastern Baltic forests to the Ural Mountains, including the Pontic-Caspian steppes to the south. Interestingly, the first samples of Bronze Age individuals from Anatolia show CHG ancestry, but not EHG. This is seen as evidence against a steppe origin for the genetic ancestors of the Hittites (Damgaard et al. 2018, Wang et al. 2018, Kristiansen et al. 2018). Moreover, a low signal of CHG is attested about 6500 BCE in several Neolithic samples from Central Anatolia. The CHG exchange may have occurred around 7000–6500 BCE across an area extended from eastern Anatolia to Transcaucasia and western Iran. In some genomes CHG is mixed together with a small amount of EHG, which suggests a contact between CHG and the EHG from the steppes earlier than the Yamnaya period. Likely, the CHG/Iran element in Yamnaya ancestry was derived from a population living in eastern Anatolia already during the Neolithic. Thus, CHG in Bronze Age Anatolian samples does not imply steppe ancestry, and the CHG/Iran element in the Yamnaya admixture should come from a third source. So far, an ancestor for the CHG/Iran element present in Yamnaya has not been identified. However, two hypotheses have been advanced. First, the Yamnaya admixture might be the result of contacts between CHG and EHG populations in the Pontic–Caspian steppes and Caucasian–Anatolian–Iranian uplands prior to the Yamnaya expansion. Second, the PIE homeland may have been the North Caucasus, and a southern genetic component may have arrived in the Yamnaya populations at some point after the Anatolian split. See David Anthony (1) and Kristian Kristiansen (2) in this volume:

1. Yamnaya ancestry may have emerged in the 4th millennium BCE in the Volga-Caucasus steppes east of the Don. Two factors support this hypothesis: First, the earliest known admixture of EHG and CHG occurred in that area in the 5th mill. BCE, i.e. before the arrival of the Yamnaya. Second, this area may be where PIE was spoken. Possibly, the speakers of an early stage of Anatolian moved from the Volga–Don region into the Danube valley around 4400–4200 BCE together with the steppe peoples of the Suvorovo culture. This would explain the admixture of EEF (Early European Farmer) genes into steppe communities before 4000 BCE. At the same time a close interaction between SE Europe and NW Anatolia increased, especially after the collapse of Old European towns in the Balkans around 4300–4200 BCE. Therefore, contacts between the Balkans and Anatolia go back to a time prior to the initial appearance of Hittite names in documents at Kanesh (1900–1800 BCE). Kroonen et al. (2018) have recently suggested that evidence for that contact may be reflected in Hittite terms attested in the archives of Ebla, which suggest that it may

be possible to trace the Anatolian branch back at least to 2500 BCE and to consider Anatolian to be contemporaneous with the Yamnaya culture (3000–2400 BCE). If this is true, the speakers of Proto-Anatolian cannot possibly descend from the Yamnaya population. That being said, the Anatolian EHG genetic signal may appear very low due to its dilution over two millennia between contacts with the Balkans and the first linguistic attestations of Anatolian. This would support the hypothesis that early PIE and Proto-Anatolian (PA) were spoken around 4500 and 3000 BCE, respectively—surely early PIE split no later than the 4th millennium BCE, leading to PA and to Proto-Indo-Tocharian, i.e. the PIE stage after the Anatolian split (Kloekhorst 2018, Kloekhorst & Pronk 2019). This presupposes that the later Anatolian-speaking peoples separated from a pre-Yamnaya steppe population.

2. CHG/Iran genes required by the Yamnaya admixture from an external-source population may come from the Maikop culture of the North Caucasus, which had a huge impact on the Yamnaya culture from around 3500 BCE onwards. Following this hypothesis, the North Caucasus may be the homeland for both Proto-Anatolian communities, which may have split off from the early Maikop culture, and PIE-speaking communities after the Anatolian split, which may coincide with the Yamnaya culture that arose through the northern expansion of the steppe Maykop culture. Indeed, genetic admixture processes between the Caucasus and Anatolia may have been ongoing since the Chalcolithic: The ancestors of the Anatolian peoples could have originated in the Caucasus and have brought CHG to Anatolia arriving from the north-east. On the other hand, the so-called Steppe Maykop culture may have been responsible for introducing pastoralism and related technologies into the steppes of the pre-Yamnaya groups (Rezepkin 2000). Moreover, the rich admixture of Maikop ancestries (Anatolian Neolithic, Levantine Neolithic, western Iranian, and CHG), which is close to the ancestry from Transcaucasia in the 4th mill. BCE and is also associated with the Kura-Araxes culture originating in the southern Caucasus, may be further evidence that the Maikop culture played an important role in this complex scenario.

Archaeological and aDNA studies seem to support the Indo-Hittite hypothesis suggested by comparative linguistics for almost a century (Sturtevant 1933: 30). They also confirm the complex interaction, during the 5th and 4th millennia BCE, between the Caucasus, Anatolia, the Levant, and the Balkans. A next step will be to define how this interaction generated new cultures and how languages are involved in that process. As for the genetic components of the

Anatolian branch, a huge contribution to the field will certainly come from the analysis of a larger number of human remains from Hittite sites and Bronze Age Anatolia.

3 The Linguistic Contribution

3.1 *Heritage and Innovation in PIE, Proto-Anatolian and Core IE*

It is generally agreed that certain significant features of Anatolian can be taken as indicators that the Anatolian branch was the first to separate: Anatolian does not show a series of traits that are instead shared by two or more non-Anatolian branches and seems to reflect, therefore, an isolated and possibly older stage of the language. The origin of these differences is not clear yet: whether the IE features missing in Anatolian have been lost in Anatolian or first developed in the successive PIE stage(s) (a.k.a. Proto-Indo-Tocharian, see Peyrot 2019) after the Anatolian split is an open issue that can only be resolved through a case-by-case investigation. However, two considerations can be made. The accepted common non-Anatolian innovations are not as numerous as previously believed, and most of them concern the formal aspect of linguistic categories, as is the case with the renewal of the dative plural *-*os*, or with semantic changes like Hitt. *nekutt-* 'twilight' *versus* non-Anatolian branches **neg^{wh}t-/nog^{wh}t-* 'night' (Melchert forthcoming). Among them, those involving functional categories, that is, the core structure of a linguistic system, belong to a very short list: as a commonly accepted post-Anatolian creation and loss see respectively the feminine gender (absent in Anatolian) and the collective plural as a still living category (present in Anatolian). This scenario does not seem to reveal an ancestor language for Anatolian radically different from the one reconstructed for the non-Anatolian IE branches.[2] However, this uncertainty about the origin of these Anatolian differences makes it still impossible to determine the exact position of Anatolian with respect to the other subgroups, since a loss and a creation process are expected to follow different paths: a loss may occur in a short period of time while the emergence of a new element, and espe-

2 *Pace* Kloekhorst & Pronk (2019), where the authors collect 23 differences between Anatolian and non-Anatolian branches and point to a radical remodeling of early PIE (a.k.a. Indo-Anatolian for the authors). However, all differences are treated individually without grouping all of them under a common denominator; this inevitably increases the number of items, see e.g. the thematisation process in (11) **h_1eḱu-* in Anatolian *versus* **h_1eḱu̯-o-* 'horse' in the non-Anatolian branches, (12) **i̯éu̯g-* (later **i̯éu̯g-o-*) in Anatolian *versus* **i̯ug-ó-* 'yoke' in the non-Anatolian branches, and (13) **$h_2$uh$_1$-ent-* in Anatolian *versus* **h_2u̯eh$_1$n̥t-o-* 'wind' in the non-Anatolian branches, which may be grouped under the single point "thematisation".

cially of a linguistic category, is expected to undergo a longer process. However, following the fact that at least the feminine gender seems to have been a post-Anatolian creation, it is very likely that Anatolian has split off from early PIE quite earlier than the other branches, and that it remained isolated for a long time. In this respect it is worth recalling that the genetic evidence suggests a very much earlier chronology and a different genetic history for the ancestors of the Anatolian communities compared to the steppe populations. In particular, see the aforementioned possibility that the Yamnaya populations, which were likely PIE-speakers, and the ancestors of the Anatolian communities, which were likely PA-speakers, were contemporaneous (see above § 2). If this reconstruction is true, the Anatolian branch may have undergone a long period of isolation from early PIE, during which it possibly preserved linguistic traits of the ancestor language. This latter, instead, continued to change during the next PIE stages, as revealed later by the innovations attested in the non-Anatolian IE branches.

Various contrasting views regarding the most prominent differences of this branch from the (other) IE branches are summarized and critically treated in Kloekhorst (2008: 7–11), Rieken (2009), Oettinger (2013/2014), Eichner (2015), Melchert (2016 and forthcoming), Adiego (2016), and Kloekhorst & Pronk (2019). Regardless of how one labels the respective stages, the issue is how radically the structure of the ancestor of all IE languages should be revised on the basis of the differences between Anatolian and all the other branches. In this volume several papers are devoted to the identification of new exclusive features of Anatolian and to the reassessment of previously suggested ones. In particular, Anatolian forms and formations may:

- preserve precious archaisms (see point 1 below) that in some cases have disappeared in other IE branches (see points 2 and 4);
- reflect the continuity of inherited patterns which did not remain unchanged in Anatolian (see point 2);
- share inherited or common independent developments with the (other) IE languages (see point 3);
- show specific developments and innovations of their own (see point 4).

A list of the contributions follows:

1. Zsolt Simon argues that Hittite and Luwian stops can be divided into voiced and voiceless, not into singles and geminates, *pace* Kloekhorst (2016) and Melchert (1994: 20, who argues in favour of geminated *versus* non-geminated stops), maintaining that they do not show any systematic contrast in length. As a litmus test of this issue, Simon examines the treatment of intervocalic voiced and voiceless stops in Anatolian loanwords attested in languages that can both express intervocalic gemination

and mark voice. They consistently reveal single reflexes of voiceless stops instead of geminates, e.g. Ugaritic *pwt* / (Ras Shamra Akkadian texts) *puwatu* / (syllabic Ugaritic) *puwatu* 'madder', Hitt./Luw. *puwatti-* 'id.(?)', and voiced instead of voiceless spelling, see e.g. Ugaritic *ủbdỉt/ủbdy* (once *updt*) '±leased land', Hitt. *upāti* 'land grant', Luw. *upātit-*. Thus, if the traditional view has to be maintained, the contrast in voice is neither a shared innovation nor a defining feature of the non-Anatolian IE languages.

2. José L. García Ramón argues that a series of Anatolian forms can only be explained assuming an inherited aspectual system in which *i*-reduplicated stems function either as an *Aktionsart* marker or as a present stem. Thus, Hitt. *mimma-*ḫḫi 'to reject, refuse' may reflect a lexicalization of PIE **mí-mn-*, i.e. an intensive *Aktionsart* formation of PIE **men-* 'to remain' (stative) with a present stem **mén-o/e-*: Gk. *μένο/ε-*. Hitt. *pippa-*ḫḫi 'to overthrow, tear up, pull down' matches Ved. 3.sg.med. (°)*pípīte* and reflects the present stem **pí-ph₂-ei* of PIE **(s)peh₂-* 'to set/get in (violent) motion', whereas Gk. *σπάο/ε-* 'to pull, draw', Arm. *hanem* 'id.' are individual innovations; the root-aorist PIE **(s)peh₂-* is continued by Luw. /oːppa-/ 'to carry (off), take (off)' (CLuw. *ūppa/i-*, HLuw. CAPERE-*u-pa-*). On the other hand, Hitt. *nakkī-* 'important' and 'difficult', a remodeling of **h₁noki-*, which replaces PIE **gʷr̥h₂ú-* 'heavy', presupposes an inherited PIE suppletive paradigm with pres. **bʰer-* 'to carry (on)', also 'to lift up', and aor. **h₁neḱ-* / **h₁enḱ-* 'to take': its basic meaning 'weight' reflects those of both roots, e.g. Hom. *φέρτερος* 'better', OLat. FERTER, and Gk. *ὄγκος* 'load'.

3. H. Craig Melchert argues that the etymology of Hitt. *ḫandā(i)-* advanced by Ziegler (2014) as derived from **h₂ent-o-* 'weave, fabric' is confirmed by the basic sense of the Hittite verb as 'to align', which may be derived from a more specific sense 'to align the threads of the warp' (Ziegler 2014: 212). This basic sense seems to be attested in Hittite as part of weaving terminology, see the derivative Hitt. GIŠ*ḫanzan-* 'upper loom beam'. Further, in Hittite this basic sense shifts to an abstract meaning with a moral connotation, see ptc. *ḫandānt-* 'just, moral, right(eous)'; cf. the similar development of Lat. *ordior* 'weave' to *ordō* 'order' (Ziegler 2014: 213–214). Whether the semantic broadening from 'to align the warp threads' to 'to align (anything)' as independently attested in Hittite and Latin reflect an early PIE situation cannot be established.

4. Riccardo Ginevra compares IE mythical traits of "non-functioning" Fertility Deities shared by the Hittite myth of Telipinu, the Greek myth of Demeter and Persephone, the Norse myth of Baldr, and the Indic myths of Cyavana. In the Greek, Norse and to some extent the Indic narratives, horses and chariots are searching for the disappeared god, while

the Hittite myth shows a bee searching for him. Through the analysis of non-trivial phraseological and narrative structures, the author suggests that the story evolved after the Anatolian split, once chariots have been invented and horses have been domesticated.

3.2 *Language Contact*

As has been shown in § 1, recent archaeological and genetic data seem to point to different degrees of interaction between peoples in prehistory, which were most likely accompanied by linguistic exchange. Looking for language-contact phenomena between IE and other language families dating back to a period before the disintegration of early PIE or to a later residual PIE stage may prove fruitful for several reasons. First, it plays a prominent role in the reconstruction of intermediate PIE nodes and in the identification of new elements introduced into IE culture during the path taken from the homeland to the historical settlements. Second, it may lead to an explanation of cases in which a term can be traced back to a prehistoric stage, yet without showing any convincing etymology. This path, which is rarely taken in historical and comparative studies, may provide new and important linguistic data on the contacts between peoples in prehistory and on their mobility. For instance, the IE vocabulary for flora and fauna that ultimately evolved into Proto-Germanic possibly stems from a non-IE language, most likely the language of the farmers who used to live in Northern Europe at the arrival of the IE-speaking peoples and who left no direct linguistic trace. A few examples are: IE **b^haw-*, *b^hab^h-* 'bean' in Old Nord. *baun*, Slav. *bobъ*, Lat. *faba*, and the appealing similarity with Figuig (a Berber language) *baw* 'bean' (Iversen & Kroonen 2017: 516). In this volume three papers focus on language contact phenomena at several stages and in different geographical areas: Anatolian and Semitic (point 1 below), Anatolian, PIE, and non-IE language families (point 2), and proto-Balkanic and substrate languages (point 3).

1. Adam Hyllested argues that Hitt. *šeppit*(*t*)- '(a kind of) wheat' may represent a loanword from Akk. *samīdu* (*pace* the interpretation as an original early PIE term by Watkins 1978); see also Aram. *semid* 'high-quality wheat flour', and the loanwords Gk. *σεμίδαλις*, Lat. *simila, simula*. Following this proposal, it is possible to hypothesise that early PIE did not have a specific terminology for 'wheat'. That seems to match the fact that the origin of the domestication of wheat may be located in Western Europe, and that wheat is absent in cultures extending from the Caspian steppe to the East.
2. With the exception of the Anatolian word for the number 'four', the decimal numerals are shared by all branches. Through an analysis of numer-

alisation strategies during the 5th–3rd millennia BCE, Rasmus Bjørn advances a new hypothesis on the provenance and formation of the IE decimal system based on the identification of patterns shared by neighboring, non-Indo-European languages. According to the author, the Balkans may have been the carrier of the decimal system from a third still unidentified source.

3. New evidence of a Balkan IE subgroup (including Greek, Armenian, Albanian, and Phrygian) and the substrate theory are treated by Rasmus Thorsø (cf. Hajnal 2003: 134–135, Kortlandt 2016: 81).[3] For instance, the exclusive correspondence between Gk. *αἴξ* 'goat', Arm. *ayc'* 'id.', and Alb. *edh* 'baby goat' and *dhi* 'nanny goat' can be traced back to a residual PIE Balkan stage **aiĝ-*, while Skt. *ajá-* 'goat' and Lith. *ožỹs*, *ožkà* 'goat' presuppose **(h_2)aĝ-*, and OCS *koza* 'nanny-goat' may go back to **kaĝʰ-*. A possible way to combine all these forms is to think of a substrate borrowing which is attested for 'goat' in several neighboring languages, such as Lat. *haedus* 'kid', Got. *gaits* 'goat' to **gʰai̯d(-o)-* and the Semitic correspondences, like Akk. *gadû* 'kid'. A third unrelated language may have worked as a carrier of the loan through Europe.

3.3 *After the Anatolian Split: Tocharian and the Italo-Celtic Unity*

The chronology of the split of the IE branches after the Anatolian split is controversial. Most likely, Tocharian, and then Italic together with Celtic, split off. Thus the second split happened when, around 800–1,000 years after the Anatolian split, the Tocharian branch split away from what we may call Proto-Indo-Tocharian (Peyrot 2019), that is the PIE residual stage after the Anatolian split (Ringe et al. 2002: 99–100, Anthony & Ringe 2015: fig. 2, Olander 2019: 238). At the beginning of the 3rd millennium BCE the speakers of a pre-stage of Tocharian probably first spread eastward to Altai, where the Afanasievo Culture arose (Allentoft et al. 2015: fig. 1). Then they went south and reached the Xinjang region, where Tocharian texts dating to the 1st millennium CE are attested. The third split happened when, around the same time, an expansion to the West took place, from which the Proto-Italo-Celtic unity probably broke off.

In some cases, Tocharian shows semantic matches with Anatolian, but shares formal innovations with the other IE branches, i.e. the so-called Core

3 However, it is commonly accepted that Greek, Armenian and Indo-Iranian may have branched out from the same PIE residual stage. Later, exclusively Greek–Armenian common traits may have arisen through language contact phenomena (Martirosyan 2013: 126) without the necessity of a Graeco-Armenian unity (Clackson 1994, Kim 2016).

IE; cf. Hitt. *ḫuwant-* 'wind' (*nt*-stem), Toch. B *yente* (plural °*i*), Toch. A *want* (*o*-stem) and Lat. *ventus* 'id.' (*o*-stem). In other cases, a Tocharian stem shows semantic and formal matches only with Anatolian, but the root has undergone replacement in Core IE. For instance, see PIE *$h_1e(h_2)g^{wh}$- 'to drink' and *$peh_3(s)$- 'swallow, take a slug'. PIE *$h_1e(h_2)g^{wh}$- is attested in Hitt. *eku-*^{mi} and Toch. B *yok* 'id.' but is replaced by PIE *$peh_3(s)$- in Core IE: see Hitt./Luw. *paš*(*š*)- 'to swallow', hence 'to drink', and the reduplicated form *$pí$-ph_3-*e*- 'gulp repeatedly, drink' in Ved. *píbati*, Lat. *bibit*, and OIr. ibid 'id.'. Furthermore, the Tocharian corpus shows a restricted vocabulary due to the typology of the available documents (almost all Buddhist texts), which does not allow a broad comparison to the Core IE vocabulary, making it most often impossible to establish whether Tocharian shares an innovation with Core IE or remains closer to Anatolian. Compare, for instance, the semantic shift of early PIE **mer-* 'to disappear': the original meaning is preserved in Anatolian, but it has changed to 'to die' in Core IE (Kloekhorst 2008: 8), and so far Tocharian has shown no trace of this root for comparison (Peyrot 2019). Thus, the classification of Tocharian remains problematic. For a recent reassessment of the Tocharian question see Weiss (2018).

Italic and Celtic probably split together after Anatolian and Tocharian. Although the topic does not remain free from doubts and skepticism (Watkins 1966, Sihler 1995: 13–15, Isaac 2007: 75–95), the shared innovations between Italic and Celtic seem to make these two branches closer to each other than to any other IE branch and to speak for a possible common node in the Indo-European family tree (Cowgill 1970; Ringe et al. 2002: 87, 100–102; Weiss 2012, Schrijver 2015: 196–197, 2016). Beside lexical innovations see e.g. the following phonological and morphological ones: */p_kʷ/ > */kʷ_kʷ/, see Lat. *quinque*, OIr. *cóic*, OW *pimp* 'five' (**kʷenkʷe* < **pénkʷe*); the thematic genitive in *-ī* as part of the thematic nominal paradigm, see Ogham Ir. MAQQI 'son', Lat. *lupī* 'Wolf' (and maybe Messapic *-a*(*i*)*hi*); the *a*-subjunctive, see Lat. *ferat* 'carry' and OIr. *bera* 'id.' (Weiss 2011: 465–466). In this volume Peter Schrijver adds a potential Italo-Celtic innovation to this list. The author reconstructs an unexpected double present for Italo-Celtic **es-* 'to be' where thematic forms with secondary endings serve as present indicatives: 1sg. **es-om*, 1pl. **es-omos*, 2sg. **es-es*, 2pl. **es-etes*, 3sg. **es-ed*, 3pl. **es-ond*. These forms look like subjunctives with full grade and secondary endings, but they lack the semantics of the subjunctive, differently from other old subjunctives—e.g. the Latin future. The situation is completely different in the other IE languages, where the verb 'to be' can be traced back to a single, athematic present older than the Anatolian split. Whether this peculiarity may cast light on the relationship between the present tense function and the subjunctive remains an open question: the present tense function may have originated as a subjunctive, or the subjunctive originated in the present that later acquired modal functions, too.

Interestingly, Italo-Celtic also shares some lexical isoglosses with Indo-Iranian, which is commonly classified as the last or one of the last branches that split off from PIE. Since these are geographically noncontiguous languages, their shared traits represent an important indication of possible contacts that occurred at a certain time and space after the Italo-Celtic split and before the arrival of the Italic and Celtic peoples in their historical settlements. In this volume, Michael Weiss offers new material on this topic. Examining the Indo-Iranian/Italo-Celtic isogloss Ved. *śraddhā́* 'trust', Lat. *crēdere* 'to believe', OIr. *creitid* 'believes', MW *credaf* 'I believe', and OBrit. *critim* 'belief', he argues for an original meaning of PIE **ḱred *d^heh_1-* as 'putting yourself or your property in the hands or power of another with the expectation that the other individual would give good in return'. Further, he brings evidence for a *s*-stem **ḱred-s-* in the collocation **ḱred-s-d^heh_1-* and interprets it as an innovation occurred after the Tocharian split (defined by the author as an Inner Indo-European innovation). Together with a series of Indo-Iranian/Italo-Celtic isoglosses of the same kind, this remodeling of a PIE lexeme likely represents a recent creation. Indeed, Tocharian and Anatolian neither have it nor have the morphological and semantic preconditions for the creation of the *s*-stem **ḱred-s-*. On the one hand, these isoglosses may derive from a period of time in which the ancestors of the Indo-Iranians could have been in a close contact with the Corded Ware culture (since Kretschmer 1896: 147, Specht 1939: 48). This may match the aDNA results indicating that the Late Bronze Age cultures of Sintashta and Andronovo—considered as likely ancestors of the Indo-Iranians—shared significant genetic traits with European Neolithic farmers. According to the author, this seems to speak for a secondary expansion from the west to the east after the formation of the Corded Ware Culture. On the other hand, they could reflect an innovative late PIE stratum (defined by the author as an Inner PIE stratum) that went lost in the intervening languages, as might be exemplified by the case of the **h_3rēĝ-s* word (Weiss 2018: 374).

Following the results of this paper, one may make one step further and suggest that the Proto-Italo-Celtic linguistic unity may belong to the end of the 3rd millennium BCE, that is, it may have been contemporaneous with the ancestors of Mycenaean Greek and Indo-Iranian, and with the early Hittite speakers.

4 Methodological Issues

In the last decades, phonological, morphological, and lexical differences between branches based on non-trivial shared innovations have been analysed mathematically in order to generate a number of possible different branching diagrams (Ringe et al. 2002; Nakhleh et al. 2005). Briefly speaking, the program selects those diagrams that occur more often than others; then, it reveals the most plausible chronological order of the branching of the IE languages. Its results match with previous comparative linguistic analyses based on shared innovations and it is usually accepted as a reliable method. However, new competing phylogenetic methods borrowed from evolutionary biology and based exclusively on lexical comparison have been tested in order to date the ancestor of all branches by dating the separation between two branches, i.e. by generating binary-tree models. These methods use a distance-based approach that aims to reconstruct the absolute chronology of the IE languages by means of a comparison of the extent of differentiation among descendent languages. However, while this approach has the advantage to provide a measurement of similarities among languages, it does also imply that similar grades of differentiation among languages reveal a similar time period of divergence and that the grade of language change is universally constant. This is simply not true. It is sufficient to recall that linguistic innovations can occur for unpredictable reasons, and that the same innovation can occur in several languages and at different time. In other words, it is risky to adapt a methodology originated in evolutionary biology to the comparison of linguistic innovations since the latter follow different paths. Moreover, probably the most evident problem of phylogenetics concerns the unexpected results on the relationship between IE languages that already have a secure position within the family tree.

For instance, in certain phylogenetic analyses Latin and Old Irish surprisingly appear not to be the direct ancestors of the Romance languages and of Modern Irish and Scottish Gaelic respectively. This is probably due to the fact that the system does not recognise parallel but independent innovations in related languages that were not present in their common ancestor. For instance, Lat. *vir* 'man' and OIr. *fer* 'id.' were replaced in Romance languages and in Modern Irish by terms with an original meaning 'human being' as Lat. *homō* and OIr. *duine*. The phylogenetic program cannot distinguish parallel innovations from inherited features. Accordingly, it assumes that an unattested close related language of Latin and Old Irish must have had *homō* and *duine* with a new meaning 'male person', which in fact develops only later. Garrett (2018: esp. 9–11) has recently discussed these issues and pointed out how such misleading results may strongly affect the family tree. Possibly, this kind of problem contributes to the unexpected results for the IE family tree from the phylogenetic analysis (Dyen et al. 1992), which strongly differ from those reached by comparative linguistics, and have led to a dramatic backdating of the ancestor language by approximately three millennia (e.g. Gray & Atkinson 2003: 437, Bouckaert et al. 2012: 959).

In this volume, Matthew Scarborough casts light on further advantages and disadvantages of the phylogenetic approach, focusing on a range of issues arisen during his collaboration with the IE-CoR database project at the *Max Planck Institute for the Science of Human History* in Jena, a worldwide leading institution in this methodology that primarily works on improving cladistic and linguistic methods through computer programs. IE-CoR uses cognate relations established between lexemes through linguistic reconstruction of IE phonology and morphology as data for phylogenetic analyses. Unfortunately, the problems with this methodology are mostly structural and have, therefore, no easy solution. First, the expectation to collect binary input data cannot be fulfilled since many IE etymologies are still uncertain, which makes the identification of corresponding cognates for certain terms impossible. This issue leads to the elimination of possible cognates and relevant lexemes as well as to the inclusion of wrong or uncertain etymologies, which deeply influences the final results. Second, a similarity between two terms is not necessarily due to common inheritance but may, for instance, result from language contact, parallel semantic shifts, or convergence processes. A prime example also mentioned by the author is the case of CHILD: PIE $*d^{h}eh_{1}(i̯)$- "(Muttermilch) saugen" (*LIV* 138–139) is common to Lyc. *tideimi-* 'child' and It. *figlio* 'child', but the system would not recognize that the latter derives from Lat. *filius* 'son'.

Differently from phylogenetics, palaeolinguistics aims to reconstruct the culture of a proto-speech community through the reconstruction of its lexicon. This approach may lead to a chronological classification of the analysed elements, which in turn may be used to estimate the order in which the branches split off from the common ancestor language. Where possible, palaeolinguists check the results obtained from linguistic analysis against the archaeological evidence and, since the last few years, the genetic material in order to achieve a more complete understanding of the historical context surrounding a given community. For instance, see the reconstruction of the wheel-vocabulary in the PIE stage after the Anatolian split (a.k.a. Proto-Indo-Tocharian), which seems to match the dating of the first findings of wheeled vehicles in Eurasia and to suggest the exclusion of the arrival of the Indo-European communities together with the Anatolian farmers (see §3). However, methodological issues arise while reconstructing cultural traits by means of the linguistic analysis. Not only is it extremely difficult to define the boundaries of a cultural trait, but it is sometimes even harder to distinguish the aspects of a given culture from 'universal' characteristics, as well as traits inherited or acquired by contact from parallel but independent developments. For instance, see above in §3 (example 3) the discussion on the impossibility to identify with certainty metaphors in PIE indicating the concept of 'being morally right' and their diffusion in the proto-speech community, although the semantic shift from 'to align' toward 'be morally right' has been identified as parallel but independent developments in at least two IE branches by the linguistic analysis.

Furthermore, in this new era of linguistic, archaeological and genetic cooperation the main risk is well known: genes, culture, and language are three separate entities that may and may not overlap. In this volume, James Johnson analyses the risk of a domino effect that starts with easy linkages between genes and culture and ends with a series of misleading results on prehistoric reality. This risk mainly lies in the overlooking and underestimation of three aspects: (1) relatively few genetic samples are used to issue proclamations about large-scale migrations and culture change; (2) culture is not a social totality fixed in space and time that can only change by replacement; (3) the equivalence between culture and genetic identity goes against the commonly recognized claims of ethnographic and archaeological research whereby culture is not defined as genetically or biologically based. In order to overcome these issues, the author explores the theoretical and methodological avenues that may help account for how ancient communities, Yamnaya in particular, underwent social change and reacted to social and demographic breakdown and relocation.

Similarly, linguistics does not necessarily go hand-in-hand with genetics, although this might occur in restricted and close communities. In this volume, David Anthony uses the new concept of genetic *mating networks*, i.e., regional populations with similar genetic ancestry measured across the whole genome. This concept implies that interaction between human groups was neither assured, nor immediate or granted in prehistory: a mixture of genetic types is rare in prehistory, and it likely always happens for a reason. The author analyses four possible mating networks which may have been the source of the genetic mixture sampled in the regions that are deemed as having been inhabited by early PIE-speaking populations. He further argues that in a quite close environment, and for instance in case of contacts of close realities through migrations, it is highly possible that languages and culture follow genetic lines. Therefore, the identification of genetic mating networks might correspond to *linguistic* and *cultural* networks, with the implication that the interaction between mating networks may be translated into genetic, linguistic, and cultural contacts.

The future of Indo-European Studies clearly cannot ignore the high potential of the cooperation between genetics, archaeology, and linguistics, in which each of these disciplines plays a prominent role. However, this new-born approach needs some regulation in order to accomplish good and long-lasting results.

Acknowledgements

I am indebted to the series editor of *Brill's Studies in Indo-European Languages & Linguistics*, H. Craig Melchert (North Carolina), to the co-editor of this volume Thomas Olander (Copenhagen), and to David Anthony (Hartwick College), Benedicte Whitehead Nielsen (Copenhagen), and Marco Santini (Princeton University) for their comments and criticism that highly improved this contribution. All mistakes are, of course, my own responsibility.

References

Adiego, Ignasi-Xavier. 2016. Anatolian languages and Proto-Indo-European. *Veleia* 33. 49–64.

Allentoft, Morten E., Martin Sikora, Karl-Göran Sjögren, Simon Rasmussen, Morten Rasmussen, Jesper Stenderup, Peter B. Damgaard et al. 2015. Population genomics of Bronze Age Eurasia. *Nature* 522(7555). 167–172. doi:10.1038/nature14507

Anthony, David W., & Don Ringe. 2015. The Indo-European homeland from linguistic and archaeological perspectives. *Annual Review of Linguistics* 1. 199–219. doi:10.1146/annurev-linguist-030514-124812

Anthony, David W. 2007. *The Horse, the wheel, and language: How Bronze-Age riders from the Eurasian steppes shaped the modern world.* Princeton: Princeton University Press.

Bouckaert, Remco, Philippe Lemey, Michael Dunn, Simon J. Greenhill, Alexander V. Alekseyenko, Alexei J. Drummond, Russell D. Gray, Marc A. Suchard & Quentin D. Atkinson. 2012. Mapping the origins and expansion of the Indo-European language family. *Science* 337. 957–960. doi:10.1126/science.1219669

Chang, Will, Chundra Cathcart, David Hall, & Andrew Garrett. 2015. Ancestry-constrained phylogenetic analysis supports the Indo-European steppe hypothesis. *Language* 91(1). 194–244. doi:10.1353/lan.2015.0005

Clackson, James. 1994. *The linguistic relationship between Armenian and Greek.* Oxford & Cambridge: Blackwell.

Cowgill, Warren. 1970. Italic and Celtic superlatives and the dialects of Indo-European. In: G. Cardona, H.M. Hoenigswald & A. Senn (eds.), *Indo-European and Indo-Europeans*, 113–153. Philadelphia: University of Pennsylvania Press.

Damgaard, Peter de Barros, Rui Martiniano, Jack Kamm, J. Víctor Moreno-Mayar, Guus Kroonen, Michaël Peyrot, Gojko Barjamovic et al. 2018. The first horse herders and the impact of Early Bronze Age steppe expansions into Asia. *Science* 360(1422). doi:10.1126/science.aar7711

Dyen, Isidore, Joseph B. Kruskal & Paul Black. 1992. An Indoeuropean classification: A lexicostatistical experiment. *Transactions of the American Philosophical Society* 82. iii–iv, 1–132.

Eichner, H. 2015. Das Anatolische in seinem Verhältnis zu anderen Gliedern der indoeuropäischen Sprachfamilie aus aktueller Sicht. In T. Krisch & S. Niederreiter (eds.), *Diachronie und Sprachvergleich. Beiträge aus der Arbeitsgruppe "historisch-vergleichende Sprachwissenschaft" bei der 40. Österreichischen Linguistiktagung 2013 in Salzburg*, 13–26. Innsbruck: Institut für Sprachen und Literaturen der Universität Innsbruck.

Gamkrelidze, Thomas V., & Vjačeslav Vs. Ivanov. 1995. *Indo-European and the Indo-Europeans: A reconstruction and historical analysis of a proto-language and a proto-culture.* Trans. Johanna Nichols. Berlin: Mouton de Gruyter.

Garrett, Andrew. 2018. New Perspectives on Indo-European Phylogeny and Chronology. *Proceedings of the American Philosophical Society* 162/1.1–14.

Gimbutas, Marija. 1977. The first wave of Eurasian steppe pastoralists into Copper Age Europe. *Journal of Indo-European Studies* 5(4). 277–338.

Gimbutas, Marija. 1970. Proto-Indo-European culture: The Kurgan culture during the fifth, fourth, and third millennia B.C. In George Cardona, Henry M. Hoenigswald & Alfred Senn (eds.), *Indo-European and Indo-Europeans*, 155–198. Philadelphia: University of Pennsylvania Press.

Gimbutas, Marija. 1956. *The prehistory of eastern Europe. Part 1.* Cambridge, MA: Peabody Museum.

Gray, Russell D., & Quentin D. Atkinson. 2003. Language-tree divergence times support the Anatolian theory of Indo-European origin. *Nature* 426. 435–439.

Haak, Wolfgang, Iosif Lazaridis, Nick Patterson, Nadin Rohland, Swapan Mallick, Bastien Llamas, Guido Brandt et al. 2015. Massive migration from the steppe was a source for Indo-European languages in Europe. *Nature* 522(7555). 207–211. doi:10.1038/nature14317

Hajnal, Ivo. 2003. Methodische Vorbemerkungen zu einer Paleolinguistik des Balkanraums. In A. Bammesberger & T. Vennemann (eds.), *Languages in prehistoric Europe*, 117–145. Heidelberg: Winter.

Heggarty, Paul. 2014. Prehistory by Bayesian phylogenetics? The state of the art on Indo-European origins. *Antiquity* 88. 566–577.

Heggarty, Paul. 2015. Prehistory through language and archaeology. In Claire Bowern & Bethwyn Evans (eds.), *The Routledge handbook of historical linguistics*, 598–626. Oxon & New York: Routledge.

Isaac, Graham. 2007. *Studies in Celtic sound changes and their chronology*. Innsbruck: Institut für Sprachen und Literaturen der Universität Innsbruck.

Iversen, Rune, & Guus Kroonen. 2017. Talking Neolithic: Linguistic and archaeological perspectives on how Indo-European was implemented in southern Scandinavia. *American Journal of Archaeology* 121(4). 511–525. doi:10.3764/aja.121.4.0511

Kim, Ronald I. 2016. Greco-Armenian: the persistence of a myth. *Indogermanische Forschungen* 123. 247–272.

Kloekhorst, Alwin. 2018. The Anatolian split and the origins of the Anatolians: a linguistic perspective. Handout, *When Archaeology Meets Linguistics and Genetics, University of Gothenburg, 3 May 2018*.

Kloekhorst, Alwin. 2016. The Anatolian stop system and the Indo-Hittite hypothesis. *Indogermanische Forschungen* 121(1). 213–247.

Kloekhorst, Alwin. 2008. *Etymological dictionary of the Hittite inherited lexicon*. Leiden & Boston: Brill.

Kloekhorst, Alwin, & Tijmen Pronk. 2019. Introduction: Reconstructing Proto-Indo-Anatolian and Proto-Indo-Uralic. In Alwin Kloekhorst & Tijmen Pronk (eds.), *The precursors of Proto-Indo-European: The Indo-Anatolian and Indo-Uralic hypotheses*. Leiden & Boston: Brill.

Kortlandt, Frederik. 2016. Baltic, Slavic, Germanic. *Baltistica* 51(1). 81–86.

Kretschmer, Paul. 1896. *Einleitung in die Geschichte der griechischen Sprache*. Göttingen: Vandenhoeck und Ruprecht.

Kristiansen, Kristian, B. Hemphill, G. Barjamovic, S. Omura, S.Y. Senyurt, V. Moiseyev, A. Gromov et al. 2018. Archaeological supplement A to Damgaard et al. 2018: Archaeology of the Caucasus, Anatolia, Central and South Asia 4000–1500 BCE. doi:10.5281/zenodo.1240516.

Kristiansen, Kristian, Morten E. Allentoft, Karin M. Frei, Rune Iversen, Niels N. Johannsen, Guus Kroonen, Łukasz Pospieszny et al. 2017. Re-theorising mobility and the formation of culture and language among the Corded Ware Culture in Europe. *Antiquity* 91(356). 334–347. doi:10.15184/aqy.2017.17

Kroonen, Guus, Gojko Barjamovic & Michaël Peyrot. 2018. Linguistic supplement to Damgaard et al. 2018: Early Indo-European languages, Anatolian, Tocharian, and Indo-Iranian. doi:10.5281/zenodo.1240516.

Mallory, James P. 1989. *In search of the Indo-Europeans: Language, archaeology, and myth*. London: Thames & Hudson.

Mallory, James P., 1997. The homelands of the Indo-Europeans. In Roger Blench &

Matthew Spriggs (eds.), *Archaeology and language*. Vol. 1. *Theoretical and methodological orientations* (One World Archaeology 27), 93–121. London & New York: Routledge.

Mallory, James P., & Douglas Q. Adams. 2006. *The Oxford introduction to Proto-Indo-European and the Proto-Indo-European world*. Oxford: Oxford University Press.

Martirosyan, Hrach K. 2013. The place of Armenian in the Indo-European language family: the relationship with Greek and Indo-Iranian. *Вопросы языкового родства* 10. 85–137.

Melchert, H. Craig. Forthcoming. The position of Anatolian. In: M. Weiss & A. Garrett (eds.), *Handbook of Indo-European Studies*. Oxford: Oxford University Press.

Melchert 2016. "Western Affinities" of Anatolian. In B. Simmelkjær Sandgaard Hansen, B. Nielsen Whitehead, T. Olander & B.A. Olsen (eds.), *Etymology and the European lexicon. Proceedings of the 14th Fachtagung der Indogermanischen Gesellschaft, 17–22 September 2012, Copenhagen*, 297–305. Wiesbaden: Reichert.

Melchert, H. Craig. 1994. *Anatolian historical phonology*. Amsterdam & Atlanta: Rodopi.

Nakhleh, Luay, Donald A. Ringe & Tandy Warnow. 2005. Perfect phylogenetic networks: A new methodology for reconstructing the evolutionary history of natural languages. *Language* 81. 382–420.

Oettinger, Norbert. 2013–2014. Die Indo-Hittite-Hypothese aus heutiger Sicht. *Münchener Studien zur Sprachwissenschaft* 67(2). 149–176.

Olander, Thomas. 2019. Indo-European cladistic nomenclature. *Indogermanische Forschungen* 124. 231–244.

Peyrot, Michaël. 2019. Indo-Uralic, Indo-Anatolian, Indo-Tocharian. In Alwin Kloekhorst & Tijmen Pronk (eds.), *The precursors of Proto-Indo-European: The Indo-Anatolian and Indo-Uralic hypotheses*. Leiden & Boston: Brill.

Reinhold, Sabine, J. Gresky, N. Berezina, A.R. Kantorovich, C. Knipper, V.E. Maslov, V.G. Petrenko, K.W. Alt & Andrew B. Belinsky. 2017. Contextualising innovation. Cattle owners and wagon drivers in the North Caucasus and beyond. In Philipp Stockhammer & Joseph Maran (eds.), *Appropriating innovations: Entangled knowledge in Eurasia, 5000–1500 BCE*, 78–97. Oxford: Oxbow.

Renfrew, Colin. 1987. *Archaeology and language: The puzzle of Indo-European origins*. New York: Cambridge University Press.

Rezepkin A.D. 2000. *Das frühbronzezeitliche Gräberfeld von Klady und die Majkop-Kultur in Nordwestkaukasien*. Rahden (Westf.): Leidorf.

Rieken, Elisabeth. 2009. Der Archaismus des Hethitischen; eine Bestandsaufnahme. *Incontri Linguistici* 32. 37–52.

Ringe, Don. 2013. The linguistic diversity of aboriginal Europe. In Shu-Fen Chen & Benjamin Slade (eds.), *Grammatica et verba, glamor and verve*, 202–212. Ann Arbor: Beech Stave.

Ringe, Donald A., Tandy Warnow & Ann Taylor. 2002. *Indo-European and computational linguistics. Transactions of the Philological Society* 100(1). 59–129.

LIV = Helmut Rix, Martin Kümmel, Thomas Zehnder, Reiner Lipp & Brigitte Schirmer (eds.), 1998. *Lexikon der indogermanischen Verben*. Wiesbaden: Reichert.

Schrijver, Peter. 2016. Sound change, the Italo-Celtic linguistic unity, and the Italian homeland of Celtic. In J.T. Koch & B. Cunliffe (eds.), *Celtic from the West*. Vol. 3. *Atlantic Europe in the Metal Ages: questions of shared language*, 489–502. Oxford: Oxbow Books.

Schrijver, Peter. 2015. Pruners and trainers of the Celtic family tree: the rise and development of Celtic in the light of language contact. In Liam Breatnach et al. (eds.), *Proceedings of the XIV International Congress of Celtic Studies*, 191–219. Dublin: Dublin Institute for Advanced Studies.

Sihler, Andrew L. 1995. *New comparative grammar of Greek and Latin*. New York: Oxford University Press.

Specht, Franz. 1939. Sprachliches zur Urheimat der Indogermanen. *Zeitschrift für vergleichende Sprachforschung* 66. 1–74.

Sturtevant, Edgard H. 1933. *A comparative grammar of the Hittite language*. Philadelphia: Linguistic Society of America & University of Pennsylvania.

Wang, Chuan-Chao, Sabine Reinhold, Alexey Kalmykov, Antje Wissgott, Guido Brandt, Choongwon Jeong, Olivia Cheronet et al. 2018. The genetic prehistory of Greater Caucasus. bioRxiv. doi:10.1101/322347

Watkins, Calvert. 1966. Italo-Celtic revisited. In Henrik Birnbaum & Jaan Puhvel (eds.), *Ancient Indo-European dialects*, 29–50. Berkeley: University of California Press.

Watkins, Calvert. 1978. Let us now praise famous grains. *Proceedings of the National American Society* 122(1). 9–17.

Weiss, Michael. 2011. *Outline of the historical and comparative grammar of Latin*. 2nd edition. Ann Arbor & New York: Beech Stave.

Weiss, Michael. 2012. Italo-Celtica: Linguistic and cultural points of contact between Italic and Celtic. In Stephanie Jamison, H. Craig Melchert & Brent Vine (eds.), *Proceedings of the 23rd Annual UCLA Indo-European Conference*, 151–173. Bremen: Hempen.

Weiss, Michael. 2018. Tocharian and the West. In Olav Hackstein & Andreas Opfermann (eds.), *Priscis Libentius et Liberius Novis. Indogermanische und sprachwissenschaftliche Studien. Festschrift für Gerhard Meiser zum 65. Geburtstag*, 373–381. Hamburg: Baar.

Ziegler, Sabine. 2014. Die Ordnung als Gewebe: Kann eine andere etymologische Erklärung für heth. *ḫandai-*[zi] "(durch Semantik) festgestellt werden"? In Cyril Brosch & Annick Payne (eds.), *Na-wa/i-VIR.ZI/A* MAGNUS.SCRIBA: *Festschrift für Helmut Nowicki zum 70. Geburtstag*, 211–215. Wiesbaden: Harrassowitz.

CHAPTER 1

Ancient DNA, Mating Networks, and the Anatolian Split

David W. Anthony

1 Introduction

The last three years of ancient DNA (aDNA) studies have revolutionized the topics about which we have solid information from past populations.[1] We can now say with some certainty who was related to whom, and how closely they were related, subjects that previously were largely speculative in reference to ancient populations. Because each person carries a genetic record of descent from hundreds[2] of recognizable individual ancestors (up to 10 generations back) and many more broadly defined ancestral groups, the *whole* genomes of a few individuals can reveal the histories of substantial populations. Applied to large samples of individuals, statistical characterizations of genetic relationships can identify migrations, reveal their demographic structure, and describe ancient mating networks—a new category of measurable human relationships. Again, these topics previously were debated or unknowable. The difficult problem of defining language groups and language borders in prehistoric landscapes, deemed a hopeless waste of time (or worse) using traditional archaeological methods (Demoule et al. 2008; Karl 2010; Sims-Williams 2012; Falileyev 2015), can and should be re-visited with these new tools. But the methodological breakthroughs that made it possible to *quickly* analyze *whole* genomes from *large samples* of prehistoric individuals were attained only after 2012, and the results were not in print before 2015, as the citations

1 Abbreviations: aDNA: ancient DNA; ANE: Ancient North Eurasian; CHG: Caucasus Hunter-Gatherer; DDII Dnieper-Donets II; EBA: Early Bronze Age; EHG Eastern Hunter-Gatherer; IE: Indo-European; LBK: *Linearbandkeramik*/Linear Pottery Culture; MtDNA: mitochondrian DNA; PIE: Proto-Indo-European; WHG: Western Hunter-Gatherer.

2 The number of distinct ancestors 10 generations before ego would be 1024 if no relatives ever married each other, but marriages between people who share a common ancestor are ubiquitous, and they reduce the number of distinct ancestors (a process called pedigree collapse) by a quantity that depends on marriage patterns, so the potential 1024 is never attained.

 | DOI:10.1163/9789004416192_003

below attest, so we are early in the process of exploring the implications and limitations of this new data.

In this essay I review the relevance of four genetically defined mating networks for the subject of the first and oldest split in the Indo-European (IE) language family, the separation of the language community that was ancestral to the Anatolian IE languages. Because mating networks are a new kind of phenomenon, first I should define this term.

2 Mating Networks, Culture, and Language

Even at this early stage in aDNA studies, one strongly supported conclusion about the inter-regional connectivity of ancient humans is clear: there was more "structure" in the geographic distribution of ancient populations than there is in modern populations (Pickrell & Reich 2014; Lazaridis et al. 2016: Fig. 3; Reich 2018; Scerri et al. 2018). Ten thousand years ago the number of humans was much lower, regional populations were more isolated genetically (and linguistically), and there was less gene flow between them, than we find today—at least in Eurasia, the continent most heavily sampled so far. These conditions created regional populations with distinctive combinations of genetic traits, referred to here as mating networks. Mating networks can be seen most clearly during chronological periods of low gene flow between largely isolated human populations—such as the peak of the last glacial period about 20,000 years ago. Even these isolated populations that lived during the glacial maximum showed genetic traces of earlier migrations and admixtures, so isolation was episodic, and no single mating network represented any kind of "pure" population. They just happened to survive the last Ice Age in different places.

Because languages usually were learned from the same parental sources that provided genes, languages probably showed at least an equivalent level of regional patterning and diversity. But genes could be shared through occasional acts while language sharing required regular face-to-face interaction and maintenance. Mating networks knitted together widely scattered human groups who ranged over large, ecologically diverse regions, where each mountain range or broad river was a potential impediment to language sharing. For these reasons we might expect ancient languages to exhibit even more regional "structure" than genes (Nettles 1998; Robb 1993; Anthony 2007: 114–116; Mallory 2008). When large population movements flowed across previously separate mating networks, like the migrations of pioneer farmers from Neolithic western Anatolia into Europe about 6500–5000 BC (Haak et al. 2015; Lazaridis et al. 2016) or the Yamnaya expansions from the steppes into Europe and Asia about 3000–2000 BC (Haak et al. 2015; Allentoft et al. 2015; Damgaard et al. 2018; Narasimhan et al. 2018), new languages must have moved with them.

Some archaeologists (Terrell 2018; Golitko 2015) seem to think that any discussion that links archaeology, genes, and language must adopt the simplest of equations between archaeological cultures, biological populations, and linguistic-ethnic groups in a dangerous replay of early 20th-century racial history. But kinship, material culture, and language need not be analyzed through early 20th-century stereotypes (see Saarikivi & Lavento 2012 or Orton 2012). Also, race and genetic ancestry are obviously different things (Anthony & Brown 2017: 28–30). Race is a social construct based on variable, culturally defined phenotypic and behavioral stereotypes with no serious attention to their genetic expression; and genetic ancestry is a statistical construct based on the frequency of shared base pairs between individual genomes with little regard for their phenotypic or behavioral expression. Skin color is a powerful element in the cultural construct of race, but the genes for skin color are a minor part of the 3.2 billion base pairs comprising the whole human genome. Our acute attention to skin color and its entanglement with modern concepts of race makes it easy for us to assume that any study that includes skin-color genes must be about them, but in fact these genes have almost no effect on how individuals are combined into mating networks, lineages, and other kinds of groups in genetic ancestry studies. It might be naïve to hope that this will insulate genetic ancestry studies from the modern politics of race, but it is wrong in both senses of the word to equate genetic ancestry studies with racism (Terrell 2018).

The most important new facts revealed by aDNA are not about archaeological cultures and their assumed social or biological correlates, but about migrations and the structure of prehistoric mating networks. When migration brought populations from distinct mating networks into contact, they repeatedly created and maintained persistent, centuries-long marriage exclusion borders rather than freely admixing with their new neighbors and trading partners. I do not suggest replacing a free-flowing, border-less, networked model of human relations with its opposite, maximally structured stereotype. But borders have been seen in anthropological archaeology primarily as zones of cultural hybridity and invention (Stark 1998; Parker & Rodseth 2005; Stockhammer 2012), not as zones of exclusion, so this newly revealed ancient reluctance to exchange mates is a surprise, and demands our attention. Material types and styles, which sometimes were widely shared, can now be compared with mating networks, which we are just beginning to perceive through samples that are still too few.

We also should distinguish between genetic mating networks, the subject of this essay, and cultural models of kinship relations. Culturally defined kinship obligations and structures were fundamental elements in ancient social organization. Gaining the ability to perceive actual genetic mating networks might therefore seem to be a major advance in understanding prehistoric social organizations. It is, but with reservations. The cultural extension of kinship to non-kin is a ubiquitous custom among humans, and that is one important difference between culturally and genetically defined mating networks—cultural notions of kinship are malleable. Nevertheless, actual "blood" relationships through shared ancestors explain many aspects of tribal socio-political behavior, and genetic mating networks do describe actual relationships through shared ancestors, so genetic mating networks give us important insights into the underlying genetic architecture of culturally defined kinship networks. However, most of the mating networks described here operated on a scale probably larger than was recognized or referenced culturally among ancient societies. All of Mesolithic Europe contained only three or four mating networks 10,000 years ago, and already they had met each other and blended into a rough cline. After the initial events of admixture between them had passed into myth, we might be able to detect their once-distinct origins better than they could, or cared to know. In contrast, some regions rich in concentrated natural resources developed distinctive local genetic populations that mated endogamously, as seems to have happened around the Dnieper Rapids (Mating Network #3 below). In this case the genetically defined network was actively maintained and small enough in geographic scale to have been recognized culturally.

In addition to small-scale (possibly cultural) genetic mating networks, there is another situation where genetic mating networks might coincide with cultural notions of kinship. This is when previously isolated populations came into contact through migration. At contact, their accumulated physical and cultural differences probably were recognized, named, and negotiated. David Reich described the genetic difference between the indigenous hunter-gatherers of western Europe and the in-migrating Anatolian farmers who carried farming into Europe between 6500–5000 BC as about the same as the difference between modern Western Europeans and East Asians, implying that they had recognizably different phenotypes, languages, and customs. These differences seem to have been recognized culturally upon contact, as the incoming migrants and indigenous hunter-gatherers mutually avoided marriage with each other in spite of sometimes robust trade exchanges of material goods and types during the initial centuries of interaction (Haak et al. 2015; Reich 2018: 101–102; Groneborn 2014). Genetic mating networks and cultural concepts of kinship might have been roughly aligned for hundreds of years on a persistent genetic border like this that also was a persistent economic and cultural border. In such cases, where intermarriage was avoided, the border probably was linguistic as well (Anthony 2007: 108–116). Of course, over the very long term, all were dynamic phenomena, and shifted through admixture and politics and time.

3 A Steppe Homeland for Late Proto-Indo-European (PIE): Summary of the Argument

I assume here that *late* Proto-Indo-European (PIE) (*classic* PIE in Kloekhorst 2016)—the parent of all known IE language branches except Anatolian—existed as a variable, innovation-sharing language community after 3500 BC in the Pontic–Caspian steppes north of the Black and Caspian Seas (Map 1). This temporal and geographic solution is supported by a growing body of ancient DNA evidence (Allentoft et al. 2016; Haak et al. 2015; Lazaridis et al. 2018), and by other arguments, including the presence of a wheel/wagon vocabulary in late PIE (Mallory & Adams 2006: 247–249; Anthony & Ringe 2015; Anthony & Brown 2017; Kristiansen 2017; Kristiansen et al. 2017). The term "innovation-sharing" describes the late PIE language community because at least ten innovations in phonology and morphology (Lehrman 2002) distinguished late PIE from the older language phase (archaic PIE, or Indo-Hittite) preserved uniquely within the Anatolian branch of IE languages. All ten had been shared and incorporated into speech, along with the wheel/wagon vocabulary, across the late Proto-Indo-European language community before it began to fragment into its known daughters.

The rapid expansion of the steppe Yamnaya population about 3300–2700 BC from the Pontic–Caspian steppes into both Europe and Asia currently represents the best archaeological and genetic vector for the expansion and multiple separations of *late* PIE populations and dialects (Anthony 2007; Haak et al. 2015; Kristiansen 2017). Wooden parts of wagons found in Yamnaya graves in the steppes are among the oldest wheeled vehicles. The oldest dated wheel in the steppes is from a four-wheeled wagon buried in a kurgan grave at the cemetery of Sharakhalsun 6, Russia, in the North Caucasus steppes, dated 3336–3105 cal BCE (4500±40 BP, GIN-12401), the same age as a wheel from the Ljubljana marshes that was previously thought to be the oldest wheel (Reinhold et al. 2017). The late PIE expansion can be dated after 3500 BC (after the invention and diffusion of wheeled vehicles) by the wheel/wagon vocabulary in late PIE, and before 2500 BC by inscriptions indicating that Anatolian (Hittite),

Greek (Linear B), and Indic (Mitanni) existed as three quite different branches by 2000–1500 BC. The Yamnaya archaeo-genetic expansion is dated independently to the same chronological window, 3500–2500 BC, so the chronological conjunction of the expansions of late PIE and the expansions of the Yamnaya people is supported independently by archaeological, genetic, and linguistic evidence.

All ancient and modern IE-speaking populations that have been sampled genetically have revealed ancestry from steppe populations—except in Anatolia. Genetic ancestry from the steppes was found in both rich and poor Mycenaean graves averaging 13–18% of their ancestry, in a political context ruled by Greek-speakers who wrote in Linear B; but not in Minoan graves on Crete, probably mostly non-IE speakers who wrote in Linear A (Lazaridis et al. 2017: 217). Steppe ancestry averaging 22% was found in 31 ancient South Asians dated 1200–800 BC from the Swat valley, but was not found in individuals dated before 2000 BC, probably associated with the Harappan civilization, indicating the arrival of this suite of genes in South Asia during the 2nd millennium BC (Narasimhan et al. 2018). IE-speakers in modern South Asia have more steppe ancestry than non-IE speakers. The part of Europe that shows the least steppe ancestry, the Mediterranean region, also exhibited the highest diversity of non-IE languages when inscriptions began to appear after 700 BC (Ringe 2013: 206–207). The modern European population with the least steppe ancestry occupies an island, Sardinia, where a non-IE language, Paleo-Sardinian (arguably related to Basque), was spoken in antiquity (Blasco Ferrer 2011). Sardinians, among all modern European populations sampled (Haak et al. 2015), have both the least steppe ancestry and the most genetic affinity to the Neolithic farmers who brought domesticated plants and animals to Europe and the Mediterranean before 5500 BC, almost certainly non-IE speakers (Anthony & Ringe 2015).

Steppe ancestry has been identified in all tested populations that arguably spoke or speak IE languages, except Bronze Age Anatolia, which remains lightly sampled. No ancient individual from a Hittite-identified city has yielded aDNA, partly because cremation was a widespread custom. Damgaard et al. (2018) sampled individuals who arguably were Hittites in a Hattic city, but their Hittite identity is uncertain. If we had aDNA from a cemetery associated with a Hittite or Luwian-speaking ancient city or fortress this paper would be much shorter. Absent that data, we cannot say when the genetic ancestors of the Hittites entered Anatolia or what they looked like genetically. The Yamnaya archaeological culture is associated more firmly with late PIE languages and genes, so we can begin there and work back towards early PIE.

4 Hunter-Gatherer Populations and Their Contributions to Yamnaya Ancestry

What can we know about the DNA of the Indo-Hittite-speaking people who separated from the archaic PIE language community perhaps a thousand years before the Yamnaya era, whose language ultimately developed into Hittite, Luwian, and the other Anatolian IE languages? Yamnaya ancestry constrains pre-Yamnaya ancestry to a certain extent. Yamnaya genomes contained two principal genetic components derived from two distinct mating networks: a majority component derived from a mating network that evolved in the northern forest zone; and a minority component derived from a southern mating network in the Caucasus or northwestern Iran. In addition, Yamnaya genomes exhibit a small third component derived from Neolithic farmers in Europe.

The northern component was designated Eastern Hunter-Gatherer or EHG (Haak et al. 2015). EHG is merely a label, first applied to hunter-gatherer samples, but it could be used for any genetically similar individuals regardless of their subsistence economy. The EHG genetic type was first defined by Haak et al. (2015: 208) on the basis of two genetically similar hunter-gatherers from Lebyazhinka IV near Samara and Oleni Ostrov in Lake Onega near the Baltic in Russia, both dated to the mid-sixth millennium BC. Additional samples have shown that Eastern Hunter-Gatherers ranged from the Urals to the Baltic and moved down the river valleys into the steppes north of the Black and Caspian Seas.

The EHG mating network was a Holocene, western regional survival of a much larger Upper Paleolithic mating network called Ancient North Eurasian (ANE), first recognized in Upper Paleolithic humans who had lived near Lake Baikal, at a site called Mal'ta about 24,000 years ago and at another site, Aftonova Gora, about 16,000 years ago (Raghavan et al. 2014). Interconnected mating networks distributed variants of the ANE genetic type across northern Eurasia during the Upper Paleolithic, when mammoths roamed across Siberia (Pavelková Řičánková 2014). These networks extended into North America on the east (where ANE averages 15–40% of Native American genomes) and into the Pontic–Caspian steppes and the Baltic forests on the west, where ANE averaged about 70% of the genomes of the EHG mating network (Haak et al. 2015). EHG averaged about 50% of the ancestry of the Yamnaya populations that have been studied to date (Haak et al. 2015; Allentoft et al. 2015; Damgaard et al. 2018).

To identify steppe ancestry among the Hittites in Anatolia, geneticists would look for EHG. Up to now, we have not seen a Bronze Age Anatolian individual

FIGURE 1.1 Sites in the Pontic–Caspian steppes and adjacent areas

with EHG ancestry, so an intrusion into Anatolia by a population derived ultimately from the steppes is not identified genetically.

The western part of Europe was occupied by a genetically distinct group of hunter-gatherers, named Western Hunter-Gatherers (WHG). This mating network emerged in Europe during the last glacial period, and eventually was distributed from Britain to the Carpathians. WHG genomes exhibited little affinity with the Paleolithic ANE, whereas EHG genomes showed very strong affinity with ANE. This contrast indicates a period of low gene flow between the WHG and EHG ancestral populations, probably during the last peak in glacial activity about 20,000 years ago. The frontier between WHG and EHG in eastern Europe was a broad zone that extended from the lower Danube valley (Iron Gates Mesolithic people were mostly WHG with some EHG ancestry) to the forests west of the Dnieper River to the western Baltic (Mathieson et al. 2018). WHG ancestry played little or no role in the evolution of the Yamnaya mating network.

The other important component of Yamnaya ancestry came not from the west, but from the south, originally from a third hunter-gatherer population that was genetically so different from the EHG and WHG that it must have remained isolated from them during most of the Upper Paleolithic (Jones et al. 2015: Fig. 2). This third group occupied the Caucasus Mountains and western Iran and was initially designated Caucasus Hunter-Gatherer (CHG). The name is derived from the location where it was first identified (Jones et al. 2015), not from the idea that the CHG type originated in the Caucasus Mountains. The first sites where CHG was defined were a late Upper Paleolithic burial at Satsurblia in western Georgia dated 11,200 BC and a Mesolithic grave at Kotias in western Georgia dated 7800–7500 BC. These individuals were later found to be quite similar genetically to hunter-gatherers dated 9100–8600 BC from level IIIb at Hotu Cave and from nearby Belt Cave in northern Iran on the southeastern Caspian coast, located 1300 km southeast of the Georgian sites and in a very different ecological setting (Lazaridis et al. 2016). People with primarily CHG ancestry also lived 750 km southwest of Hotu Cave, at Early Neolithic Ganj Dareh near Kermanshah, dated 7000 BC (Lazaridis et al. 2016).

Because people with CHG ancestry lived on the northern (Hotu Cave) and southern (Ganj Dareh) margins of the western Iranian plateau, a similar CHG population probably was distributed across western Iran and the Caucasus at the beginning of the Neolithic, about 8000 BC. In recent papers CHG ancestry is sometimes designated "Ganj Dareh" or "Iran-N" (for Iran-Neolithic) or "CHG/Iran" but these various labels do not designate a different genetic type or variant—they refer to the same genetically defined mating network, including Hotu Cave (Caspian Sea coast) and Kotias Cave (Georgia), which here is CHG. Diluted CHG ancestry appeared in some Neolithic individuals at Tepecik-Çiftlik in central Anatolia dated 6500 BC. Tepecik-Çiftlik can be seen as the far western edge, the western tail of the curve of the CHG mating network, around 6500 BC (Kliniç et al. 2017). Most of the genetic ancestry of the Neolithic farmers from Tepecik-Çiftlik was derived from local Anatolian Farmers, who lived in central and western Anatolia and were genetically distinct from the CHG populations in the Caucasus and western Iran.

Variation existed within the CHG group. The Late Upper Paleolithic/Mesolithic individuals from Georgia exhibited a little admixture with an EHG population, probably reflecting contact with the EHG populations in the steppes north of the North Caucasus Mountains, or possibly indicating penetration into the mountains by some EHG explorers. We do not know exactly where or when the CHG element that was a robust part of Yamnaya ancestry entered the steppes—an important question.

The presence of CHG by itself in a Bronze Age Anatolian sample would not indicate steppe ancestry, because CHG was present in Anatolia during the Neolithic. A nearly 1/1 combination of CHG and EHG was the defining feature of Yamnaya ancestry as it was first defined (Haak et al. 2015; Allentoft et al. 2015).

5 The Caucasian Scenario for the Ancestry of the Hittites

If the EHG/CHG Yamnaya admixture happened in the steppes long before the Yamnaya period, then Yamnaya ancestry (and language) could have evolved entirely in the steppes. In this case the Anatolian branch could have separated from an older, pre-Yamnaya steppe population that already exhibited a mixture of CHG/EHG ancestries, through a migration from the steppes toward Anatolia. A suitable migration can be identified archaeologically, flowing from the Pontic steppes into the Danube valley and the Balkans about 4400–4200 BC, contemporary with the burning and abandonment of dozens, possibly hundreds of tell settlements and the sudden end of Old European traditions associated with the Varna-Gumelnitsa-Karanovo VI cultures (Govedarica & Kaiser 1996; Anthony 2007: 230–262; Ivanova 2007; Dergachev 2007; Bicbaev 2010). The Suvorovo-culture migrants from the steppes are not yet sampled for aDNA. Archaeologically, they seem to have admixed with the local population to produce the post-Gumelnitsa Cernavoda I culture. We also have no genetic samples from this important culture. The later Cernavoda III culture exchanged material culture styles with northwest Anatolia (Nikolova 2008), so an archaeological vector (really more than one) can connect the steppes with southeastern Europe, and southeastern Europe with Anatolia long before the initial appearance of Hittite names in documents dated 1900–1800 BC at Kanesh. But the absence of any EHG ancestry in the initial handful of Bronze Age individuals from Anatolia (Damgaard et al. 2018; Kristiansen et al. 2018) is now seen as evidence against a steppe origin for the Hittites' genetic ancestors.

If, on the other hand, the Yamnaya admixture required an extra component of CHG genes from the south, then that southern donor region could have contributed its language with its genes, particularly if economic, political, and technological innovations were introduced to the steppes by that same southern population—a description that was thought to fit the Maikop culture of the North Caucasus and its relationship with the steppes around 3500 BC, just before Yamnaya began. In that case the North Caucasian homeland of the CHG donor population (Maikop) could also have been the source of the Anatolian branch of IE languages, which could have entered Anatolia from the northeast, through Transcaucasia, although this region in later times was home to largely non-IE languages such as Urartian and Hurrian.

Reich (2018: 107–109, 120) and Kristiansen et al. (2018) suggested that a Caucasian homeland for archaic PIE (pre-Maikop and Maikop) could be combined with a steppe homeland for late PIE (Yamnaya), if Yamnaya could be derived culturally and genetically (and then, arguably also linguistically) from Maikop. Yamnaya clearly had southern (CHG) genetic ancestry and was influenced culturally by Maikop, adopting several new technologies from Maikop—arsenical bronze-making, bivalve casting molds, cast copper tanged daggers, cast copper shaft-hole axes, and possibly wheeled vehicles (Korenevskii 2012; Kohl 2007: 72–86). But it was unknown whether Maikop could have been the genetic source of CHG ancestry in Yamnaya, because a good sample of Maikop and older genomes from graves in the North Caucasus piedmont and steppes had not been published.

A very recent paper by Wang et al. (2019) changed that. The Wang et al. paper presented new data on ancient DNA from Maikop and pre-Maikop graves in the North Caucasus. The Maikop culture represented the northwestern frontier of the enormous expansion in trade for metals, gem stones, timber, and other commodities that emanated from the world's first cities during the fourth millennium BC, called the Uruk Expansion (Rothman 2014; Algaze 2005). The richest Maikop graves contained Mesopotamian symbols of power (golden lions, not native to the North Caucasus, paired with golden bulls; rosettes; and cylinder seals) as well as new metal types (arsenical bronzes) and technologies (shaft-hole axes, bivalve molds) that were borrowed by Yamnaya people after about 3300 BC (Korenevskii 1980; Chernykh 1992: 88; Ivanova 2012). Wheel-made pottery first appeared on the steppe margins with Maikop, and the oldest dated wheeled vehicle in the steppes was found in a grave in the North Caucasus steppes in a region where Maikop and Yamnaya cultural practices hybridized (Reinhold et al. 2017: Wang et al. 2019: Supplementary Information). Maikop kurgans copied earlier and simpler Eneolithic steppe burial mounds (Korenevskii 2012), but the richest Maikop burial mounds were much larger and more monumental than any of the graves they copied, and their grand scale might have inspired the widespread adoption of kurgan graves across the Pontic–Caspian steppes during the Yamnaya period. But where did the Maikop people come from? Were they Mesopotamian immigrants exploring the gold and silver resources of the North Caucasus Mountains? And did they intermarry with steppe people just before the Yamnaya culture appeared in the steppes?

Wang et al. (2019) found that individuals from both rich and poor Maikop graves had ancestries inherited from earlier Eneolithic farmers in the North

Caucasus piedmont. The first farmers in the North Caucasus piedmont came from the south, probably from western Georgia and Abkhazia, today home to Northwest Caucasian languages. They are called the Darkveti–Meshoko culture by Trifonov in Wang et al. (2018), and are the ideal archaeological candidate for the founders of the Northwest Caucasian language family. From sites like Darkveti Cave on the Georgia/Abkhazia side of the mountains, a region where northwest Caucasian languages are spoken today, they migrated over the North Caucasus ridge into the upper Belaya river valley, the other principal region where Northwest Caucasian languages are spoken today. Their earliest known arrival is dated about 4600–4500 BC at Unakozovskaya Cave in the upper Belaya River valley (Wang et al. 2018). Rapidly afterward, walled agricultural settlements such as Meshoko spread down the Belaya valley to the edge of the steppes (Svobodnoe) before 4000 BC. They established farming (wheat) and domesticated animal herding (cattle, pigs, sheep & goats) in the northwest Caucasus region, and also founded the genetic mating network that later would characterize the people of the Maikop culture, their direct descendants. Their Y-chromosome (paternal) haplogroups were L, J, and G2, which were typical of southern males, but generally were not shared with northern steppe males. They showed an admixture of ancestries, largely CHG, but with about 30–40% Anatolian Farmer ancestry, which had spread into the Caucasus from the west after about 5000 BC. A similar admixture characterized most of the sampled people who lived across Transcaucasia in the fourth millennium BC, associated with the Kura-Araxes culture. This Maikop/Kura-Araxes genetic admixture played only a minor role, if any, in the formation of Yamnaya ancestry, because the 30–40% Anatolian Farmer component was not seen in steppe ancestries.

Maikop cannot be regarded as the source of "southern" CHG ancestry in Yamnaya because Maikop genomes had too much ancestry from Anatolian Farmer populations. Yamnaya genomes had only 10–18% Anatolian Farmer ancestry, and Wang et al. (2019) identified most of that as derived from Europe, from Globular Amphorae and late Tripol'ye populations. If Wang et al (2019: 9) are correct that Yamnaya and all later steppe populations "deviate from the [pre-Yamnaya steppe population] towards European populations in the West" then Caucasus populations are left to play only a small role in Yamnaya ancestry. Yamnaya men had almost exclusively R1b Y-haplogroups, and pre-Yamnaya Eneolithic Volga–Caspian–Caucasus steppe men were principally R1b, with a significant Q1a minority. Maikop men did not father a significant number of Yamnaya males. If there was any Maikop gene flow into Yamnaya, it could have been through a small number of Maikop females whose 30–40% Anatolian Farmer ancestry was diluted in their descendants, and whose skeletons have not yet been found or analyzed.

If Maikop people rarely married into or mated with or were taken as concubines by Yamnaya people, then one of the most powerful vectors of language shift—intermarriage between people from different language groups—is removed. It then becomes more difficult to derive the Yamnaya language, presumed to be late PIE, from Maikop. In any case, Maikop is geographically more likely to represent the ancestor of today's Northwest Caucasian languages, as argued above.

If Maikop was not the source of the CHG in Yamnaya, then another alternative could be that CHG ancestry came from an unknown and undocumented southern source that entered the steppes at an unknown time. But the dataless places where such a source could be hidden are shrinking. A previously unknown genetic population actually was identified in Wang et al. (2019), but it was a peculiar relict-seeming group related to Paleo Siberians and American Indians (Kennewick) that had survived isolated somewhere in the Caspian steppes or perhaps in the North Caucasus Mountains. The Maikop people *did* admix with this previously isolated Siberian/Kennewick population in graves labeled "Steppe Maikop" in Wang et al. (2019).

But this just makes it clearer that a cultural choice motivated the Maikop people to exclude marriages with Yamnaya and pre-Yamnaya people specifically, even while exchanges of material goods, ideas, and technologies continued. Neither the Maikop nor the North Caucasus/Siberian/Kennewick population can be the source of most of the CHG ancestry in Yamnaya. In order to narrow down when and where CHG ancestry entered the steppes, we must widen our geographic frame beyond the Caucasus.

6 Four Eneolithic Mating Networks in the Pontic–Caspian Steppes

Four mating networks in the Pontic–Caspian region are relevant for determining Yamnaya genetic ancestry and origins. The first mating network was that of Eneolithic farmers and the later Maikop people in the forested zone of the North Caucasus Mountains, just described. The second mating network linked together populations in the middle Volga steppes (Khvalynsk) and the North Caucasus steppe foothills (Progress-2), a north-south distance of over 1000 km taking in the Volga steppes, Caspian steppes, North Caucasus steppes, and the lower Don steppes. The third mating network was much smaller, connecting cemeteries in the middle Dnieper region about 200 km apart. The middle Dnieper was a strategic ecotone richly endowed with Eneolithic cemeteries, so while small, the region is important. The fourth network linked together the Neolithic and Copper Age or Eneolithic farmers of southeastern Europe, who subsisted on rainfall agriculture, lived in large farming villages and towns, and were quite distinct from the first three. We have important voids in the DNA evidence, one of being the absence of any samples from the coastal part of the Pontic steppes in Ukraine, a potential bridge between the steppes and Network #4, and it will be critical to study such samples in the future.

6.1 *Mating Network # 1: The North Caucasus Network, 4500–4000 BC*

The Eneolithic farmers of the North Caucasus Mountains, the parent population of the later Maikop population, appeared in the upper Belaya River drainage on the north side of the North Caucasus Mountains around 4600–4400 BC (the age of Eneolithic graves in Unakozovskaya Cave). They crossed the mountains from western Georgia and Abkhazia on the south side, carrying with them a genetic admixture that subsequently linked populations on both sides of the North Caucasus ridge (Wang et al. 2019). An inviting low gap (maximum 2000 m elevation) leads directly into the upper Belaya headwaters from near Sochi and Adler on the Black Sea coast. The North Caucasus ridge forms a permanently glaciated wall up to 5400 m high (at Mt Elbrus) for a solid 350 km east of the eastern peak (Mt. Chugush) that defines this gap. Therefore this gap is the first place explorers in western Georgia moving westward along the southern mountain foothills could have easily crossed the mountains to their north side. Visible from the south as a depression between two glacier-capped peaks (Mt. Chugush on the east and Mt. Fisht on the west, each rising to ca. 3000 m), the pass to the upper Belaya River is so steep and winding that no paved road exists today, but summer hikers regularly backpack through the area. This geographic feature could explain why the oldest Eneolithic sites on the north side of the North Caucasus are found in the upper Belaya valley, why the oldest and richest Maikop graves are located there, and why Maikop and Meshoko populations were so similar genetically to those on the south side of the North Caucasus.

Eneolithic agricultural settlements (Meshoko, Yasenova Polyana) and rock-shelter occupations (Unakozovskaya Cave) were clustered in the upper Belaya but extended down the Belaya River valley to the steppe border (Svobodnoe). The Eneolithic farmers built protective walls around their agricultural villages (earth at Svobodnoe, stone at Meshoko), herded pigs and cattle, and traded material goods and ideas with the steppe population but did not marry them. The huge Maikop chieftan's kurgan (early Maikop, 3600–3300 BC) was erected in the middle Belaya valley, and the even richer Klady or Novosvobodnaya kurgan cemetery (late Maikop, 3300–2900 BC) was erected not far from Maikop. Because they came from a genetically and geographically distinct population, and avoided marriage with the steppe population of Mating Network #2, it is

FIGURE 1.2 Mating networks in and near the Pontic–Caspian steppes dated 4500–4000 BC

likely that both the Svobodnoe-Meshoko people and their Maikop descendants spoke a Caucasus-derived language distinct from that of the steppes.

6.2 *Mating Network # 2: The Volga-Caucasus Network 4500–4000 BC*

A population showing a mixture of EHG and CHG ancestries existed in the Volga-Caucasus steppes during the Eneolithic period. This Yamnaya-like admixture was established before 4500 BC, the approximate date of Khvalynsk. Published samples (Mathieson et al 2018; Wang et al 2019) from two cemeteries 1000 km apart, Progress-2 and Khvalynsk, dated about 4500–4300 BC, define this population, and a third published sample might be added to the very end of this period from Aleksandriya in eastern Ukraine, dated about 4000 BC. Samples from two other Volga-steppe Eneolithic cemeteries, Ekaterinovka Mys and Khlopkov Bugor, are now under study at the Reich lab at Harvard but are not published. They exhibit dominant EHG ancestry, typical of this mating network, with CHG. The percentage of CHG ancestry declines south-to-north, from Progress-2, where CHG is 30–50%, to Khvalynsk (CHG 20–

30%) to Ekaterinovka (perhaps 5%, but not yet published). Eneolithic individuals generally had less CHG than Yamnaya, but their EHG/CHG admixture ranges overlapped with those from Yamnaya samples, according to Wang et al. 2019: Figure 2C. The Khvalynsk-Progress-2 mating network makes a plausible genetic ancestor for Yamnaya, but Yamnaya was more homogeneous genetically than the Eneolithic cemeteries, particularly in male genetic traits on the Y-chromosome.

Most Khvalynsk males belonged to Y-chromosome haplogroup R1b1a, like almost all Yamnaya males, but at least five Khvalynsk males, including some very richly endowed, were Q1a1b. Single males were R1a1, J1, and I2a2a. The Q1a1b males probably were linked to the north, where this haplogroup is found in ancient samples from Siberia, the Altai Mountains, and across the forest zone to the Baltic. The J1 male at Khvalynsk probably was linked to the south, since he belonged to the same Y-haplogroup as the CHG type specimen from Satsurblia Cave in Georgia, confirming affinity with CHG in the Khvalynsk population. The I2a2a male was descended from a haplogroup common among Mesolithic WHG's in the Danube valley, and the R1a1 male belonged to a minority type within the EHG. But Yamnaya individuals chosen for kurgan burial seem to have been drawn from a narrower subset of these, almost all of them R1b1a, suggesting that those buried under Yamnaya kurgans in the Pontic–Caspian steppes belonged to a restricted patrilineal group of some kind—probably a clan or related set of clans.

The samples from the North Caucasus steppes came from three Eneolithic graves at Progress-2 and Vonyuchka, both dated about 4300–4100 BC (4336–4173 cal BCE/5397±28 BP/MAMS-110563; and 4233–4047 cal BCE/5304±25 BP/MAMS-11210). These three males were very similar genetically to Khvalynsk males—they showed a mixture of EHG/CHG ancestry and Y-chromosome haplogroups R1b1 and Q1a2, closely related to the most common haplogroups at Khvalynsk, R1b1 and Q1a1b (Wang et al. 2019). They lived near the Svobodnoe-Meshoko farmers higher up in the North Caucasus mountain valleys, but showed no genetic connections with them. They exhibited higher proportions of CHG than at Khvalynsk, overlapping the Yamnaya proportions.

Finally, one individual from a Sredni Stog culture cemetery on the Donets River at Aleksandriya in eastern Ukraine is dated 4000 BC (4045–3974 cal BCE/5215±20 BP/PSUAMS-2832). He exhibited about 70–80% CHG/EHG ancestry, like Khvalynsk and Progress-2, but also about 20% Neolithic farmer ancestry of the type that spread from western Anatolia into Europe with the advent of farming. His Y-chromosome haplogroup was R1a–Z93, similar to the later Sintashta culture and to South Asian Indo-Aryans, and he is the earliest known sample to show the genetic adaptation to digesting milk in adults, lactase per-

FIGURE 1.3 Khvalynsk II, female (sister) and male (brother) skeletons 24 & 25 decorated with hundreds of shell beads, 13 copper rings, 3 copper tubes, a copper spiral ornament, beaver incisor belts, and a boar's tusk pendant, with a polished stone mace-head at center right and bones of sheep and goat offerings at lower right.

sistence (I3910-T). The Sredni Stog culture has for decades been recognized (Telegin et al. 2001) as an Eneolithic predecessor of Yamnaya in Ukraine that also showed links with Khvalynsk in the Russian steppes (similar grave rituals) and with the European farmer cultures to the west (copper trade). This Sredni Stog individual was much more admixed with European farmers than any previous sample in the steppes. His primary ancestry showed the expansion westward of Network #2 into the North Pontic steppes.

These samples indicate that a mating network with mixed EHG/CHG ancestry, a good candidate for an ancestor to Yamnaya, occupied the 1000 km of steppes between the middle Volga and the North Caucasus foothills during the late Eneolithic, 4500–4000 BC. By 4000 BC, a significant component of European farmer ancestry had spread eastward to Aleksandriya in eastern Ukraine. With the addition of European farmer ancestry (similar to Anatolian farmer ancestry), the genetic cocktail typical of the Yamnaya culture was formed in eastern Ukraine (and perhaps elsewhere) many centuries before the Yamnaya culture began.

This is not surprising from an archaeological perspective. S.N. Korenevskii (2012; 2016: 11) already identified the Eneolithic archaeological cultures of this steppe region (Khvalynsk, Sredni Stog, and steppe Caucasus) as the extended proto-Yamnaya community within which the practice of erecting a burial mound, a kurgan, first appeared within the steppes, though not at Khvalynsk. The body pose and grave ritual at the Khvalynsk cemetery, without mounds, was recognized as similar to the Nalchik cemetery in the North Caucasus, with mounds, by the archaeologists who excavated Khvalynsk in 1977 (Agapov, Vasiliev & Pestrikova 1990; Vasliev 2003: 74). Nalchik was excavated mostly before World War II, but the grave rituals there (body posed on the back with raised knees, ochre on the grave floor, shape of the grave pit, N-NE orientation, and even some artifact types) were similar to Khvalynsk, as well as other cemetery sites on the lower and middle Volga excavated later (Anthony 2007: 186–187; Vasiliev 1981, 2003). As we receive more aDNA samples from Eneolithic cemeteries in the Volga–Caspian–Caucasus steppes it is anticipated that they will exhibit variants of this same EHG/CHG genetic ancestry, admixed with European farmer ancestry after about 4000 BC.

We still do not know when or where CHG people first entered the steppes, but it was definitely before 4500 BC. Hunter-gatherer populations of the CHG type probably migrated northward into the steppes from the southern end of the Caspian Sea, perhaps during the early Holocene, and were integrated into EHG mating networks that extended down the Volga from the forest zone, producing a hybrid steppe population that was fairly homogeneous genetically from the middle Volga to the North Caucasus steppes by 4500–4300 BC. But at 4500 BC they had not yet married into the emerging cattle-keepers whose biggest cemeteries were on the Dnieper Rapids, far to the west, as we will see below.

6.3 *Mating Network # 3: The Middle Dnieper Network 5000–4500 BC*

Three early Eneolithic cemeteries on the Dnieper River, Dereivka-1, Vil'nyanka, and Vovnigi, yielded aDNA that was notably different from Khvalynsk and Progress-2 (Mathieson et al. 2018; Jones et al 2017). Two of the three Dnieper cemeteries, Dereivka_1 and Vil'nyanka, together yielded aDNA from 31 graves; the third, Vovnigi, yielded a single individual, for a total of 32. All three cemeteries can be attributed to the Dnieper-Donets II (DDII) culture, so had similar artifacts and rituals (Lillie et al. 2009; Anthony 2007: 174–182; Telegin & Potekhina 1987). Human bones from the two heavily sampled cemeteries are dated about 5400–4800 BC, not adjusting for reservoir effects. Their true age might be more like 5100–4500 BC, centuries older than Khvalynsk. The Vovnigi individual was dated 4500–4400 BC, so about contemporary with Khvalynsk. Dnieper-Donets II cemeteries were large and contained bodies laid out in extended positions beside each other in trenches or long pits, some of which contained three or four layers of superimposed skeletons. This mortuary ritual was different from that of Khvalynsk and Progress-2, as was the Dnieper-Donets II pottery distinct from Khvalynsk ceramics.

Dereivka-1 was located in the transitional forest-steppe ecological zone, 100 km north of the Dnieper Rapids, and Vil'nyanka and Vovnigi were located in the steppes beside the Dnieper Rapids. The Rapids (flooded today by dams) fell 50 m in elevation from north to south over a distance of 90 km in seven named whitewater falls. They were strategic fishing places and river crossings, and were the first place in the Pontic–Caspian steppes to attract populations that created formal cemeteries, beginning in the early Mesolithic about 11,000–10,500 BC (Lillie et al. 2009; Jones et al 2017: Supp. Mat. p. 9).

At the whole-genome level all three DDII cemetery populations were very similar to each other. They were also similar to the Mesolithic population of the Dnieper Rapids, but the Mesolithic fishers had less WHG ancestry than their DDII fisher-herder descendants. The Dnieper region seems to have experienced an influx of WHG ancestry between the Mesolithic and Neolithic, perhaps when European farmers moved into former WHG territories in Moldova and Romania, pushing the indigenous people eastward.

All 32 tested DDII individuals were admixtures of EHG (primarily) and WHG (variable minor amounts) with no CHG ancestry. The absence of CHG distinguishes the middle Dnieper populations from the Volga-Caucasus mating network to the east.

Looking at Y-chromosome haplogroups (Mathieson et al. 2018: Supplementary Data), the Dereivka males were largely R1b1a with a few I2a2a, similar to Khvalynsk, but without the Q1a2 element that comprised an important minority at Khvalynsk; and also without the J1 individual that linked Khvalynsk to the Caucasus. Vil'nyanka was surprisingly homogeneous, as all of the tested males had I2a2a or a less defined variant of I ancestry. This again was more typical of WHG than EHG populations, perhaps suggesting that the Neolithic–Eneolithic increase in WHG admixture in the Dnieper region was sex-biased toward WHG males.

At Vil'nyanka at least one grave, 38, contained the burned bones of a sacrificed domesticated bull (Anthony 2007: 179; Telegin & Potekhina 1987: 113).

The domesticated stock from which this animal came probably originated among Linear Pottery villages in the east Carpathian foothills, from where domesticated cattle slowly spread eastward into steppe communities after 5500 BC. The people buried at Vil'nyanka might have enjoyed domesticated beef, but they showed no trace of genetic admixture with European farmers. They seem to have harbored a European farmer captive or refugee at Dereivka-1, where DNA revealed a single anomalous male in Grave 102, not the expected EHG/WHG admixture seen in all other graves, but instead a 100% European farmer of the Linear Pottery–Tripol'ye genetic type (Mathieson et al. 2018: 200). He was a captive, trader, or refugee who left no genetic imprint on his hosts. His radiocarbon date was a little later than most of the others at Dereivka-1 (4949–4799 BC, 5995±25 BP/PSUAMS-2303) so perhaps he was buried when the cemetery was in decline. He was found at the end of a row of eight, the other seven apparently indigenous EHG/WHG individuals buried shoulder-to-shoulder (graves 95–102)—his adopted family/owners? Captive-taking would not be unexpected (Cameron 2016) between a population of immigrant Linear Pottery–Tripol'ye farmers and indigenous former hunter-gatherers (WHG/EHG) who were beginning to adopt the herding aspect of the farmers' economy.

The earliest dated admixture between European farmers and Network #3 was a female in the Dereivka-1 cemetery. She was dated 1500 years after the Eneolithic graves, so was an isolated burial in a long-abandoned cemetery directly dated 3600–3400 BC, just before the Yamnaya kurgan-grave horizon spread across the steppes (grave 73, 3634–3377 cal BCE/4725±25 BP/UCIAMS-186349). She showed about 20% European farmer ancestry, similar to the Aleksandriya individual dated 4000 BC; but she showed less CHG than Aleksandriya and more Dereivka-1 ancestry, not surprising for a Dnieper valley sample (Mathieson et al. 2018: 200). Her mtDNA group was J2b1, which was rare in both European farmer and EHG/WHG populations.

No DD II individual showed ancestry from the European farmer populations to the west, or CHG ancestry from the herders to its east. They were a distinct, locally derived population that seems to have limited its mating network to the rich, strategic region it occupied, centered on the Rapids. We do not have samples from the coastal steppes below the Rapids, so we do not know the southern border of this mating network. But it would not be surprising if they spoke a different language from that of the Volga-Caucasus steppes, which is beginning to look like the region where the genetic type associated with IE languages appeared earliest.

6.4 *Mating Network # 4: European Farmers and Admixture with the Steppe 4600–4300 BC*

Most of the 48 individuals that yielded aDNA from 16 Neolithic and Copper Age (Eneolithic) cemeteries in Bulgaria and Romania exhibited standard European farmer ancestries (Mathieson et al. 2018). They were descended mostly from Neolithic west Anatolian Farmers and probably spoke languages derived from Neolithic western Anatolia. Some showed admixtures with the former indigenous population, WHG, usually less than 10% of their ancestry, indicating occasional and remote hunter-gatherer ancestors (Mathieson et al. 2018).

But two individuals had significant steppe ancestry of the Volga-Caspian EHG/CHG type (Network #2); and a third, the richest grave at Varna, probably had distant ancestry of this type. These individuals are dated 4650–4450 BC (Krauss et al. 2016: 282). A few families in the tell towns of northeastern Bulgaria at their peak period of development had ancestors from Network #2—certainly a surprise. It must be stressed that 95% of the Neolithic and Chalcolithic individuals tested showed no identifiable steppe ancestry.

Two of the five graves at Varna I that yielded aDNA, or 40% of those successfully sampled, had or probably had EHG & CHG ancestry. The least secure case is described first. The famous golden male in Grave 43, now dated about 4550–4450 BC (MAMS 15095/5662 ± 27), was buried in the latest (sixth) phase of the cemetery (Krauss et al. 2016: 282), with seven heavy copper implements, more than 1000 gold items, ornaments made of the shells of *Spondylus* and imported minerals, and highly sophisticated flint tools. His steppe ancestry was not strong enough to make him a statistically significant outlier from the European farmer population, but Grave 43 did deviate away from European farmer central values in the direction of EHG/CHG, suggesting a distant ancestor who was genetically from the Volga-Caucasus EHG/CHG mating network.

The second individual from Varna that showed steppe ancestry was in one of the oldest graves, grave 158, assigned to phase 1 of the cemetery, dated 4711–4550 BC, possibly 200 years older than Grave 43 (5787±30 BP/OxA-13688; 5755±24 BP/MAMS-30944) (Mathieson et al. 2018: Supplementary Data Table and Supplementary Information p. 14). Grave 158 contained the remains of a 5–6-year-old girl who had about 20% steppe ancestry of EHG/CHG type, enough to make her a statistically significant outlier from her Neolithic/Copper Age European farmer population (Mathieson et al. 2018: 201). Her steppe ancestry was consistent with a grandparent or great-grandparent from the Volga-Caucasus steppes. She was furnished with Varna-culture ceramic vessels and large quantities of Varna-culture ornaments made of *Spondylus* and beads of various minerals—a rich grave in its phase (Mathieson 2018, Supplementary Materials, p. 14). Her mtDNA haplogroup was H7a1, like a woman in the Yunatsite tell in Bulgaria and another buried in a Neolithic Impresso-ware site in Croatia (Mathieson 2018: Supplementary Data Table), and unlike any steppe MtDNA lineage. This indicates that her maternal ancestry was a local farmer lineage, so her steppe ancestor more probably was male. Steppe ancestry does not seem to have hindered people at Varna from achieving high status.

The third individual with steppe ancestry was buried at Smyadovo, Bulgaria, in a grave much like the others in this Late Copper Age cemetery. Grave 29 contained a male 20–25 years old, posed like the others in a grave like the others, buried with a flint tool, two typical ceramic vessels, and beads of serpentine, bone and *Spondylus*—a well-equipped grave. Like the girl in Grave 158 at Varna, he had about 20 % steppe CHG/EHG ancestry, enough to make him a statistically significant outlier. Grave 29 was dated 4550–4455 BC (5680±30 BP/Beta-432803), about the same age as Varna Grave 43. His MtDNA haplogroup was HV15, not a common haplogroup in ancient Europe, but variants of HV do occur in Middle Neolithic European sites, so his matriline could be considered a European farmer type. His Y-chromosome haplogroup could not be defined closely, but it was a variant of R, quite common in the steppes. Again, his steppe ancestor more likely was a male, and again, his steppe ancestry was not an impediment to being buried in a well-equipped grave.

A scenario that would be consistent with these observations would be for some higher-status Old European families in northeastern Bulgaria to have accepted a small number of steppe males as marriage partners to secure peaceful interactions and exchanges under the umbrella of kinship. These marriages were infrequent or absent everywhere except Varna. If they involved only higher-status families, this could explain why the three steppe-related individuals at Varna and Smyadovo had well-equipped graves—it was because they belonged to elite families, and only elite families in northeastern Bulgaria had steppe ancestors. Whatever rules or conditions prevented European farmers from mating with steppe people elsewhere were dropped in these exceptional cases. The admixed offspring remained in the Varna region and identified as members of their native elite families. Alliance-making, or relational wealth (Mulder et al. 2010: 37–39) is one of the principal foundations of power in tribal societies. Steppe kinship perhaps was seen as an advantageous element of relational wealth in some Varna leaders.

It is intriguing that the type of steppe ancestry that appeared in Varna and Smyadovo was the Volga-Caucasus type, EHG/CHG (I. Mathieson, personal communication), not the middle Dnieper type, EHG/WHG. The middle Dnieper is much closer to Varna. People with middle Dnieper-type ancestry (Network #3) continued to live in that region until well after the Varna period, since the female from Dereivka dated 3800–3600 BC still had mostly Neolithic Dereivka-1 ancestry. People in the Dnieper Rapids region certainly acquired many copper artifacts from Old Europe during the "Skelya" period, 4500–4200 BC, a period of increased trade between the steppes and southeastern Europe named by Rassamakin (2002) after a site on the Dnieper Rapids, Stril'cha Skelya (not sampled for DNA). But Mating Network #2, the Volga-Caucasus genetic type, appeared in Varna; not Mating Network # 3, the middle Dnieper type. The Sredni Stog grave at Aleksandriya shows that before 4000 BC, people with primarily Volga-Caucasus ancestry, EHG/CHG, occupied the steppes west of the Don. Perhaps they moved through the coastal steppes south of the Rapids to meet and seal agreements with elite families who lived in the tell towns of the lower Danube. Khvalynsk-type ancestry, which contained the essential elements of Yamnaya ancestry (EHG/CHG with R1b1), except for the European farmer component, expanded across the steppes from east to west with the Sredni Stog culture.

7 The 4300 BC Event and the Anatolian Split

Dueling archaeological scenarios have envisioned migrations from the steppes into southeastern Europe, as described above, and from southeastern Europe into the steppes. This dispute can now be revisited with evidence from aDNA.

In the farmer-into-the-steppes scenario, European farmers migrated in large numbers from Tripol'ye C1 super-towns (larger in area than Uruk-phase cities) in modern Moldova and Ukraine into the steppes about 3500 BC. This Tripol'ye-to-the-steppe migration was partly responsible for the origin of the Yamnaya culture, regarded in this theory as a semi-pastoral outgrowth of the more advanced Tripol'ye culture on one side and the metal-rich Maikop culture on the other (Mileto et al. 2017; Kaiser 2010; Kohl 2007: 236–237; Manzura 2005; Rassamakin 1999, 2002). This set of ideas overturned and replaced Gimbutas's (1963, 1977) long-criticized hypothesis that IE-speaking mounted nomads rode on horseback westward out of the steppes and into Europe. Rassamakin (1999, 2002) and Manzura (2005) proposed and defended in detail the archaeological foundation for this theory, giving concrete archaeological support to a more abstract western critique of migration theories in general.

However, the farmer>steppe theory also denied any agency or originality to steppe societies, particularly those in the Volga steppes, painting them as peripheral, egalitarian, unwarlike, horse-less, sedentary hunters and hoe cultivators, and unimaginative imitators of more advanced neighboring cultures: "… the Volga zone was a region that received innovations and was not a point of origin …" (Rassamakin 1999: 108). The indigenous steppe herders prior to the hypothesized migration of 3500 BC were, in P. Kohl's phrase, "impoverished cowboys" (Kohl 2007: 237). In this theory the Skelya period about 4500–4200 BC witnessed the transfer of copper metallurgy from Varna and Tripol'ye to the Dnieper Rapids, making the Rapids region the dominant center of a Pontic–Caspian trade system; followed by a hiatus in exchanges after the decline of the Varna-Karanovo VI cultures; and ending with a major demographic expansion of European farmers into the steppes about 3500–3000 BC.

The low level of European farmer ancestry (10–18%) in Yamnaya individuals from the Ukrainian, Volga, and North Caucasus steppes, combined with the low level of potential Maikop ancestry in Yamnaya genomes discussed above, speaks strongly against this theory as it relates to the origin of the Yamnaya population. No demographic wave of European farmers or Maikop pastoralists flowed into the steppes; on the contrary, most of the Yamnaya population was derived primarily from older steppe populations. I have argued elsewhere (Anthony 2013; 2016) against the characterization of Eneolithic steppe pastoralism as "primitive" or "unsophisticated" during the first two millennia of steppe pastoralism, 5500–3500 BC; or as focused exclusively on cattle imported from Tripol'ye after 3500 BC. Eneolithic (pre-Yamnaya) steppe pastoralism was not universally primitive or anything else; it varied from region to region. In some places, including Khvalynsk and the middle Volga region, domesticated animals were more important as a ritual currency used in funeral feasts than in the daily diet (Anthony 2013), but this is far from an "unsophisticated" (Mileto et al. 2017: 72) use of domesticated animals. Before and after Yamnaya appeared, some sites were sheep-dominant and others were cattle-dominant—cattle were not the universal mainstay of all Yamnaya or Early Bronze Age (EBA) economies (Anthony 2016: 22–23). The 3500 BC date for the admixture of significant European farmer ancestry into the steppe populations must also be wrong, because European farmer ancestry was present at Aleksandriya in eastern Ukraine in a person who died about 4000 BC (before the biggest Tripol'ye C1 towns appeared). This earlier date for admixture with European farmers favors the second theory.

The second theory hypothesizes a migration of steppe people of the Suvorovo culture (a Danube-delta group of graves probably derived from the Sredni Stog culture in Ukraine) into the Danube valley about 4400–4200 BC, consistent with European farmer admixture at Aleksandriya at 4000 BC (Gheorgiu 1994; Govedarica & Kaiser 1996; Ivanova 2007; Anthony 2007; Dergachev 2007; Heyd 2016). In addition to creating the Suvorovo graves in the steppes north of the Danube delta, some steppe migrants also apparently moved into the Balkans, the eastern Carpathian Basin, and Transylvania (Alexandrov 2010;

Gogâltan & Ignat 2011). Gimbutas proposed a similar migration, her Wave 1 of IE expansions (Gimbutas 1963, 1977), but in my estimation her Wave 1 went too far geographically and its motivations were poorly articulated (Anthony 2007: 230–262). Dergachev (2007), however, accepted her description of this event as essentially correct. It begins archaeologically with the appearance of Suvorovo-type graves in the Danube delta about 4400–4300 BC and ends with the end of Karanovo VI and Gumelnitsa A2 and of almost all of the material culture traditions they embodied about 4300–4200 BC.

One of the hallmarks of the Suvorovo (Telegin et al. 2002) or Skelya (Rassamakin 1999) period was the appearance of new kinds of polished stone mace heads made in specific Volga-Caspian steppe styles, different from Dnieper mace-head styles, in both Cucuteni–Tripol'ye towns and in the tell towns in the lower Danube and the Balkans (Karanovo VI). This transfer of Volga-Caucasus polished stone mace styles accompanied a contemporary transfer of Volga-Caucasus genes into the leading families of northeast Bulgaria. At the same time, copper from the Balkans flowed into steppe communities. Hundreds of copper ornaments apparently made from Balkan ores were recovered from Eneolithic graves in the Dnieper-Azov steppes, where they are associated with Skelya and Sredni Stog cultures; and at Khvalynsk on the Volga, 373 copper ornaments were recovered from 27 graves among 201 excavated (14% of graves), the largest copper assemblage from a fifth-millennium BCE site anywhere in the steppes (Agapov 2010). At least five Khvalynsk ornaments examined by Ryndina (2010: 239–240) must have been imported from southeastern Europe as finished objects. Balkan-derived copper also reached both Svobodnoe (Courcier 2014: 586) and Progress-2-type steppe graves in the North Caucasus (Korenevskii 2016). Ornaments of Balkan copper, exotic ornamental shells (*Glycemeris, Antalis*), long lamellar flint blades, polished stone maces, and perhaps people and animals were exchanged across the Pontic–Caspian steppes from Varna to Khvalynsk and Svobodnoe. But Eneolithic regional marriage networks exhibited persistent structure while material and technological exchanges flowed between the marriage blocks.

This period of exchange, interaction, and migration was followed by a catastrophic culture change that accompanied the abandonment of all tell settlements in the lower Danube valley and the Balkans and the end of their material culture traditions about 4300–4200 BC (Todorova 1995; Ivanova 2007; Nikolova 2008; Gogâltan & Ignat 2011; Georgieva 2014). In the following centuries the immigrants from the steppes seem, from archaeological evidence, to have mixed with the remnants of the tell populations to become the steppe-influenced but admixed Cernavoda I culture. (Again, we have no aDNA yet from this important population.)

The language of the Suvorovo migrants and of their Cernavoda I descendants is unknown, and their DNA has not been reported. At this early moment in the publication of aDNA, it seems to me that the most likely place for the archaic PIE (Indo-Hittite) homeland would be in the Volga-Caucasus steppes east of the Don, where the oldest admixture of EHG and CHG occurred in the fifth millennium BC or earlier; from which the Varna chiefs accepted a few mates; and where Yamnaya ancestry emerged in the fourth millennium BC. An archaic dialect of PIE, the parent of Anatolian, could have moved from the Volga-Don region into the Danube valley with the Suvorovo migrants and their Volga-Caucasus-style stone maces.

Limited movements from southeastern Europe into northwestern Anatolia might have occurred immediately after the collapse of Old European towns in the Balkans, before 4000 BC, although the cited evidence is thin (Georgiev 2014). Or, the steppe immigrants could remain in the Balkans for a millennium until the Baden-Cernavoda III and Troy I period around 3100–3000 BC, when archaeology shows more robust material connections between Bulgaria and northwest Anatolia (Nikolova 2014; Krauss et al. 2016). This EBA date would fit with the estimate from Kloekhorst (2018) that Proto-Anatolian was spoken about 3000 BC. But by 3000 BC the original steppe genes would have been diluted by a millennium or more of admixture in southeastern Europe before the move into Anatolia, and then another millennium of admixture in Anatolia before the first Hittite names appeared in documents. The EHG signal in Bronze Age Anatolia might be very weak when and if it is found.

On the other hand, recent aDNA studies should make all archaeologists wary of depending too much on archaeology to solve questions about migration. In particular, we cannot expect to equate ancient migrations with the introduction of an easily recognizable archaeological material culture derived from the homeland of the migrants. Sometimes that happened, but migrants often used material culture in inventive ways that concealed their origin, perhaps intentionally, which only aDNA can then reveal. The most surprising recent cautionary case was the origin of Corded Ware. The Corded Ware material culture package looked like it was indigenous to northern Europe using excellent archaeological methods that were well-matched to explanatory theories (Furholt 2015). But aDNA (Allentoft et al. 2015; Haak et al. 2015) showed that the Corded Ware people clearly were migrants who came overwhelmingly, more than 70% of their ancestry, from a Yamnaya steppe origin genetically. Their migrant origin was obscured by their shift from Yamnaya to Corded Ware material cultures probably within a century (3000–2900 BC) at the beginning of a major expansion of range. Corded Ware material culture incorporated specific artifact types (globular amphorae, polished stone hammer-axes) taken from indigenous Middle Neolithic cultures in northern Europe. It could be seen as a material advertisement by the Corded Ware migrants directed at their Yamnaya parents and grandparents, warning of new political alliances with indigenous Middle Neolithic populations—an active material statement of political separation that contained pointed references to new allies. Whatever it represented, the creation of the Corded Ware package was an active and creative use of material culture to forge a new cultural identity among migrants who had separated themselves geographically from their parent group, although they remained genetically and probably linguistically much alike. A major regional shift in material culture occurred in the middle of a migration stream, like a dye introduced to a river. The introduction of the dye (the material culture shift) was an important, even critical cultural event, but it did not change the biological species in the river fundamentally. So the search for an *archaeological* signal of a migration into Anatolia is interesting, but we must depend on aDNA, and hope that it tells a clear story, if we are to decide whether Hittites had biological ancestry that flowed out of the steppes, like other populations that spoke or speak IE languages.

References

Agapov, S.A., I.B. Vasiliev & V.I. Pestrikova, 1990. *Xvalynskij èneolitičeskij mogil'nik.* Saratov: Izd. Saratovskogo universiteta.

Agapov, S.A. (ed.) 2010. *Xvalynskie èneolitičeskie mogil'niki i xvalynskaja èneolitičeskaja kul'tura: Issledovanija materialov.* Samara: SROO IEKA "Povolž'e".

Alexandrov, Stefan. 2010. Prehistoric barrow graves with extended inhumations between the Danube and the Balkan Range. *Studia Praehistorica* (Bulgaria) 13. 277–292.

Algaze, G. 2005. *The Uruk world system.* 2nd edition. Chicago: University of Chicago Press.

Anthony, David W. 2007. *The horse, the wheel, and language: How Bronze Age riders from the Eurasian Steppes shaped the modern world.* Princeton: Princeton University Press.

Anthony, David W. 2013. Two IE phylogenies, three PIE migrations, and four kinds of steppe pastoralism. *Journal of Language Relationship* (Moscow) 9. 1–22.

Anthony, David W., & D.R. Brown 2017. Molecular archaeology and Indo-European linguistics: Impressions from new data. In Bjarne S.S. Hansen, Adam Hyllested, Anders R. Jørgensen, Guus Kroonen, Jenny H. Larsson, Benedicte Nielsen Whitehead, Thomas Olander & Tobias M. Søborg (eds.), *Usque ad radices: Indo-European studies in honour of Birgit Anette Olsen*, 25–54. Copenhagen: Museum Tusculanum.

Anthony, David W., & D.R. Brown. 2011. The secondary products revolution, horse-riding, and mounted warfare. *Journal of World Prehistory* 24(2). 131–160.

Anthony, David W., & Don Ringe. 2015. The Indo-European homeland from linguistic and archaeological perspectives. *Annual Review of Linguistics* 1. 199–219.

Allentoft, Morten E., Martin Sikora, Karl-Göran Sjögren, Simon Rasmussen, Morten Rasmussen, Jesper Stenderup, Peter B. Damgaard et al. 2015. Population genomics of Bronze Age Eurasia. *Nature* 522. 167–172. doi:10.1038/nature14507

Bicbaev V. 2010. The Copper Age cemetery of Giugiuleşti. In D.W. Anthony & J. Chi (eds.), *The lost world of Old Europe: the Danube valley, 5000–3500 BC*, 212–224. New York: Institute for the Study of the Ancient World.

Cameron, Catherine M. 2016. *Captives: How stolen people changed the world.* Lincoln: University of Nebraska Press.

Courcier, Antoine. 2014. Ancient metallurgy in the Caucasus from the sixth to the third millennium BCE. In B.W. Roberts & C.P. Thornton (eds.), *Archaeometallurgy in global perspective*, 579–664. New York: Springer.

Czebreszuk, J., & M. Szmyt. 2011. Identities, differentiation and interactions on the central European plain in the 3rd millennium BC. In S. Hansen & J. Müller (eds.), *Sozialarchäologische Perspektiven: Gesellschaftlicher Wandel 5000–1500 v. Chr. zwischen Atlantik und Kaukasus*, 269–294. Darmstadt: Philipp von Zabern.

Damgaard, Peter de Barros, R. Martiniano, J. Kamm, J.V. Moreno-Mayar, G. Kroonen, M. Peyrot, G. Barjamovic et al. 2018. The first horse herders and the impact of Early Bronze Age steppe expansions into Asia. *Science* 360(1422). doi:10.1126/science.aar7711

Davidski (blogger). 2018. Likely Yamnaya incursion(s) into Northwestern Iran. *Eurogenes*, 22 April 2018. https://eurogenes.blogspot.com/2018/04/likely-yamnaya-incursions-into.html

Demoule, Jean-Paul, B. Laks, S. Cleuziou & P. Encrevé. 2008. Origins and evolution of languages: retrospectives and perspectives. In Bernard Laks (ed.), *Origin and evolution of languages: Approaches, models, paradigms*, 1–28. London: Equinox.

Ecsedy, István (ed.). 1979. *The people of the pit-grave kurgans in eastern Hungary*. Budapest: Akadémia Kiadó.

Fansa M., & S. Burmeister (eds.). 2004. *Rad und Wagen: der Ursprung einer Innovation: Wagen im vorderen Orient und Europa*. Mainz: Philipp von Zabern.

Falileyev, Alexander. 2015. Introduction: A folk who will never speak: Bell Beakers and linguistics. In Maria Pilar Prieto Martínez & Laure Salanova (eds.), *The Bell Beaker Transition In Europe: Mobility and local evolution during the 3rd millennium BC*, 1–7. Oxford: Oxbow.

Georgieva, Petya. 2014. Opportunities for tracing the influence of the Balkans on Anatolia during the end of the 5th and the beginning of the 4th millennium BC. *e-Journal of Archaeology* (Bulgaria) 4. 217–236.

Gheorgiu, Drago. 1994. Horse-head scepters—first images of yoked horses. *Journal of Indo-European Studies* 22(3–4). 221–250

Gimbutas, Marija. 1977. The first wave of Eurasian steppe pastoralists into Copper Age Europe. *Journal of Indo-European Studies* 5(4). 277–338.

Gimbutas, Marija. 1963. The Indo-Europeans: Archaeological problems. *American Anthropologist* 65. 813–835.

Gogâltan, Florin, & Ana Ignat. 2011. Transilvania şi spaţul Nord-Pontic. Primele contacte (cca 4500–3500 a. Chr). *Tyragetia* 5(1). 7–38.

Golitko, Mark 2015. Migration, admixture, and human populations. *Science Dialogues*, 30 June 2015. https://sciencedialogues.com/articles/biological/migration-admixture-and-human-populations/

Govedarica, B., & E. Kaiser. 1996. Die äneolithischen abstrakten und zoomorphen Steinzepter Südost- und Osteuropas. *Eurasia Antiqua* 2. 59–103.

Groneborn, Detlef. 2014. The persistence of hunting and gathering: Neolithic western and central Europe. In V. Cummings, P. Jordan & M. Zvelebil (eds.), *The Oxford handbook of the archaeology and anthropology of hunter–gatherers*, 1–14. Oxford: Oxford University Press.

Haak, Wolfgang, I. Lazaridis, N. Patterson, N. Rohland, S. Mallick, B. Llamas, G. Brandt et al. 2015. Massive migration from the steppe was a source for Indo-European languages in Europe. *Nature* 522(7555). 207–211.

Heyd, Volker, 2012. Yamnaya groups and tumuli west of the Black Sea. In E. Borgna & S. Müller Celka (eds.), *Ancestral landscapes: Burial mounds in the Copper and Bronze Ages*, 536–555. Lyon: Maison de l'Orient et de la Méditerranée—Jean Pouilloux.

Heyd, Volker. 2016. Das Zeitalter der Ideologien: Migration, Interaktion und Expansion im prähistorischen Europa des 4. und 3. Jahrtausends v. Chr. In M. Furholt, R. Großmann & M. Szmyt (eds.), *Transitional landscapes? The 3rd millennium BC in Europe*, 53–84. Bonn: Habelt.

Ivanov, V.V., & T.V. Gamkrelidze. 1995. *Indo-European and the Indo-Europeans*. 2 vols. Berlin & New York: Mouton de Gruyter.

Ivanova, Mariya. 2012. Kaukasus und Orient: Die Entstehung des "Maikop-Phänomens" im 4. Jahrtausend v. Chr. *Praehistorische Zeitschrift* 80(1). 1–28.

Ivanova, Mariya. 2007. Tells, invasion theories and warfare in 5th-millennium BC northeastern Bulgaria. In Tony Pollard & Iaian Banks (eds.), *Warfare and sacrifice: Studies in the archaeology of conflict*, 33–48. Leiden: Brill.

Jones, Eppie R., Gloria Gonzalez-Fortes, Sarah Connell, Veronika Siska, Anders Eriksson, Rui Martiniano, Russell L. McLaughlin et al. 2015. Upper Palaeolithic genomes reveal deep roots of modern Eurasians. *Nature Communications* 6. 8912.

Jones, E.R., G. Zarina, V. Moiseyev, E. Lightfoot, P.R. Nigst, A. Manica, R. Pinhasi & D.G. Bradley, 2017. The Neolithic Transition in the Baltic was not driven by admixture with Early European Farmers. *Current Biology* 27. 1–7.

Kaiser, E., 2010. Ègalitarnoe pastušeskoe obščestvo *versus* voiny-kočevniki. *Stratum plus* 2. 99–120.

Karl, R. 2010. The Celts from everywhere and nowhere. In B. Cunliffe & J.T. Koch (eds), *Celtic from the West*, 39–64. Oxford: Oxbow.

Kılınç, G.M., D. Koptekin, Ç. Atakuman, A.P. Sümer, H.M. Dönertaş, R. Yaka, C.C. Bilgin et al. 2017. Archaeogenomic analysis of the first steps of Neolithization in Anatolia and the Aegean. *Proc. Royal Society B* 284(1867). doi:10.1098/rspb.2017.2064

Kloekhorst, Alwin. 2016. The Anatolian stop system and the Indo-Hittite hypothesis. *Indogermanische Forschungen* 121(1). 213–248.

Koivulehto J. 2001. The earliest contacts between Indo-European and Uralic speakers in the light of lexical loans. In C. Carpelan, A. Parpola & P. Koskikallio (eds.), *Early contacts between Uralic and Indo-European: linguistic and archaeological considerations*, 235–263. Helsinki: Suomalais-Ugrilainen Seura.

Korenevskii, S.N. 1980 O metalličeskix veščax I utevskogo mogil'nika. In A.D. Prjaxin (ed.), *Arxeologija vostočno-evropejskoj lesostepi*, 59–66, Voronež: Izd. Voronežskogo universiteta.

Korenevskii, S.N. 2016. Problemnye situacii "post-Ubajdskogo perioda" v Predkavkaz'e (4500–3500 let do n.è.). *Stratum plus* 2. 1–26.

Krauss, R., C. Schmid, D. Ciobotaru & V. Slavchev. 2016. Varna und die Folgen—Überlegungen zu den Ockergräbern zwischen Karpatenbecken und der nördlichen Ägäis. In M. Bartelheim, B. Horejs & R. Krauss (eds.), *Von Baden bis Troia. Ressourcennutzung, Metallurgie und Wissenstransfer: Eine Jubiläumsschrift für Ernst Pernicka*, 273–315. Rahden: Leidorf.

Kristiansen, Kristian. 2017. Migration, archaeology and DNA: Interview with Kristian Kristiansen. *Revista ArkeoGazte* (Vitoria-Gasteiz, Spain) 7. 169–172.

Kristiansen, Kristian, Morten E. Allentoft, Karin M. Frei, Rune Iversen, Niels N. Johannsen, Guus Kroonen, Łukasz Pospieszny et al. 2017. Re-theorising mobility and the formation of culture and language among the Corded Ware Culture in Europe. *Antiquity* 91(356). 334–347.

Kristiansen, Kristian, B. Hemphill, G. Barjamovic, S. Omura, S.Y. Senyurt, V. Moiseyev, A. Gromov et al. 2018. Archaeological supplement A to Damgaard et al. 2018: Archaeology of the Caucasus, Anatolia, Central and South Asia 4000–1500 BCE. doi:10.5281/zenodo.1240516

Lazaridis, Iosif, D. Nadel, G. Rollefson, D.C. Merrett, N. Rohland, S. Mallick, D. Fernandes et al. 2016. Genomic insights into the origin of farming in the ancient Near East. *Nature* 536(7617). 419–424.

Lazaridis, Iosif, A. Mittnik, N. Patterson, S. Mallick, N. Rohland, S. Pfrengle, A. Furtwängler et al. 2017. Genetic origins of the Minoans and Mycenaeans. *Nature* 548. 214–218.

Lehrman, Alexander 2001. Reconstructing Proto-Hittite. In Robert Drews (eds.), *Greater Anatolia and the Indo-Hittite language family*, 106–130. Washington: Institute for the Study of Man.

Lillie, Malcolm, C. Budd, I. Potekhina, and R. Hedges. 2009. The radiocarbon reservoir effect: new evidence from the cemeteries of the middle and lower Dnieper basin, Ukraine. *Journal of Archaeological Science* 36: 256–264.

Mallory, J.P. 2008. Migrations in prehistoric Eurasia: problems in the correlation of archaeology and language. *Aramazd (Armenian Journal of Near Eastern Studies)* 3(2). 7–37.

Mallory, J.P., & D.Q. Adams. 2006. *The Oxford introduction to Proto-Indo-European and the Proto-Indo-European world.* Oxford: Oxford University Press.

Manzura, Igor. 2005. Steps to the steppe: or, how the North Pontic region was colonized. *Oxford Journal of Archaeology* 24(4). 313–338.

Mathieson, Iain, I. Lazaridis, N. Rohland, S. Mallick, N. Patterson, S.A. Roodenberg, E. Harney et al. 2015. Genome-wide patterns of selection in 230 ancient Eurasians. *Nature* 528. 499–503.

Mathieson, Iain, S.A. Roodenberg, C. Posth, A. Szécsényi-Nagy, N. Rohland, S. Mallick, I. Olalde et al. 2018. The genomic history of southeastern Europe. *Nature* 555. 197–203.

Mileto, S., E. Kaiser, Y. Rassamakin & R.P. Evershed. 2017. New insights into the subsistence economy of the Eneolithic Dereivka culture of the Ukrainian North-Pontic region through lipid residue analysis of pottery vessels. *Journal of Archaeological Science: Reports* 13. 67–74.

Mulder, Monique B., I. Fazzio, W. Irons, R.L. McElreath, S. Bowles, A. Bell, T. Hertz & Leela Hazzah. 2010. Pastoralism and wealth inequality: Revisiting an old question. *Current Anthropology* 51(1). 35–48.

Narasimhan, Vagheesh M., N. Patterson, P. Moorjani, I. Lazaridis, M. Lipson, S. Mallick, N. Rohland et al. 2018. The genomic formation of South and Central Asia. *bioRxiv*. doi:10.1101/292581

Nettle, D. 1998. Explaining global patterns of linguistic diversity. *Journal of Anthropological Archaeology* 17. 354–374.

Nikolova, Lolita. 2008. Balkan-Anatolian cultural horizons from the fourth millennium BC and their relations to the Baden complex. In M. Furholt, M. Szmyt & A. Zastawny (eds.), *The Baden Complex and the outside world*, 157–166. Bonn: Habelt.

Ortman, S.G. 2012. *Winds from the North: Tewa origins and historical anthropology*. Salt Lake City: University of Utah Press.

Pavelková Řičánková, V., J. Robovský & J. Riegert. 2014. Ecological structure of recent and last glacial mammalian faunas in northern Eurasia: The case of Altai-Sayan refugium. *PLoS ONE* 9(1). e85056.

Parker, Bradley J., & Lars Rodseth (eds.). 2005. *Untaming the frontier in anthropology, archaeology, and history*. Tucson: University of Arizona Press.

Pickrell, J.K., & David Reich. 2014. Toward a new history and geography of human genes informed by ancient DNA. *Trends in Genetics* 30(9). 377–389.

Rassamakin, Yuri. 2002. Aspects of Pontic steppe development (4550–3000 BC) in the light of the new cultural-chronological model. In Katie Boyle, Colin Renfrew & Marsha Levine (eds.), *Ancient interactions: East and West in Eurasia*, 49–74; Cambridge: McDonald Institute.

Raghavan, M., P. Skoglund, K.E. Graf, M. Metspalu, A. Albrechtsen, I. Moltke, S. Rasmussen et al. 2014. Upper Palaeolithic Siberian genome reveals dual ancestry of Native Americans. *Nature* 505. 87–91.

Reich, David. 2018. *Who we are and how we got here: Ancient DNA and the new science of the human past.* Oxford: Oxford University Press.

Reinhold, Sabine, J. Gresky, N. Berezina, A.R. Kantorovich, C. Knipper, V.E. Maslov, V.G. Petrenko, K.W. Alt & Andrew B. Belinsky. 2017. Contextualising innovation. Cattle owners and wagon drivers in the North Caucasus and beyond. In Philipp Stockhammer & Joseph Maran (eds.), *Appropriating innovations: Entangled knowledge in Eurasia, 5000–1500 BCE*, 78–97. Oxford: Oxbow.

Ringe, Don. 2013. The linguistic diversity of aboriginal Europe. In Shu-Fen Chen & Benjamin Slade (eds.), *Grammatica et verba, glamor and verve*, 202–212. Ann Arbor: Beech Stave.

Robb, John. 1993. A social prehistory of European languages. *Antiquity* 67. 747–760.

Rothman, Mitchell S. 2014. Interpreting the role of Godin Tepe in the "Uruk expansion". In Cameron A. Petrie (ed.), *Ancient Iran and its neighbors: Local developments and long-range interactions in the fourth millennium BC*, 75–91. Oxford: Oxbow Books.

Ryndina, N.V. 2010. Mednye naxodki xvalynskogo I mogil'nika: Itogi texnologičeskogo issledovanija. In S.A. Agapov (ed.), *Xvalynskie èneolitičeskie mogil'niki i xvalynskaja èneolitičeskaja kul'tura: Issledovanija materialov*, 234–257. Samara: SROO IEKA "Povolž'e".

Saarikivi, Janne, & Mika Lavento. 2012. Linguistics and archaeology: A critical view of an interdisciplinary approach with reference to the prehistory of northern Scandinavia. *Suomalais-Ugrilaisen Seuran Toimituksia* 265. 177–216.

Scerri, Eleanor M.L., M.G. Thomas, A. Manica, P. Gunz, J.T. Stock, C. Stringer, M. Grove et al. 2018. Did our species evolve in subdivided populations across Africa, and why does it matter? *Trends in Ecology & Evolution* 2399. doi:10.1016/j.tree.2018.05.005

Shishlina, N.I., E.P. Zazovskaya, J. van der Plicht, R.E.M. Hedges, V.S. Sevastyanov & O.A. Chichagova. 2009. Paleoecology, subsistence, and 14C chronology of the Eurasian Caspian steppe Bronze Age. *Radiocarbon* 51(2). 481–499.

Sims-Williams, P. 2012. Bronze- and Iron-Age Celtic speakers: what don't we know, what can't we know, and what could we know? Language, genetics and archaeology in the twenty-first century. *Antiquaries Journal* 92. 427–449.

Stark, Miriam T. (ed.). 1998. *The archaeology of social boundaries.* Washington: Smithsonian Press.

Stockhammer, P.W. (ed.). 2012. *Conceptualizing cultural hybridization.* Heidelberg: Springer.

Telegin, D.Y., & I.D. Potekhina. 1987. *Neolithic cemeteries and populations in the Dnieper Basin*. Oxford: BAR.

Telegin, D.Y., A.L. Nechitailo, I.D. Potekhina & Y.V. Panchenko. 2001. *Srednestogovskaja i Novodanilovskaja kul'tury èneolita Azovo-černomorskogo regiona*. Lugansk: Šljax.

Terrell, John. 2018. "Plug and Play" genetics, racial migrations and human history. *Scientific American Blog Network*, 29 May 2018. https://blogs.scientificamerican.com/observations/plug-and-play-genetics-racial-migrations-and-human-history

Todorova, Henrietta. 1995. The Neolithic, Eneolithic, and transitional in Bulgarian prehistory. In Douglass W. Bailey & Ivan Panayotov (eds.), *Prehistoric Bulgaria*, 79–98, Madison, WI: Prehistoric Press.

Vasiliev, I.B. 1981. *Èneolit Povolž'ja*. Kujbyšev: Kujbyševskij gosudarstvenyj pedagogičeskij institut.

Vasiliev, I.B. 2003. Xvalynskaja èneolitičeskaja kul'tura Volgo-Ural'skoj stepi i lesostepi (nekotorye itogi issledovanija). *Voprosy Arxeologii Povolž'ja* (Samara) 3. 61–99.

Wang, C.-C., S. Reinhold, A. Kalmykov, A. Wissgott, G. Brandt, C. Jeong, O. Cheronet et al. 2019. Ancient human genome-wide data from a 3000-year interval in the Caucasus corresponds with eco-geographic regions. *Nature Communications* 10. 590. doi:10.1038/s41467-018-08220-8.

CHAPTER 2

Nouns and Foreign Numerals: Anatolian 'Four' and the Development of the PIE Decimal System

Rasmus Bjørn

1 Introduction

1.1 *Anatolian and Core Indo-European*

Proto-Anatolian **mei̯-(e)u-* 'four', for the moment not-withstanding its etymology, is unique among the ancient Indo-European branches in that it emphatically departs from the otherwise canonical treatment of the decimal numerals (Kloekhorst 2008: 572). Perhaps more perplexing is the fact that Anatolian seems to continue all other attested simple numerals; something is certainly awry with the numeral 'four'. Aligning previously presented arguments into a comprehensive numeral typology for PIE and the prehistoric region in fact suggests that the entire decimal system betrays areal and typological phenomena that attest to the process of numeralization of previously nominal or foreign elements in a relatively shallow time frame. Excellent works exist both on the attestations (in particular Gvozdanović 1992) and research history (e.g. Blažek 1999) of Indo-European numerals, allowing this treatment to focus on the broader lines of development and, in particular, the loanword hypotheses.

1.2 *Methodology*

> [I]n the absence of any additional information we can only conclude that at the stage of PIE which we can reconstruct with the comparative method, the names of the numerals had no further significance.
>
> CLACKSON (2007: 200)

> Ohne Kühnheit kommt man in der Forschung nicht vorwärts, wenn es sich um schwierige Fragen handelt.
>
> COLLINDER (1965: 109)

Beyond the threshold of the established proto-languages, otherwise tantalizing comparanda easily become unamenable to the requirements of the comparative method as many strong loanword indicators, e.g. relative chronologies and

 | DOI:10.1163/9789004416192_004

phonetic match (cf. Campbell 2013: 61–66), are severely impeded or lost, and the demonstration of relatedness comes to rely on weaker domains like geography and culture. While accepting that isolated comparanda remain beyond our ability to properly evaluate, I have previously argued in favor of a methodological framework to deal coherently with prehistoric loanwords (Bjørn 2017: 1–21): nouns have been shown to have their spread mirrored in archaeology ("Wörter und Sachen", e.g. for the spread of Gr. πέλεκυς, Ved. *paraśú-* 'ceremonial axe', see Makkay 1998), but purely linguistic phenomena may, too, be bolstered by circumstantial evidence in semantic spheres. Numerals present a particularly good case for testing such systemic features: the decimal row is closed and the meaning by default relates one-to-one as opposed to connotational accidents of common nouns.

As Proto-Semitic and Proto-Indo-European are unlikely to have been immediate neighbors even at the proto-stages, I posit an intermediary language ("Balkanic") to account for the (near) correspondences. While it is inherently unattractive to posit forms from an unattested language, the prehistorical circumstances demand that a (set of) culturally significant language(s) was spoken in the Balkans within the relevant timeframe, and unlike other plausible substrate theories (e.g. Schrijver 2003, Carling 2005: 52–54), this even purports to relate to known phyla. None of the above considerations render the issue settled in any degree, but are gathered to present a methodologically defensible scenario subject to further scrutiny. Most exhaustive are thus the discussions on 'six', 'seven', and 'eight', which all betray signs of borrowing, although the common etymologies for the rest of the simplex decimal numerals are included to show their most probable etymologies.

1.3 *The Smaller "Subitizing" Numerals*

1–3 belong to the core vocabulary in most languages, and in Proto-Indo-European they show none of the signs of recent numeralization as the higher numerals do.[1] They are here referred to as the "subitizing numerals", a term borrowed from the cognitive sciences that denotes quantities that are readily discernible at a glance:

> [S]ubitizing range is nowadays usually considered to range from one to about three or four objects in adults, and from one to about two to three in children under school age.
>
> RAILO & HANNULA-SORMUNEN 2012: 3233

1 The reason why 'one' seems to fluctuate between branches (cf. Blažek 1999: 154–157) is its function in the intersection between numeral, adverb, pronoun, and article, thus making multiple roots continuously compete for the numeral slot.

2 How Many Indo-European Numerals for 'Four'?

'Four' introduces issues to an otherwise consistent decimal series. Three different words with the meaning 'four' have been proposed at the Proto-Indo-European horizon: Core IE **kʷetu̯or*, PA **mei̯-(e)u-*, and the purported antecedent of a dual 'eight', PIE **(H)oḱt-*. While I intend to show that the latter number is a mirage, the mere existence of a competition within the system indicates that it was not fully numeralized and that different strategies of describing sets of four were employed by the speakers.

2.1 *Core PIE* *kʷetu̯or- *'Four'*

- Toch. A *śtwar*, Toch. B *śtwer*; Lat. *quattuor*; OIr. *cethair*; Goth. *fidwor*; Lith. *keturì*; OCS *četyre*; Alb. *katër*; Myc. *qe-to-ro-po-pi* 'four-footed', Gr. *τέσσαρες*; Arm. *cʿorkʿ*; Ved. *catvā́raḥ*, YAv. *caϑβārō*.

The consistency with which the numeral has been passed on in all branches apart from Anatolian securely establishes the proto-form to an early stage of Proto-Indo-European. The lack of an obvious loan relation or a transparent etymology (although a plethora of explanations have been proposed, see Schmid 1989: 23–24, Blažek 1999: 209–215 and Szemerényi 1996: 222–223) suggests that the numeral can be traced further back, most likely predating the split of Anatolian. Hit. *kutruuan* 'witness', widely considered a derivative of **kʷetu̯or-* (e.g. Eichner 1992: 80–82 and Kloekhorst 2008: 500–501), could in this regard cement its ancient status and is preferable to the alternative yet tenuous connection with Lithuanian *gudrùs* 'clever, cunning, wily' (Puhvel 1997: 299–300, Kassian 2009a: 68 n. 8). The numeral etymology gains further credibility in light of Hit. *tariyala-* 'mediator' and HLuw. *tariwana-* 'righteous judge [i.e. prince]' as the 'third' (Eichner 1992: 70–73), cf. also Lat. *testis* 'witness' (de Vaan 2008: 618). Another striking feature of **kʷetu̯or-* is that it inflects like the subitizing numerals (1-2-3) opposing the uninflected higher set (5–10). This positive interpretation of the noun requires the specialized meaning to have developed already by the split of Proto-Anatolian from Core Indo-European.[2]

2 Relative chronology thus dictates that the legal function must have been attained by the split of Proto-Anatolian into its constituents. With Anatolian judge ('four') and an Italic witness ('three'), the court is almost set and these forms should consequently aid in the reconstruction of the PIE legal system.

2.2 *Proto-Anatolian* *mei̯-(e)u- *'Four'*

- Hittite: *mieu-*, *miu-*, e.g. *mi-e-wa-as-* (Eichner 1992: 76)
- Cuneiform Luwian: *maauua-*, e.g. *ma-a-u-wa-a-ti pa*[*-aa-*]*r-ta-a-ti* 'with four sides' (Eichner 1992: 78)
- Lycian: *mupm̃m* 'fourfold?' (Shevoroshkin 1979: 188; Kloekhorst 2008: 571; Neumann 2007: 227)

Consistent use of securely attested forms of the numeral in at least Hittite and Luwian, and possibly also Lycian, establishes **mei̯-(e)u-* as the Proto-Anatolian numeral 'four'. Ablaut is required to account for the attested forms, indicating that the formation is internal (Melchert, p.c., Tischler 1990: 178; Heubeck 1963: 202; Eichner 1992: 77–78) and that the numeral was still treated as nominally derived at the split of Anatolian.

The most widely accepted etymology relates it to Myc. *me-wi-jo* 'less', Gr. *μείων* 'smaller', and thus a native formation referring to a, presumably already fixed, numeral value of 'five' (e.g. Martínez 1999: 207, see §3.1). Other known strategies for adding numerals come from borrowing (cf. Kassian 2009a: 65), and a sub- or superstratum loan would offer the best alternative, necessarily through special circumstances either elevating the foreign item as cultic or debasing the inherited form through taboo. There is, however, no external candidate for a numeral 'four' in the known high cultures around Anatolia at the time, and the ablauting paradigm is similarly indicative of a native formation.

2.3 *Pre-PIE* *(H)oḱt- *'[Four]'* → *Pre-PIE Dual* *(H)oḱtō(u) *'Two [Four]s'* → *PIE* *(H)oḱtō(u) *'Eight'*

- YAv. *ašti* 'breadth of four fingers'

With the hypothesized logical antecedent of 'eight' as a petrified grammatical dual of PIE **h₂oḱ-t-* 'Handspitze', possibly attested in a related form YAv. *ašti* 'breadth of four fingers' (Henning 1948), a third numeral 'four' enters the Proto-Indo-European horizon. The reconstruction is further enlivened by the probable loan relation with Proto-Kartvelian **otxo* 'four' (see further §3.4). The dual interpretation is not secured (Mayrhofer 1992: 142, Sihler 1995: 414), and a negative evaluation would cut the internal morphological connection with 'four' and the Young Avestan etymon.

2.4 *PIE 'Four' in Summation*

Up to three distinct forms thus inhabit the last common stage of the Indo-European languages. The trajectories from Pre-Proto-Indo-European through to the first uncontested stage are presented below.

TABLE 2.1 The Indo-European words for 'four' and their development

Proto-form	Pre-PIE	PIE	P-Anat.	Core-IE
**kʷetu̯or-*	'four'	'four'	'witness' (der.)	'four'
**mei̯-(e)u-*	'smaller'	'four'/'smaller'	'four'	'smaller'
**(H)oḱt-*	'Handspitze'	'eight'/'Handspitze'	'eight'	(Av. 'width of four fingers')

2.5 *'Four' in Proto-Anatolian*

If even a true PIE quantifier, there is no reason to assume that **(H)oḱt-* should have carried the meaning 'four' far, if at all, into Proto-Anatolian, which then must have shed it early on. The two other designations appear to have been in simultaneous use with **kʷetu̯or-* ultimately displaced. There is no obvious external pressure on the numeral value of 'four' to warrant a shift. A taboo exclusion of the numeral is not evident either, and would have had to have happened within Proto-Anatolian. The lack of **mei̯-(e)u-* as 'four' in Core-Indo-European does, however, suggest that the numeral function only developed in Proto-Anatolian, although Eichner takes the semantic shift as an indication that it is of Proto-Indo-European date (1992: 77–78).

3 The Remaining Higher Numerals of the Decimal System

The remaining Proto-Indo-European numerals appear to be consistent throughout the individual branches, with occasional Anatolian evidence defying the scribal convention of hiding their phonological reality behind ideograms.

3.1 *Core-IE* *penkʷe *'Five'*

- Toch. A *päñ*, Toch. B *piś*; Lat. *quīnque*; OIr. *cōic*; Goth. *fimf*; Lith. *penkì*; OCS *pętĭ*; Alb. *pesë*; Gr. *πέντε*; Arm. *hing*; Ved. *páñca*, YAv. *paṇca*.

There is no Anatolian evidence for the form.[3] Polomé's connection to Hit. *panku-* 'all, whole' (1969: 99–101) is a tantalizing attempt at an etymology

3 Possible Luwian material mentioned in Bjørn (2017: 123) should be abandoned (Melchert, p.c.).

but remains disputed (cf. Kloekhorst 2008: 624–626). There are no external numeral comparanda, and the formation is probably native,[4] although not readily decipherable. Secondary connections with the Germanic words for *fist* and *finger*, and also ORuss. *pjastʹ* 'fist' (cf. Kroonen 2013: 141, Szemerényi 1960: 113–114, 1996: 223 n. 9), underpin the 'referential' numerals ('four' as 'smaller' [§ 2.2] and 'six' as 'grow' [§ 3.2]) along with the semantics of a word like Gr. *πεμπάζω* 'to count on the five fingers', suggesting that the numeral represents a central and potentially early fixed point in Indo-European counting. The Indo-European evidence is thus not conclusive, but the hands are typologically common nominal bases for 'five' (and 'ten' [§ 3.6]), thus also in Semitic (cf. Lipiński 1997: 287; and, more broadly, Winter 1992: 18).

3.2 *PIE *(s)u̯eḱs 'Six'*

- Toch. A *ṣäk*, Toch. B *ṣkas*; Lat. *sex*; Welsh *chwech*; Goth. *saíhs*; Lith. *šešì*, OPrus. *us(ch)ts* 'sixth'; OCS *šestĭ*; Alb. *gjashtë*; Myc. *we-pe-za* 'six-footed', Gr. *ἕξ*; Arm. *vecᶜ*; Ved. *ṣáṭ*, YAv. *xšuuaš*.

Blažek suggests that the Hittite measurement *wakšur* derives from **(s)u̯eḱs-* (2012), potentially establishing evidence for the numeral in Proto-Indo-European proper. Even if this etymology is accepted, the actual numeral value may still technically have been replaced and the formation be a relict like Hit. *kutruuan* 'witness' opposed to **mei̯-(e)u-* 'four' (§ 2.2). There is no consensus as to a Proto-Indo-European derivational basis (cf. Mayrhofer 1996: 680–681), and the attempt to connect to the verbal root **h₂u̯eks-* 'grow' (e.g. Klimov 1994; Szemerényi 1960: 79), potentially referring to the fixed value 'five' and semantically mirroring the standard etymology for Anatolian 'four' as 'smaller' (§ 2.2), suffers from a plain velar and is thus unlikely. A native formation may be corroborated by the Old Prussian ordinal that appears to be a zero-grade (Stang 1966: 278–279); the initial **s-* is in this scenario sequentially assimilated from 'seven'. There is still no easy way to reconcile all attestations in the branches and this incompatibility has been addressed by various scholars, both in defense of a native formation (e.g. Blažek 2012; Szemerényi 1960: 79 n. 55; Winter 1992: 14–15, Sihler 1995: 413) and as a sign of foreign influence (Mallory & Adams 1997: 402; Martínez 1999: 208–209). Regardless of the ultimate origin of the form it must be presupposed that the numeral was integrated into the decimal, and consequently grammatical, system before the dissolution of Proto-Indo-European,

4 A Uralic nominal **piŋз* 'palm' has been proposed (Čop 1970: 161, Trombetti 1923: 549), but is irrelevant to the numeral argument.

and potential foreign sounds have been neutralized. For this reason, "independent borrowings" into individual branches, as Mallory & Adams tentatively suggest (1997: 402), are highly unlikely. Rather, a proto-linguistic borrowing may have been reinterpreted, possibly through folk-etymological associations, e.g. to **h_2u̯eks-* 'grow', and assumed native traits such as ablaut.

The proposed comparanda are:

- Kartvelian **ekws-* > Georgian *ekvs-*, Mingrelian *amšv*, Laz *a*(*n*)*š*-, Svan *usgwa*
- NW Caucasian: *(*s*)*əxwə* > Kabardian *хы*, Abkhaz *ҩба*
- Hurrian *šeše*
- Semitic **šidt* > Akk. *šeššet*, Syr. *štā'*, etc.
- Egyptian *śrś.w* > Coptic *sow*

With a mercurial initial sibilant and an occasional labial element, the external comparanda show great variation that nonetheless appear to mirror the problems encountered within Indo-European. As Proto-Indo-European may have borrowed 'seven' (§ 3.3), and possibly also 'eight' (§ 3.4), it is likely that 'six', with comparanda from the same neighboring language families, could have entered the system from the outside. Two Caucasian proto-languages have similar forms: Proto-NWC *(*s*)*əxwə* 'six' (Colarusso 1997: 144) on the Black Sea littoral in close proximity to the Pontic Steppes is particularly interesting if it stands scrutiny, but the reconstruction of this language family is severely inhibited by morphosyntactic and attestational circumstances, rendering definite answers hard to reach (cf. Dolgopolsky 1989: 16). South of the Caucasus range, Proto-Kartvelian **ekws* (Klimov 1998: 48; Georg 2002; Fähnrich 2007: 151–152) appears less obviously connected, although Blažek makes a case for a borrowing from an Indo-European dialect, possibly Iranian (1999: 83, but see discussion of the age of Proto-Kartvelian numerals in § 3.4). The Semitic connection is even less robust, the forms are thus unlikely to relate directly in the same temporal or linguistic stratum, and intermediary languages could in this regard help bridge the phonological gap (see further § 5.5).

3.3 *PIE* *septm̥ *'Seven'*

- PAnat. **septam* → Hit. *si-ip-ta-mi-ya* 'drink of seven (ingredients?)'; Toch. A *ṣpät*, Toch. B *ṣukt*; Lat. *septem*; OIr. *secht*^{N}; Goth. *sibun*; Lith. *septynì*; OCS *sedmĭ*; Alb. *shtatë*; Gr. *ἑπτά*; Arm. *ewtʿn*; Ved. *saptá*, YAv. *hapta*.

The Anatolian evidence was secured by Neu in demonstrating the identity of the forms *si-ip-ta-mi-ya* and *VII-mi-ya*, both 'drink of seven (ingredients?)' (1999). Scholars treating Indo-European numerals, while defending internal analyses of 'six' and 'eight', have grappled with the abstract nature of 'seven' and most, more or less hesitantly, concede the possibility of a loan from Semitic (e.g.

Winter 1992: 13; Martínez 1999: 209). See Schmid (1989: 13–14) for an attempt at an internal explanation that ultimately relies on secondary meanings of **sep-* '(richtig) behandeln, (in Ehre) halten' (LIV²: 534).

The proposed external comparanda are:

– Semitic **t͡sabʕa-t-Vm* (masc.def.) > Akk. *sebet*, Syr. *šabʿā*, etc.
– Egyptian *śfḫ* > Coptic *sašif*
– Kartvelian **šwid-* > Georgian *švid-*, Mingrelian *škvit-*, Laz *šk(v)it-*, Svan *išgwid*

In favor of a direct transfer from Proto-Semitic to Proto-Indo-European, Dolgopolsky posits the morphological complex masc.def. Proto-Semitic form **šabʿa-t-Vm* (1993: 243). Juxtaposed with the unanalyzable ending in Proto-Indo-European it constitutes a strong argument in favor of a borrowing (cf. Campbell 2013: 63–64), but a reception in (pre-)Proto-Indo-European is not straightforward and has some phonotactic gaps to bridge:[5]

1 The *e*-vocalism could be attributed to the undefined status of PIE **a* (cf. Lubotsky 1989, Sihler 1995: 44–45).
2 The Proto-Semitic form is trisyllabic as opposed to the disyllabic Proto-Indo-European counterpart.
3 The Proto-Semitic phoneme */ʕ/ is not immediately reflected in Proto-Indo-European, which is generally assumed to have three distinct laryngeals.
4 The stressed final syllabic resonant in Proto-Indo-European seems at odds with the full-vowel ending in Proto-Semitic.
5 The refined reconstruction of an initial **t͡s-* in Proto-Semitic (van Putten & Suchard, p.c.) changes little in terms of how the onset can be expected to appear in (pre-)Proto-Indo-European.

The comparison is consequently not as immaculate as Dolgopolsky would have it. It is similarly troublesome to pinpoint a geographic location for the transfer to have occurred, with Proto-Semitic and Proto-Indo-European on opposite sides of the Caucasus range with all it entails of linguistic variety. These difficulties do not, however, exclude the comparison altogether, but only highlight the need for an intermediate stage (cf. § 5.5), and necessarily with a formation grammatically related to that in Semitic proper. This form could stem either from a language closely related to Semitic or an unrelated language that borrowed the term wholesale from Proto-Semitic and passed it on to Proto-Indo-European (see further in § 5). The inflected form would still indicate that the borrowing very concretely denoted a concept of high value,

5 I am indebted to the anonymous reviewer for the concrete points of incompatibility.

which Nichols suggests is of agricultural origin (1997: 127), which is highly conceivable considering the sustained cultic significance of the *sabbath*. The borrowability of 'seven' is corroborated by more recent transfers from different Indo-European continuants into Uralic languages, potentially on more than one occasion (Joki 1973: 313), and likely also into Chinese and Turkic (Napolskikh 2001: 373, Schuessler 2007: 419, contra Starostin et al. 2003: 960). Turning to the Caucasus, PK **šwid-* (Klimov 1998: 251, Fähnrich 2007: 531, Georg 2002), just as the case was with 'six' (§ 3.2), is not likely to have been in direct contact with Proto-Indo-European either, but they do appear to belong to the same stock.[6] Proto-Indo-European as the ultimate purveyor even to Semitic and Egyptian is technically possible, but this particular case presents such compelling directionality and morphological transparency to warrant a clear source in the Middle East (cf. § 5.4).

3.4 *PIE* *(H)oḱtoH *'Eight'*

- Toch. A *okät*, Toch. B *okt*; Lat. *octō*; OIr. *ocht*^{N}; Goth. *ahtau*; Lith. *aštuonì*; OCS *osmĭ*; Alb. *tetë*; Gr. ὀκτώ; Phr. **o(t)tuos*; Arm. *owt*^{c}; Ved. *aṣṭā́*, *aṣṭáu*, YAv. *ašta*.

Neumann has suggested that the numeral may also be found in Lycian *ait-ãta* (2007: 8). The most plausible attempt at an internal etymology is from a grammaticalized dual of PIE *h_2*oḱ-t-* 'Handspitzen' (Mayrhofer 1992: 142), semantically collocated in ἄκρων χειρῶν τε καὶ ποδῶν (Her. I, 119, cf. Blažek 1999: 269–271); while plausible, it remains speculative and continues surmising a basic value 'four' competing with the canonical Core Indo-European and Anatolian items (§ 2.4).

The proposed external comparanda are:

- Kartvelian **otxo* 'four' > G. *otx-*; Ming. *otx-*; Laz *o(n)txo-*/*otxu-*; Svan *wostx(w)* /*wosdxw*
- Berber **okkuz* > e.g. Tamahaq *ŏkkoẓ*, Zenaga *akkuṯ*^{h}

The similarity between PIE *(H)oḱtoH* 'eight' and PK **otxo* 'four' (Fähnrich 2007: 325–326, Klimov 1998: 145–146) is formally attractive, but suffers on the semantic side; this is supposedly offset by three factors:

1 PIE 'eight' is believed to be a solidified dual formation (cf. already Brugmann 1904: 365), indicating an underlying value 'four' (see also § 2.3).
2 YAv. *ašti* 'breadth of four fingers' (Henning 1948, see also Schmid 1989: 14–15).

6 Note also Hurrian *šind(i)*, Basque *zazpi* and Etruscan *semp*^{h}, all 'seven', effectively covering known forms in ancient languages of Northwestern Eurasia and Northern Africa.

3 The cross-linguistic connection between 'four' and 'eight' appears typologically viable; the most notable example is PK **arwa* 'eight' from PS **rbaʿ-* 'four' (§ 5.2), but also Hurrian *tumni* 'four' ~ PS **tmn-* 'eight', Proto-Aymara **puši* 'four' ~ Proto-Quechua **pusaq* 'eight' (Klimov 1985: 206, 1994: 472, 1998: 3).

The majority view thus follows Klimov (1994) in that the Proto-Kartvelian numeral represents a loanword from Proto-Indo-European or one of its descendants (e.g. Blažek 1999: 82; Fenwick 2017: 315), although the exact circumstances are left unexplained. There are three possibilities:

1 An Iranian source may be indicated by the similar phenomenon in PK **usx-* 'sacrificial ox' from an Iranian continuant of PIE **ukʷs-* 'ox' (cf. Greppin 1997), but identical treatment of palatal and non-palatals is suspicious, and both vowel quality and dating are unresolved, if not problematic, for this scenario (cf. Testelec 1995: 14); the transfer must thus have happened at a time before the de-facto split of Proto-Indo-Iranian.
2 Armenian is phonetically incompatible, arriving at *owtᶜ* only through **opto-* (Schmitt 1981: 130), and is unlikely even to have been neighbors of Proto-Kartvelian at a sufficiently early stage (cf. Solta 1963: 80–81).
3 Proto-Anatolian only poses a viable source with an entry through the Caucasus, but the branch is unlikely to have possessed **(H)oḱt-* with the meaning 'four' (alongside **mei̯-(e)u-* and possibly **kʷetu̯or-*, cf. § 2); in a hypothetical scenario Proto-Kartvelian should rather have borrowed one of these for the numeral four.

With indisputable reconstructions to both proto-languages, the chronological argument becomes moot, and the reverse trajectory, i.e. from a precursor of Kartvelian to pre-Proto-Indo-European, remains formally possible (cf. Pisani 1980; Kassian 2009a: 68). Estimates vary as to the age of Proto-Kartvelian, but it is generally believed to be somewhat younger than Proto-Indo-European (Smithermann 2012: 517; Gamkrelidze & Ivanov 1995: 777 n. 19). Most indicative would be a more precise dating of the Semitic numeral loans in Proto-Kartvelian: in addition to 'eight' from 'four', PK **a(ś)t-* 'ten' may also have been borrowed from PS **ʿaśr-* (cf. Nichols 1997: 142; Klimov 1998: 2). If they represent a sufficiently late stratum it may be surmised that Proto-Kartvelian was similarly susceptible to influence from an Indo-European neighbor. If, however, the Semitic elements represent a comparatively older stage, they may be indicative of a numeral "push" (cf. Mallory & Adams 1997: 398, Helimski 2001: 190–192, Kassian 2009b: 426 fn. 72) northward that first reached the Kartvelians in the Caucasus before arriving with the Proto-Indo-Europeans on the steppes soon after.

A period of contact between Proto-Indo-European and Proto-Kartvelian may be linguistically warranted, both in terms of lexical (e.g. PK *(*m-*)*ḳerd* 'chest' ~ PIE **ḱerd* 'heart', cf. Klimov 1998: 123) and typological influence (cf. esp. Gamkrelidze & Ivanov 1995: 5–6, contra Harris 1990). The contact need not have been direct either, as Nichols points out (1997: 127–129), and the words for 'seven' do show clear signs of different trajectories, although both ultimately from Semitic (§ 3.3). The discrepancies that still do haunt the comparison of PIE *(*H*)*oḱtoH* 'eight' ~ PK **otxo* 'four' could similarly have arisen through intermediary languages (cf. § 5.5).

3.5 *PIE* *(h₁en)néu̯n̥ *'Nine'*

– Toch. A *ñu*; Lat. *novem*; OIrish *noí*; Welsh *naw*; Goth. *niun*; Lith. *devynì*; OCS *devętĭ*; Alb. *nëntë*; Gr. *ἐννέ*(*ϝ*)*α*; Arm. *inn*; Ved. *náva*, YAv. *nauua*.

Anatolian evidence may be found in the unspecified Lycian numeral *nuñtãta* (see Neumann 2007: 245). A common etymological interpretation requires 'nine' to be newer (Szemerényi 1960: 173, Mayrhofer 1996: 24–25), i.e. more recently numeralized, than 'eight' and 'ten', and, ostensibly, the missing link between a quaternary system possibly visible in a dual 'eight' (§ 3.4, Edelman 1999: 235 n. 2) and the decimal system of the two hands (§ 3.1 and § 3.6). This etymology finds further support in the interpretation of the Greco-Armenian initial vowel as a prepositional prefix **h₁en-* (akin to 'a-new') and the independent innovations of 'nine' across the Iranian dialects, where both the Ossetic *farad* ('beyond') and Chorasmian *š'δ* ('increase') similarly describe their relation to 'eight' (cf. Emmerick 1992: 300, Kassian 2009a: 68), although the comparison is not immaculate (Winter 1992: 13–14) and could be secondarily associated through folk etymology. There are no external comparanda for the form and it is most likely a native formation.

3.6 *PIE* *déḱm̥[7] *'Ten'*

– Toch. A *śäk*; Lat. *decem*; Welsh *deg*; Goth. *taíhun*; Lith. *dẽšimt*; OCS *desętĭ*; Alb. *djathtë*; Gr. *δέκα*; Arm. *tasn*; Ved. *dáśa*, YAv. *dasa*.

Anatolian evidence may be found in CLuw. *ti-na-ta-za*, interpreted by Hawkins as 'tithe' (2000: 466 § 28, 470 § 26), logically connected to the numeral 'ten' (Melchert, p.c.). The etymology remains disputed (cf. Mayrhofer 1992: 709),

7 Note that the stress is realized on the first syllable, as opposed to PIE 'seven' that carries it on the final resonant (§ 3.3).

although it is commonly related to PIE **deḱ-s* 'right hand', continued in Latin *dexter*, Bret. *dehou* 'right, south', Myc. *de-ki-si-wo*, Alb. *djathtë*, Goth. *taíhswa* etc. (Mallory & Adams 1997: 403; de Vaan 2008: 168), and ultimately to the verbal root **deḱ-* '(an-, auf-, wahr-)nehmen' (LIV²: 109–112). There are no external comparanda, and the formation must be assumed to be native.[8]

4 Proto-Indo-European Numeral Etymologies

While the etymologies for all simplex numerals in PIE can be contested, the sequence 'six', 'seven', and 'eight' present particular difficulties as their proposed internal sources either suffer from formal constraints or strained semantics. Anatolian evidence may be gleaned for all numerals except for 'five', ensuring the reconstruction of all numerals to Proto-Indo-European proper. The preceding discussions may thus be summed up in the following list:

1 Subitizing, old formation
2 Subitizing, old formation
3 Subitizing, old formation
4 Old formation (Core-Indo-European) / semantic shift (Anatolian)
5 Related to the hand (no Anatolian evidence)
6 No internal etymology
7 No internal etymology
8 Dubious internal etymology (see § 3.4)
9 Semantic shift
10 Related to the hand

The internal strategies used for forming the Proto-Indo-European simplex numerals are thus subitizing (1–3, maybe 4), relating to the hand (5, 10), and semantic shift (Anat. 4, 9). The remaining numerals (6, 7, 8) also happen to be the only three with formally similar external comparanda, albeit none so perfect as to warrant a direct borrowing between known proto-forms.

4.1 *Numeral or Lexical Substitution?*

In the attested Indo-European languages numeral substitution is exceptionally rare; the most comprehensive examples in the simplex numerals are from the Romani dialects, inextricably tied to their constant status of minority language with very clear origins of their borrowings (Matras 2009: 201–202, Friedman

8 Its presence in a number of Uralic dialects is obviously secondary, incl. possibly in Fenno-Volgaic 'eight' and 'nine' (cf. Hakulinen 1946: 33, contra Itkonen 1973: 337).

2010). Along with the two isolated Iranian instances of substitution of the inherited 'nine' (see § 3.5), the Anatolian substitution of the numeral 'four' constitutes an oddity in the setting of otherwise canonically stable numerals. The Old Irish personal numeral substantive *mórfes(s)er* 'seven men' (lit. 'big six'), derived from *sesser* 'six men' (Greene 1992: 518), only changes in its nominal form. It thus appears that the phenomenon of numeral substitution only occurs within a nominal context: If the numeralization of the higher basic numbers in Proto-Indo-European is relatively recent, it allows for a preceding descriptive system, and the designation for 'four' could have changed like any other noun before the decimal system solidified.

5 The Proto-Indo-European Decimal System in Its Context

As demonstrated in §§ 2–4, internal evidence suggests that the PIE decimal system is a relatively recent innovation when Anatolian splits off: with an ancient core of subitizing numerals, 1–4, the strategies for PIE 5, 9, 10 and Anatolian 4 appear reasonably organically from internal material, and either belong to the hand or arise from a transparent semantic drift. When 6–8 fail to formally satisfy any of these criteria, and are unlikely subitizing (i.e. ancient) candidates, we may look for alternative linguistic strategies for supplying these numerals, including borrowings.

With two exceptionally well-understood language families both north and south of the Pontic Steppes, Proto-Indo-European is thus surrounded by strong comparable data that can help frame the spread of the decimal system.

5.1 *Uralic*

As opposed to Proto-Indo-European, only the numeral 'two' is reconstructable to Proto-Uralic (Napolskikh 2003), i.e. numerals were, at most, only subitizing. Proto-Indo-European has some affinity to this northern language family, whether adstrate or genetic, and they are believed to originate in close areal and temporal proximity on the northern reaches of the Volga (cf. Anthony 2007: 93–97; Carpelan & Parpola 2001; Parpola 2013). Although tantalizing similarities exist between these two proto-languages (e.g. Helimski 2001), the numeral systems are fundamentally different: as demonstrably attractive items to borrow, the lack of comparable numerals in Proto-Uralic suggests that the period of close contacts predates a fully formed Proto-Indo-European decimal system. 'Seven' eventually appears in different branches of Uralic, but at a decisively later point in time and from various Indo-European dialects rather than the proto-language itself (cf. § 3.3).

TABLE 2.2 Northern Afro-Asiatic numerals. All forms and analyses from Lipiński (1997: 282–288), all masc. Related forms are etched grey.

	'three'	'four'	'five'	'six'	'seven'	'eight'	'nine'	'ten'
P-Sem.	_*ślaṯ-_	_*rbaʿ-_	_*ḫamš-_	_*šidṯ-_	_*šabʿ-_	_*ṯmān-_	_*tišʿ-_	_*ʿaśr-_
P-Berb.	_*k̠raḍ / *sarḍ_	_*kkuẓ_	_*səmmus / *afus_	_*sḍis_	_*sa_	_*tam_	_*tẓa_	_*mraw_
Egyptian	_ḫmt-w_	_fd-w_	_di̓-w_	_śrś-w / śi̓ś-w_	_śfḫ-w_	_ḫmn-w_	_pśḏ-w_	_mḏ-w_

5.2 *Semitic and Afro-Asiatic*

Semitic, on the other hand, is a candidate as the source of PIE 'seven' and, less obviously, 'six'. The three northern branches of Afro-Asiatic, viz. Semitic, Egyptian, and Libyco-Berber are particularly interesting for two reasons:

1. As opposed to the general consistency of numerals in the Indo-European languages, the process of numeralization was happening as the branches split up (from subitizing in Afro-Asiatic to decimal system in, e.g., Proto-Semitic, see table 2.2). This might give clues to how Proto-Indo-European arrived at the fixed system.
2. Early speakers of Afro-Asiatic appear to have held a central position in the early Neolithic (cf. Militarev 2002), whose cultural impact also reached Proto-Indo-European (e.g. through the Uruk expansion and Maikop north of the Caucasus, cf. Anthony 2007: 290).

Certain features are directly comparable to the phenomena seen in Indo-European: in the extended family of Afro-Asiatic, 'four' sets Berber, Egyptian, and Semitic apart while many other basic numerals are shared, suggesting a looser affiliation of 'four' than, e.g., that of 'six' and 'seven', potentially mirroring the situation surrounding the unique numeral 'four' in Anatolian (§ 2.2). Numerals could on the other hand have spread through the diversifying Afro-Asiatic dialects as borrowings and would consequently be difficult to distinguish from shared heritage (cf. Blažek 2001: 22, Lipiński 1997: 287–288, Marwan Kilani, p.c.), thus adding another potential layer to the borrowability of the higher decimals. It is thus typologically significant that the same three numerals that all three northern Afro-Asiatic branches agree upon are the exact same three Proto-Indo-European appears to share with Kartvelian.

5.3 *'Seven' and the Big Language Families*

Three of the best understood proto-languages are thus intersected by the same or a similar numeral 'seven' (§3.3): Semitic (in the larger context of Afro-Asiatic), Indo-European, and Uralic. The comparative analysis matched with their respective homelands produces a clear relative chronology of Semitic as the ultimate purveyor, Proto-Indo-European as recipient and secondary purveyor, and various descendants of Uralic as the ultimate recipients, see table 3. The axes are focused on the branching of the individual families as compared to their respective stage of developing a numeral category from more or less nominal quantifiers.

5.4 *The Caucasus*

The most direct route from the Fertile Crescent to the Pontic Steppes runs through the Caucasus. But with much tighter geographic distribution and fewer extant languages than Uralic, Indo-European, and Afro-Asiatic, the Caucasian languages are significantly more difficult to assess. Kartvelian may hold important clues to the source of PIE 'eight', although the exact trajectory still defies a final verdict; similarly, NW Caucasian may continue the spread of at least 'six' in close association with Kartvelian, and 'eight' (cf. Abkhaz *aaба*) is likely ultimately a continuation of Semitic 'four' (see §3.4). The diverse NE Caucasian languages appear not to partake in this particular numeral spread.[9]

Ideally these languages also belong in table 3 below, but a simpler schematization of the process might serve to include the scattered data that do exist. Kartvelian and the NW Caucasian languages are, for all we know, autochthonous in their current distribution (although Nichols proposes to retroactively repatriate Kartvelian further east, 1997: 128), and Semitic is located smack in the hotbed of the Neolithic revolution and everything that came with it in terms of complex societies. A tentative trajectory for the numerals can be thus posited and a simple diagram can be found in table 4.

Loan relations are obviously complicated and cannot easily be reduced, but the value of trajectories constitutes one possibly interpretation of the data. In essence, the directionality is straightforward in terms of Proto-Semitic → Proto-Indo-European → Uralic, less so with the Caucasian languages, but it should be evident that certain numerals do have a tendency to pervade several linguistic clades in succession. If their position in relation to the spread of complex society and typology carries any meaning, table 4 is a valid hypothetical point of departure.

9 The typical form cited is Khinalug *zäk* 'six', but the resemblance seems to be accidental (Blažek 1999: 83).

TABLE 3 Numeralization in the major language families

<table>
<tr><td colspan="3">Proto-Uralic
subitizing only</td><td colspan="2">Pre-PIE
subitizing only</td><td colspan="3">Proto-Afro-Asiatic
subitizing only</td></tr>
<tr><td>Samoyedic
numeralization
‘seven’ borrowed</td><td colspan="2">Fenno-Ugric
[~3000 BC]
incipient
numeralization</td><td colspan="2">PIE
[~4000 BC]
intensive
numeralization;
‘seven’, ‘six’, and
‘eight’ borrowed</td><td colspan="3">“Northern Afro-Asiatic”
Semitic, Egyptian, Berber(, Balkanic?)
[before 5000 BC]
incipient numeralization;
‘six’ and ‘seven’ appear</td></tr>
<tr><td>
system</td><td>Ugric
‘seven’
borrowed
system</td><td>Fenno-Permic
‘seven’
borrowed
system</td><td>P-Anat.
system</td><td>Core IE
system</td><td>P-Semitic
system</td><td>P-Egyptian
system</td><td>P-Berber
system</td></tr>
</table>

5.5 *Numerals Through the Balkans?*

An alternative route from the Fertile Crescent to the Steppes runs west of the Black Sea through the Balkans. It is simply not known what languages were spoken in Southeastern Europe prior to the arrival of the Indo-Europeans, but a qualified guess places an Afro-Asiatic language closely related to Semitic in contact with Proto-Indo-European on its western perimeter in modern Ukraine (cf. Vennemann 2003; Anthony 2007: 164–166; for speakers of Afro-Asiatic as Neolithic revolutionaries, see Militarev 2002).[10] This scenario helps account for some of the similarities that nonetheless cannot have come about in direct contact: other attractive items for borrowing pertain to a purported agricultural substrate that predominantly appears to have affected the western branches of Indo-European.[11] Based on the known Afro-Asiatic forms (cf.

10 While the Vinča symbols remain enigmatic, they represent the off-chance that the present hypothesis may even be tested against evidence in the future. Until then, it remains part of the reconstructional exercise of presenting hypothetical proto-forms to account for known forms. A different hypothesis might depart from Kartvelian, where the same three numerals appear to exist, or a third altogether unrelated language.

11 E.g. PIE **b^{h}ar-*(*s*-) ‘barley’ ~ Semitic **bVrr-* ‘cereal, wheat’; PIE **d^{h}oHn-* ‘grain’ ~ Semitic **dúχn-* ‘millet’ (for discussion and further references, see Bjørn 2017: 47–48, 53, 142).

TABLE 4 Numerals in flux, south to north

Distance from Neolithic epicenter				
Semitic	**Kartvelian**	**NW Cauc.**	**Indo-European**	**Uralic**
'four'	→ 'eight'	→ 'eight'		
	'four'		→ 'eight'	
'six'	→ 'six'	→ 'six'	→ 'six'	
'seven'	→ 'seven'		→ 'seven'	→ 'seven'

§ 5.2) and the numerals attested in Indo-European, the following 'Balkanic' numerals may be posited:

- ?**okk-tu*^{m} 'four': Based on the Berber numeral **okk-* 'four' with an ending morphologically similar to the definite masculine form in 'seven' (§ 3.3). This presupposes a different form or stratum for the transfer since the endings have been treated differently in Proto-Indo-European. Lipiński bases his Berber reconstruction on a verbal root (1997: 287, contra van Putten, p.c.) and does not include the initial vowel for Proto-Berber, but it appears only to be missing in most of the North Berber attestations, while South and East Berber all retain the vowel (Prasse 1974 apud Blažek 1999: 58–60).
- ?**šiḱ-t-* 'six': Based on the Egyptian and Semitic numerals for 'six'. The combined Afro-Asiatic evidence hints that such a construction could be viable, and it would help explain the discrepancies between otherwise tantalizingly similar forms in Proto-Semitic, Proto-Indo-European, and, to a lesser extent, Proto-Kartvelian.
- ?**šap-t*$_{a}$*m* 'seven': With a few phonological developments, the full grammatical shape of the Semitic form has been extrapolated to the hypothetical Balkanic language.
- ?**okk-t-ō* 'eight': an internal Balkanic dual formation of a numeral 'four' (cf. Pisani 1980), thus already with the meaning 'eight' by the absorption into Proto-Indo-European. Kartvelian 'four' would then still be related, although with a different trajectory. Proto-Semitic forms dual nouns through vowel lengthening (cf. Lipiński 1997: 236–237), which would help explain the discrepancy between the endings of 'seven' and 'eight' if from the same source. Accepting PIE *(*H*)*oḱtōH* as a loan from either Proto-Kartvelian or Balkanic allows us to rid Proto-Indo-European of a superfluous value 'four'.

6 Conclusion

The decimal numerals belong to the core vocabulary of the Indo-European language family and can be securely reconstructed for all branches but Anatolian, where *four* is expressed differently while most other numerals seem to correspond to the rest of Indo-European. The etymologies throughout the series are contested, and the question of their origin has seemed beyond the reach of the comparative method, but a study of numeralization strategies suggests that Proto-Indo-European partook in a wider regional tendency occurring roughly 5000–3000 BC.

a The neighboring language families all betray signs of their numeralization process: Kartvelian through numeral borrowings from the Afro-Asiatic stock, which itself both grammaticalized nominals and borrowed certain numbers through its dispersing dialects; Uralic did not have a fixed decimal system and only late started forming their series dialectally from borrowings from Indo-European languages and internal developments.

b Of the non-subitizing numerals, 'four' is expressed with the most different terms across the reconstructed languages of northern Afro-Asiatic and Indo-European: Berber, Egyptian, Semitic, Anatolian, and Core-Indo-European each has its own unique term. This enigma still lacks a satisfactory explanation.

c The compounded evidence from neighboring language families suggests that pre-PIE borrowed the numerals 'six', 'seven', and 'eight'.

d The lack of evidence for direct transfers suggests that a culturally significant language provided pre-Proto-Indo-European with the numerals, most likely through the Balkans. The material likely ultimately derives from Afro-Asiatic but could have transferred through unrelated extinct intermediaries in Anatolia and the Balkans.

e Without internal numerals for said numbers, it is likely that pre-Proto-Indo-European, like Proto-Uralic, lacked a fixed decimal series and only finally grammaticalized quantitative terms as a reaction to the imported numerals.

The cultural developments that became the "Indo-Europeanization" of the Steppe cultures likely coincided with the complexity of society increasing and, as a correlate, the institution of a decimal system from a simpler subitizing strategy, closely linked to impulses from Neolithic societies on its western perimeter.

References

Anthony, David. 2007. *The horse, the wheel, and language*. Princeton: Princeton University Press

Bjørn, Rasmus G. 2017. *Foreign elements in the PIE vocabulary*. MA thesis, University of Copenhagen. Available at www.loanwords.prehistoricmap.com

Blažek, Václav. 1999. *Numerals: Comparative–etymological analyses of numeral systems and their implications*. Brno: Masarykova univerzita.

Blažek, Václav. 2001. Etymologizing the Semitic cardinal numerals of the first decade. In Andrzej Zaborski (ed.), *New data and new methods in Afroasiatic linguistics: Robert Hetzron in memoriam*, 13–38. Wiesbaden: Harrassowitz.

Blažek, Václav. 2012. Hittite *wakšur*. In Stephanie Jamison, Craig Melchert & Brent Vine (eds.), *Proceedings of the 23rd Annual UCLA Indo-European Conference*, 17–28. Bremen: Hempen

Brugmann, Karl. 1904. *Kurze vergleichende Grammatik der indogermanischen Sprachen*. Strassburg: Trübner.

Campbell, Lyle. 2013. *Historical linguistics: An introduction*. Third edition. Edinburgh: Edinburgh University Press.

Carling, Gerd. 2005. Proto-Tocharian, Common Tocharian, and Tocharian—on the value of linguistic connections in a reconstructed language. In Karlene Jones-Bley, Martin E. Huld, Angela Della Volpe & Miriam Robbins Dexter (eds.), *Proceedings of the Sixteenth Annual UCLA Indo-European Conference*. Washington, DC: Institute for the Study of Man.

Carpelan, Christian, & Asko Parpola. 2001. PIE, Proto-Uralic and Proto-Aryan. In Christian Carpelan, Asko Parpola & Petteri Koskikallio (eds.), *Early contacts between Uralic and Indo-European: Linguistic and archaeological considerations. Papers presented at an international symposium held at the Tvärminne Research Station of the University of Helsinki, 8–10 January 1999*, 55–150. Helsinki: Société Finno-Ougrienne.

Clackson, James. 2007. *Indo-European linguistics: An introduction*. Cambridge: Cambridge University Press.

Colarusso, John. 1997. Proto-Pontic: Phyletic links between Proto-Indo-European and Proto-Northwest Caucasian. *Journal of Indo-European Studies* 25(1–2). 119–151.

Collinder, Björn. 1965. *Hat das Uralische Verwandte?* Uppsala: Almquist & Wiksell.

Čop, Bojan. 1970. Indouralica XV. *Zeitschrift für vergleichende Sprachforschung* 88. 41–58.

Cunliffe, Barry. 2015. *By steppe, desert, and ocean. The birth of Eurasia*. Oxford: Oxford University Press.

Dolgopolsky, Aron. 1989. Cultural contacts of Proto-Indo-European and Proto-Indo-Iranian with neighbouring languages. *Folia Linguistica Historica* 8. 3–36.

Dolgopolsky, Aron. 1993. More about the IE homeland problem. *Mediterranean Language Review* 6–7. 230–248.

Edelman, Džoj I. 1999. On the history of non-decimal systems and their elements in numerals of Aryan languages. In Gvozdanović 1999, 221–241.

Eichner, Heiner. 1992. Anatolian. In Gvozdanović 1992, 29–96.

Emmerick, Ronald. 1992. Iranian. In Gvozdanović 1992, 289–345.

Fenwick, Rhona S.H. 2017. An Indo-European origin of Kartvelian names for two maloid fruits. *Iran and the Caucasus* 21(3). 310–323.

Friedman, Victor A. 2010. Numerals and language contact: Albanian, Slavic, and Romani. In Giovanni Belluscio & Antonio Mendicino (eds.), *Scritti in onore di Eric Pratt Hamp per il suo 90 compleanno*, 109–114. Cosenza: Università della Calabria.

Gamkrelidze, Thomas V., & Vjaceslav V. Ivanov. 1995. *Indo-European and the Indo-Europeans*. Translated from Russian by Johanna Nichols. Berlin: Mouton de Gruyter.

Georg, Stefan. 2002. Clusters, affricates, and the numerals 'six' and 'seven' in Kartvelian. In Fabrice Cavoto (ed.), *The linguist's linguist: A collection of papers in honour of Alexis Manaster Ramer*, 175–181. München: Lincom Europa.

Greene, David. 1992. Celtic. In Gvozdanović 1992, 497–554

Grepin, John A.C. 1997. A note on Georgian USX- and Indo-Europeanisms in the Kartvelian languages. *Journal of Indo-European Studies* 25(3–4). 383–386.

Gvozdanović, Jadranka (ed.). 1992. *Indo-European numerals*. New York & Berlin: Mouton de Gruyter.

Gvozdanović, Jadranka (ed.). 1999. *Numeral types and changes worldwide. International Conference on Historical Linguistics, 12, 1995, Manchester, England*. New York & Berlin: Mouton de Gruyter.

Hakulinen, Lauri. 1946. Suomen kielen rakenne ja kehitys. Helsinki: Otava.

Hawkins, John D. 2000. *Corpus of Hieroglyphic inscriptions*. Vol. 1. *Inscriptions of the Iron Age, Part 2*. New York & Berlin: Walter de Gruyter.

Helimski, Eugene. 2001. Early Indo-Uralic linguistic relationships. In Christian Carpelan, Asko Parpola & Petteri Koskikallio (ed.), *Early contacts between Uralic and Indo-European: Linguistic and archaeological considerations. Papers presented at an international symposium held at the Tvärminne Research Station of the University of Helsinki 8–10 January 1999*, 187–205. Helsinki: Suomalais-Ugrilainen Seura.

Henning, Walter B. 1948. Oktō(u). *Transactions of the Philological Society* 1948. 69.

Heubeck, Alfred. 1963. "Digamma"-Probleme des mykenischen Dialekts. *Die Sprache* 9(2). 193–202.

Itkonen, Erkki. 1973. Zur Geschichte des Partitivs. *Finno-Ugrische Forschungen* 40. 278–339.

Joki, Aulis. 1973. *Uralier und Indogermanen. Die älteren Behrührungen zwischen den uralischen und indogermanischen Sprachen*. Helsinki: Suomalais-ugrilainen Seura.

Kassian, Alexei. 2009a. Anatolian **meyu-* '4, four' and its cognates. *Journal of Language Relationship* 2. 65–78.

Kassian, Alexei. 2009b. Hattic as a Sino-Caucasian language. *Ugarit-Forschungen* 41. 309–448.

Klimov, Georgij A. 1985. Zu den ältesten IG-semitisch-kartwelischen Kontakten im Vorderen Asien. In Hermann M. Ölberg & Gernot Schmidt (eds.), *Sprachwissenschaftliche Forschungen. Festschrift für Johann Knobloch*, 205–210. Innsbruck: Amos.

Klimov, Georgij A. 1994. L'analogie kartvélienne de l'IE *ok'tō(w)=. In Roland Bielmeier & Reinhard Stempel (eds.), *Indogermanica et Caucasica. Festschrift für Karl Horst Schmidt zum 65. Geburtstag*, 472–478. New York & Berlin: Mouton de Gruyter.

Klimov, Georgij A. 1998. *Kartvelian etymological dictionary*. New York & Berlin: Mouton de Gruyter.

Kloekhorst, Alwin. 2008. *Etymological dictionary of the Hittite inherited lexicon*. Boston & Leiden: Brill.

Kroonen, Guus. 2013. *Etymological dictionary of Proto-Germanic*. Boston & Leiden: Brill.

Lipiński, Edward. 1997. *Semitic languages: Outline of a comparative grammar*. Leuven: Uitgeverij Peeters & Departement Oosterse Studies.

LIV^2 = Rix, Helmuth et al. 2001. *Lexikon der indo-germanischen Verben*. Zweite Auflage. Wiesbaden: Reichert.

Lubotsky, Alexander. 1989. Against a Proto-Indo-European phoneme **a*. In Theo Vennemann (ed.), *The new sound of Indo-European*, 53–66. Berlin & New York: Mouton de Gruyter.

Makkay, János. 1998. Greek *ἀξίνη* and *πέλεκυς* as Semitic loan-words in Greek and the corresponding axe type. In Mikasa no Miya Takahito (ed.), *Essays on ancient Anatolia in the second millennium B.C.*, 183–198. Wiesbaden: Harrassowitz.

Mallory, James P., & Douglas Q. Adams (eds.). 1997. *Encyclopedia of Indo-European culture*. Chicago & London: Fitzroy Dearborn.

Martínez, Eugenio R.L. 1999. The Indo-European system of numerals from '1' to '10'. In Gvozdanović 1999, 199–219.

Matras, Yaron. 2009. *Language contact*. Cambridge: Cambridge University Press.

Mayrhofer, Manfred. 1992. *Etymologisches Wörterbuch des Altindoiranischen*. Vol. 1. Heidelberg: Winter.

Mayrhofer, Manfred. 1996. *Etymologisches Wörterbuch des Altindoiranischen*. Vol. 2. Heidelberg: Winter.

Militarev, Alexander. 2002. The prehistory of a dispersal: the Proto-Afrasian (Afroasiatic) farming lexicon. In Peter Bellwood & Colin Renfrew (eds.), *Examining the farming/language dispersal hypothesis*, 135–150. Oxford: Oxbow Books.

Napolskikh, Vladimir. 2001. Tocharisch-uralische Berührungen. In Christian Carpelan, Asko Parpola & Petteri Koskikallio (eds.), *Early contacts between Uralic and Indo-European: Linguistic and archaeological considerations. Papers presented at an international symposium held at the Tvärminne Research Station of the University of Helsinki 8–10 January 1999*, 367–384. Helsinki: Suomalais-Ugrilainen Seura.

Napolskikh, Vladimir. 2003. Uralic numerals. *Linguistica Uralica* 39(1). 43–54.

Neu, Erich. 1999. Zum hethitischen Zahlwort für 'sieben'. In Peter Anreiter & Erzsébet

Jerem (eds.), *Studia Celtica et Indogermanica. Festschrift für Wolfgang Meid*, 249–254. Budapest: Archaeolinga.

Neumann, Günter. 2007. *Glossar des Lykischen*. Wiesbaden: Harrassowitz.

Nichols, Johanna. 1997. The epicentre of the Indo-European linguistic spread. In Matthew Spriggs & Roger Blench (eds.), *Archaeology and language*. Vol. 1, 122–148. London & New York: Routledge.

Parpola, Asko. 2013. Formation of the Indo-European and Uralic (Finno-Ugric) language families in the light of archaeology. In Riho Grünthal & Petri Kallio (eds.), *A linguistic map of prehistoric northern Europe*, 119–184. Helsinki: Suomalais-Ugrilainen Seura.

Pisani, Vittore. 1980. Indoeuropeo **oḱtōu*. *Paideia* 35. 47.

Polomé, Edgar C. 1968. The Indo-European numeral for 'five' and Hittite *panku-* 'all'. In J.C. Heesterman et al. (eds.), *Pratidānam: Indian, Iranian, and Indo-European studies presented to Franciscus Bernardus Jacobus Kuiper on his sixtieth birthday*, 98–101. Den Haag & Paris: Mouton.

Puhvel, Jaan. 1984–2001. *Hittite etymological dictionary*. Vols. 1–5. New York & Berlin: Mouton de Gruyter.

Railo, Henry, & Minna M. Hannula-Sormunen. 2012. Subitizing. In Norbert M. Seel (ed.), *Encyclopedia of the sciences of learning*, 3233–3235. Boston, MA: Springer.

Schmid, Wolfgang P. 1989. *Wort und Zahl. Sprachwissenschaftliche Betrachtungen der Kardinalzahlwörter*. Stuttgart: Steiner.

Schmidt, Karl Horst. 1962. *Studien zur Rekonstruktion des Lautstandes der südkaukasischen Grundsprache*. Wiesbaden: Deutsche morgenländische Gesellschaft.

Schmitt, Rüdiger. 1981. *Grammatik des Klassisch-Armenischen mit sprachvergleichenden Erläuterungen*. Innsbruck: Institut für Sprachwissenschaft der Universität Innsbruck.

Schrijver, Peter. 2003. Early developments of the vowel systems of North-West Germanic and Saami. In Alfred Bammesberger & Theo Vennemann (eds.), *Languages in prehistoric Europe*, 195–244. Heidelberg: Winter.

Schuessler, Axel. 2007. *ABC Etymological Dictionary of Chinese*. Honolulu: University of Hawaii Press.

Shevoroshkin, Vitalij V. 1979. On the Hittite–Luwian numerals. *Journal of Indo-European Studies* 7(3–4). 177–198.

Sihler, Andrew L. 1995. *New comparative grammar of Greek and Latin*. Oxford: Oxford University Press.

Smitherman, Thomas. 2012. Ancient Kartvelian-Indo-European lexical contacts. In Benedicte Nielsen Whitehead, Thomas Olander, Birgit Anette Olsen & Jens Elmegård Rasmussen (eds.), *The sound of Indo-European*, 501–521. Copenhagen: Museum Tusculanum.

Solta, Georg R. 1963. Die armenische Sprache. In Gerhard Deeters & Georg Renatus Solta (eds.), *Armenisch und kaukasische Sprachen*, 80–128. Leiden & Köln: Brill.

Stang, Christian S. 1966. *Vergleichende Grammatik der baltischen Sprachen*. Oslo, Bergen & Tromsø: Universitetsforlaget.

Szemerényi, Oswald. 1960. *Studies in the Indo-European system of numerals*. Heidelberg: Winter.

Szemerényi, Oswald. 1996. *Introduction to Indo-European linguistics*. Oxford: Oxford University Press.

Testelec, J.G. 1995. Sibiljanty ili kompleksy v protokartvel'skom? (Klassičeskaja dilemma i nekotorye novye argumenty). *Voprosy jazykoznanija* 1995(2). 10–28.

Tischler, Johann. 1977–2010. *Hethitisches etymologisches Glossar*. Lieferung 1–15. Innsbruck: Institut für Sprachen und Literaturen der Universität Innsbruck.

Trombetti, Alfredo. 1923. *Elementi di glottologia*. Bologna: Zanichelli.

de Vaan, Michiel. 2008. *Etymological dictionary of Latin and the other Italic languages*. Boston & Leiden: Brill.

Vennemann, Theo. 2003. *Europa Vasconica—Europa Semitica*. Berlin & New York: Mouton de Gruyter.

Wegner, Ilse. 2000. *Einführung in die hurritische Sprache*. Wiesbaden: Harrassowitz.

CHAPTER 3

Proto-Indo-European Continuity in Anatolian after the Split: When Hittite and Luwian Forms Require a Proto-Indo-European Source

José L. García Ramón

1 Anatolian development vs. PIE heritage[1]

The characteristic look of Hittite, like that of the other Anatolian languages, is basically due to the coexistence of peculiar features of different character, origin and chronology.

Some of them may be traced back to Proto-Indo-European (PIE) without major problems: this is the case with features which are shared with at least one of the oldest Indo-European (IE) languages. The same applies to archaisms of Anatolian as against innovations shared by Core IE (e.g. the sense 'run' of *$*h_2e\underset{^}{u}h_1$-* in Hitt. *ḫu̯u̯ai-*^{ḫḫi}, previous to its semantic shift to 'help, assist' in Core IE: Ved. *av*^{i}, Lat. *(ad)iuuō, -āre*).[2] In such cases it may safely be assumed that Anatolian reflects the PIE situation, although for exclusive coincidences between Hittite and/or other Anatolian languages and Greek an explanation in terms of language contact remains open and must be checked case by case. On the other hand, features which are not shared by any other language—and can hardly be an *unus testis* of a PIE inheritance—may be understood as specific Anatolian innovations, developed after the split from PIE, e.g. the Hittite abstracts in *-eššar / -ešnaš*, which surely reflect a conflation of stems in **-es-* and **-r/n-*, and the Anatolian infinitive formations.

A special position is taken by features attested in Anatolian whose form and/or function or meaning cannot be explained *ex Anatolico ipso*, but exclusively in the light of comparison or, more precisely, in terms of lexicalization and/or remodelling of inherited PIE patterns. This is, for instance, the case with

1 Standard works are quoted according to the current conventions. Hittite translations are normally taken from *CHD* or from the dictionaries of Puhvel 1984—or Tischler 1983–; Vedic and Avestan translations are taken from (or rely on) those of Jamison & Brereton (2014) and of Humbach (1991) respectively.

2 Cf. García Ramón 2016. On further PIE archaisms in Anatolian cf. the overviews by Eichner 2015 and Melchert forthcoming a.

 | DOI:10.1163/9789004416192_005

Hitt. *šanḫ-*^{mi} 'to look for, search, strive for' (also with infinitive), the meaning of which is hardly compatible with that of *$^*senh_2$-* *'to reach', a telic momentative lexeme for which a root-present PIE *$^*senh_2$-ti* is not expected, even less with the meaning 'search': Hitt. *šanḫ-* 'to search, strive for' is only understandable as the lexicalization of the conative realization 'tries to reach' of the durative present stem *$^*s\mathring{n}$-néh_2- / $^*s\mathring{n}$-n-h_2-´* 'is about reaching', which has been formed from the zero-grade *$^*s\mathring{n}$-n-h_2-´*, as I have tried to show.[3] The sense of the telic lexeme 'reach, achieve' lives on in *šanḫu-*^{mi} 'to roast', which is in turn a lexicalization of inherited *$^*s\mathring{n}h_2$-éu̯- / $^*s\mathring{n}h_2$-u̯-´* (Ved. *sanó-*^{ti} 'to reach', 'win', Gk. *ἀνύο/ε-* 'to accomplish', 'to bring to end, fulfill'), as pointed out by H. Eichner.[4]

The present contribution will focus on some forms and formations of Hittite and Luwian that are rather opaque in an approach *ex Anatolico ipso*, and can be explained *only* in the light of our knowledge of Proto-Indo-European or Core Indo-European, namely as lexicalizations or remodellings of inherited patterns that existed before the split of Proto-Anatolian and were transformed in the Anatolian languages. The cases in point are: firstly, two verbs that have exact counterparts in other languages that can only be traced back to an inherited aspectual system in which *i*-reduplication marked present stems or *Aktionsart* depending on the different lexemes, namely Hitt. *mimma-*^{ḫḫi} 'to reject, refuse' (§ 2) and *pippa-*^{ḫḫi} 'to set/get in (violent) motion' (§ 3); in addition, CLuw. *ūppa-*, HLuw. (CAPERE$_2$)*u-pa* 'to carry (off), take (off)' (§ 4) and Hitt. *nakkī-* 'important, prominent', and 'difficult', also as a neuter substantive (§ 5), the meaning of which is only understandable on the assumption of a PIE suppletive paradigm with pres. *$^*b^her$-* and aor. *$^*h_1ne\hat{k}$- / $^*h_1en\hat{k}$-*.

2 Hitt. *mimma-*^{ḫḫi} 'to reject, refuse' (: Gk. *μίμνο/ε-*), PIE *$^*mí$-mn-* 'to resist' (intensive *Aktionsart*, *$^*men$-*: pres. *$^*mén$-o/e-*)

The meaning and constructions of Hitt. *mimma-*^{ḫḫi} (OH+) are clear, namely 'to reject' (acc.), 'to refuse (to do)' (with infinitive, coreferential), also without object:

> KBo 6.3 ii 9–10 *takku attaš=a annaš mimmai* (Laws § 28, OH/NS)
> 'but if father and mother refuse … (*scil.* to pay)'

3 García Ramón 2002: 131 ff. PIE *$^*s\mathring{n}$-n-h_2-o/e-* may underlie OHG *sinnan* 'strive, seek for', OE *sinnan* 'to take care' (with **senn-* by remodeling of PGm. **sunna-*), i.e. basically the same meaning as Hitt. *šanḫ-*, and PCelt. **san-na-* (OIr. *seinnid* 'gets, reach').

4 Eichner 1979: 55 n. 42 with reference to Hitt. *zeari* 'cooks, is cooked' (stative *$^*t/séih_1$-o-*) beside causat. *zinna/i-* 'to stop, finish with' (*$^*t/sineh_1$-*).

KUB 17.10 i 8–9 UDU-*uš=za* SILA$_4$-*SU mimmaš* GUD=*ma* AMAR-*ŠU mimmaš* (Telipinu myth, OH/MS)
'The ewe rejected her lamb, the cow rejected her calf'

KUB 14.1 obv. 18 (MH/MS) ᵐ*Madduu̯attaš=a=z* KUR ḪUR.SAG*Ḫārii̯ati ašānna mimmaš*
'Madduwatta refused to settle in the Mt. Ḫariyati district'

Hitt. *mimma-*, with consistent spelling ⟨*mi*⟩ in the oldest texts,[5] stands isolated in Anatolian: there is no nominal or verbal derivative of the lexeme, and the coincidence with CLuw. *mimma-* 'to look at, favor' (**mí-mn-*, of PIE **men-* 'to think') is purely formal.[6] The interpretation of *mimma-* as a reflex of **mí-mn-*, a reduplicated formation of PIE **men-* 'to remain' as shown by Edward H. Sturtevant,[7] is, to my mind, correct: a proto-form **mí-mn-* (3sg. **mí-mn-e*), underlying a verb of the *ḫi*-conjugation in Hittite, as well as a thematic present in Greek (and probably in Core IE) as per J. Jasanoff (2003), has an obvious match in Hom. *μίμνο/ε-* 'to stand fast, stand firm, tarry', also 'to remain'. On the other hand, the semantic shift from 'stand firm' to 'refuse, reject' is perfectly conceivable (cf. in Germanic, OFris. *warna* 'to refuse, deny' [PGmc. **warnō-ja-*], a denominative of **warnō-* 'resistance, obstacle, defence').[8] The alternative interpretation as a verb formed from prohibitive **mḗ* (Gk. *μή*, Ved. *mā́*), namely **mi-móh$_1$-ei* / **mi-mh$_1$-énti*[9] offers no recognizable advantages: it relies on a fully unusual type of formation from the prohibitive particle and ignores a Greek comparandum, which is formally and semantically perfect, in order to favour an explanation of *mimma-* as an idiosyncratic Hittite creation.

---

5 For the whole dossier cf. *CHD* L–N: s.v. **mimma-**, **memma-**. On the coherence of *i*-spellings cf. Melchert 1984: 100 n. 53.

6 Cf. Melchert 1988: 218 ff. The form confirms the existence of formations with *-i-* reduplication in Anatolian which have no correspondence in other IE languages.

7 Sturtevant 1933: 133; Jasanoff 2002: 128 ff. ("an exact word equation"); García Ramón 2010b: 44–45 (with a short presentation of the ideas set forth here).

8 Riccardo Ginevra (p.c.). Kloekhorst's strictures (2008: 581–582, s.v.), namely "a semantic connection between 'to refuse' and 'to stay' is far from evident …" and "no other examples of thematic verbs in Anatolian can be found", with the conclusion "I therefore reject this etymology", are hardly understandable. On the one hand, it is common wisdom that Hom. *μίμνο/ε-*, like *μένο/ε-*, also means 'to resist, stand firm' (not only 'to stay'), and a shift to 'to refuse' does not not need further justification. Besides, Hitt. *mimma-* is *not* a thematic present, but a verbal stem of Jasanoff's **h$_2$e*-conjugation (3sg.**mí-mn-e*), to which the thematic conjugation of Core IE may also be traced back.

9 With generalization of *-mm-* by extension from 3pl. **mimmanzi* (Kloekhorst *loc.cit.*, following Oettinger 1979: 496 ff.).

On the assumption that Hitt. *mimma-* and Hom. *μίμνο/ε-* are a perfect equation, to be traced back to PIE **mí-mn-* 'to stand firm' (**men-* 'to remain'), the specific meaning of the Hittite verb ultimately goes back to a lexicalization of the inherited meaning of the reduplicated stem, which may be an aspectual present or a formation of intensive *Aktionsart*. The Hittite evidence does not help by itself to decide: a contrastive approach to test whether *mimma-* expresses a specific *Aktionsart* is impossible, as the non-reduplicated stem of **men-* does not live on in Hittite. It is therefore only the comparative, especially Greek, evidence which may help provide an interpretation of PIE **mí-mn-*. Two possible interpretations remain open for Hitt. *mimma-* (and Hom. *μίμνο/ε-*):

1 as the continuants of a PIE present stem **mí-mn-*[10] beside an *-s*-aorist **mḗn/mén-s-* (Gk. *μεινα-*, Lat. *mansī*) in the framework of an inherited aspectual system. This would imply that Gk. *μένο/ε-* (Hom.+) is a secondary formation, like other marked presents attested in other languages (see below), a possibility which, however, hardly fits into the pattern of a stative lexeme like 'remain', for which one expects a root-present (athematic or thematic), cf. for instance, **ḱéi̯-(t)o(i̯)* 'lies' (Ved. *sáye*, Gk. *κεῖται*), **tḱéi̯-t(i)* 'dwells, settles' (Ved. *kṣéti*, OAv. *šaēitī̆*, Myc. 3pl. *ki-ti-je-si /ktiensi/*), **séĝʰ-o/e-* 'to hold, retain' (Ved. *sáh-a-* : Gk. *ἔχο/ε-*). If one makes the alternative assumption that **men-* was a telic, non-stative root with the meaning "come to a halt, not to continue, to get left" (Ch.R. Barton),[11] which is, in my opinion, untenable, the existence of a root-present (even thematic) as **mén-o/e-* (: *μένο/ε-*) would remain a major problem. Moreover, the tenet "*μένω* and *μίμνω* have no counterpart elsewhere and need not be old"[12] simply ignores the existence of Hitt. *mimma-*.

2 as the continuants of an *Aktionsart* formation **mí-mn-*, namely intensive 'to resist, stand firm', which coexisted with the aspectual present of **mén-o/e-* of **men-* 'to remain'. This fits into the well-known pattern [stative lexeme : root-present], as against a marked aorist, which in our case should be **men-s-* (: Gk. *μεινα-*, Lat. *mans-ī*,[13] with *a*-vocalism extended

10 Cf. Kümmel, *LIV*² s.v. **men-* "bleiben, warten" (**mi-mén/mn-*); Jasanoff 2003: 128 ff.

11 Barton 1990–1991: 44. *Contra* Kümmel, *LIV*² s.v. **me-mon-* (replaced by *μεμένηκα*).

12 Barton 1990–1991: 44 ff. According to the author, the paradigm of **men-* had a root aorist (replaced in Greek by sigmatic **men-s-*) and a perfect **me-mon-*, which, being homonymous with **mémon-e* 'has in mind' (: PIE **men-*¹ 'to think'), was replaced by Gk. *μεμένηκα* (with *-μένη-* from stative **mn-eh₁*).

13 Accordingly, the aor. *ἔμεινε* (**men-sa-*) is [ingressive] (entry into the state expressed by the stative lexeme, as per Ruipérez 1954: 80 ff.), i.e. 'he got into the state of staying', cf. *Il.* 14.286 *ἔνϑ' Ὕπνος μὲν ἔμεινε πάρος Διὸς ὄσσε ἰδέσϑαι* 'there Sleep came to a halt before the eyes of Zeus caught sight of him'.

> from the present *man-ē-*). Whether an intensive reading of the reduplicated formation is recognizable can exclusively be checked in Homeric Greek, the only language in which both stems coexist (and even occur in one and the same line, see below). It must be stressed, however, that a clear opposition between both stems is extremely difficult to state: the present stem (aspect!), being unmarked as to *Aktionsart*, may also express the intensive reading—and, conversely, the function of the marked stem may have faded out, to become a mere synonym of the non-reduplicated present. A contrast between intensive *μίμνο/ε-* 'to resist' and *μένο/ε-* 'to remain, stand firm' with acc. *Ἄρηα* (i.e. 'war', which the god personifies) might only be assumed in *Il.* 17.720–721 *οἵ τὸ πάρος περ / μίμνομεν ὀξὺν Ἄρηα παρ' ἀλλήλοισι μένοντες* '(we) who in the past have been accustomed to withstand the bitter Ares, remaining beside each other', although the reading 'stand firm, resist' is also expressed by means of *μένο/ε-* (cf. *Il.* 11.836 … *ὃ δ' ἐν πεδίῳ Τρώων μένει ὀξὺν Ἄρηα* 'the other in the plain is resisting the bitter Ares of the Trojans'). It must be noted, in any case, that the sense 'wait for' with accusative with infinitive (which excludes any connotation of resistance) is attested only with *μένο/ε-*, e.g. *Il.* 4.247 *ἦ μένετε Τρῶας σχεδὸν ἐλθέμεν ἔνθά τε νῆες* '… or are you waiting for the Trojans to come close …?'.[14]

Greek thus turns out to reflect the inherited situation, i.e. the coexistence of a present *μένο/ε-* (**mén-o/e-*) and an intensive stem *μίμνο/ε-* (**mí-mn-*) of PIE **men-* 'to remain, stay', which may both be considered as inherited. The original present stem has been replaced by other formations in the daughter languages: Lat. *manēre* 'to remain' (**man-ē-i̯o/e-*: stative **mn̥-é*h_1-), OP *mānaya-* : OAv. *mānaiia-*, YAv. *mąniia-* (**mon-ei̯o/e-*), Arm. *mnam* (probably a denominative),[15] as well as Toch. BA *mäsk-* 'to be', 'to become' (**mn̥-sḱ-o/e-*).

The situation in Hittite may easily be explained in the framework of this reconstruction: the inherited present has left no trace in Hittite, whereas the (also inherited) intensive stem (3sg. **mí-mn-e*) 'to resist, stand firm' lives on in *mimma-* lexicalized as 'to reject, refuse'.

---

14 The situation stated for *μίμνο/ε-* : *μένο/ε-* is similar to that of the pair *ἴσχο/ε-* : *ἔχο/ε-* (both Hom.+) for a stative lexeme 'to have, hold in one's hand' (PIE **seĝʰ-*). Whether *ἴσχο/ε-* may be understood as intensive 'retain, hold with strength' as against *ἔχο/ε-* remains a matter of intuition in *δέος μ' ἴσχει* (*Il.* 5.812) and *σέβας μ' ἔχει* (*Od.* 3.123).

15 Denom. **mēne*h_2*-i̯o/e-* or remodelled from **mn̥-é*h_1- (Klingenschmitt 1982: 91–92), *aliter* Barton 1990–1991: 45 (**men-*h_1*i̯é-*). For *mna-*, Kölligan 2014: 159 mentions the possibility of a denominative **munāi̯o/e-* from Arm. **mun*(*a*)- (**moné*h_2-: Gk. *μονή*).

3 Hitt. *pippa-*^{ḫḫi} 'to overthrown, tear up, pull down' (: Ved. (°)*pípīte* 'moves'), pres. PIE **pí-ph₂-* (*(*s*)*peh₂-* 'to set/get in (violent) motion', cf. Gk. *σπάο/ε-* 'to pull, draw' and Arm. *hane-* 'id.')

Hitt. *pippa-*^{ḫḫi}, med. *pippa-*^{tta} (OH+) has a series of readings mostly in connection with an adverb indicating the direction of the motion: 'to overthrow, tear up, pull down' (an altar; a throne (^{GIŠ}ŠÚ.A); a temple (É.ḪI.A) or house (É.ḪI.A-*TIM*); a city (URU); a wall (BÀD-*eššar*) or a gate (KÁ.GAL)), especially with *arḫa* 'away', whence 'overturn', 'destroy', 'pull out of the ground', as well as in the expression $^{(TÚG)}$*šeknun/-uš šarā* (: UGU) *pipp*(*a*)- 'to turn up the robe', i.e. 'to show one's genitals' as a gesture of cursing.[16] All senses[17] may be reduced to a basic meaning 'put in motion violently'. The voice opposition beween transitive *pippa-*^{ḫḫi} and intransitive *pippa-*^{tta}[18] may be traced back to the original paradigm (s. below):

> KUB 33.10 ii 12 [… URU?.DIDLI.ḪI.]A-*uš pippaš* É.ḪI.A-*TIM píp*[*paš*] (OH/MS, Telipinu myth)
> 'he overthrew [citie]s(?), [he] overthr[ew] houses'[19]

> KUB 34.22 rev. i 8–9 *nu a-pa-a-at* ^{GIŠ}ŠÚ.A […] *arḫa pippattari* (LH/LS)
> 'that throne will be overthrown'

> KBo 22.6 iv 23 [(^{URU}*Pu-*)]*rušḫandaš* BÀD-*eššar* KÁ.GAL *ḫanti pippandu* (OH?/NS)
> 'let them break down the wall (and) the gate of Purušḫanda separately'[20]

The verb, which stands isolated in Hittite, has been associated since Karl Hoffmann[21] with Ved. *ut-pipīte* 'rises' (TS 3.2.10.2) of a root *pā*³ 'to move', as persua-

---

16 As per Melchert 1983: 141ff. This usage is specific and is not helpful for phraseology.

17 *CHD* P s.v. **pippa-** ("1. to knock down / apart / off, tear down, overthrow, destroy, 2. to turn up, throw up (usually with *šarā*)").

18 Thus Jasanoff 2003: 131: 3sg.act. **pí-pH-e* as against intrans. med. **pí-pH-o*(*r*), like *kānki* 'hangs' as against *gangattari* (intransitive).

19 KUB 31.124 ii 10–12 (MH) *nu kētaš ANA* KUR.KUR.ḪI.A *šumenzan ŠA* ⟨DINGER.MEŠ⟩ É.ḪI.A DINGIR.MEŠ=*KU-NU kue ēšta n=at* LÚ.MEŠ ^{URU}*Gašga arḫa pípper* 'the Kaskeans have destroyed what temples (É.ḪI.A) of you ⟨O gods⟩ were in these lands'.

20 Also KBo 18.54 rev. 18' (letter, late MH/MS) *nu mān* BÀD *kuuapi arḫa UL píppanzi* 'if they do not knock/break down the wall (BÀD) someplace …'.

21 Hoffmann *apud* Oettinger 1979: 498 (with reference to aor. 3sg. *pās-ta* AV); Kümmel, *LIV*² s.v. **peH-* "sich bewegen"; Jasanoff 2003: 131, 146 (with reference to med. *pippattari* 'topples' as a semantic bridge with Ved. (°)*pipīte*).

sively argued by T. Burrow.[22] This is surely right, both from a formal and from a semantic point of view. The evidence for Vedic *pā*^{3} 'move', med. 'get in motion' (3sg. *pipīte*, pl. °*pipate* : **pi-pH-toi̯*, **pi-pH-n̥toi̯*], perhaps aor. *pā-s-* impv.3sg. *pāsta* AV)[23] matches basically that of Hitt. *pippa-*: the different meanings of *pā*^{3}, like those of Hitt. *pippa-*, are conditioned by local preverbs,[24] namely *ud*° 'up' (also *prati-ud*°, *an-ud*°) and *vi*° 'apart' whence *út-pā* 'rise' (3sg. *ud-pipīte*), *ví-pā* 'move apart' (*vi-pipīte* 'separates himself' or 'for himself' Br), e.g.[25]

> TS 1.6.10.1 *yá evaínaṃ pratyutpípīte tám úpāsyate*
> 'Verily he overthrows him who rises against him'

The equation Hitt. *pippa-* : Ved. *pipī-* obviously points to **pí-pH-*, a reduplicated present stem of PIE **peH-* 'to move, get in motion' ("sich bewegen", Kümmel, *LIV*^{2} s.v.). However, the evidence from both languages does not allow for the reconstruction of the exact shape of the PIE root (which laryngeal?), and it is commonly assumed that the semantic connection between Hitt. *pippa-* and Ved. *pā*^{3} needs to be specified in detail in view of the diversity of readings.[26] Moreover, there is a crucial point that has not been given adequate attention: the dossier of the root is not limited to Hittite and Vedic, but it also includes Gk. *σπάο/ε-* 'to draw violently' and Arm. *hanem* 'id.', as I have tried to show,[27] which are currently traced back to **(s)peh*$_2$- 'pull, draw': Gk. *σπάο/ε-* (aor. *σπασ(σ)α-*) is formed from zero-grade **spə*$_2$-, and Arm. *hanem* 'id.' (aor. *ehan*) reflects **pā-no/e-*.[28] Their meanings and collocations are the same (also specified or conditioned by preverbs, see below) as those of Hitt. *pippa-* : Ved.

---

22 Burrow 1973, with an extremely fine analysis of the Vedic facts, except that his assumption of a root-present of this root (1973: 92ff.) cannot be retained, as the alleged instances of *pā-*^{ti} actually belong to *pā*^{2} 'to protect'.

23 Cf. AV XII 3.43b *kravyā́t piśācá ihá mā́ prá pāsta* "… and may the flesh-eating *piśāca* not come here" (Burrow), but *prá pāsta* of *pā*^{1} 'drink' is also possible ("let the flesh-eating *Piśācá* not have a draught here", Whitney).

24 The only exception is *pípāna-* lexicalized as 'burly' (AV IX 4.21).

25 This is a specific development within the language of Vedic ritual, referring to the separation of a liquid from another liquid, whence a reading 'to suck (in / out)' (for a selection of data, all from Burrow's study, cf. García Ramón 2009: 136).

26 Kümmel, *LIV*^{2} s.v. ("Die semantische Anknüpfung bedürfte der Präzisierung"); Kloekhorst 2008: 676 s.v. ("this is not evident semantically").

27 García Ramón 2009: the proposed **(s)peh*$_2$- subsumes the two roots currently assumed to be different, namely **peH-* "sich bewegen" and **(s)peh*$_2$- "(heraus)ziehen" (Kümmel in *LIV*^{2} s.vv.).

28 As proposed by Kölligan 2014: 153, Arm. *spananem* 'kill' may be traced back to a neo-root **span(a)*- (from a compound **z(u)-peh*$_2$- 'draw', with pres. **(zu)-p-n̥(e)-h*$_2$- : *spanane-*).

°*pipīte* (*pā* 3), i.e., form and semantics of the different verbs allow us to assume that they all belong to one and the same lexeme: **peH-* may therefore be specified as **(s)peh₂-* (with *s- mobile*, attested only in Greek) 'to put / get in (violent) motion', a telic–momentative root, for which a reduplicated present stem **pí-ph₂-* is perfectly conceivable. For the sake of clarity, the paradigm of **(s)peh₂-* may be reconstructed as follows:

Present 3sg. **pí-ph₂-e*[29]	:	Hitt. *pippa-ḫḫi*, Ved. °*pipīte*
		→ **spə₂-éi̯o/e-* or PGk. **spa-i̯o/e-* (σπάο/ε-)[30]
		→ **péh₂-no/e-* : Arm. *hanem*
Aorist **(s)péh₂-* / **(s)pə₂-´*	:	Ved. *pās-* (probably)
		→ **spə₂-s-* or PGk. **spa-s-* (σπασ(σ)α-)

Let us recall some parallels between Hitt. *pippa-* and Gk. *σπάο/ε-* (with *ἀνα°*, *ἀπο°*, *δια°*), namely with 'wall' (Hitt. BÀD-*eššar*, Gk. *ὑποτείχισις*) or with 'gate' (KÁ.GAL, *πύλαι*)

> KBo 22.6 iv 23 [(URUPu-)]*rušḫandaš* BÀD-*eššar* KÁ.GAL *ḫanti pippandu* (OH? / NS)
> 'let them break down the wall (BÀD-*eššar*) (and) the gate (KÁ.GAL) of Purušḫanda separately'

Cf. Thuc 6.100.3 *τήν τε ὑποτείχισιν καθεῖλον καὶ τὸ σταύρωμα ἀνέσπασαν* 'they pulled down the counter-wall (*ὑποτείχισιν*), and tore up the stockade'; Hdt. 3.159 *τὰς πύλας πάσας ἀπέσπασε* 'he tore out all the doors (*πύλας*)'.

The constructions of Hitt. *pippa-* with 'cities', 'houses' or 'throne' as the object (see above) basically match the semantics of Gk. *ἀνα-σπάο/ε-* with objects as 'pavilion', and 'statues' which are torn from their foundation (Hdt. 7.119 … *τήν τε σκηνὴν ἀνασπάσαντες* '… having rent the pavilion (*σκηνήν*) from the ground', 5.86 … *πρὸς τὰ ἀγάλματα· οὐ δυναμένους δὲ ἀνασπάσαι ἐκ τῶν βάθρων* … '… to the statues (*ἀγάλματα*); but as they could not tear them from their foundations …').

The synonymity of Ved. *pā*³ with Gk. *σπάο/ε-* and Arm. *hanem* is evident in some constructions which are not attested with Hitt. *pippa-*: for instance, intransitive Ved. *ud-pípīte* 'raises up' matches medial *σπάο/ε-*, cf. TS 3.2.10.2 *yó na … abhidā́sati bhrā́tr̥vya utpípīte śubhas* "the enemy who … is hostile to us,

29 Reanalyzed from 3.pl. **pi-ph₂-ént(i)*. There is no trace of a putative ablauting stem **pi-péh₂-* / **pi-ph₂-´*.

30 From **sph₂-ei̯o/e-* (Klingenschmitt 1982: 132) or directly from PGk. **spa-*, i.e. *σπάο/ε-* :: *σπασ(σ)α-* according to the pattern of *ἐλάο/ε-* :: *ἐλασ(σ)α-*, *κεράο/ε-* :: *κερασ(σ)α-*.

who rises up against us",[31] and Soph. *Trach.* 786 ἐσπᾶτο γὰρ πέδονδε καὶ μετάρσιος / βοῶν, ἰύζων· 'he pulled himself to the floor and up (μετάρσιος), screaming, yelling'. The same applies to the collocations 'to draw a liquid' (Vedic, Greek), and 'to draw a ship (from the water)', 'to tear a part of the body', or 'to take someone away/to' (Greek, Armenian).[32]

To sum up: Hitt. *pippa-*^{hhi} can only be explained in a comparative perspective, namely as the lexicalization of the present stem **pí-ph$_2$-* (3sg. **pi-ph$_2$-e*) of PIE **(s)peh$_2$-* 'to set in motion (violently)', med. 'to get in motion' (telic–momentative), which is represented in Ved. *pā* 3, Gk. σπάο/ε- and Arm. *hanem* as well. The different senses are determined by the presence of local adverbs in the different languages, and the common appurtenance to one and the same root is evident in the light of a series of common collocations. The inherited reduplicated present (i.e. morphologically marked) **pí-ph$_2$-*, which is in *aspectual* opposition to root-aorist **(s)péh$_2$-t*, med. **(s)pə$_2$-tó*, lives on in Hittite (*ḫi*-conjugation) and in Vedic, and has been remodelled in Greek and in Armenian, whereas the aorist stem has disappeared in Hittite and has been remodelled in Greek, in Armenian, and perhaps in Vedic (*pās-*?).

4 CLuw. *ūppa/i-* 'to carry (off), take (off)', HLuw. (CAPERE$_2$-*u-pa-* (/oːppa-/), root-aorist PIE **(s)péh$_2$-*

CLuw. *ūppa-* 'to carry (off), take (off)' (also *ūppanna-* 'id.'), HLuw. (CAPERE$_2$)*u-pa* 'id' (in what follows Luw. /oːppa-/), the meaning of which has been elucidated by H.C. Melchert,[33] is isolated in Luwian. Some instances:

> KBo 13.260 iii 13–15 *a=tta ādduu̯an=za parii̯an adduu̯alii̯an u̯attanii̯an uppannandu* (NS)
> 'Let them carry the evil over to an evil land' (Yakubovich 2010: 237, text [133])

> KARKAMIŠ A 11*b*+*c* §13 **a-u̯a/i-ta* (SCALPRUM.CAPERE$_2$)*u-pa-ní-zi a-tá* / (CAPERE$_2$)*u-pa-ha*.

---

31 Cf. also TB 3.2.9.10 *mū́laṃ vā́ … rákṣāṃsy anū́tpipate* "Verily the Rakṣases rise against (attack, assail) that root which stands above the ground".

32 For the data, cf. García Ramón 2009: 144ff. and 142ff. respectively.

33 Melchert 2004: 371ff., and especially forthcoming b (with discussion of the dossiers of both Luw. /oːppa-/ and Hitt. *uppa/i-* 'to send'). Luw. /oːppa-/ is surely different from CLuw. *upa-* 'to grant, furnish' (HLuw. (PES$_2$)*pa-(za)-*), Lyc. *ube-* 'dedicate' (Melchert 2004: 371, 375–376).

'(I devastated these countries) and I brought in the spoils' (or 'I carried off')[34]

KARKAMIŠ A1*a* §7 **a-u̯a/i-tú pa+ra/i-i-ha-´* / (SCALPRUM.CAPERE$_2$)*u-pa-ní-i-na* / (CAPERE$_2$)*u-pa-ha*
'I destroyed the city (Alathana) and I brought forth the spoils to him'

Luw. /o:ppa-/ is difficult to interpret *ex Anatolico ipso*.[35] A connection with Hittite *uppa/i-* ^{ḫḫi} 'to send', which relies only on the formal similarity, is surely to be ruled out: 'to send' is not compatible with 'to bring, carry (off), take (off)', and CLuw. *ūppa-* shows plene spelling ⟨*u-up-*⟩ (i.e. *u-up-pa-* /o:ppa-/), whereas Hitt. *uppa/i-* does not.[36] H.C. Melchert (forthcoming b) has convincingly identified the outcome of **au̯-(s)p(e)h$_2$-* *'to take away, remove' in Luw. /o:ppa-/, whence 'to carry (off), take (off)', and then just 'to carry', with **au̯°* 'off, away' (as Lat. *auferō* 'I carry off'), and a second member **(s)peh$_2$-* 'to set / get in (violent) motion', which he endorses in the terms proposed above (§3). This interpretation fits the semantics of **(s)peh$_2$-*, especially with 'spoils' as its object, i.e. something that one takes away, after seizing it (note the determinative (CAPERE$_2$)*u-pa* in Hieroglyphic Luwian), with a violent motion.

In my opinion, it is possible to get a step further, and to assume that Luw. /°ppa-/ in /o:ppa-/ is the counterpart of Hitt. (°)*pippa-* ^{ḫḫi} (more precisely, the continuant of the inherited aorist stem **(s)peh$_2$-*). This finds support in some occurrences of *σπάο/ε-* 'to seize' by violence and *ἄγο/ε-* 'to carry off' with 'booty' with spoils or booty (*λεία*) as the object, e.g.

Plb. 2.26.8 ... *ἐπιτηρεῖν δὲ μᾶλλον καιροὺς καὶ τόπους εὐφυεῖς ἑπόμενος, ἐάν πού τι βλάψαι τοὺς πολεμίους ἢ τῆς λείας ἀποσπάσαι δυνηθῇ*
'... to hang on the enemy's rear and watch for times and places favourable for inflicting damage on them or wresting some of the spoil from their hands'

---

34 Melchert 2004: 372, with reference to the *figura etymologica* in *upaninzi upaha*.

35 The verb is considered as "etymologically valueless" (Kloekhorst 2008: 922 s.v. *uppa-ⁱ* / *uppi-*).

36 Hitt. *uppa/i-* 'to send' has been persuasively explained by Melchert (ftch. b) as a deadverbial verb of the *ḫi*-conjugation built on the directional preverb **upo* (Skr. *úpa*), of the type *āppai-* 'to go back' (pre-Hitt. **opi*, Luw. /a:ppi/, *p(a)rā-* 'to appear' (*parā* 'forth', *šanna-* 'to conceal' (*šanna-* 'isolated, secret') as per Melchert 2009). The current explanation of *uppa/i-* (Oettinger 1979: 489) as a compound with *au̯°* and *pai-/pii̯e* ^{ḫḫi} 'give' reappears in Kloekhorst 2008: 922 s.v ("I support wholeheartedly"), beside "PIE **h$_2$ou* + **h$_1$p-oi-ei* / **h$_1$p-i-enti*" ibid. 921).

X.*Cyr.* 5.3.1 *καὶ ἧκον πολλοὶ μὲν αὐτῶν κατακεκυλισμένοι ἀπὸ τῶν ἵππων, πολλοὶ δὲ καὶ λείαν πλείστην ἄγοντες*
'And many of them were thrown from their horses and came back, but many of them also came bringing a great quantity of plunder' (cf. also E. *Tro.* 614 *ἀγόμεθα λεία σὺν τέκνῳ* 'I am taken hence with my child as booty' (speaks Andromache))

The connection between 'carry' and 'booty' underlies Athena's epithet *ἀγελείη* (*Ἀθηναίην ἀγελείην Il.* 5.765 et al.), a transparent compound '(she) who takes away the plunder' (: *ἄγουσα λείαν*, as per Eustathius[37]), and eventually '(she) who helps (*scil.* the warriors she helps) to take away the plunder',[38] which may also be a group of women (*ληϊάδας*), cf. *Il.* 20.193 ... *αὐτὰρ ἐγὼ τὴν / πέρσα μεθορμηθεὶς σὺν Ἀθήνῃ καὶ Διὶ πατρί,/ ληϊάδας δὲ γυναῖκας ἐλεύθερον ἦμαρ ἀπούρας / ἦγον* (Achilles to Aeneas) 'but going after you I stormed that place, with the help of Athene and father Zeus, and the captive women, after taking them off the day of liberty, I lead away'.

In conclusion: Luw. /oːppa-/ (CLuw. *ūppa-*, HLuw. CAPERE$_2$-*u-pa-*) 'carry off, take (off)' (with a violent motion) may be easily explained as the lexicalization of the aorist stem of *(*s*)*peh*$_2$- 'to draw, pull' ('to set in violent motion').

5 Hitt. *nakkī*- (**h*$_1$*noki*-) 'important, prominent' (also 'importance, prominence'), 'difficult', replacing PIE **g*^{w}*r̥h*$_2$*ú*- 'heavy'

Hitt. *nakkī*- (: DUGUD, Akkad. *kabtu*), with a twofold meaning (1) 'important, prominent', 'powerful', and (2) 'difficult, arduous, inaccessible [of places]'), is well attested (MH+), with a series of derivatives, namely neuter *nakkī*- 'importance, prestige' (continued by *nakkii̯atar*- 'id.' NH), and stative *nakke*-^{mi}, fientive *nakkešš*-^{mi}, factitive *nakkiaḫḫ*-^{tta}. It refers practically to all types of referents, including humans (often kings or queens), deities, places, matters, and words.

Both readings of *nakkī*- may be subsumed under one, namely 'weighty', in the good sense (1) *'having much weight', whence 'important' (Span. *de peso*, Germ. *wichtig*) and in the bad one (2) *'onerous', whence 'difficult'. The seman-

37 The conception of Athena as helper to the one who desires booty and invokes her as *ἀγελεία* is evident in the commentary by Eustathius (*ad Il.* vol. 2, p. 319) *Ὅτι ὥσπερ ὁ ἐφιέμενος λείας ἀγελείαν Ἀθηνᾶν ἐπεκαλεῖτο, οὕτως ... οἱ περὶ σωτηρίας πόλεως χεῖρας αὐτῇ ἀνέχοντες ... ἐρυσίπτολιν Ἀθηνᾶν ἐπεβοῶντο.*

38 Cf. *Il.* 4.128 ... *πρώτη δὲ Διὸς θυγάτηρ ἀγελείη et alibi*, *Od.* 16.207 *Ἀθηναίης ἀγελείης* (also *Il.* 6.269 *et alibi*).

tics of *nakkī-* is clear, but its word formation is not, because of its unexpected /-ī/ and its non-ablauting paradigm, which fits into the pattern of a noun inflection, not into that of an adjective (see below).[39] The two cognates proposed for *nakkī-* by E.H. Sturtevant (1930: 21, 1934: 267) are of different value: Hitt. *nini(n)k-* 'to rise', transitive 'to raise' (**ni-n-k-*) surely belongs to another root (PIE **nei̯k-* 'to raise (oneself)', Lith. *su-ninkù* 'fall upon', OCS *vъz-nikǫ* 'rise', Gk. *νεῖκος* 'strife'), whereas the connection with Gk. *ἐνεγκεῖν* raises some semantic difficulty, as *nakkī-* does not match the original meaning of *ἐνεγκεῖν* (PIE **$h_1$neḱ-* /**$h_1$enḱ-* 'to take, obtain': Toch. B /eṅk-/ 'id.', *ἕνεκα* *'because of', cf. § 5.4), i.e. previous to its integration as the aorist of a suppletive paradigm with **b^her-*. Only two possibilities remain open: either to assume that *nakkī-* has no recognizable etymology, which is surely wrong,[40] or to admit the connection with *ἐνεγκεῖν*—and try to find an explanation for the semantic difficulty. This is surely right, as is the reconstruction of a proto-form **$h_1$noḱ-i-* (in fact a "Transponat") as proposed by Calvert Watkins, who explains *nakkī-* as an Anatolian innovation which replaces PIE **g^wr̥h_2ú-*[41] and crucially evokes the semantic connection with **b^her-*.[42]

In line with Watkins' interpretation, the final /-ī/ and the non-ablauting inflection of the epithet *nakkī-* 'weighty' speaks for a former deinstrumental formation **$h_1$nóki-h_1* 'with weight' from a deverbal abstract **$h_1$nók-i-* 'weight, quality of being weighty (in both senses)' created as a nominalization of an

39 As is well known, an ablauting paradigm is characteristic of *i*-adjectives, with *o*-grade like *šalli-* 'big, vast' (cf. PIE **solH-u̯o-*: Ved. *sárva-* 'all', Gk. *ὅλος*) or *daluki-* 'long' (PAnat. **dol(H)ug^h-i-*, as against **dol(H)ig^hó-*: Gk. *δολιχός* and **dl̥Hg^hó-* : Ved. *dīrghá-*) or with zero-grade like *palḫi-* 'wide, broad' (PAnat. **pl̥h_2-i-*).

40 Kloekhorst 2008 s.v. *nakkī-*, 593–594, questions a connection of *nakkī-* 'important' and **$h_1$neḱ-* 'to seize, carry' as "semantically difficult", with the argument that this would only be possible if *nakkī-* meant 'heavy', which is excluded by *CHD* L–N **nakki-** s.v. ("a meaning 'heavy' cannot be established"). Such a tenet ignores that 'weighty' and 'heavy' (: having weight) are very close to each other, as well as to 'carry, bear', cf. e.g. Span. *de peso* (: *importante* [Lat. *importāre*!] vs. *pesado* (: *heavy, onerous*), Lat. *importāre*, Germ. *wichtig* beside *gewichtig, Gewicht*).

41 Also Puhvel 1984–, vol. 5: 50. According to Yakubovich 2011: 173, PIE **g^wr̥h_2ú-* lives on in Hitt. *u̯arḫui-* 'shaggy, rough, leafy, unshaven', e.g., of sheep (/w-/ as the phonetic outcome of /g^w-/). Apart from the semantic differences, and the fully anomalous reflex of a labiovelar as /w-/ ⟨u̯-⟩ in Hittite (for which Yakubovich alternatively proposes an interference between Hittite und Luwian), *u̯arḫui-* may perfectly reflect **u̯erh_2-u̯-ih_2* (Melchert 1987: 13 n. 21 after Neumann 1958: 90, Oettinger 1979: 549 "zu *εἶρος* 'Vließ'"). Kloekhorst's remark "This preform does not yield the Greek form by regular sound change" (2008: 961, s.v. *u̯arḫui- / u̯arḫuu̯ai-*), is certainly right, but hardly a counterargument: *εἶρος* may obviously be traced back to **u̯érh_2u̯-es-*.

42 Watkins 1971: 72 n. 24.

-*o*-stem *$^*h_1$nok-ó-* 'burden, weight (borne)' corresponding to an action noun PIE *$^*h_1$nók-o-* 'carrying, bearing'. The final /-ī/ of the neuter noun *nakkī-* 'importance' (*'weight') reflects the use of the neuter of the epithet as equivalent to the abstract.[43]

5.1 *Semantics of Hitt.* nakkī, daššu- *'strong'*

Two remarks on the semantics of Hitt. *nakkī-* and its synonyms are in order. The term shares basic meaning and collocations with the reflexes of PIE *$^*g^w$r̥h_2ú-* 'heavy, weighty' in other languages (Skr. *gurú-*, Gk. *βαρύς*, Lat. *grauis etc.*), also in a good and bad sense, e.g. Skr. *gurú-* 'heavy' (*gurúm bhārám* 'heavy burden' RV IV 5.6), beside (1) 'teacher' (Sū +) and (2) 'heavy (to endure)' (RV I 147.4cd *mántro gurúḥ púnar astu só asmā ánu mr̥kṣīṣṭa tanvàm̥ duruktaíḥ* 'let this heavy spell be back at him: he should bring harm upon his own body by his evil words').

On the other hand, within Hittite, *nakkī-* is a partial synonym of *daššu-* (DUGUD) 'strong' (PIE **dn̥sú-*, originally 'compact' : Hom. *δασύς* 'densely overgrown, hairy, leafy', Lat. *dēnsus*), which shares with it the basic meanings 'weighty, strong' and 'heavy' (*daššu* GUN-*an* 'heavy load'), as well as both readings (1) and (2). The overlapping of *nakkī-* and *daššu-*, an actual merger, represents a specific Anatolian development.[44]

A distinction between (1) and (2) is not always easy. When the referents themselves are negative concepts ('enemy' and 'enmity', 'evil(ness)', 'grievous(ness)', 'war' and the like), it is their lexeme itself which conditions the reading of the epithet,[45] e.g. *nakkī kurur* 'bitter enmity' (KUB 24.9 ii 9 MH/NS), like Ved. *gurú dvéṣaḥ* 'heavy hatred' (RV VII 56.19), Hom. *ἔριδα ... βαρεῖαν* (*Il.* 20.55), *πόλεμος ... βαρύς* (Dem. 18.241), *ἔχθραι βαρύταται* 'the heaviest enmities' (Pla. *Leg.* 9.934d),[46] Lat. *graue bellum, ... grauior ... seditio* (Liv. 6.11.1).

43 The same explanation applies to the type *τρόπις* "qualité de tourneur", *στρόφις* "qualité de ce que se tord", *τρόχις* "qualité du coureur" (Lefeuvre 2016, especially 200–201). According to Widmer 2005: 199, 201–202, the base form of *nakkī-* from **(H)nok̂íh₁-* "mit Gewicht seiend; gewichtig" would be an abstract **Hnók-o-* "Gewicht", like Ved. *rathī́-* 'driver of the chariot' beside *rathá-*, as a nominalization of a former instr. **(H)nok̂-íh₁* to **(H)nok̂o-* "Gewicht". Other proposals may be recalled at this point, namely those of Zucha 1988: 313 (*nakki-* like *τρόφι* 'well-nourished') and of Puhvel 1984–, vol. 5: 49 (adjective *nakí-* beside substantive *náki-* "noun masquerading as an epithetic or appositional adjective").

44 Puhvel *HED* 49–50.

45 The close connection between 'heavy' (*$^*g^w rh_2$-ú-*, *$^*g^w rh_2$-í-*) and 'evil', 'war' is evident in the etymology of OHG *krēg* 'stubbornness', the predecessor of NHG *Krieg* (**krīya-* aus *$^*g^w rh_2$i-kó-* as persuasively argued by Kölligan 2013, Appendix "Germanic 'War'"; differently Kroonen 2013: 304, who posits **kriaga-*).

46 Cf. Massetti 2016: 38, with reference to other referents: *κακότης* (Hom.), *νεῖκος* (Pi.), *κότος* (A., also *βαρύκοτος* A.), *ὀργή* and *μῆνις* (S.).

5.2 *Collocations of Hitt.* nakkī-

Some instances of collocations of *nakkī-* (with reference to comparanda with *daššu-* and with the reflexes of **gʷr̥h₂ú-*, as well as indication of (1) good sense and (2) bad sense, if possible), namely with (a) deities, (b) names (*laman-*), (c) matters (*uttar*) (d) places, and (e) words (*memiyan-, uttar*), speak for themselves:[47]

a Deities: (1) KUB 24.3 i 29–34 [*z*]*ik=za* ᵈUTU ᵁᴿᵁ*Arinna nakkiš* DINGIR-*LIM-iš nu=tta=kkan ŠUM-an lamnaš ištarna nakki* ... 'you, Sun-Goddess Arinna, you are an honored deity, and your name is honored among names'; (2) KBo 18.15: 6–7 *nu=*[*šši*] *ŠA ABI=ŠU* DINGIR.MEŠ.ḪI.A *nakkiškantat* 'his father's gods became oppressive' (cf. Theocr. 1.100 *Κύπρι βαρεῖα, Κύπρι νεμεσσατά* ...).—With *daššu-*: KUB 36.106 obv. 9′ *na=an kē daššauẹ*[*s* / *NIŠ* DINGIRᴹᴱŠ *appant*[*u* 'might these mighty oath-gods seize them'.

b Names: (1) *ŠUM-an lamnaš ištarna nakki* cf. (a) above.—With *daššu-*: KUB 31.141:4 *ŠUM-an=tit daššu* 'your name is important' (hymn to Istar, NH).

c Matters: (1) KUB 36.114 rt. col. 29 [...]x-*pát* 1-*EN uttar nakki ēšdu* 'and let a single matter be important' (MH/MS); (2) *kēdani* MU.KAM-*ti nakkii̯atar UL namma kuiški* [-*tki*?] *ēšzi* 'there will be no further difficulty this year' (KUB 40.1 rev! 18–23, NH).[48]—With *daššu-*: KUB 23.72 rev. 54 *nu mališku* / [*uttar lē tašn*]*ụttani taššu=ma uttar lē mališkunụtan*[*i* ... 'and do not make an unimportant matter important, but do not make an important matter unimportant' (MH/MS).

d Places: (1) KUB 29.4 iii 26–28 *nakkiš=za* DINGIR-*LUM* NÍ.TE=*KA paḫši* ... *nu edass=a ANA* É.ḪI.A GIBIL.ḪI.A *ehu nu=za nakki pēdan ēp* 'you, honoured goddess, take care of your person! ... come to these new temples and take (them as your) important places' (NH);[49] (2) KUB 14.17 iii 22–23 *na=aš=kan nakki pēdi* [*aš*(*anza*)] 'and it (the city of Ura) is [situa]ted in a place hard to reach' (Ann. Mursilis).—With *daššu-*: *tašša⟨u⟩i pēdi hamikta ulipanan* '(the river) bound the leopard to a strong place' KBo 3.8 iii 10 (NS). Cf. also *loca grauissima* (Cato, *Agr.*131 *uti* (*loca*) *quaeque grauissima et aquosissima erunt*).

e Words: (1) KUB 33.106+KBo 26.65 i 25–26 [*kuu̯*]*at =u̯a ŠA* ᵈU EN [= *YA*] *nakkin memian UL išt*[*amašmi*] 'why do I not hear the important word of

47 For a larger selection with slightly different criteria cf. García Ramón 2010a: 75–80.

48 It is difficult to decide whether factitive *nakkii̯aḫḫ-* (medial) reflects (1) or (2) in KBo 4.6 vs. 24–26 *namma=šši apāt uttar nakkii̯aḫtāt* 'and then that matter became a concern to her'.

49 García Ramón 2010a: 84; Massetti 2016: 169.

the Storm God, of my Lord?' (*Ullikummi*).[50]—With *daššu-*: KUB 17.7 + iii 42' *nu kī dašša*[*u̯u̯a*] INIM^{MEŠ}-*ar* ^{D}*Irširaš pe⟨r⟩an memi* "e (Kumarbi) pronuncia queste parole forti davanti agli dei di Irširra" (Dardano 2012: 62). The collocation [PROMINENT (: STRONG)—WORD(S)] (*daššau̯a* INIM^{MEŠ}: MS, NS copies of OH) is normal in oaths, cf. KUB 43.38 rev. 26–28 *kaš=u̯a* NA_4 *maḫḫan d*[*aššus*] / [EGIR-*and*]*a=wa=šan NIŠ* DINGIR^{LIM} *inann=a INA* [ŠÀ=*KUNU*] *daššišdu* "wie dieser Stein schwer ist, ebenso soll nachher der Eid und die Krankheit in [eurem innerem] schwer werden" (Oettinger 1976: 20–21). It underlies the name of the oath god *Ḫantitaššu-*.[51] Cf. also for (1) Pl. *Trin.* 385 *grauius tuom erit unum verbum ad eam rem quam centum* 'more important is a single word of you for that matter than a hundred of mine' (also Cic. *Brut.* 109) and *λόγων φερτάτων* in Pindar (cf. 5.5 below). For (2) cf. Pi. *P.* 2.52–56 *εἶδον γὰρ … ἐν ἀμαχανίᾳ ψογερὸν Ἀρχίλοχον βαρυλόγοις ἔχθεσιν πιαινόμενον* […] 'for I have seen Archilochus the blamer often in straits as he fed on dire words of hatred'.[52]

5.3 *Hitt.* nakkī- *and Gk.* ὄγκος, *OLith.* naštà *'load': semantics*

On the assumption that *nakkī-* (protoform *$^*h_1$noḱi-*) is connected with Gk. *ἐνεγκο/ε-* (*$^*h_1$ne-h_1nḱ-o/e-*, cf. YAv. *nąsat̰*)[53] and that both go back to PIE *$^*h_1$neḱ-* / *$^*h_1$enḱ-* 'to take, take away' (root with Schwebeablaut),[54] a first look outside

50 García Ramón 2010a: 76; Massetti 2016: 169, with reference to the association of *φραδαί* 'instructions' with *φέρτατος Ζεύς* (Ba. 19.12–18 … *φεῦγε χρυσέα βοῦς, / εὐρυσθενέος φραδαῖσι φερτάτου Διός* '… the golden cow had to flee according to the instructions of the mighty, highest Zeus').

51 Cf. Tischler 1983—T,D/2: 261 with references. Appurtenance of Lyc. *tese/i-* 'oath, vow', pl. *tasa*, loc. *tesi* 'under oath' (also *tesẽti* 'id.', *Tesẽti* 'divine agent', cf. Melchert 2005 s.vv.) to *daššu-* is most dubious (Hajnal 1993: 76, 186: protoform **teksé/í-* < **toksó/í-*, also Serangeli 2015: 39).

52 On *βαρύλογος* 'of dire words' cf. Massetti 2016: 37 ff.

53 Beekes 1979: 18 ff.; Strunk 1988: 573 ff.; García Ramón 1999: 61–62, 73–74.

54 The assumption of a root *$^*h_1$neḱ-* / *$^*h_1$enḱ-* with Schwebeablaut like others (cf. Schindler 1970) raises no problem, to my mind, and is in any case better than tracing *ὄγκος* back to *$^*h_2$enk-* 'to bow' or to connect it with Ved. *áṃśa-* 'portion, share' : Av. *ąsa-* 'id.', which actually reflect *$^*h_2$ónḱ-o-* (of a different root *$^*h_2$enḱ-*: Hitt. *ḫe/i(n)k-^{mi}* 'to offer, bestow' [*$^*h_2$énḱ-*]), and are connected with Hitt. *ḫe/inkan-* 'death, doom, plague' (*'share'). PIE *$^*h_2$enḱ-* 'offer' is in turn the Schwebeablaut variant of *$^*h_2$neḱ-* 'to reach' (OIr. pres. [*ro-*]*icc* 'id.', perf. *·ánaic*, also Ved. *naś* : Av. *nas*, Ved. pres. *aśnóti* : Av. *ašnaoiti*, aor. *ā́naṭ*, perf. *ānā́śa, ánaṃśa*), as I have tried to show (García Ramón 1999). The lexicalization of 'reach' as 'offer' (*$^*h_2$enḱ-*), as attested also in some instances of Ved. *naś* (*$^*h_2$neḱ-*), may be traced back to a reading *'reach something to someone' (as is the case with Hitt. *ēp-* / *app-^{mi}* 'grasp', whence 'offer') or to agentive 'to let reach' (Span. *alcanzar*, Germ. *reichen*, e.g. *alcánzame*

Anatolian leads to the substantives OLith. *naštà* 'load' ("onus"), Latv. *nasta* 'id.' and Gk. *ὄγκος* 'bulk' and 'dignity', beside 'arrogance', which may easily be traced back to (actually *transposed* as) *$h_1$noḱ-téh$_2$-* and (*h_1óńk-o-*)[55] respectively.

The meaning of OLith. *naštà* 'load', Latv. *nasta* is straightforward and perfectly fits Lith *nèšti*, Latv. *nest* 'to carry', cf. MžG 468.13 Ps. 37/38,5 *kaipo naſchta ſunki* "sicut onus graue". It fully matches the semantics of *g^wr̥h$_2$u-* 'heavy' and the basic sense of Hitt. *nakkī-*.

Gk. *ὄγκος* 'bulk, weight' (*βραχεῖ σὺν ὄγκῳ* S.*OC* 1341, *θαυμαστὸν ὄγκον … τοῦ μύθου* 'a marvellous mass of myth') matches the semantics of the neuter Hitt. *nakkī-* 'importance' (and *nakkii̯atar*) in the sense (1) 'dignity, pride, loftiness', as well as (2) 'pretension, arrogance'.[56] It also shares some referents and collocations with adjectival *nakkī* (see below). Some instances:

S.*Phil.* 717 *ἔχει τιν' ὄγκον Ἄργος Ἑλλήνων πάρα*
'Argos has some weight among the Hellenes'[57]

S.*Tr.* 817–818 *ὄγκον γὰρ ἄλλως ὀνόματος τί δεῖ τρέφειν*
μητρῷον, ἥτις μηδὲν ὡς τεκοῦσα δρᾷ;
'Why should she nurture the dignity of mother's name, she who does nothing as one who has born?'

The term is used for diction in both senses, (1) 'high, majestic', i.e. 'loftiness, majesty of diction', and (2) 'bombastic, tiresome', 'bombastic pomp', especially of tragedy (Aeschylus), and also 'vulgar'.

---

el libro, reiche mir das Buch). Differently Kümmel, *LIV*² 268, who posits an independent root PIE *$h_2$enḱ- "zuteilen" (*unus testis*: Hitt. *ḫe/i(n)k-*) beside *$h_2$neḱ- "erreichen" (ibid. 282–283).

55 Beekes 1969: 132, *GED* s.v. ("what is carried, load, burden"). The term has no connection with *$h_1$onk-ó-* (Ved. *aṅká-* 'hook, clamp' : Lat. *uncus* 'hook', also *ὄγκη· γωνία* Hsch.) which belongs to a different root with non-palatal dorsal, namely PIE *$h_2$enk-* 'to bow, fold' ("biegen" *LIV*² s.v., p. 268), well attested in Hitt. *ḫi(n)k-*$^{ti/tta/a}$ 'bow reverentially', Ved. *añc* 'bow' (pres. *ác-a-*^{ti} RV, *áñc-a-*^{ti} AV), also *ἀγκών* 'elbow', *ἀγκύλη* 'bend of the arm' (*$h_2$enk-*). The attempt to trace back the sense 'burden' of *ὄγκος* to 'swelling' and ultimately to 'curvature' (as per J. Jouanna *apud* Beekes, *GED* [*non uidi*]) is hopeless.

56 The basic meaning is clear, although limits between dignity and arrogance are not always sharp, cf. Eur. *Tr.* 1158 *ὦ μείζον' ὄγκον δορὸς ἔχοντες ἢ φρενῶν* '(O you Achaeans), more reason have you to boast of your spear than your wisdom'.

57 Cf. also *τῷ … γένους ὄγκῳ* (Pl. *Alc.* 121b, D.C. 57.6.4).

Arist. *Rhet.* 407b 26 *εἰς ὄγκον δὲ τῆς λέξεως συμβάλλεται τάδε, τὸ λόγῳ χρῆσθαι ἀντ' ὀνόματος,*
'to the pomp of style contributes the using of a definition instead of a name'[58]

S.*OC* 1162 *βραχὺν … μῦθον οὐκ ὄγκου πλέων*
'a short talk, not full of pretensions'.

In both senses *ὄγκος* is conceived as weight that one bears, or carries or raises. The expression *ὄγκον αἴρειν* 'to exalt (raise) one's dignity' mirrors the action as that of raising or bearing a burden:

S.*Aj.* 128–129 *μηδέν ποτ' εἴπῃς αὐτὸς ἐς θεοὺς ἔπος,/ μηδ' ὄγκον ἄρῃ μηδέν(α)*
'see that you yourself never utter an arrogant word against the gods, nor assume any swelling pride', cf. also Pl.*Plt.*277b *θαυμαστὸν ὄγκον ἀράμενοι τοῦ μύθου* 'having taken up a marvellous mass of myth'.

5.4 *PIE* *$h_1$neḱ-/*$h_1$enḱ- *'to take' and* *b^her- *'to carry on, lift up'* (*OHG* burlîh *'sublimis, excellens' and cognates*)*: a suppletive pair*

Once we have established that Hitt. *nakkī-*, Gk. *ἐνεγκο/ε-*, Lith. *naštà* (**$h_1$neḱ-*), as well as Gk. *ὄγκος* (**$h_1$enḱ-*) (1) 'dignity', 'loftiness' and (2) 'pretension, tiresomeness' have a basic meaning 'weight' (i.e. a load that one carries on, or bears), with an adjective 'weighty' (:*grauis*), it must be stated that this meaning cannot easily be reconciled with that of PIE **$h_1$neḱ-* / **$h_1$enḱ-*, actually 'to take (for oneself, away)',[59] as is recognizable in Toch.B /*eṅk*-/ 'take', A *ents* (**$h_1$enḱ-* / **h_1n̥ḱ-*) or in the original meaning of *ἕνεκα*, Myc. *e-ne-ka* 'because of' (acc. **$h_1$néḱ-m̥*), namely 'to the taking of' + genitive,[60] which is surely earlier than the constitution of the suppletive pair *φέρο/ε-* :: *ἐνεγκο/ε-*.

In fact, 'weight', 'weighty' is only reconcilable with to 'to carry (on), bear', i.e. with one of the original meanings of PIE **b^her-*. This is evident in the light of some of its derivatives, e.g. **b^hór-o-* (Ved. *bhára-* ntr. 'action of bearing', dat. *bhárāya* 'for bearing'),[61] and, by internal derivation, **b^hor-ó-* *'concerning the

58 Arist. *Poet.* 1459b *ὑφ' ὧν οἰκείων ὄντων αὔξεται ὁ τοῦ ποιήματος ὄγκος. ὥστε τοῦτ' ἔχει τὸ ἀγαθὸν εἰς μεγαλοπρέπειαν …*, Plut. *quomodo* 16b7 *οὔτε γὰρ μέτρον οὔτε τρόπος οὔτε λέξεως ὄγκος.*

59 "erhalten, (weg)nehmen" (García Ramón 1999), "erhalten, nehmen" (Kümmel, *LIV*² s.v.).

60 On the Tocharian forms cf. Hackstein 1995: 229 with n. 1; on *ἕνεκα* (and Myc. *e-ne-ka*), cf. García Ramón 1999: 72–73 (the meaning of *ἕνεκα* is previous to the insertion in a suppletive paradigm with *φέρο/ε-* :: aor. *ἐνεγκ-ο/ε-*, perf. *ἐνήνοχα*).

61 AV 9.1.13 *āpā́m tvā goṣṭhó adhyarukṣad bhárāya* "the stall of the waters has ascended thee for bearing" (Whitney).

action of carrying',[62] whence the noun *rei actae* Ved. *bhārá-* 'load, burden' (ntr.), and *φόρος* (with accentual retraction, lexicalized as 'payment, tribute'), which lives on in *φόρτος* 'load' (Hom.+), also (2) 'rudeness', *φορτικός* 'tiresome, vulgar, wearisome', e.g.[63]

> D. 5.4 *τὸ λέγειν περὶ ὧν αὐτὸς εἶπέ τις …, οὕτως ἡγοῦμαι φορτικὸν καὶ ἐπαχθές* 'to talk about what oneself spoke, I feel that it is so vulgar and so burdensome'

The connection between 'weigh' and **bʰer-* is evident also in Ossetic (*bharyn* 'to weigh': Iran. **bāraya-*) and Bengali (*bhari* 'heavy' : Indo-Ar. *bharika-*),[64] and in the Germanic languages; cf. Goth. *baurþei* "*φορτίον*" (**burþīn-*), ONorse *byrð(r)* (PGmc. **burþ/di-*),[65] OE *byrð/den* 'burden' (**burþ/dinjo-*).

Of special interest for our purposes is OHG *bor, por* "prestigium" (Notker), *burlîh* "praestans, sublimis, excellens", 'lofty, exalted' (PGmc. **bur-līka-*: ME *borlich* "burly", OE *borlice* 'eminently, excellently', cf. PGmc. **bur-a-* 'high', 'height', **burjan* 'to raise, lift': OHG *burien, burren* "ascendere, surgere"), which is practically a synonym of Hitt. *nakkī*. OHG *burlîh* (with abstract *burlîchî* "eminentia, excellentia, elatio", and denominative *burlîchôn* "exaltare, sublimare") refers to, *inter alia*, persons and places, e.g. Notker Martianus Capella II (King 1979: 150) *athlantis tóhterôn scônista . búrlichíu hárto* 'the most beautiful daughter of Atlas, very eminent', I (ibid. 47) *kestáteta sî dóh ín êinemo búrlîchemo séze* 'but he sat down on a prominent seat' (and adverbial *burlihho* 'highly' I (ibid. 27) *únde dâr sâhen sie filium púrlicho latonę in hóhemo chúningstuôle sízzenten* 'and there they saw Latona's son, sitting high in a high throne'), also Notker Boethius *De Consolatione Philosophiae* II (Tax 1986: 78) collocatę tamen infra excellentiam uestram. *îo dóh fóne íuuérro búrlichi férro geskéidene.*[66]

To conclude so far: Hitt. *nakkī-* 'weighty' and 'weight' (originally *h_1*noḱ-i-*), in both senses (1) 'important' and (2) 'onerous' reflects, like *ὄγκος* (*h_1*ónḱ-o-*) and Lith. *naštà*, the semantics of **bʰer-* 'to carry on, bear', not that of *h_1*neḱ-* / *h_1*enḱ-* 'to take'. More precisely, Hitt. *nakkī-*, like *ὄγκος*, is equivalent to **bʰoró-* 'bur-

62 The internal derivative **bʰoró-* may also be agentive 'carrier': Ved. °*bhará-* (*puṣṭim-bhará-* 'who carries the growth', *bhāra-bhṛ́t-* 'who carries a load'), Gk. °*φόρος* (and *φορός* Arist.).

63 In metaphorical sense cf. Ar. *Pax* 748–749 *Τοιαῦτ' ἀφελὼν κακὰ καὶ φόρτον καὶ βωμολοχεύματ' ἀγεννῆ / ἐπόησε τέχνην μεγάλην ἡμῖν* 'He took that kind of ugliness and the annoyance and the unworthy vulgarity and created a fine art for us', *Nub.* 524 *εἶτ' ἀνεχώρουν ὑπ' ἀνδρῶν φορτικῶν / ἡττηθείς* 'then I had to resign, defeated by crude rivals'.

64 Watkins 1971: 72 n. 24 (= *Sel. Writ.*, 167).

65 Casaretto 2004: 296; Schaffner 2001: 374 ff., 455.

66 Thanks are due to Riccardo Ginevra for discussion and references.

den, load', continued by *φόρτος* 'load' (also 'rudeness', *φορτικός* 'onerous'), and Goth. *baurþei* "φορτίον", OE *byrðen* 'burden' and cognates. The positive sense of *nakkī-* (1) 'important, prominent' has a perfect parallel in OHG *burlîh* "praestans, sublimis, excellens", 'lofty, exalted' (with its derivatives) and cognates. We can therefore assume that the basic meaning 'weight, weighty' of the nominal derivatives of *$h_1$neḱ- / *$h_1$enḱ- in three different languages is *inherited*, although secondary, as it reflects that of *b^her-. This points to a suppletive paradigm *b^her- :: *$h_1$neḱ-, subsuming the meanings of both roots, which must therefore be inherited as well. In fact, the suppletive pair is well attested in Greek and Avestan (*bar* :: *nas*, with -*s*-aorist *nāš̆-*),[67] and may be safely assumed for a prehistoric phase of Baltic and Slavic,[68] given that Lith. *nešù* (*nèšti*) 'to bear, bring' (also *nešióti* 'id.'), OCS *nesǫ* (*nesti*) "φέρειν, βαστάζειν" (also *nositi*) continue *$h_1$neḱ-, but have the semantics of *b^her-.[69]

5.5 *Hitt.* nakkī-, *Hom.* φέρτερος *'better'* (*OLat.* Ferter), φέριστος *'excellent': semantics and collocations*

A last, remarkable semantic comparandum of *nakkī-* in its lexicalized sense (1) 'important, prominent' may be recalled at this point, namely comparative *φέρτερος* 'better' (Hom.+, 34×), originally a contrastive *b^hértero- (with a perfect match in the name OLat. FERTER) vs. superlative *φέρτατος* (10×, also MN *Φέρτατος* in Athens 2×), and *φέριστος* 'excellent, the best' (7×, also MN *Φέριστος* in Cyrene, also Plut.*Tim*.25). The latter has a formal match in Av. (°)*bairišta-* (3×) 'the best to bring', but the equation fails as to the semantics: °*bairišta-* does not reflect the lexicalized sense 'important', but the meaning of *bar* itself (and has even an object in accusative).[70]

---

67 Cf. Y. 70.4 *yaϑa īža vācim nāšīma yaϑa vā saošiiaṇtō dax́iiunąm … suiiamna vācim barəṇti* "like the īžā, may we (now) lift our voice (*vācim nāšīma*)! or the way the revitalizers of the lands … lift their voice (*vācim barəṇti*)" (Prods O. Skjaervo, p.c.); cf. also Y. 44.13 *kaϑā drujəm nīš ahmat̰ [nīš.]nāšāmā / tāṇg ā auuā yōi …* "how can we drive deceit out of ourselves …" beside Yt. 4.5 *ϑβąmca +drujimca nižbarām* "dich und die Drug schaffe ich fort" (García Ramón 1999: 59–60).

68 García Ramón 1999: 60 ff., 65 ff.; 2010b: 86 ff.

69 Cf. Lith. *nèšti kám pagálbą* 'bring help to someone', OCS *i pridǫ kъ njemu nosęšte oslabljenь žilami* Mk 2.3 "καὶ ἔρχονται πρὸς αὐτὸν παραλυτικὸν φέροντες" (: Goth. *ja qemun at imma usliþan bairandans*). The continuants of *b^her- have assumed other meanings, namely Lith. *beȓti* [*beriù*] 'strew' (intens. *barstýti*), OCS *bьrati* (*berǫ*) 'put together' "τρυγᾶσθαι", but the old sense of *b^her- lives on in residual forms like Lith. *bérnas* 'young man', OLith. *bernẽlis* 'child', Latv. *bȩ̀rns* 'id.'.

70 Namely with objects *bāgəm* (OAv. *bāgəm aibī.bairištəm* 'the best bringer of a share': Y. 51.1a *vohū xšaϑrəm vairīm bāgəm aibī.bairištəm* … "the good command, which is what most (often) brings the well-deserved share"), and *drujəm* 'druz, deceit' (YAv. *drujəm nižbairišto* "which most (often) gets rid": Yt.11.3 *mąϑrō spəṇtō mainiiəuuīm drujəm nižbairištō* "the

Gk. *φέρτερος, φέρτατος, φέρτιστος* 'important, prominent' shares some referents, namely (1) humans (also OLat. *Ferter*) and (2) deities, also (3) places and (4) words, with *nakkī-* and *daššu-* and cognates (§5.2):[71]

1 Humans: *Il.* 3. 430–431 *πρίν γ'εὔχε'(ο) ... Μενελάου / σῇ τε βίῃ καὶ χερσὶ καὶ ἔγχεϊ φέρτερος εἶναι* 'once it was your boast that you were a better man than Menelaos with your might and hands and spear', 12. 246 *ἐξ ἔλεϑ', οἵ χερσίν τε βίηφί τε φέρτατοι ἦσαν*, 6.123 *τίς δὲ σύ ἐσσι φέριστε καταϑνητῶν ἀνϑρώπων*. OLat. FERTER, the name of the king of the Aequicoli (*FERTER RESIUS* | *REX AEQUEICOLUS*, Elogium CIL I^2 p. 202, Claudius's times, with a correct spelling[72]), beside gentilicium *Fertrius* (*AT. FERTRIO* CIL $I^2$2, 476.2) obviously goes back to **b^hér-tero-*. The old term turned out to be opaque, and its semantics lives on in the gentilices *Melior, Optumus / Optimus*, also *Eccellens, Egregius*.[73]

2 Deities: *Il.* 21.264 *ϑεοὶ δέ τε φέρτεροι ἀνδρῶν* 'for gods are mightier than men', 15.247 *τίς δὲ σύ ἐσσι φέριστε ϑεῶν ὅς μ' εἴρεαι ἄντην;*

3 Places: Bacch. 19.12 *πρέπει σε φερτάταν ἴμεν / ὁδὸν παρὰ Καλλιόπας λα/χοῖσαν ἔξοχον γέρας* 'it is good that you go the best way, you who have received the excellent honor of Kalliope' (the poetry is referred to as a path).

---

revitalizing divine thought, which most (often) gets rid (*nižbairištō*) of the druz in the other world"; translations by Skjaervo, p.c.). JAv. *nižbairišto* in Yt. 12.7–8, an obscure text, stands in parallel with a series of superlatives, all of them reflecting the meaning of their lexemes, among others *dūraēdarštəma* '(you) who is the best to see from afar') and with *nijaγništa* '(you) who is the best to defeat' (*rašnuuō dūraēdarštəma rašnuuō † arəϑamat̰ bairišta rašnuuō tāiiūm nijaγništa* (with v.ll. *arəϑəmat̰* F1; *ərəϑmat̰* J10; Prods O. Skjaervo, p.c.) "o Rašnav, (der) du in die Ferne am besten siehst, (der) du dem Beklagten am besten beistehst, (der) du den Dieb ... am besten niederschlägst" (Wolff), and the discussions by Tucker 2009: 523–524 and Dieu 2011: 163–164).

71 Other referents of *φέρτερος* are shared with non-Anatolian languages and are therefore not directly relevant for our purposes. This is, for instance, the case with 'fame' (*φέρτατον ... κῦδος* 'important, best fame': Ba. 6.2 *λάχε φέρτατον πόδεσσι / κῦδος ἐπ' Ἀλφεοῦ προχοαῖσ*['(Lachon) obtained the best fame in the course of Alpheios floods'), on which cf. Massetti 2016: 131–132., with reference to Pi. *N.* 3.40 *συγγενεῖ δέ τις εὐδοξίᾳ μέγα βρίϑει* "One with inborn glory carries great weight" and to the comparanda Goth. *wulþaus kaurei "βάρος δόξης"* (k 4.17B *aiweinis wulþaus kaurei "αἰώνιον βάρος δόξης"* 'weight of everlasting glory') and Toch B *käre-perne* (T128b4 *käre-perne lantuññe* 'a glorious kingship'), with *käre°* (**g^wr̥h_2-os-°* or **g^wr̥h_2-ú-°*), *°perne* 'glory' (OP *farnah-* 'bright', Av. *x^varənah-* 'id.': **su̯él-nes-*).

72 The form has been wrongly transmitted as *Fertor*, a *lectio facilior* (*Lib. de praen.* I ... *primum eorum regem et Fertorem Resium, qui ius fetiale constituit*) and actually a ghost-word which is currently assumed to a be a perfect correspondence of Umb. **ař̌fertur**, *arfertur*.

73 A name *Fertor* must indeed have existed, as strongly suggested by the attestation of a gentilicium *Fertōrius* (*vasa arretina* CIL XI 6700, 319, 320), according to the pattern *-tor* :: *-tōrius* (e.g. *Sertor* :: *Sertōrius*) (García Ramón 2013: 111–112; on the semantic continuity of MN *Ferter* in synonyms, 113).

4 Words: P. *P.* 5.46–49 *μακάριος, ὃς ἔχεις καὶ πεδὰ μέγαν κάματον / λόγων φερτάτων μναμήϊ'(α)* 'blessed you, who after great hardship have a memorial of most important words'. The collocation *φέρτατος λόγος* matches Hitt. *nakkin memian* 'important word', also *daššauu̯a* INIM^{MEŠ} 'important (: strong) words', as well as Lat. *graue uerbum* 'id.' (cf. § 5.1): the basic sense 'weighty', with the intransitive reading of *$h_1$neḱ- and *b^her-, points to a collocation [IMPORTANT—WORD], i.e. a word which has a weight, which in spite of being expressed by different lexemes may be inherited. The possibility that an [IMPORTANT (*$h_1$noḱ-i-, *b^hér-tero-)—WORD] is referred to as [HIGH—WORD], i.e. a word that is carried on or lifted (*b^her- and synonyms) to a *high position*— and therefore turns out to be *important*[74]—cannot *a priori* be excluded,[75] but is not supported by the evidence for the collocations [HIGH—WORD/VOICE], [*b^her-—WORD/VOICE] or [*b^her-—HIGH—WORD] attested in different languages. On the one hand, [HIGH—WORD/VOICE] (Ved. *bṛhán vácas-*, YAv. *bərəzəm vācim*)[76] refers to the high tone of the voice, not to its superiority or importance (e.g. RV VII 96.1a *bṛhád u gāyiṣe vácaḥ* 'I shall sing a lofty speech'). On the other hand, [b^her-—WORD/VOICE] (Ved. *bhar—vā́cam*, OAv. *vācəm … baraitī*, Hom. *μῦθον / φάτιν φέρειν*, Lat. *uocem adferre*, OIr. *do·beir guth*)[77] is a periphrasis for 'speak'[78] or means, in some cases, 'raise the voice' (e.g. Y. 50.6a *yə̄ mąϑrā vācəm mazdā baraitī* "the disciple who raises his voice, O Wise One"), but simply with reference to the tone,[79] not to importance or dignity of the content, and the same applies to [*b^her-—HIGH—WORD] (Ved. *bhar—bṛhánt—vácas-* :: YAv. *bar—bərəz-—vāc-*) regardless of how its internal structure is (either [HIGH—WORD] as a formula, or a predicative [*b^her-—HIGH]), cf. RV III 10.5a *prá hótre pūrvi̯yáṃ váco 'gnáye bharatā bṛhát* 'bring forward (*prá … bharatā*) the first lofty speech for the

74 A different case is that of the reference to the crucial component of an utterance as 'summit of the speech', cf. P. *Ol.* 7.68 *λόγων κορυφαί / ἐν ἀλαθείᾳ πετοῖσαι* 'summits of words which fell into reality', *P.* 4.116 *ἀλλὰ τούτων μὲν κεφάλαια λόγων / ἴστε* 'But you know the main parts of this story' (Massetti 2016: 181–182., with reference to OIr. *taulcha … bríathar* 'summit of the speech').

75 Note that *ὄγκος*, a cognate of *nakkī-* is also object of *αἴρο/ε-*, like *φέρο/ε-* in the reading 'raise, lift, puff up', cf. *ὄγκον ἄρασθαι* (S.*Aj.* 129), *θαυμαστὸν ὄγκον ἀράμενοι τοῦ μύθου* (Pl. *Plt.* 277b).

76 From [*b^hṛ$\hat{g}^h$-ónt- *u̯ék^{w}es-], [*b^hṛ$\hat{g}^h$-—*u̯ok^w-] respectively.

77 Schmitt 1967: 255–256 (with reference to Mayrhofer, *KEWAi* 2,445–446. s.v. *bṛhánt-*); Campanile 1999: 119–120 (= 1993).

78 The same applies to Ved. *matím bhar* 'bring forth a thought/poem' is one for 'recite', e.g. RV I 157.1b *taváse matím bhare* 'for the mighty one I bring forth my thought', like *μέλος φέρειν* (P. *P.*2.3), *Μοῦσαν φέρειν* (P. *P.* 3.28), as pointed out by Massetti 2016: 198.

79 Also with synonyms *$h_3$er- (Ved. *i̯yár-*, Gk. *ὀρ-*), and in Greek *αἴρο/ε-*, and *μῦθον, φάτιν*.

Hotar, for Agni', Yt. 17.61e *bərəzəm barāt̰ zaota vācim* 'loudly should the Zaotar raise his voice'.

The lexicalized meaning of *φέρτερος, φέρτατος / φέρτιστος* is transparent: it fully matches the positive reading of *nakki-* (1) 'important, prominent'. Its origin, however, does not. Two possibilities remain open: (a) an intransitive reading of *φέρειν, προφέρειν* 'stand out', 'be distinguished' cf. *προφερής* 'carried before, excelling', French *il se porte bien* (con *προφερέστερος, -τατος*), of humans (*Od.*8.221 *τῶν δ' ἄλλων ἐμέ φημι πολὺ προφερέστερον εἶναι*, 21.134 *βίῃ προφερέστερος*) or Muses (*προφερεστάτη ἐστὶν ἁπασέων* Hes.*Th.*79,361), etc. (b) A transitive reading with elliptic object, cf. French *l'emporter sur*, for instance *κράτος* 'power' (*Il.* 18.308 *ἤ κε φέρῃσι μέγα κράτος*), *κλέος* (*Od.* 3.204 *οἴσουσι κλέος εὐρὺ*), *ἀέθλια / ἄεθλον* 'price' (*Il.* 23.413 *φερώμεθα χεῖρον ἄεθλον*), or the like,[80] as it is the case with transitive Av. °*bairišta-*, the only difference being that the latter has accusative object. Both (a) and (b) are perfectly plausible, and opting for one of them to the detriment of the other is impossible: this makes it difficult to give a conclusive answer to the question whether the lexicalized meaning 'prominent, important' in *h_1*nok̑-i-* and **bʰér-tero-* reflects one and the same original reading of **bʰer-* :: *h_1*nok̑-i-*: in the case of *nakkī-* 'weighty' (whence 'important') it is clear that the referent is conceived as something *having a weight*, a load, i.e. something that is borne (*portātum*), and the same may also apply to *φέρτερος* etc. (a), i.e. to its intransitive reading:[81] someone or something *is carried before*, or *high*: in this case the semantic match between both forms is perfect also in its origin. Anyway, and regardless of the original meaning of *φέρτερος* etc., it is a fact that the semantic match between *nakkī-* (1) and *φέρτερος* etc. is perfect.

5.6 *Hitt.* **nakkī-** *as a derivative of PIE aor.* ***$h_1$nek̑-/*$h_1$enk̑-** *:: pres.* ***bʰer-**

To conclude so far with regard to PIE *h_1*nek̑-* and **bʰer-*, the situation in Hittite reflects *disiecta membra* of an inherited system which may be traced back to PIE proper.

*h_1*nek̑-*, as the suppletive aorist of **bʰer-*, lives on in Hitt. *nakkī-* (*h_1*nok̑i-*) (1) 'important, prominent' and (2) 'difficult, arduous'. These are specializations in the good and in the bad sense of a basic meaning 'weighty', i.e. 'that which

80 For further possible objects cf. García Ramón 2009a: 85–86. Other interpretations: *φέρτατος* "der im Tragen leistungsfähigste", whence "der stärkste" (Seiler 1954: 94 ff.); "davontragend" (Osthoff 1910: 167 ff.), "der am besten davontragende" in a contest (Janda 2013: 173 ff.). Differently Dieu 2011: 164 ff., 2015: 207 ff.: *φέρτερος, φέρτατος* originally epithets of deities, referred to as "apporteuses", "dispensatrices de biens", "providers of goods".

81 The assumption of a (°)*φερτός* as the starting point (Seiler 1950: 96) is hardly convincing (García Ramón 2010a: 85 n. 53).

one bears, carries on' (like a load). Hitt. *nakkī-* is thus a perfect synonym of PIE *g^wr̥h_2ú- 'heavy', which actually has both senses (1) and (2) and is in fact its replacement, in addition to being a partial replacement of Hitt. *daššu-* 'strong' in some collocations.

The semantics of *nakkī-* matches, on the one hand, that of its cognates, the substantives *ὄγκος* (1) 'dignity, honor' and (2) 'boasting, arrogance' and Lith. *naštà* "*onus*", 'load' (that one bears). The common basic meaning 'weight' does not mirror that of *$h_1$neḱ- / *$h_1$enḱ- 'to take, get', but that of the *b^her-: this leads to the conclusion that *nakkī-* and cognates mirror one of the accumulative meanings of a suppletive pair *b^her- :: *$h_1$neḱ- 'carry, take', as well as 'bear'. This meaning may well be inherited, like the suppletion itself, which is attested in Greek and in Avestan, and must be assumed for Baltic and Slavic as well. On the other hand, *nakkī-* in its positive sense (1) matches OHG *burlîh* "praestans, sublimis, excellens" and Hom. *φέρτερος* : OLat. *Ferter* (*b^hér-tero-), *φέριστος* (: Av. (°)*bairišta-* : *b^hér-isth_2o-), *φέρτατος*, regardless of whether it reflects an intransitive 'excelling' (like *προφερής*) or a transitive 'who takes (all, the best, etc.)'. The phraseological collocations of Hitt. *nakkī-* and *φέρτερος*, *φέρτατος* with HUMAN and GOD, with PLACE and especially with WORD made the semantic match evident.

PIE *b^her- does not live on as a verb in Anatolian, with the exception of CLuw. *par(a)-*, *papra-* 'carry (off)' (Melchert 2016:203–206): its meanings are taken over by other verbs, some of which continue PIE roots, among others *peḫute-*^{mi} 'to carry out' (°*u̯ed^h-), *uu̯ate-*^{mi} 'to lead' (°*u̯od^h-ei̯e-), *u̯eda-*^{mi} 'to bring' and denominative *u̯edae-*^{mi} 'id.' (*u̯ed^h-), as well as *pipeda-*^{tta} 'to carry out', *uda-*^{ḫḫi} 'id' (both with °*deh_3-), and *park(ii̯a)-*^{mi} 'to raise, lift' (*b^herĝ^h-, cf. for the sense *τλῆναι*, Lat. *ferō* :: *tulī*, and *tollō*). It is highly probable that *b^her- lives on only residually in Hitt. $^{(PÉŠ)}$*kapirt-* 'mouse', if it conceals [kabērt-] (*ka-pí-ir-t°*, *ka-pár-t°*), a compound *k/ga-pir-t-* (*kom-bhḗr-t- "Zusammenträger" as persuasively proposed by N. Oettinger)[82] with *ka°* (: *kan-* in proclisis, cf. Lat. *com°*) and °b^hḗr-t- 'carrier' (cf. PIE *b^hṓr-: *φώρ*, Lat. *fūr* 'thief').[83]

82 Cf. Oettinger 1995: 44–46 (and the remarks by Brosch 2008), with references. If the term is Indo-European (*pace* Kloekhorst 2008 s.v. $^{(PÍŠ)}$*kapart-/kapirt-*; Kroonen 2016) this proposal, supported by the parallel of Skr. *mū́ṣ-* 'mouse' beside *muṣṇā́-*^{ti} 'to steal', is preferable to the interpretation of °b^hēr-t- 'one who carries' (Lat. *forāre*, Kimball 1992: 85) or to that as *kapa/i- + *rd- "Klein-Nager" (Neumann 1985: 20–23).

83 With *-t*-enlargement as in Hitt. *sā-u̯idis-t* 'yearling' (*sā́-* 'one'), Ved. *úpa-stu-t-* 'invocation', Gk. *προ-βλη-τ-* 'jutting out' (Oettinger 1995: 45).

6 Conclusions

To sum up:

Hitt. *mimma-*[ḫḫi] 'to reject, refuse' (: Gk. *μίμνο/ε-*) reflects a lexicalization of PIE **mí-mn-*, an intensive *Aktionsart* formation of PIE **men-* 'to remain' (stative), the present of which is **mén-o/e-* (Gk. *μένο/ε-*). Hitt. *pippa-*[ḫḫi] 'to overthrown, tear up, pull down' perfectly matches Ved. 3sg.med. (°)*pípīte* reflects the present stem **pí-ph*$_2$- of PIE **(s)peh*$_2$- 'to set/get in (violent) motion' (momentative, telic), to which Gk. *σπάο/ε-* 'to pull, draw' and Arm. *hanem* 'id.' belong (in all of them the direction of the motion is made explicit by means of preverbs). Both verbs can only be explained on the assumption of an inherited aspectual system with *-i-*reduplicated stems in the function of a present stem (3.sg. **pí-ph*$_2$*-ei̯*) or of an *Aktionsart* marker (3.sg. **mí-mn-ei̯*). For its part. CLuw. *ūppa/i-* 'to carry (off), take (off)', HLuw. (CAPERE$_2$)-*u-pa-* (/o:ppa-/) continues the root-aorist PIE **(s)péh*$_2$-.

The semantics of Hitt. *nakkī-* (a remodelling of **h*$_1$*noki-*) 'important, prominent' (also neuter 'importance, prominence'), as well as 'difficult', which is the replacement of PIE **g*^{w}*r̥h*$_2$*ú-* 'heavy', points to a basic meaning 'weighty', 'weight', which may also be assumed for the cognates *ὄγκος*, Lith. *naštà* 'load' and ultimately for PIE **h*$_1$*neḱ-* / **h*$_1$*enḱ-*, which has in fact another basic meaning, namely 'to take'. In fact they display the meaning of **b*^{h}*er-*'to carry on, lift up', with an identical good sense as OHG *burlîh* "sublimis, excellens" and cognates, and Hom. *φέρτερος* 'better' (OLat. *Ferter*), *φέριστος* 'excellent'. The meaning of *nakkī-* turns out to be only understandable on the assumption of an inherited PIE suppletive paradigm with pres. **b*^{h}*er-* :: aor. **h*$_1$*neḱ-* / **h*$_1$*enḱ-*.

The present contribution has made the case for the existence of forms and formations in Anatolian which can only be explained satisfactorily on the assumption that they reflect the continuity of inherited PIE patterns which did not live on unchanged in Anatolian. It implies a serious *caveat* against any attempt to reconstruct the prehistory of Anatolian languages as a result of idiosyncratic developments for which the consideration of comparative IE material is dispensable—but does obviously not exclude that the Anatolian languages have specific developments and innovations of their own or that they, contrarily, preserve PIE precious archaisms which have disappeared in other languages and in Core IE itself.

Acknowledgements

This article has been written in the framework of the Research Project "Estudio diacrónico de las instituciones socio-políticas de la Grecia Antigua y de sus manifestaciones míticas" (FFI2016-79906-P), MEC Universitat Autònoma de Barcelona / Agencia Estatal de Investigación (AEI, España), Fondo Europeo de Desarrollo Regional (FEDER).

It is a pleasant duty to express my gratitude to Riccardo Ginevra and Daniel Kölligan (Köln), Laura Massetti (Copenhagen) and Matilde Serangeli (Jena), as well as José Virgilio García Trabazo (Santiago de Compostela), Prods O. Skjærvø (Harvard), the anonymous reviewer and especially Craig Melchert (North Carolina) for their indications and criticism; and to Johanna Narten (Erlangen), who kindly put at my disposal (1993) her invaluable *Materialien* to Ved. *pā*[3] ("[3]*pā* 'sich (in eine Richtung) bewegen'"). Thanks are also due to Benedicte Nielsen Whitehead (Copenhagen) for her stylistic and grammatical corrections.

References

Beekes, R.S.P. 1979. Gav. *uzirəidyāi* and *rārəša-*. Appendix: Skt. *irayā́ti*; *ínakṣati*, *ānā́śa*, *ἐνεγκεῖν*. *Münchener Studien zur Sprachwissenschaft* 38. 9–20.

Brosch, C. 2008. *Nominalkomposita und kompositionsähnliche Strukturen im appellativen Wortschatz des Hethitischen.* MA thesis, Humboldt-Universität zu Berlin.

Burrow, Th. 1973. Sanskrit *pā-* 'go, move, pass, traverse'. *Indo-Iranian Journal* 15. 81–108.

Barton, Ch R. 1990–1991. On the denominal *a*-statives of Armenian. *Revue des Études Armeniennes* 22. 29–52.

Campanile, E. 1999. Réflexions sur la reconstruction de la phraséologie poétique indo-européenne. In M.P. Bologna et al. (eds.), *Saggi di linguistica comparativa e ricostruzione culturale*, 119–127. Pisa & Roma: Istituti editoriali. (Originally published in *Diachronica* 10, 1993, 1–12.)

Casaretto, A. 2004. *Nominale Wortbildung der gotischen Sprache. Die Derivation der Substantive.* Heidelberg: Winter.

CHD = H.G. Güterbock, H.A. Hoffner & Th.P.J. van den Hout (eds.). 1980–. *The Hittite dictionary of the Oriental Institute of the University of Chicago.* Chicago: Oriental Institute of the University of Chicago.

Dardano, P. 2012. Il vento, i piedi e i calzari: i messaggeri degli dei nei miti ittiti e nei poemi omerici. In N. Bolatti-Guzzo, S. Festucia & M. Marazzi (eds.), *Quaderni della Ricerca Scientifica. Centro Mediterraneo Preclassico. Studi e Ricerche.* Vol. 3. *Studi vari di egeistica, anatolistica e del mondo mediterraneo*, 53–87. Napoli: Università degli Studî Suor Orsola Benincasa.

Dieu, É. 2011. Le supplétisme dans les formes de gradation en grec ancien et dans les langues indo-européennes. Genève: Droz.

Dieu, É. 2015. Review of Janda 2014. *Bulletin de la Societé de Linguistique* 110(2). 203–215.

Eichner, H. 1979. Hethitisch *gĕnuššuš, ginušši, ginuššin*. In E. Neu & W. Meid (eds.), *Hethitisch und Indogermanisch: vergleichende Studien zur historischen Grammatik und zur dialektgeographischen Stellung der indogermanischen Sprachgruppe Altkleinasiens*, 41–61. Innsbruck: Institut für Sprachwissenschaft der Universität Innsbruck.

Eichner, H. 2015. Das Anatolische in seinem Verhältnis zu den anderen Gliedern der indoeuropäischen Sprachfamilie aus aktueller Sicht. In Th. Krisch & St. Niederreiter (eds.), *Diachronie und Sprachvergleich: Beiträge aus der Arbeitsgruppe "Historisch-vergleichende Sprachwissenschaft" bei der 40. Österreichischen Linguistiktagung 2013 in Salzburg*, 13–26. Innsbruck: Institut für Sprachen und Literaturen der Universität Innsbruck.

García Ramón, J.L. 1999. Zur Bedeutung indogermanischer Verbalwurzeln: *$h_2$neḱ- 'erreichen, reichen bis', *$h_1$neḱ- 'erhalten, (weg)nehmen'. In J. Habisreitinger et al. (eds.), *Gering und doch von Herzen: 25 indogermanistische Beiträge: Bernhard Forssman zum 65. Geburtstag*, 47–80. Wiesbaden: Reichert.

García Ramón, J.L. 2002. Zu Verbalcharakter, morphologischer Aktionsart und Aspekt in der indogermanischen Rekonstruktion. In H. Hettrich (ed.), *Indogermanische Syntax—Fragen und Perspektiven*, 105–136. Wiesbaden: Reichert.

García Ramón, J.L. 2009. Idg. *(*s*)*peh*$_2$- 'in (heftige) Bewegung setzen, ziehen': Ved. *pā* 3, heth. *pipp*(*a*)-*ḫḫi* und gr. *σπάω*, arm. *hanem*. In R. Lühr & S. Ziegler (eds.), *Protolanguage and prehistory. Akten der XII. Fachtagung der Indogermanischen Gesellschaft vom 11. bis 15.10.2004 in Krakau*, 134–138. Wiesbaden: Reichert.

García Ramón, J.L. 2010a. Hethitisch *nakkī*- und homerisch *φέριστος*: avestisch [°]*bairišta*-, homerisch *φέρτερος, -τατος*. In J. Klinger et al. (eds.), *Investigationes Anatolicae: Gedenkschrift für Erich Neu*, 73–89. Wiesbaden: Harrassowitz.

García Ramón, J.L. 2010b. On Hittite verbs of the type *mimma-ḫḫi* 'refuse': *Aktionsart* and aspect in the Indo-European reconstruction. In R. Kim et al. (eds.), *Ex Anatolia lux: Anatolian and Indo-European studies in honor of H. Craig Melchert on the occasion of his sixty-fifth birthday*, 40–54. Ann Arbor & New York: Beech Stave.

García Ramón, J.L. 2013. Italische Personennamen, Sprachkontakt und Sprachvergleich: I Einige oskischen Namen, II *Ferter Resius* ³ *rex Aequeicolus*. In J.L. García Ramón et al. (eds.), *Sprachkontakt und Kulturkontakt im Alten Italien: Onomastik und Lexikon. 10 Jahre nach Jürgen Untermanns Wörterbuch des Oskisch-Umbrischen* (*Arbeitstagung Köln, 21.–23.4.2010*), 103–117. Roma & Pisa: Linguarum Varietas.

García Ramón, J.L. 2016. Vedic *indrotá*- in the Ancient Near East and the shift of PIE *$h_2$eu̯h_1- 'run' → Core IE 'help, favor'. In D. Gunkel et al. (eds.), *Sahasram ati srajas. Studies in honor of Stephanie W. Jamison*, 64–81. Ann Arbor & New York: Beech Stave.

Hackstein, O. 1995. *Untersuchungen zu den sigmatischen Präsensstammbildungen des Tocharischen*. Göttingen: Vandenhoeck & Ruprecht.

Hajnal, I. 1995. *Der lykische Vokalismus. Methode und Erkenntnisse der vergleichenden anatolischen Sprachwissenschaft, angewandt auf das Vokalsystem einer Kleinkorpussprache*. Graz: Leykam.

Janda, M. 2014. *Purpurnes Meer. Sprache und Kultur der homerischen Welt*. Innsbruck: Innsbrucker Beiträge zur Kulturwissenschaft.

Jasanoff, J. 2003. *Hittite and the Indo-European Verb*. Oxford: Oxford University Press.

Kimball, S.E. 1992. The phonological pre-history of some Hittite *mi*-conjugation verbs. *Münchener Studien zur Sprachwissenschaft* 53. 160–181.

King, J.C. (ed.). 1979. *Notker der Deutsche, Martianus Capella, "De nuptiis Philologiae et Mercurii"*. Tübingen: Niemeyer.

Klingenschmitt, G. 1982. *Das altarmenische Verbum*. Wiesbaden: Reichert.

Kloekhorst, A. 2008. *Etymological dictionary of the Hittite inherited lexicon*. Leiden & Boston: Brill.

Kölligan, D. 2013. *"Οβριμος Ἄρης*. Handout, Colloquium of the DAAD-VIGONI-Project "Divine Epithets in Ancient Greece" (Milan, 14.2.2013).

Kölligan, D. 2014. *Indogermanisch und Armenisch. Studien zur historischen Grammatik des Klassisch-Armenischen*. Habilitation thesis, Universität zu Köln.

Kroonen, G. 2013. *Etymological dictionary of Proto-Germanic*. Leiden: Brill.

Kroonen, G. 2016. Hitt. *kapart-/kapirt-* 'small rodent' and Proto-Semitic **ʕkbr-t-* 'mouse, jerboa'. *Indogermanische Forschungen* 121(1). 53–62.

Le Feuvre, C. 2016. Le type *τρόπις*, *στρόφις*, *τρόφις* et le problème de *τρόφι κῦμα* (*Il.* 11,307). *Nouveaux acquis sur la formation des noms en grec ancien*, 179–202. Louvain: Peeters

*LIV*² = H. Rix (ed.). 2001. *Lexikon der indogermanischen Verben*. Wiesbaden: Reichert.

Massetti, L. 2016. *Phraseologie und indogermanische Dichtersprache in der Sprache der griechischen Chorlyrik: Pindar und Bakchylides*. PhD thesis, Universität zu Köln.

Melchert, H. Craig. 1983. Pudenda Hethitica. *Journal of Cuneiform Studies* 35. 137–145.

Melchert, H. Craig 1984. *Studies in Hittite historical phonology*. Göttingen: Vandenhoeck & Ruprecht.

Melchert, H. Craig 1988. Luvian lexical notes. *Historische Sprachwissenschaft* 101. 210–243.

Melchert, H. Craig 2004. A Luwian dedication. In J.H.W. Penney (ed.), *Indo-European perspectives: Studies in honour of Anna Morpurgo Davies*, 370–379. Oxford: Oxford University Press.

Melchert, H. Craig 2005. *A dictionary of the Lycian languague*. Ann Arbor & New York: Beech Stave.

Melchert, H. Craig 2009. Hittite *ḫi*-verbs from adverbs. In R. Lühr & S. Ziegler (eds.), *Protolanguage and prehistory. Akten der XII. Fachtagung der Indogermanischen Gesellschaft vom 11. bis 15.10.2004 in Krakau*, 335–339. Wiesbaden: Reichert.

Melchert, H. Craig 2016. New Luvian verb etymologies. In H. Marquardt, S. Reichmuth & J.V. García Trabazo (eds.), *Anatolica et Indogermanica. Studia linguistica in honorem Johannis Tischler septuagenarii dedicata*, 203–212. Innsbrück: Innsbrucker Beiträge zur Sprachwissenschaft.

Melchert, H. Craig. Forthcoming a. Hittite and Luvian *uppa-* and Hittite *uiya-*. In A. Süel (ed.), *Uluslararası Hititoloji Kongresi Bildirleri, Çorum, 01–07 Eylül 2014. Acts of the 9th International Congress of Hittitology, Çorum, September 01–07 2014*, 643–654. Ankara: T.C. Çorum Valiliği.

Melchert, H. Craig. Forthcoming b. The position of Anatolian. In A. Garrett & M. Weiss (eds.), *Handbook of Indo-European studies*. Oxford: Oxford University Press.

Neumann, G. 1958. Hethitische Etymologien. *Zeitschrift für Vergleichende Sprachforschung* 75. 87–90.

Neumann, G. 1985. Hethitisch-luwische Wortstudien und Etymologien IV. *Zeitschrift für Vergleichende Sprachforschung* 98. 20–25.

Oettinger, N. 1976. *Die militärischen Eide der Hethiter*. Wiesbaden: Harrassowitz.

Oettinger, N. 1979. *Die Stammbildung des hethitischen Verbums*. Nürnberg: Hans Carl.

Oettinger, N. 1995. Anatolische Etymologien. *Historische Sprachwissenschaft* 108. 39–49.

Osthoff, H. 1910 *Morphologische Untersuchungen auf dem Gebiete der indogermanischen Sprachen*, VI. Leipzig: Hirzel.

Puhvel, J. 1984–. *Hittite etymological dictionary*. Berlin & New York: de Gruyter.

Ruipérez, M.S. 1954. *Estructura del sistema de aspectos y tiempos en griego antiguo. Análisis funcional sincrónico*. Salamanca: Publicaciones de la Universidad.

Schaffner, St. 2001. *Das Vernersche Gesetz und der innerparadigmatische grammatische Wechsel des Urgermanischen im Nominalbereich*. Innsbruck: Institut für Sprachwissenschaft der Universität Innsbruck.

Schindler, J. 1970. Review of R. Anttila, *Proto-Indo-European Schwebeablaut*, Berkeley & Los Angeles, 1969. *Kratylos* 15. 146–152.

Schmitt, R. 1967. *Dichtung und Dichtersprache in indogermanischer Zeit*. Wiesbaden: Harrasowitz.

Seiler, H.J. 1950 *Die primären griechischen Steigerungsformen*. Hamburg: Heitmann.

Serangeli, M. 2015. *Sprachkontakt im alten Anatolien: Das Lykische aus synchroner und diachroner Perspektive*. PhD thesis, Universität zu Köln.

Strunk, K. 1988. Über Laryngale und einige reduplizierte Verbalstämme. In A. Bammesberger (ed.), *Die Laryngaltheorie und die Rekonstruktion des indogermanischen Laut- und Formensystems*, 563–582. Heidelberg: Winter.

Sturtevant, E.H. 1933. *A comparative grammar of the Hittite language*. Philadelphia: Linguistic Society of America.

Sturtevant, E.H. 1934. Adjectival *i*-stems in Hittite and in Indo-European. *Language* 10. 266–273.

Tax, P.W. (ed.).1986. *Notker der Deutsche, Boethius "De consolatione Philosophiae", Buch I/ II*. Tübingen: Niemeyer.

Tischler, J. 1983–. *Hethitisches etymologisches Glossar*. Innsbruck: Institut für Sprachwissenschaft der Universität Innsbruck.

Tucker, E.F. 2009. Old Iranian superlatives in *-išta-*. In W. Sundermann et al. (eds.), *Exegisti monumenta: Festschrift in honour of Nicholas Sims-Williams*, 509–526. Wiesbaden: Harrassowitz.

Watkins, C., 1971. Hittite and IE studies: the denominative statives in **-ē-*. *Transactions of the Philological Society*. 51–93. (Reprinted in *Selected Writings* 1, 1994, 146–188.)

Widmer, P. 2005 [2007]. Der altindische *vr̥kī́*-Typus und hethitisch *nakkī-*: Der indogermanische Instrumental zwischen Syntax und Morphologie. *Die Sprache* 45(1–2). 190–208.

Yakubovich, I. 2010. *Sociolinguistics of the Luvian language*. Leiden: Brill.

Yakubovich, I. 2011. Review of *Investigationes Anatolicae: Gedenkschrift für Erich Neu*, Wiesbaden, 2010. *Kratylos* 56. 172–181.

Zucha, I. 1988. *The nominal stem types in Hittite*. PhD dissertation, University of Oxford.

CHAPTER 4

Myths of Non-Functioning Fertility Deities in Hittite and Core Indo-European

Riccardo Ginevra

1 Introduction[1]

It is a well-known fact that the Hittite god Telipinu, who was associated with fertility, was the protagonist of one of the most intriguing mythical narratives attested in 2nd millennium BCE Anatolia, namely the myth about his rage and disappearance (CTH 322–324).[2] The fact that Telipinu's name is Hattic (it means something like 'impetuous lad', cf. Haas 1994: 442–443) has been taken to indicate a pre-Indo-European origin for his cult. As long recognized, however, the Telipinu myth has parallels in other Indo-European (IE) mythical traditions, namely in the Greek myth of Persephone's abduction and Demeter's rage (cf. Burkert 1979: 123–142) and the Norse myth of the death of Baldr (cf. Schröder 1962: 354–356), two myths which have long been compared with each other as well (cf. already Bugge 1889: 244–248). To these we may add the Indic narratives about the decrepitude, blindness and rage of the seer Cyavana and about the imperfect godhood of the Aśvins, which, as argued in this contribution, have correspondences in all of the above. The Hittite myth about the rage and disappearance of Telipinu may thus conceivably reflect features of an inherited Proto-Indo-European (PIE) mythical theme, which was

1 The translations of Greek passages are adapted from those of the Loeb Classical Library; other translations are adapted from Davies 2007 (*Branwen ferch Llŷr*), Dronke 1997 (*Vǫluspá*), Eggeling 1885 (*Śatapathabrāhmaṇa*), Faulkes 1987 (*Gylfaginning*), Ganguli 1883–1896 (*Mahābhārata* 13), Gray 1982 (*Cath Maige Tuired*), Jamison & Brereton 2014 (*Rigveda*), Hoffner 1998 (Telipinu myth), Vijñanananda 1890 (*Devībhāgavatapurāṇa*), Vira-Candra 1954 (*Jaiminīyabrāhmaṇa*). Unless otherwise noted, Hittite texts are quoted on the basis of Rieken et al. 2012 (KUB 17.10 + KBo 55.8), 2009a (IBoT 3.141 + KUB 33.5), 2009b (KUB 33.10), 2009c (KUB 33.11), 2009d (KUB 33.19) and Fuscagni 2012 (KBo 22.178 + KUB 48.109).

The following abbreviations for literary sources are used: *BFL* = *Branwen ferch Llŷr*; *CMT* = *Cath Maige Tuired*; *DBP* = *Devībhāgavatapurāṇa*; *Gylf.* = *Gylfaginning*; *HAph.* = *Homeric Hymn to Aphrodite*; *HDem.* = *Homeric Hymn to Demeter*; *JB* = *Jaiminīyabrāhmaṇa*; *MBh.* = *Mahābhārata*; *ŚB* = *Śatapathabrāhmaṇa*; *Vsp.* = *Vǫluspá*.

2 On the Telipinu myth in general, cf. e.g. Haas 1994: 707–719; Haas 2006: 103–115; Hutter-Braunsar 2011; Asan 2014.

 | DOI:10.1163/9789004416192_006

at some point associated with a pre-existing Hattic fertility deity or superimposed upon its pre-existing mythology. This may also explain why the narrative elements and phraseology of the Telipinu myth closely match those attested in other Hittite mythical narratives about the disappearance of deities who are not specifically Hattic and who actually show reflexes of Indo-European heritage, namely the Storm-god (CTH 325) and the mother-goddess Ḫannaḫanna (CTH 334).[3]

In the present contribution, an attempt will be made to demonstrate that, on the one hand, all these IE myths preserve features which reflect inherited PIE poetics and themes, and that, on the other hand, the Hittite narrative lacks one feature which is attested in the Greek, Norse and Indic myths. On the assumption that generic similarities between mythological texts may often reflect universal motifs or areal diffusion,[4] and not necessarily common inheritance, we shall focus on the specific "ready-made surface structures" (Watkins 2004: 77) by which these traditional texts were composed, namely formulas and narrative structures, in order to determine whether the correspondences between the myths may reflect a shared heritage. After a brief presentation of the mythical traditions examined (§2), eight parallels between the Hittite, Greek, Norse and Indic narratives will be identified by comparing the phraseology and themes employed to describe the existential conditions of the main characters and the features of the cosmos around them (§3). These correspondences will be shown to match poetic devices generally employed in several IE languages to describe any character in conditions of distress and any environment suffering from cosmic disorder, thus pointing to a PIE origin for these elements (§4). The Greek, Norse and Indic narratives will be shown to share one further feature as well, namely a type-scene involving horses or chariots reaching the main character; the absence of this feature in the Hittite narratives suggests that it reflects an innovation which took place after the split between Proto-Anatolian, the linguistic ancestor of Hittite, and Core Indo-European, from which Greek, Old Norse and Sanskrit later developed (§5).

3 The Storm-God is the protagonist of a serpent-slaying narrative whose PIE background has been conclusively demonstrated by Calvert Watkins (1995: 321ff.; 355–356; 444ff.); Ḫannaḫanna's name is a reduplicated formation of the inherited term *ḫanna-* 'grandmother' (PIE *h_2*enH-o-* 'id.', cf. Latin *anus* 'old woman'; *HED*, s.v.).

4 Cf. e.g. Watkins 1995: 448ff. on Anatolian and Greek myths.

2 Indo-European Non-Functioning Fertility Deity Myths

Let us briefly recall the essentials of the (1) Hittite, (2) Greek, (3) Norse and (4) Indic narratives which are especially relevant for the purpose of the present study. The motifs that are discussed in detail are marked in bold.[5]

1. The Hittite Myth of Telipinu.

> For unknown reasons, Telipinu becomes enraged and disappears. Cosmic disorder follows his disappearance: **mothers do not care about their children, plants do not grow** and **gods do not get satiated** at their own feasts anymore. The goddess Ḫannaḫanna sends a bee to search for Telipinu, who is **sleeping/lying down** on a meadow near Lihzina. The bee finds him and forcibly makes him **stand up** and **speak.** Telipinu is not happy about the coercion and becomes even more enraged. Several ritual acts are required to appease him: among other things, the god is told to **eat and drink.** In the end, cosmic order is restored, as **mothers care about their children** and plants grow properly again.

2. The Greek Myth of Demeter and Persephone (*Homeric Hymn to Demeter* et al.).[6]

> While playing with other maidens, Persephone is kidnapped by Hades, Lord of the Dead. Persephone stays calm as long as she can **see the sun** and the upper world, but Hades forcibly takes her **to the darkness** of the Realm of the Dead. Persephone's mother Demeter searches for her, with no success. Distressed, Demeter wanders on the earth and **does not eat or drink.** She ends up in the countryside near the city of Eleusis. Grieved, she **sits in the shadow**, assuming the appearance of an **old woman.** Demeter is found there by some Eleusinian maidens, who bring her to the royal palace, where, sorrowful, the goddess **sits** on a stool and does **not speak** to anyone. After being made to laugh by a woman named Iambe, Demeter **drinks** the sacred beverage cyceon and starts talking again. After some more misadventures, she "**thrusts old age away**" from herself. Meanwhile,

5 The summaries do not differentiate between the various versions of the Hittite myth of Telipinu and of the Indic myth of Cyavana, Sukanyā and the Aśvins: any version, even more recent ones, may attest ancient motifs which are not preserved by other versions.

6 On the *Homeric Hymn* and on Demeter's myth in general, cf. e.g. Richardson 1974: 1–135; Foley 1993; Janda 2000 and 2005 *passim.*

cosmic disorder has arisen after her disappearance: **plants do not grow**, men are starving and **gods are deprived of sacrifices.** Zeus takes notice and sends Hermes to bring Persephone **back to the light from the darkness** of the Realm of the Dead. Hermes arrives in the Underworld and finds Hades **seated** on a couch with Persephone, who is heavily distressed. Hades tells Persephone she's free to leave and she **springs up** out of happiness. Hermes **takes** Persephone **by chariot to the place where Demeter is.** Cosmic order is restored: **plants grow** again, men prosper and gods receive their offerings.

3. The Norse Myth of Baldr (*Gylfaginning* 49 et al.).[7]

Pierced by a mistletoe twig thrown by his brother Hǫðr, the god Baldr **falls** dead. The other gods are so shocked that they are not even able to **lift him up.** Baldr's death is associated with cosmic disorder, as it is explicitly stated to be the unluckiest deed that ever happened among gods and mortals. Baldr's mother Frigg sends the god Hermóðr to bring Baldr back from Hel, the Realm of the Dead. He **rides a horse to the place where Baldr is**, and finds him **seated.** All efforts to bring Baldr back from the dead fail for the moment; when cosmic order will be restored after the End of Time, however, Baldr will come back and **cornfields will grow** without sowing.

4. The Indic Myth of Cyavana, Sukanyā and the Aśvins (*Śatapathabrāhmaṇa* 4.1.5, *Jaiminīyabrāhmaṇa* 3.120–128, *Mahābhārata* 3.122–125 et al.).[8]

The seer Cyavana has become very **old** and **lies down** near a lake. King Śaryati arrives with his people and Cyavana is harassed by them, e.g. **blinded** by Śaryati's daughter Sukanyā. Cosmic disorder follows, as Cyavana becomes enraged and makes **mothers not recognize their sons, fathers fight with sons** and **brothers with brothers.** To appease the seer, Śaryati **takes** Sukanyā **by chariot to where Cyavana is** and marries her to the seer. Cosmic order is thus restored and **discord among the tribe mem-**

7 On the myth of Baldr in general, cf. e.g. de Vries 1956–1957: 2, 214–238; Lindow 1997; Liberman 2016: 197–241.

8 On the myth of Cyavana in general, cf. e.g. Hopkins 1905; Witzel 1987; West 2017. On the etymology of his name (*Cyávāna-* in the RV, *Cyávana-* in later sources, a change whose reasons are unknown), cf. García Ramón 1999. The name is conventionally spelled Cyavana throughout this paper (but Cyavāna within quotations from Jamison & Brereton 2014).

> **bers ends**, i.e. **they recognize their children and siblings** again. Later on, the Aśvins approach Sukanyā as suitors and are thereafter told by Cyavana that they are not whole, because they do **not drink soma, the food of the gods**; he also tells them that the **gods do not sacrifice properly**, a sign of cosmic disorder. The Aśvins make Cyavana **young** again, **removing his old age "like a cloak"**, and they make him **see** again. Cyavana, thankful, instructs the Aśvins on how to sacrifice properly together with the gods. The Aśvins become whole again (by joining the other gods and **drinking soma** with them) and restore cosmic order (by making the gods sacrifice properly).

Some relevant motifs are also attested in the apparently unrelated narrative about Cyavana's rage against King Kauśika (*MBh.* 13.52–55):

> Cyavana is angry at King Kauśika and goes to live in his palace in order to test him in several ways. For instance, he tells the king not to wake him up while he **lies down sleeping** for weeks. When he finally does **rise up of his own will**, he does **not speak** to anyone. Cyavana thus hopes that Kauśika will forcibly wake him up or make him speak, as such disrespectful acts would allow him to curse the king. Kauśika, however, does nothing of the sort and, after several of these tests, he wins Cyavana's favor back.

Cyavana does not appear often as a main character in Indic myths and his NON-FUNCTIONING state of anger in this narrative justifies its inclusion among the comparanda.

The provenance and date of composition of all these Indo-European narratives is diverse, ranging from Scandinavia to India and from the Bronze Age to the Middle Ages. Nonetheless, they all may be integrated in a common basic mythical theme, which essentially consists of two main elements:

a Some sort of distress in which one (or more, as in the case of Greek and Indic) of the main characters find themselves: they are angry, sad, blind, resting, asleep, old, dead or in the Realm of the Dead; we may conventionally label this their "NON-FUNCTIONING state", as against the "FUNCTIONING state" in which they are supposed to be and which they desire to return to.

b A cosmic disorder, which we may label "NON-FUNCTIONING cosmos", somehow linked to (and usually caused by) the NON-FUNCTIONING state of the protagonist(s); this prompts other characters to try and restore cosmic order (the "FUNCTIONING cosmos") by eliminating the distress of the main character(s) (bringing them back to a FUNCTIONING state).

The indissoluble connection between the well-being of the cosmos, often associated with the growth of crops, and the well-being of the protagonists is precisely what justifies their conventional definition as "fertility deities", even though the Norse god Baldr is never explicitly connected with fertility (but has several correspondences with the Norse fertility god Freyr)[9] and the Indic seer Cyavana is actually a "human" character (who, however, acts like a powerful god, even defeating the king of the gods, Indra, in *MBh.* 3.125).[10] In what follows, all these narratives will thus be conventionally referred to as "Non-Functioning Fertility Deity Myths". As we shall see, they share several further devices which are attested in the Hittite tradition as well, whereas one specific feature is attested only in the later IE traditions, namely Greek, Norse and Indic. Let us first turn our attention to those features which are attested in Hittite as well, namely the poetic devices which describe the existential conditions of the main characters and of the cosmos around them.

3 Parallels between the myths: a System of Structural Oppositions

The descriptions of the NON-FUNCTIONING state of the protagonists and of the NON-FUNCTIONING cosmos allow for the establishment of several parallels and ultimately of a system of structural oppositions. This may be summarized as in the following table:

IE non-functioning fertility deity myths		Status of the main character	
		NON-FUNCTIONING	FUNCTIONING
Features of the main character	(1) STAND, MOVE UPWARDS	–	+
	(2) SEE, BE IN THE LIGHT	–	+
	(3) EAT, DRINK	–	+
	(4) SPEAK	–	+
	(5) (SEXUALLY) VIGOROUS	–	+
Features of the cosmos	(6) FAMILY TIES WORK	–	+
	(7) PLANTS GROW	–	+
	(8) SACRIFICES WORK	–	+

9 Cf. Dietz 1974: 78–79. For parallels between Baldr and certain West-Asian fertility deities, cf. Neckel 1920; Schier 1995.

10 In contrast, Telipinu, Persephone, Demeter and the Aśvins are deities explicitly associated with fertility.

Whenever a main character is NOT FUNCTIONING properly (because he/she is angry, sad, dead, etc.), he/she is explicitly said, inter alia, to (1) NOT STAND or (2) NOT SEE. These may at first seem unmarked features; they must however be analysed as marked, as they stand in structural opposition to the acts of (1) STANDING or (2) SEEING, with which the main characters' FUNCTIONING state is explicitly associated in the texts. The same is valid for the descriptions of the NON-FUNCTIONING cosmos, which is linked to the main characters' distress: among other things, if a main character is NOT FUNCTIONING, (6) FAMILY TIES DO NOT WORK anymore within the cosmos around him/her; in contrast, once the main character is FUNCTIONING again, (6) FAMILY TIES WORK. In what follows, each of these associations (1–8) will be illustrated by a selection of passages quoted from the Hittite, Greek, Norse and Indic myths.

1. The NON-FUNCTIONING main character is said to NOT STAND (i.e. SIT, LIE DOWN, SLEEP) or MOVE DOWNWARDS (i.e. FALL).

> Hittite myth: KUB 33.10 ii 7–8 *šumeš=a=wa=mu* ***šašandan*** [*kuwat aranutten*] "[Why] did you [make] me (Telepinu) [rise], **when I was sleeping/lying?"**
>
> Greek myth: *HDem.* 197–201 (Demeter) *ἔνθα* ***καθεζομένη*** *προκατέσχετο χερσὶ καλύπτρην: / δηρὸν δ' ἄφθογγος τετιημένη ἧστ' ἐπὶ δίφρου,* [...] / *ἧστο πόθῳ μινύθουσα βαθυζώνοιο θυγατρός* "**Sitting** there, she held her veil before her face, and for a long time she **sat on the stool** in silent sorrow. [...] **She sat** there pining for her deep-girt daughter;" *HDem.* 343–344 (Persephone) **ἥμενον** ἐν λεχέεσσι **σὺν αἰδοίηι παρακοίτι** / πόλλ' ἀεκαζομένηι μητρὸς πόθωι "(Hermes found Hades) **seated** on his couch **with his modest consort**, who was full of resistance from longing for her mother."
>
> Norse myth: *Gylf.* 49 [...] *ok* ***fell*** *hann dauðr til jarðar.* [...] *Þá er Baldr* ***var fallinn*** *þá fellusk ǫllum Ásum orðtǫk ok svá hendr* ***at taka til hans*** [...] "and he **fell** dead to the ground. [...] When Baldr **had fallen**, then all the Æsir's tongues failed them, as did their hands **for lifting him up;**" [...] *sá þar* ***sitja í ǫndugi*** *Baldr* [...] "there he saw Baldr, **sitting in the seat of honour.**"
>
> Indic myth: *ŚB* 4.1.5.5 (Cyavana) [...] *púruṣa evā̀yaṃ jī́rṇiḥ kr̥tyā́rūpaḥ* ***śete*** [...] "Yonder **lies** a man, decrepit and ghostlike"; *MBh.* 13.52.31ab *na prabodhyo* ***'smi saṃsupta*** *ity uvācātha bhārgavaḥ* "The son of Bhr̥gu (Cyavana) said to them, 'Do not, **while I sleep**, awake me.'"

In contrast, the FUNCTIONING main character must STAND or MOVE UPWARDS (i.e. RISE).

Greek myth: *HDem.* 370–371 [...] *γήθησεν δὲ περίφρων Περσεφόνεια, / καρπαλίμως δ' ἀνόρουσ' ὑπὸ χάρματος* [...] "So he spoke, and prudent Persephone was delighted, and promptly **jumped up in joy.**"

Indic myth: *MBh.* 13.52.36ab (Cyavana) *bhārgavas tu* ***samuttasthau svayam*** *eva* [...] "The son of Bhrigu **rose of his own accord.**"

2. The NON-FUNCTIONING main character is said to NOT SEE or NOT BE IN THE LIGHT (i.e. BE IN THE SHADOW/DARKNESS).

Greek myth: *HDem.* 80–81 (Persephone) [...] *ὃ δ' ὑπὸ ζόφον ἠερόεντα / ἁρπάξας ἵπποισιν ἄγεν* [...] "He (Hades) seized her, and was taking her on his chariot **down to the misty darkness**"; *HDem.* 98–100 (Demeter) *ἕζετο δ'* [...] *τετιημένη ἦτορ,* [...] / *ἐν σκιῇ* [...] "She had sat down [...] sick at heart [...] **in the shade.**"

Indic myth: *DBP* 7.3.37b–38a [...] ***andhasya*** [...] / [...] *jarārtasya krodhanasya viśeṣataḥ* "of the **blind**, oppressed by old age, and, above all, very irritable (Cyavana)."

In contrast, the FUNCTIONING main character is said to SEE (THE LIGHT) or BE IN THE LIGHT.

Greek myth: *HDem.* 33–37 (Persephone) *ὄφρα* [...] / *λεῦσσε θεὰ* [...] / *αὐγάς τ' ἠελίου,* [...] / *τόφρα οἱ ἐλπὶς ἔθελγε μέγαν νόον* [...] "Now so long as the goddess **could still see the light of the sun,** [...] so long her great mind had the comfort of hope [...];" *HDem.* 336–338 ὄφρ' Ἀΐδην μαλακοῖσι παραιφάμενος ἐπέεσσιν / ἁγνὴν Περσεφόνειαν ἀπὸ ζόφου ἠερόεντος / ἐς φάος ἐξαγάγοι [...] "(Zeus sent Hermes to the Underworld) to persuade Hades with soft words and **bring** chaste Persephone **out from the misty dark to the daylight.**"

Indic myth: *DBP* 7.5.46 (Cyavana) [...] *andhasya ca ativṛddhasya bhogahīnasya kānane / yuvābhyāṃ* ***nayane datte*** *yauvanaṃ rūpam adbhūtam* "I was blind, very aged and without any enjoyment in the forest, through you two **I was given eyes**, youth and exquisite beauty."

3. The NON-FUNCTIONING main character is said to NOT EAT and/or NOT DRINK anything or a specific (sacred) food.

Greek myth: *HDem.* 49–50 (Demeter) *οὐδέ ποτ' ἀμβροσίης καὶ νέκταρος ἡδυπότοιο / πάσσατ' ἀκηχεμένη* [...] "and in her grief **she did not once taste ambrosia and the nectar sweet to drink;**" *HDem.* 200–201 (Demeter) ἀλλ' ἀγέλαστος ἄπαστος ἐδητύος ἠδὲ ποτῆτος / ἧστο, πόθωι μινύθουσα βαθυζώνοιο θυγατρός "but she sat there unsmiling, **tasting neither food nor drink**, pining for her deep-girt daughter."

Indic myth: *JB* 3.124.4 (Aśvins) [...] *yuvaṃ vā asarvau stho yau devau santāv* ***asomapau*** *sthaḥ* [...] "You are not complete, who, being gods, are **not soma-drinkers.**"

In contrast, the FUNCTIONING main character must EAT and/or DRINK something or a specific (ritual) food (cyceon in the Greek myth, soma in the Indic one).

Hittite ritual: KUB 33.11 ii 11–12 [*nu=za*] ***išpāi*** [...] [*nu=za*] ***ninga*** "[...] [and] **satisfy your hunger** (Telipinu)! | [...] [and] **satisfy your thirst!**"

Greek myth: *HDem.* 208–211 (Demeter) [...] *ἄνωγε δ' ἄρ' ἄλφι καὶ ὕδωρ / δοῦναι μίξασαν* ***πιέμεν*** *γλήχωνι τερείνῃ. /* [...] ***δεξαμένη*** *δ' ὁσίης ἕνεκεν πολυπότνια Δηώ* "she (Demeter) told her to mix barley and water with the graceful pennyroyal and give it to her **to drink.** [...] The lady Deo (Demeter) **took it** for custom's sake."

Indic myth: *JB* 3.127 (Aśvins) [...] *tāv adhvaryū āstām tat tāv* ***apisomāv abhavatām*** [...] "they (the Aśvins) acted as two Adhvaryus and **became partakers of Soma.**"

4. The NON-FUNCTIONING main character is said to NOT SPEAK.

Hittite myth: KUB 33.10 ii 8 [*nu=wa=mu*] ***šāntan*** *kuwat* ***memanutten*** "[And] why did you **make** [me] (Telipinu) **speak, when I was sullen**?"

Greek myth: *HDem.* 198–199 *δηρὸν δ'* ***ἄφθογγος*** *τετιημένη ἧστ' ἐπὶ δίφρου, /* ***οὐδέ τιν' οὔτ' ἔπεϊ προσπτύσσετο οὔτε τι ἔργῳ*** "For a long time she sat there on the stool in **silent** sorrow. **She greeted no one with word or movement.**"

Indic myth: *MBh.* 13.55.3b ***akiṃcid uktvā*** *gamanaṃ bahiś ca* [...] "(Cyavana, what was thy object in) going out **speaking to no one?**"

In contrast, a FUNCTIONING main character is said to SPEAK.

Greek myth: *HDem.* 202–207 πρίν γ' ὅτε δὴ χλεύῃς μιν Ἰάμβη κέδν' εἰδυῖα / πολλὰ παρασκώπτουσ' ἐτρέψατο πότνιαν ἁγνήν / μειδῆσαι γελάσαι τε καὶ ἵλαον σχεῖν θυμόν· / [...] **ἔφασκεν** "(Demeter did not speak,) until at last dutiful Iambe with ribaldry and many a jest diverted the holy lady so that she smiled and laughed and became benevolent. [...] (Then, Demeter) **said** [...]."

5. The NON-FUNCTIONING main character is said to be NOT (SEXUALLY) VIGOROUS, i.e. DECREPIT.

> Greek myth: *HDem.* 101–102 (Demeter) *γρηὶ παλαιγενέι ἐναλίγκιος, ἥτε τόκοιο / εἴργηται δώρων τε φιλοστεφάνου Ἀφροδίτης* "she looked like **an ancient crone, debarred from motherhood and the blessings of garland-loving Aphrodite.**"
>
> Indic myth: *ŚB* 4.1.5.5 (Cyavana) [...] *púruṣa evā̀yaṃ jī́rṇiḥ kṛtyā́rūpaḥ śete* [...] "Yonder lies a man, **decrepit** and ghostlike."

In contrast, the FUNCTIONING main character is described as (SEXUALLY) VIGOROUS, i.e. YOUNG. Old age is removed as if it were a material object.

> Greek myth: *HDem.* 275–276 (Demeter) *ὣς εἰποῦσα θεὰ μέγεθος καὶ εἶδος ἄμειψε / γῆρας ἀπωσαμένη* [...] "With these words the goddess changed her form and stature, **thrusting old age away.**"
>
> Indic myth: RV 5.74.5 (Cyavana) ***prá cyávānāj jujurúṣo / vavrím átkaṃ ná muñcathaḥ / yúvā yádī kṛtháḥ púnar / ā́ kā́mam ṛṇve vadhúvaḥ*** "**You remove the covering like a cloak** from Cyavāna, **who had become old**; **as a youth**—since you made him so again—**he meets the desire of his wife.**"

Let us now turn to the descriptions of the NON-FUNCTIONING cosmos caused by the main character's distress.

6. When the main character is NON-FUNCTIONING, FAMILY TIES DO NOT WORK: parents do not recognize their children, brothers fight against each other.

> Hittite myth: KUB 17.10 + KBo 55.8 i 8–9 UDU-*uš=za* **SILA$_4$-*ŠU* *mimmaš*** GU$_4$=*ma* **AMAR-*ŠU* *mimmaš*** "The ewe **rejected her lamb.** The cow **rejected her calf.**"
>
> Indic myth: *ŚB* 4.1.5.3 *sá śāryātébhyaś cukrodha tebhyó 'saṃjñāṃ cakāra* ***pitā̀vá putréṇa yuyudhe bhrā́tā bhrā́trā*** "He (Cyavana) was wroth with the Sâryâtas, and sowed **discord** among them: **father fought with son, and brother with brother**"; *JB* 3.121.3–4 [...] *so 'saṃjñāṃ śāryātyebhyo 'karot* ***tan na mātā putram ajānān, na putro mātaram*** [...] "He (Cyavana) sowed **discord** among Śaryāta's people: **then the mother did not recognize her son, nor the son his mother.**"

In contrast, when the main character is FUNCTIONING, FAMILY TIES WORK again: parents recognize their children again.

Hittite myth: KUB 17.10 + KBo 55.8 iv 24–25 ***nu=za annaš*** **DUMU-*ŠU penništa*** UDU-*uš* **SILA$_4$-*ŠU penništa*** GU$_4$ **AMAR-*ŠU penništa*** "**The mother nurtured her child.** The ewe **nurtured her lamb.** The cow **nurtured her calf.**"

Indic myth: *ŚB* 4.1.5.7 [...] *tásya ha táta eva* ***grā́maḥ saṃjajñe*** [...] "And from that same time **his tribe was at peace.**"

7. When the main character is NON-FUNCTIONING, PLANTS DO NOT GROW anymore.

Hittite myth: KUB 17.10 + KBo 55.8 i 13–17 *nu namma* ***ḫalkiš*** **ZÍZ-*tar UL māi*** [...] ***n=ašta par(a)šduš UL wēzzi*** "Therefore **barley and wheat no longer ripen** [...] **shoots do not come (forth).**"

Greek myth: *HDem.* 306–307 [...] ***οὐδέ τι γαῖα / σπέρμ' ἀνίει***, *κρύπτεν γὰρ* [...] *Δημήτηρ* "The land **allowed nothing sown to come up**, for fair-garlanded Demeter kept it hidden."

In contrast, when the main character is FUNCTIONING, PLANTS GROW.

Norse myth: *Vsp.* 62$^{1-4}$ ***Muno ósánir | acrar vaxa*** / *bǫls mun allz batna | Baldr mun koma* "without sowing **cornfields will grow**; all harm will be healed, Baldr will come."

Greek myth: *HDem.* 470–471 [...] *Δημήτηρ / αἶψα δὲ* ***καρπὸν ἀνῆκεν*** *ἀρουράων ἐριβώλων* [...] "Demeter quickly **made the produce** of the loam-rich ploughlands **come up.**"

8. When the main character is NON-FUNCTIONING, SACRIFICES or DIVINE FEASTS DO NOT WORK.

Hittite myth: KUB 17.10 + KBo 55.8 i 19–20 GAL-*iš=za* ^{d}UTU-*uš* EZEN$_4$-*an yēt nu=za* 1 *LIM* DINGIR^{MEŠ} *ḫalzaīš* ***eter n=e UL išpiyēr ekwiēr=ma n=e=za UL ḫašš[i]kker*** "The Great Sun God made a feast and invited the Thousand Gods. **They ate but couldn't get enough. They drank but couldn't quench their thirst.**"

Greek myth: *HDem.* 311–312 [...] *γεράων τ' ἐρικυδέα τιμὴν / καὶ θυσιῶν ἤμερσεν Ὀλύμπια δώματ' ἔχοντας* "(Demeter) **would have deprived** the Olympians **of their honorific privileges** and **their sacrifices.**"

Indic myth: *JB* 3.126 [...] *devā vā ete kurukṣetre* ***'paśīrṣṇā yajñena*** *yajamānā āsate* ***te taṃ kāmaṃ nāpnuvanti yo yajñe kāmaḥ*** [...] "The gods are now sacrificing in the Field of the Kurus; but **their sacrifice has no head. They do not obtain what they desire to obtain with the sacrifice.**"

In contrast, when the main character is FUNCTIONING, SACRIFICES or DIVINE FEASTS WORK again.

Hittite myth: KUB 33.19 iii 8–9 (CTH 327.1 "The Storm-god of the Queen Ḫarapšili") [*azzik*]*kanzi* ***n=at=za išpiyēr*** ˹***namma***˺ [*akkušk*]*anzi=ma* ***n=at=za ḫaššikke***[*r*] ˹***namma***˺ "They (the gods) [a]te, **and they satisfied their hunger again.** They [dran]k, **and they quenche[d] their thirst.**"

Indic myth: *ŚB* 4.1.5.15 [...] *tā́v adhvaryū́ yajñásyābhavatāṃ tā́v etád* ***yajñásya śíraḥ práty adhattāṃ*** [...] "those two (Aśvins) became the Adhvaryu priests of the sacrifice, **and restored the head of the sacrifice.**"

The Hittite, Greek, Norse and Indic mythical traditions appear to have several close correspondences. These may of course reflect (mass-scale) borrowing or areal diffusion. As we shall see, however, this assumption seems simply unnecessary once we compare the phraseology and themes shared by these mythical narratives with phraseology occurring in non-related IE texts.

4 Parallels in Non-Related Texts: Indo-European "Biopoetics"

From the perspective of IE poetic language, STAND, SEE, EAT, and the other concepts discussed above share the same contiguity relations and (trivial) semantic associations with the higher concept FUNCTION AS A LIVING ANIMATE, i.e. LIVE FUNCTIONALLY, what Marcello Durante (1976: 117) called "pienezza della vitalità psicofisica", different from the plain biological condition of being alive (which we today mostly identify with having a pulse or breathing). This semantic contiguity is evident for instance in RV 10.125.4ab *máyā só* ***ánnam atti*** *yó* ***vipáśyati*** / *yáḥ* ***prā́ṇiti*** *yá īṃ* ***śr̥ṇóti uktám*** "Through me he **eats food**—whoever **sees**, whoever **breathes**, whoever **hears what is spoken**," i.e. whoever is functionally alive.[11]

Some "biopoetic"[12] devices of this kind have already been shown to be inherited: the formulaic contiguity of the concepts LIE DOWN (PIE **ḱei̯-*) and BE

11 Cf. Jamison & Brereton 2014 ad loc.: "[...] Eating is essential to life: one can't see, breathe, or hear without being alive [...]." Contiguity-driven features of the poetic language such as merisms were most probably learned in blocks: as noted by Calvert Watkins (1995: 209), the employment of several "inherited formulaic merisms in a row" is "a recurrent feature of early Indo-European traditional texts, which may indicate that these formulas were learned in groups".

12 Just like English *bioethics* refers to "ethical issues relating to the practice of medicine and

SLAIN (PIE *g^{wh}*en-*), as demonstrated by Calvert Watkins (1995: 500–506), the collocation NOT SEE LIGHT as a metaphor for BE DEAD (Marcello Durante 1976: 116–118, George Dunkel 1993: 106–108 inter alia), the collocation EAT AND DRINK as a metaphor for LIVE (Watkins 1995: 209). Further similar poetic devices are attested in several texts in IE languages which describe the existential conditions of dead, cursed, sick and other NON-FUNCTIONING characters. In a similar way, parallels for the NON-FUNCTIONING cosmos, which is associated with the main character's distress in our myths, may be found in various IE narratives about the "End of Time" (e.g. Ragnarök, the Norse apocalypse), the time *par excellence* when the universe will become NON-FUNCTIONING.

Fragments of the system of structural oppositions which was set up above for the "Non-Functioning Fertility Deity Myths" may thus be recognized in texts which are not directly connected to these narratives. In what follows, seven semantic associations corresponding exactly to the first seven shared features of the "Myths of Non-Functioning Fertility Deities" will be illustrated by a selection of passages.

1. A NON-FUNCTIONING character is said to NOT STAND, i.e. SIT, LIE DOWN, or SLEEP.

> As pointed out by Watkins (1995: 500–506), a character who has been SLAIN (*g^{wh}*en-*) is often said to LIE (**ḱei̯-*) by formulaic association:
>
> Greek: *Il.* 18.20 ***κεῖται*** *Πάτροκλος, νέκυος δὲ δὴ ἀμφιμάχονται γυμνοῦ* "**Low lies** Patroclus, and around his corpse they are fighting—his naked corpse."
>
> Vedic: RV 1.32.10d *dīrgháṃ táma* ***ā́śayad*** *índraśatruḥ* "He whose rival was Indra **lay** there in the long darkness (of death)."
>
> Avestan: *Yt.* 10.80 *yahmi* ***sōire*** *miϑrō.drujō / aipi vīϑiši jata / pauruua mašiiākåŋhō* "At whose divinatory trial men false to contract **lie** in masses, slain." (tr. Watkins)

A SLAIN or IMPURE character may also SLEEP (Watkins 1995: 506–507); Vedic attests the figurative employment of MAKE SLEEP for MAKE DIE, i.e. SLAY (Jamison 1982–1983: 11). The association of the concept SIT with the condition of being DEAD and that of LIE with other NON-FUNCTIONING states such as OLD AGE or SADNESS are attested as well, cf. e.g. *Od.* 11.142 ("[Odysseus' dead mother Antikleia] **sits** in silence near the blood"); 11.195 ("[Odysseus' old father Laertes] **lies** sorrowing, and nurses his great grief in his heart").

---

biology" (*OED*, s.v.), the term *biopoetics* could be used to refer to those poetic devices which relate to cultural conceptions of health, healing and life in general.

2. A NON-FUNCTIONING character is said to NOT SEE or NOT BE IN THE LIGHT. As mentioned above, the figurative use of LIGHT as a metonymy for LIFE has been widely treated.[13]

Greek: *Il.* 5.119–120 [...] *οὐδέ μέ φησι / δηρὸν ἔτ' ὄψεσθαι λαμπρὸν φάος ἠελίοιο* "and declares that **not** for long **shall I look on the** bright **light of the sun** (= I will die);" Eur. *Hec.* 706 *ὦ τέκνον, οὐκέτ' ὄντα Διὸς ἐν φάει* "o child, now **no more within the light of Zeus** (= dead)."

Vedic: RV 1.32.10d *dīrgháṃ* ***táma ā́śayad*** *índraśatruḥ* "he whose rival was Indra **lay** there **in the** long **darkness** (**of death**)."

Conversely, a LIVING character is said to SEE or BE IN THE LIGHT:

Hittite: KUB 24.5, 8 *nu=wa* **ᵈUTU AN-*E*** IGI.ḪI.A-*it* ***ušgallu*** "**Let me see the sun of heaven** with my eyes (= let me **live**)." (Dunkel 1993).

Old Norse: *Helgakviða Hjǫrvarðssonar* 39[3–4] *buðlungr, sá er* ***var****, baztr* ***und sólu*** "the king, who **was** the best **under the sun** (= the best who **lived**)."

3. A NON-FUNCTIONING character is said to NOT EAT and/or NOT DRINK properly.

Hittite: KBo 22.178 + KUB 48.109 iii 4–5 [*āšš*]*u adatar* ***UL adanz***[***i***] *āššu akuwatar=mi*[*t U*]***L akuwanzi*** "they (the dead) **do not eat** [goo]d food; they **do** [**no**]**t drink** my good drink."

Greek: Hes. *Th.* 796 *οὐδέ ποτ' ἀμβροσίης καὶ νέκταρος ἔρχεται ἆσσον / βρώσιος, ἀλλά τε κεῖται* [...] "(the cursed god) does **not** go **near to ambrosia and nectar for nourishment**, but lies there."

Old Norse: *Gylf.* 34 [...] ***Hungr*** *diskr hennar,* ***Sultr*** *knífr hennar* [...] "her (the death goddess Hel's) dish (is) **Hunger**, her knife (is) **Famine.**"

Conversely, the Hittite verb-phrase merism EAT (AND) DRINK means to BE ALIVE (Watkins 1995: 209) and is employed as a banishment formula in opposition to the death sentence (Dardano 2012: 627–633):

---

13 Cf. the aforementioned Durante 1976: 116–118 and Dunkel 1993: 106–108, as well as West 2007: 86–87. Cf. also Bremer 1976: 37 and Kölligan 2007: 254, 274 (Greek); Roesler 1997: 264–265 and Oberlies 1998: 455–458 (Vedic).

Hittite: KBo 3.1+ ii 13–15 ***nu=wa=za azzikkandu akkuškandu*** *idālu=ma=šmaš=kan lē ku*[*itki*] *taggašši* "**Let them eat and drink** (= let them live). Let no one do harm to them"; KUB 1.16 ii 33–34 ***nu azzikkeddu akkuškedd***[***u*** *mān=aš āššuš*] *n=ašta šarā uiškettaru* "**Let him continue to eat and drink** (= let him live). [So long as he is on good behavior,] let him continue to come up (to the palace)."[14]

4. A NON-FUNCTIONING character is said to NOT SPEAK.

Greek: *Od.* 11.142 *ἡ δ' ἀκέουσ' ἧσται σχεδὸν αἵματος, οὐδ' ἑὸν υἱὸν / ἔτλη ἐσάντα ἰδεῖν οὐδὲ προτιμυθήσασθαι* "she (Odysseus' dead mother Antikleia) sits **in silence** near the blood and **cannot bring herself** to look upon the face of her own son or **to speak to him**"; Hes. *Th.* 797 [...] *ἀλλά τε κεῖται ἀνάπνευστος καὶ ἄναυδος* [...] "but (the cursed god) lies there without breath and **without voice.**"

Middle Welsh: *BFL* 44.10 *Ac yna y byrywyt y* ***kalaned*** *yn y peir* [...], *ac y kyuodyn tranoeth y bore yn wyr ymlad kystal a chynt, eithyr* ***na ellynt dywedut.*** "Then they threw **the corpses** into the cauldron [...], and they (= the dead) would get up the next morning fighting as well as before except that **they could not talk.**"

5. A FUNCTIONING character is expected to be VIGOROUS and NOT DECREPIT: OLD AGE is like a COVERING which may be removed.

The connection between a FUNCTIONING hero and the concept YOUTH is of course very well attested, cf. e.g. Gk. *ἥρως* 'hero', which is the reflex of **Hi̯eh₁ro u̯-* 'the (masculine) personification of the period of bloom' (García Ramón 2016: 53–56). In the passage of the Sanskrit myth of Cyavana quoted above, however, this association is paired with the peculiar poetic image of OLD AGE as a COVERING which can be removed, cf. RV 5.74.5ab: ***prá cyávānāj jujurúṣo / vavrím átkaṃ ná muñcathaḥ*** "**You remove the covering like a cloak** from Cyavāna, **who had become old.**" This feature may be inherited, as it matches closely the Homeric formulaic expression *γῆρας ἀποξῦσαι* "to strip away old age," which is attested as a poetic periphrasis for MAKE YOUNG AGAIN, cf. *Il.* 9.445–446 [...] *οὐδ' εἴ κέν μοι ὑποσταίη θεὸς αὐτὸς / γῆρας ἀποξύσας θήσειν νέον ἡβώοντα* "not even if a god himself should undertake **to strip from me my old age** and render me

---

14 Cf. also KBo 4.8 ii 10–12, where a banished priestess is said to LIVE, SEE the sun (cf. *supra*) and EAT "the bread of life" (H. Craig Melchert, p.c.).

strong in youth."[15] In *HDem.* 275–276 (quoted above, § 3 [5]) a similar, though not identical, expression *γῆρας ἀπωσαμένη* "thrusting away old age" is attested at the beginning of the hexameter as well, reflecting the same poetic image of OLD AGE as a MATERIAL which can be removed.

Let us now focus on the descriptions of cosmic disorder which occur in texts in IE languages.

6. Within any NON-FUNCTIONING cosmos, FAMILY TIES DO NOT WORK: parents do not recognize their children and siblings fight against each other.

> Hittite: KBo 22.178 ii 3–7 + KUB 48.109 ii 4–8 (Realm of the Dead) *anna-nekē[š UL kan]ēššanzi* ***pappa*-ŠE[ŠMEŠ *UL kan*]*ēššanzi annaš=za* DUMU-*a*[*n UL k*]*anēšzi*** [**DUMU-*aš=za*]** **AMA-*a*[*n UL k*]*anēšzi*** "Sisters having the same mother do [not] recognize (each other). **Brothers having the same father** do [**not**] **recognize** (each other). **A mother** does [**not**] **recognize** [her] own **child.** [A **child**] does [**not**] **recognize** [its own] **mother**" (Hoffner 1998: 34).
>
> Greek: Hes. *Erga* 183–185 (End of Time) ***οὐδὲ πατὴρ παίδεσσιν ὁμοίιος οὐδέ τι παῖδες***, [...] / ***οὐδὲ κασίγνητος φίλος ἔσσεται***, *ὡς τὸ πάρος περ* "**Father** will **not** be **like-minded with sons**, nor the sons (with their father), [...] **nor** will **the brother** be **dear** (**to his own brother**), as he once was."[16]
>
> Old Norse: *Vsp.* 45 (End of Time) ***Brœðr muno beriaz*** | *oc at bǫnom verðaz* / *muno* ***systrungar*** / ***sifiom spilla*** "**brothers will fight** and kill **each other, sisters' children** will **defile kinship.**"[17]
>
> Old Irish: *CMT* 838–840 (End of Time) ***Foglaid cech mac.*** *Ragaid mac i lligie a athar. Ragaid athair a lligi a meic.* [...] ***immera mac a athair*** "**Every son an enemy** (**of his father**). The son will go to the bed of his father, the father will go to the bed of his son. [...] **Son will betray his father.**"

Hittite *kanēš-* 'recognize' is a reflex of PIE *$\acute{g}neh_3$- 'recognize, discern, perceive' and therefore a cognate of Ved. *jñā-* 'id.'.[18] A collocation MOTHER **NOT REC-**

---

15 Cf. also *Nostoi* fr. 7 Bernabé. S. Douglas Olson (2012, ad loc.) points out a peculiar use of the phrase in *HAph.* 223–224.

16 Cf. also Hes. *Erga* 185–189.

17 It should be noted that both the myth of Baldr and the myth of the End of Time (as well as several other Norse myths) are attested in the *Vǫluspá* and in the *Gylfaginning*, which, therefore, strictly speaking, are related to our myths.

18 Cf. *LIV*²: 168–170; *HED*, s.v. *ganes*(*s*)-, *kanes*(*s*)-; García Trabazo 2007: 293–297; Kloekhorst 2008, s.v. *kane/išš-zi*.

OGNIZE (*ǵneh₃-) SON thus underlies both this Hittite text and the passage of Cyavana's myth quoted above (§ 3 [6]: *JB* 3.121.4 [...] *tan* ***na*** *mātā putram* ***ajānān*** [...] "then the mother **did not recognize** her son").

7. Within any NON-FUNCTIONING cosmos, PLANTS DO NOT GROW anymore.

> Old Norse: *Gylf.* 51 (End of Time) [...] *vetr sá kemr er kallaðr er* ***fimbulvetr****. Þá drífr snær ór ǫllum áttum. Frost eru þá mikil ok vindar hvassir. Ekki nýtr sólar. Þeir vetr fara þrír saman ok* ***ekki sumar*** *milli* "[...] a winter will come called '**mighty winter**'. Then snow will drift from all directions. There will then be great frosts and keen winds. The sun will do no good. There will be three of these winters together and **no summer** between."
>
> Old Irish: *CMT* 831 (End of Time) *Ni accus bith nombeo baid:* ***sam cin blatha*** [...] "I shall not see a world which will be dear to me: **summer without blossoms.**"

The same motif occurs in the Iranian mythical tradition as well (cf. e.g. Mallory & Adams 1997: 182).

Let us summarize the conclusions reached so far. The poetic devices employed in the IE "Non-Functioning Fertility Deity Myths" to describe the NON-FUNCTIONING state of the main character(s) and the consequent NON-FUNCTIONING cosmos have several correspondences (§ 3). These poetic devices reflect phraseology and themes which are independently attested in several IE traditions and are most probably reflexes of inherited PIE poetic culture (§ 4). The most economical way to explain the parallels between the Hittite, Greek, Norse and Indic myths is therefore to assume that they reflect an inherited PIE mythical theme, the peculiarity of which consisted of the (causal) link between the (variously described) NON-FUNCTIONING state of one or more main characters and the (variously described) NON-FUNCTIONING condition of the cosmos around them.

5 Parallels Limited to Core Indo-European: an Inherited Type-Scene

A further common feature of "Non-Functioning Fertility Deity Myths" is the occurrence of a scene involving characters who ride horses or drive chariots in order to reach the NON-FUNCTIONING main character. These scenes are exclusively attested in the non-Hittite narratives, namely in the Greek myth of Demeter and Persephone, in the Norse myth of Baldr, and, partially, in the Indic myth of Cyavana, Sukanyā and the Aśvins:

Greek myth: *HDem.* 375–385

ἵππους *δὲ προπάροιθεν ὑπὸ χρυσέοισιν ὄχεσφιν*
ἔντυεν *ἀθανάτους Πολυσημάντωρ Ἀιδωνευς.*
ἢ δ᾽ ***ὀχέων ἐπέβη****, πάρα δὲ κρατὺς Ἀργειφόντης*
ἡνία καὶ μάστιγα λαβὼν μετὰ χερσὶ *φίλῃσι*
σεῦε *διὲκ μεγάρων: τὼ δ᾽ οὐκ ἀέκοντε* ***πετέσθην.***
ῥίμφα δὲ μακρὰ κέλευθα διήνυσαν: οὐδὲ θάλασσα
οὔθ᾽ ὕδωρ ποταμῶν οὔτ᾽ ἄγκεα ποιήεντα
ἵππων *ἀθανάτων* ***οὔτ᾽ ἄκριες ἔσχεθον ὁρμήν,***
ἀλλ᾽ ὑπὲρ αὐτάων *βαθὺν ἠέρα τέμνον ἰόντες.*
στῆσε δ᾽ ἄγων, ὅθι μίμνεν *ἐυστέφανος* ***Δημήτηρ,***
νηοῖο προπάροιθε θυώδεος [...]

Then the Major General Aïdoneus **harnessed his** immortal **steeds** at the front under the golden chariot. She (Persephone) **got into it**, while beside her the strong Argus-slayer **took the reins and the goad in his hands and urged the horses** out through the halls, and they **flew forward** without demur. Swiftly they accomplished the long legs of their journey: neither sea nor flowing rivers nor grassy glens **nor mountain peaks stayed the** immortal **steeds' impetus**, but **they passed over them** cleaving the deep air. **He brought them to a halt where** fair-garlanded **Demeter was waiting**, in front of her fragrant temple.

Norse myth: *Gylf.* 49

[...] *Þá reið Hermóðr þar til er hann kom at Helgrindum. Þá sté hann af hestinum ok* ***gyrði hann fast, steig upp*** *ok* ***keyrði hann sporum.*** *En hestrinn* ***hljóp svá hart ok yfir grindina at hann kom hvergi nær. Þá reið Hermóðr heim til hallarinnar*** *ok steig af hesti, gekk inn í hǫllina,* ***sá þar*** *sitja í ǫndugi* ***Baldr bróður sinn*** [...]

Then Hermod rode on until he came to Hel's gates. Then he dismounted from the horse and **tightened its girth, mounted** and **spurred it on.** The horse **jumped so hard and over the gate that it came nowhere near.** Then **Hermod rode up to the hall** and dismounted from his horse, went into the hall, **saw** sitting **there** in the seat of honour **his brother Baldr.**

Indic myth: *ŚB* 4.1.5.6

*sa **rátham** **yuktvā́***
sukanyā́ṃ** śāryātī́m **upādhā́ya** **prásiṣyanda** sa **ā́jagāma** **yatra** **ṛṣir** **ā́sa** **tát

He (king Śaryati) **yoked** his **chariot**, and **putting** his daughter **Sukanyâ thereon**, he **set forth**, and **came to the place where the Rishi** (**Cyavana**) **was**.

The scenes appear to have several structural and phraseological matches. The elements shared by these passages may be summarized as follows:

a A HORSE/CHARIOT is harnessed.
b Someone (a maiden in the Greek and Indic narratives) mounts/is put on the HORSE/CHARIOT.
c The HORSE/CHARIOT sets forth.
d The HORSE/CHARIOT flies/jumps over an OBSTACLE (not in Indic).
e All contact between the HORSE/CHARIOT and the OBSTACLE is denied (not in Indic).
f The HORSE/CHARIOT reaches the place where the NON-FUNCTIONING main character is.

The elements (a–f) occur in identical order in Greek, Norse and (to some extent)[19] in Indic, and therefore point, in my opinion, to an inherited narrative structure. This kind of ready-made thematic structures, called "traditional type-scenes" in the terminology of scholars of oral literature, were first observed in Homeric poetry by Walter Arend (1933). However, if we compare the horse/chariot-scenes in our myths with Homeric type-scenes of the type "ride on a chariot" (Arend 1933: 86ff.), parallels may be found only for the realistic elements (a–c, f), whereas there are not matches for the fantastic elements (d–e, the horse/chariot flying over all obstacles).

In the Hittite myth of Telipinu, the god is reached by a flying object as well, namely a bee, sent by the goddess Ḫannaḫanna to search for Telipinu, whom the bee finds lying on a meadow (e.g. KUB 33.9 ii 11–12 + KUB 33.10 ii 4–5). No horses or chariots are involved; the only further correspondence with the other mythical traditions is the employment in both the Hittite and Greek scenes of the same collocation EARTH AND WATER as a merism for WORLD UNDER THE SKY.[20]

19 The myth of Cyavana does not attest the elements (d–e), but the chariot ride seems to be a traditional motif, as it occurs in the Kauśika narrative as well, cf. *MBh.* 13.55.5; 22.

20 Over which both the Hittite bee and the Greek chariot fly, cf. KUB 33.5 ii 17–19; *HDem.* 380–383.

The attestation of structurally comparable scenes involving horses or chariots in the Greek, Norse and (at least partially) Indic narratives and the absence of the same feature in the Hittite narratives points to an innovation of the poetic devices associated with the "Non-Functioning Fertility Deity Myths": the innovation must have taken place after the split between Proto-Anatolian and so-called Core Indo-European, from which Greek, Old Norse and Sanskrit (among others) later developed. If the Greek, Norse and Indic scenes indeed reflect an inherited Core-Indo-European ready-made narrative structure, the type-scene must have originally involved horses, as chariots are first attested by archaeological sources around the 21st century BCE (Anthony 2007: 462), too late to correspond to the time of Core-Indo-European unity.[21] The chariots employed in the Greek and Indic narratives must therefore reflect an even younger innovation, which may have spread together with chariot technology in the context of long-distance cultural contact attested by the archaeology of Bronze Age Eurasia (cf. e.g. Kristiansen-Larsson 2005: 197 ff.; Anthony 2007: 456–457). This would not be unparalleled, as the same must indeed be assumed for the poetic image of the "Chariot of the Sun" attested by several Indo-European traditions, which for the same reasons cannot be reconstructed as an inherited feature (cf. West 2007: 210).

6 Conclusions

The conclusions of this study may be summarized as follows:

1 A series of phraseological and thematic parallels between the Hittite myth of Telipinu, the Greek myth of Demeter and Persephone, the Norse myth of Baldr and the Indic myths of Cyavana may be identified. These parallels concern the poetic devices employed in the narratives to describe the NON-FUNCTIONING state of the main character and the consequent NON-FUNCTIONING cosmos: the NON-FUNCTIONING main characters appear to share the features NOT STAND/MOVE UPWARDS, NOT SEE/BE IN THE LIGHT, NOT EAT/DRINK, NOT SPEAK and NOT BE (SEXUALLY) VIGOROUS, while the NON-FUNCTIONING environments around them share the features FAMILY TIES DO NOT WORK, PLANTS DO NOT GROW and SACRIFICES DO NOT WORK. The opposite features occur once the main character(s) and (consequently) the surrounding cosmos are back to a FUNCTIONING state.

21 Greek and Indo-Aryan (differentiated from Iranian) are already attested as separate branches by the 16th century BCE.

2 These parallels match phraseological collocations and themes which are well attested independently in several IE traditions to describe the existential conditions of any NON-FUNCTIONING character (e.g. DEAD characters) and of any NON-FUNCTIONING cosmos (e.g. the world at the End of Time), respectively; the use of these poetic devices is therefore a reflex of inherited PIE poetic culture.
3 Even though the possibility of borrowing and areal diffusion remains open, the most economical way to explain the numerous parallels between the Hittite, Greek, Norse and Indic myths is to assume that they reflect an inherited PIE mythical theme about "Non-Functioning Fertility Deities", in which the NON-FUNCTIONING state of one or more main characters was intimately linked with the NON-FUNCTIONING condition of the cosmos around them.
4 The Greek, Norse and (partially) Indic narratives attest structurally comparable scenes involving horses or chariots. The absence of the same feature in the Hittite narratives suggests that it reflects an innovation of the poetic devices associated with the mythical theme of the "Non-Functioning Fertility Deity" which must have taken place after the split between Proto-Anatolian and Core Indo-European, from which Greek, Old Norse and Sanskrit later developed.
5 The inherited Core-Indo-European type-scene must have originally involved horses; the chariots employed in the Greek and Indic narratives reflect an even younger innovation which may have spread together with chariot technology (after the 21st century BCE).

Acknowledgements

For valuable help, criticism and discussion, it is my pleasure to thank Andrea Lorenzo Covini, Paola Dardano, Manfred Hutter, Sylvia Hutter-Braunsar, Alwin Kloekhorst, Daniel Kölligan, Kristian Kristiansen, Guus Kroonen, Matilde Serangeli, Michael Weiss and especially José Luis García Ramón and H. Craig Melchert, who engaged in detailed discussion of the final version of the present contribution. I also wish to thank Benedicte Nielsen Whitehead and Robert Tegethoff for improving my English version, as well as the anonymous reviewer for her/his helpful remarks. The usual disclaimers apply.

References

Anthony, David W. 2007. *The Horse, the wheel, and language: How Bronze-Age riders from the Eurasian steppes shaped the modern world.* Princeton: Princeton University Press.

Arend, Walter. 1933. *Die typischen Szenen bei Homer.* Berlin: Weidmann.

Asan, Ali Naci. 2014. *Der Mythos vom erzürnten Gott.* Wiesbaden: Harrassowitz.

Bremer, Dieter. 1976. *Licht und Dunkel in der frühgriechischen Dichtung: Interpretationen zur Vorgeschichte der Lichtmetaphysik.* Bonn: Bouvier.

Bugge, Sophus. 1889. *Studien über die Entstehung der nordischen Götter- und Heldensagen.* München: Kaiser.

Burkert, Walter. 1979. *Structure and history in Greek mythology and ritual.* Berkeley, Los Angeles & London: University of California Press.

Dardano, Paola. 2012. Die Worte des Königs als Repräsentation von Macht: Zur althethitischen Phraseologie. In Gernot Wilhelm (ed.), *Organization, representation, and symbols of power in the Ancient Near East. Proceedings of the 54th Rencontre Assyriologique Internationale at Würzburg 20–25 July 2008*, 619–636. Winona Lake, IN: Eisenbrauns.

Davies, Sioned. 2007. *The Mabinogion.* Oxford: Oxford University Press.

Dietz, Karin. 1974. *Mythos und Kult des Gottes Freyr in der Überlieferung der Nordgermanen.* Hamburg: Universität Hamburg.

Dronke, Ursula. 1997. *The Poetic Edda.* Vol. 2. *Mythological poems.* Oxford: Clarendon.

Dunkel, George E. 1993. Periphrastica Homerohittitovedica. In Bela Brogyanyi & Reiner Lipp (eds.), *Comparative–historical linguistics: Indo-European and Finno-Ugric: Papers in honor of Oswald Szemerényi.* Vol. 3, 103–118. Amsterdam & Philadelphia: Benjamins.

Durante, Marcello. 1976. *Sulla preistoria della tradizione poetica greca.* Vol. 2. *Risultanze della comparazione indoeuropea.* Roma: Ateneo.

Eggeling, Julius. 1885. *The Śatapatha-Brāhmaṇa. According to the text of the Mādhyandina School.* Oxford: Clarendon.

Faulkes, Anthony. 1987. *Edda. Snorri Sturluson. Translated from the Icelandic and introduced.* London: Viking Society for Northern Research & University of London.

Foley, Helene P. 1993. *The Homeric hymn to Demeter.* Princeton: Princeton University Press.

Fuscagni, Francesco (ed.). 2012. hethiter.net: CTH 457.7.2 (INTR 2012-12-19)

Ganguli, Kisari Mohan. 1883–1896. *The Mahabharata of Krishna-Dwaipayana Vyasa translated into English prose.* Calcutta: Bhārata.

García Ramón, José Luis. 1999. Védico *Cyávāna-* : Griego *Σύμενος* (Rodas). *Minerva* 13. 55–65.

García Ramón, José Luis. 2016. Hera and hero: Reconstructing lexicon and god-names. In: D.M. Goldstein, S.W. Jamison & B. Vine (eds.), *Proceedings of the 27th Annual*

UCLA Indo-European Conference. Los Angeles, October 22–23 2015, 41–60. Bremen: Hempen.

García Trabazo, José Virgilio. 2007. Die hethitischen Verben für 'wissen, erkennen' im indogermanischen Kontext. *Studi Micenei ed Egeo-Anatolici* 49 (*VI Congresso Internazionale di Ittitologia [Roma, 5–9 settembre 2005], Parte 1*). 293–303.

Gray, Elisabeth A. 1982. *Cath Maige Tuired: The second battle of Mag Tuired*. Kildare: Irish Texts Society.

Haas, Volkert. 1994. *Geschichte der hethitischen Religion*. Leiden: Brill.

Haas, Volkert. 2006. *Die hethitische Literatur*. Berlin & New York: de Gruyter.

HED = Jaan Puhvel. 1984–. *Hittite etymological dictionary*. Berlin & New York: De Gruyter Mouton.

Hoffner, Harry A., Jr. 1998. *Hittite myths*. Atlanta, GA: Scholars Press.

Hopkins, E. Washburn. 1905. The fountain of youth. *Journal of the American Oriental Society* 26. 1–67.

Hutter-Braunsar, Sylvia. 2011. Vergleichende Untersuchungen zu den Texten über eine aus Zorn verschwundene Gottheit. In Manfred Hutter & Sylvia Hutter-Braunsar (eds.), *Hethitische Literatur. Überlieferungsprozesse, Textstrukturen, Ausdrucksformen und Nachwirken. Akten des Symposiums vom 18. bis 20. Februar 2010 in Bonn*, 129–144. Münster: Ugarit.

Jamison, Stephanie W., & Joel Peter Brereton. 2014. *The Rigveda. The earliest religious poetry of India*. Oxford: Oxford University Press.

Jamison, Stephanie W. 1982–1983. "Sleep" in Vedic and Indo-European. *Zeitschrift für vergleichende Sprachforschung* 96(1). 6–16.

Janda, Michael. 2000. *Eleusis. Das indogermanische Erbe der Mysterien*. Innsbruck: Institut für Sprachwissenschaft der Universität Innsbruck.

Janda, Michael. 2005. *Elysion. Entstehung und Entwicklung der griechischen Religion*. Innsbruck: Institut für Sprachen und Literaturen der Universität Innsbruck.

Kloekhorst, Alwin. 2008. *Etymological dictionary of the Hittite inherited lexicon*. Leiden: Brill.

Kölligan, Daniel. 2007. *Suppletion und Defektivität im griechischen Verbum*. Bremen: Hempen.

Kristiansen, Kristian & Thomas B. Larsson. 2005. *The rise of Bronze Age society. Travels, transmissions and transformations*. Cambridge & New York: Cambridge University Press.

Liberman, Anatoly. 2016. *In prayer and laughter. Essays on Medieval Scandinavian and Germanic mythology*. Moscow: Paleograph.

Lindow, John. 1997. *Murder and vengeance among the gods: Baldr in Scandinavian mythology*. Helsinki: Suomalainen tiedeakatemia.

LIV[2] = Helmut Rix (ed.). 2001. *Lexikon der indogermanischen Verben*. Wiesbaden: Reichert.

Mallory, James P., & Douglas Q. Adams (eds.). 1997. *Encyclopedia of Indo-European culture*. London & Chicago: Fitzroy Dearborn.

Neckel, Gustav. 1920. *Die Überlieferungen vom Gotte Balder. Dargestellt und vergleichend untersucht*. Dortmund: Ruhfus.

Oberlies, Thomas. 1998–1999. *Die Religion des Rgveda: Das religiöse System des Rgveda*. Vienna: Sammlung De Nobili.

Olson, S. Douglas. 2012. *The Homeric hymn to Aphrodite and related texts*. Berlin: de Gruyter.

Richardson, Nicholas. 1979. *The Homeric hymn to Demeter*. Oxford: Clarendon.

Rieken, Elisabeth, et al. (ed.). 2012. hethiter.net/: CTH 324.1 (INTR 2012-05-10)

Rieken, Elisabeth, et al. (ed.). 2009a. hethiter.net/: CTH 324.2 (INTR 2009-08-12)

Rieken, Elisabeth, et al. (ed.). 2009b. hethiter.net/: CTH 324.3 (INTR 2009-08-12)

Rieken, Elisabeth, et al. (ed.). 2009c. hethiter.net/: CTH 324.4 (INTR 2009-08-12)

Rieken, Elisabeth, et al. (ed.). 2009d. hethiter.net/: CTH 327.1 (INTR 2009-08-12)

Roesler, Ulrike. 1997. *Licht und Leuchten im Ṛgveda. Untersuchungen zum Wortfeld des Leuchtens und zur Bedeutung des Lichts*. Swisttal-Odendorf: Indica et Tibetica.

Schier, Kurt. 1995. Gab es eine eigenständige Balder-Tradition in Dänemark? In Edith Marold & Christiane Zimmermann (eds.), *Nordwestgermanisch*, 125–153. Berlin & New York: de Gruyter.

Schröder, Franz Rolf. 1962. Balder-Probleme. *Beiträge zur Geschichte der deutschen Sprache und Literatur* 84. 319–357.

Vijñanananda, Swami. 1890. *The Śrīmad Devī Bhāgavatam*. Allahabad: Panini Office.

Vira, Raghu, & Lokesh Chandra. 1954. *Jaiminīyabrāhmaṇa*. Nagpur: International Academy of Indian Culture.

Vries, Jan de. 1956–1957. *Altgermanische Religionsgeschichte*. Berlin: W. de Gruyter.

Watkins, Calvert. 1995. *How to kill a dragon: Aspects of Indo-European poetics*. New York: Oxford University Press.

Watkins, Calvert. 2004. The third donkey: Origin legends and some hidden Indo-European themes. In J.H.W. Penney (ed.), *Indo-European perspectives: Studies in honour of Anna Morpurgo Davies*, 65–80. Oxford: Oxford University Press.

West, Emily. 2017. The transformation of Cyavana: A case study in narrative evolution. *Oral Tradition* 31(1). 77–122.

West, Martin L. 2007. *Indo-European poetry and myth*. Oxford: Oxford University Press.

Witzel, Michael. 1987. On the origin of the literary device of the 'frame story' in Old Indian literature. In U. Schneider & H. Falk (eds.), *Hinduismus und Buddhismus: Festschrift für Ulrich Schneider*, 380–414. Freiburg: Falk.

CHAPTER 5

Did Proto-Indo-European Have a Word for Wheat? Hittite *šeppit*(*t*)- Revisited and the Rise of Post-PIE Cereal Terminology

Adam Hyllested

1 PIE 'Wheat' and a Suffix for Foodstuffs

Since Watkins 1978, Hittite *šeppit*(*t*)- has been widely regarded as the lone survivor of an original PIE term for '(a type of) wheat', **sép-it*, which was lost and replaced by innovative designations in all other branches than Anatolian. Despite the meager evidence, Watkins considered Hitt. *šeppit*(*t*)- to be an inherited Indo-European word because of its seemingly archaic morphology: Neuter nouns with nom.-acc. sg. in *-*it* comprise an excessively rare and unproductive stem class—containing, in fact, just two other members:[1]

a the undisputed **mél-it* 'honey' with widespread reflexes in the daughter-languages (e.g., Hitt. *milit*-, Luv. *mallit*-, Gk. *μέλι*, gen. *μέλιτος*, OIr *mil*, Lat. *mel*, Alb. *mjaltë*, Goth. *miliþ*, all 'id.'; Mallory & Adams 2006: 271)[2] and

b *h_2*élbʰit* (or **albʰit*) 'barley' reconstructed on the basis of Gk. *ἄλφι*, gen. *ἄλφιτος*; Alb. *elb*, def. *elbi*; and a range of Eastern Iranian forms comprising Pashto *orbəša*, pl. *ōrbašē*, dial. Afridi *warbaše*, Wanetsi *urbūsa*, *arbasa*, pl. *arbaši*, *arbusi*, *arbəšē*, Waziri *rebəše*; Wakhi *arbəsi*; Sanglechi *urwəs*, *vərvəs*; Ishkashimi *urvəs*; and Yidgha *yɛršio*.[3]

The 'barley'-word is generally regarded as derived from the root in the adjective 'white' *h_2*élbʰ-o-s*.[4] The Eastern Iranian forms, however, are not directly

1 Using broader categorizations, they are often grouped with other heteroclitics showing an alternation -*i*-/-*n*-, which, however, apart from this combination display quite heterogeneous paradigms among themselves (see, e.g., Olsen 1999: 169 and Oettinger 2017 *passim*).

2 Arm. *metr* is generally regarded a contamination of **mél-it* and **médʰu* 'mead' (Olsen 1999: 168–169; Clackson 2017: 112 with references).

3 Forms taken from Blažek 2017: 53 and Kümmel 2017: 281. According to Kümmel, they cannot be connected to Khotanese *rrusā*- and Khwarezmian *rsy* as proposed by Bailey (1979: 374) because these go back to a protoform **rucā*- in Common Iranian, obviously far from **arpucyā*-.

4 Sometimes reconstructed as **álbʰ-o-s* because of the missing laryngeal in Hitt. *alpaš* 'cloud', but loans into Uralic such as Finnish *kalvas*, *kalpea*, both 'pale' secure a laryngeal in this

 | DOI:10.1163/9789004416192_007

compatible with the Greek and Albanian ones since they point to an original sequence **-lp-* or **-rp-*, not **-lbʰ-* (Kümmel 2017: 282; *pace* Mallory & Adams 2006: 165, Joseph 2017: 271 n. 19). Thus, a reconstruction **$h_2$élbʰit* (or **albʰit*) in fact only makes sense for the precursor of Greek and Albanian, and we may speculate whether we are dealing with a form that did not appear until the arrival of Indo-European languages in the Balkans (in that case, reconstructing a laryngeal is probably anachronistic).

2 A Transferred Epithet

Watkins further analyzed Gk. *ἄλφι* and Alb. *elb* as having arisen secondarily from a Proto-Indo-European fixed formula of noun and epithet, **$h_2$élbʰom sépit* or **sépit $h_2$élbʰom* representing one possible manifestation of WHITE + GRAIN where the noun (**sépit*) was ultimately lost while the adjective left behind (**$h_2$élbʰom*) acquired its inflection, forming a new noun (**$h_2$élbʰ-it*).

This formula WHITE + GRAIN would have continued as a structure in Hom. *ἄλφιτα λευκά* 'white barley' and *κρῖ λευκά* 'white grain' after the original noun (**sépit*) had been lost and the adjective had acquired its inflection. In other words, **$h_2$élbʰit* (or **álbʰit*) is not an original noun reconstructable for PIE. The consequence of this analysis is that only **sép-it* and **mél-it* remain as primary members of their class.

That Hitt. *šeppit(t)-*, despite its lack of cognates within the family, as well as its suffix **-it-*, represents a PIE archaism was nonetheless Watkins' conclusion (thus also Watkins 1996: 63): "A curious athematic suffix **-it* marking elemental foodstuffs is found in **mel-it* 'honey' (…) and **sep-it* 'wheat' (…)".[5] Furthermore, it is generally accepted in standard handbooks where scholars basically paraphrase Watkins, sometimes with hesitation, thus Fortson (2004: 112 = 2010: 125): "[A] suffix of (…) some interest is **-it-* (…) perhaps it was a "foodstuffs" suffix"; and Mallory & Adams (2006: 166): "(…) the archaic and unproductive morphology would argue that the word could not have been created in Anatolian but must be earlier (…)". In a similar vein, Kloekhorst (2008: 745) states: "because of the similarity in formation with *militt-* 'honey' (…) it is not unlikely that *šeppit(t)-*, too, is of Indo-European origin".

word, and because the semantics provides a motivation for borrowing, the Hittite term is best regarded a loanword from another Indo-European dialect (Hyllested 2011).

5 In the 2nd ed. of the Italian version (Ramat & Ramat 1997), the equivalent passage appears on p. 79, reading "Un curioso suffisso atematico **-it*, che marca sostanze commestibili basilari si trova nelle parole **mel-it* 'miele' (…) e **sép-it* 'frumento'".

However, no good candidates for cognates are known. Like Kloekhorst (2008: 745), I find Rieken's (1999: 185–186) attempt at connecting it to Hittite *šeba-* 'sheaf (?)' too uncertain. Furthermore, as pointed out to me by Craig Melchert (pers. comm.) the unlenited variant **šeppitt-* is quite mysterious by the derivation from **sépit*, with fixed initial accent. In any case, no such variant is known of the noun *milit-* 'honey', and the corresponding adjective *mlittu-* (*ma/i-li-it-tu-*) is too far away to have influenced *šeppit*(*t*)-.

3 A New Etymology for Hittite *šeppit*(*t*)-

While the seemingly archaic morphology speaks against the stem of *šeppit*(*t*)- having arisen in Hittite, or Anatolian for that matter, there is another possibility: That it was borrowed from a foreign source lock, stock and barrel, and that its second syllable was subsequently interpreted as a domestic stem formation.

Akkadian *samīdu* 'high-quality wheat flour' and its cognates in other Semitic languages, such as Aramaic *semid*, are already known to have spread into Mediterranean Indo-European languages in ancient times. In Greek it is known as *σεμίδαλις* from where it has entered Latin as *simila, simula*. The latter evolved into Mod.It. *semola* 'bran', the diminutive of which, *semolina* 'coarse meal', is the source of Eng. *semnel* and terms for semnel in other modern European languages (Sallares 1991).

Crucially, a similar Hittite substitution -*p*(*p*)- for Akkadian -*m*(*m*)- occurs in at least two other famous culture-words:

- Hitt. *kappani-* 'cumin' ← Akk. *kamūnu*(*m*), *kamannu*(*m*)
- Hitt. *šapšama* 'sesame' from ← Akk. *šammašammu-*

It could be argued that *šapšama-* is different, seeing that -*p*- from -*m*- occurs in preconsonantal position, and perhaps it can be added that the repetitive structure of the word is less than typical; but *kappani-* at least constitutes a direct parallel to *šeppit* from a Semitic form **semid-* vel sim.

Rieken (1999: 185–186) argues that sporadic occurrences of the genitive *šeppit*(*t*)*aš* with -*d-* in Old Hittite, i.e. *šeppidaš*, points to an early regular lenition of *-*t*- in post-tonic position (as from Proto-Anatolian **šépitaš*), while most forms show a later generalization of the unlenited alternant, geminate *-*tt*- throughout the paradigm. As mentioned in the previous section, however, it is unclear where the unlenited variant would have come from in the first place if the accent was fixed on the initial syllable. The only other comparable noun, *milit-* 'honey', is always lenited. Thus, the lenited variant is not the one that needs an explanation. In any case, if the word has a foreign source with voiced -*d-* from the outset, the variation in Old Hittite between lenited and unlenited stops may simply reflect different strategies for rendering the foreign sound. As is well known, variation between similar sounds is typical in borrowings, because of different phonetic or phonotactic differences between the counterparts in the source and receiving languages. I would thus interpret the variation in and of itself as yet another sign of foreign provenance.

4 Latin *sibitillus* ~ *simitillus*

Latin may provide additional evidence for a Semitic origin of *šeppit-*. A denasalized variant of Akk. *samīdu*—or one of its counterparts in the other Semitic languages—possibly surfaces in Latin if the otherwise opaque *sibitillus* ~ *simitillus* 'a kind of bread' is an independent Mediterranean loan from the same ultimate source (this time not via Greek, where only a shape *σεμίδ-* is attested). The variant *sibit-* need not be a Hittite-style rendering of an original **-m-*; it can have arisen internally in Latin from an earlier **simbit-* since such an alternation is known from other loanwords in Latin, e.g., *sabūcus* alongside *sambūcus* 'elder (tree)'.

One may envision that **-m(m)-* in the Semitic source was pronounced something like **-bm-* which was initially rendered as a prenasalized stop with facultative variants **-b-* or **-mb-* as today in Modern Greek—but there are many other possibilities. The key point is that Akkadian *-m(m)-* is frequently substituted for Hittite *-pp-*, and that a similar consonant alternation shows up in an otherwise unetymologized Latin word of the same structure from the same semantic sphere.

5 'Barley' on the Balkans—a Turkic Loan?

As mentioned above, the Balkan Indo-European words for 'barley', Greek *ἄλφι*, pl. *ἄλφιτα* and Albanian *elb* are incompatible with the Eastern Iranian forms, which means they cannot regularly hark back to the same Indo-European source. The Pashto cluster *-rb-* can only reflect original **-rp-*, and the Common Iranian protoform would be **arpucyā-* (Kümmel 2017: 282).

Robbeets (2017) has suggested that Turkic **arpa* 'barley' is an old borrowing from Iranian and thus of Indo-European provenance. Kümmel and Blažek are indifferent as to the connection between the Turkic and Iranian words, but the shape and distribution of the Iranian words speak against it;[6] conversely,

6 I first made this point in a paper read at the workshop "The language of the first farmers" in Naples, 3 September 2016 (Hyllested 2016).

the word occurs in all Turkic languages, mostly as *arpa* (Stachowski 2008: 10–12, Witczak 2003) and can be reconstructed for Proto-Turkic as **arpa*. Furthermore, also Mongolian has *arbai* 'barley', and it even occurs in Manchu, a Tungusic language, as *arfa* 'barley; oats' (regularly < **arpa*). These terms are compatible in Altaic according to Sevelyev (2017).[7]

The remaining members of the 'barley'-word family in Indo-European correspond regularly to each other, although the genitive **albʰitos* is not directly reflected in Albanian *elb*, which can only prove an *-i-* suffix because of the umlaut from **a* > *e*. Conversely, Alb. *mjaltë* 'honey' points to Proto-Alb. **meltV-* with early syncope of the *-i-* although there is a slight possibility that *-të* is a productive suffix which was added later.

I have earlier argued (Hyllested 2016) that the conclusion to be drawn from this, rather than regarding neighboring 'barley'-words as incidentally similar, is that the Turkic 'barley'-word was transferred as an early loan into Balkan Indo-European. This was first suggested by Vasmer (1921: 16) and supported by Jokl (1926: 92); see most recently Manzelli (2013) for a thorough treatment of the material and further references. Another IE/Turkic parallel displaying the same oscillation may provide a clue:

Proto-Turkic **arba* 'sorcery; to bewitch, enchant', likewise widespread among the Turkic languages, seems to constitute a parallel. Hitt. *alpant-* 'swoon' ~ *alwanz-* 'being bewitched, affected by sorcery' etc. have disputed origins, and the very connection between the two forms is not certain either (Kloekhorst 2008: 170–171; Yakubovich 2008). They are sometimes regarded as loanwords from some non-Indo-European source because of the irregular variation between *-p-* and *-w-*. We may identify Turkic as their ultimate source; not only do they appear similar to the Turkic item, but the latter is already known to be an early culture-word, having entered into Proto-Fenno-Ugric[8] as **arpa* 'remedy for sorcery' (Rédei 1988: 16; Campbell 1998: 117). Since Proto-Fenno-Ugric did not possess voiced or lenited stops, PFU *-*p*- was the natural substution for Proto-Turkic *-*b*-. A voiced labial stop in the source language would explain the alternation between an unvoiced stop *-p-* and a voiced approximant *-w-* in Hitt. *alpant-* ~ *alwanz-* as two different renderings of a foreign sound.

The *-l-* in Greek and Albanian 'barley' could theoretically reflect another attempt at rendering slightly different phonetics of a foreign consonant, but

7 Robbeets adds Old Japanese *apa* 'millet' to the family, but according to Alexander Francis-Ratte (pers. comm.) this stumbles upon formal difficulties.

8 Not necessarily for Proto-Uralic since no cognates are known from Samoyedic languages.

in this case the change is more likely to reflect inner-Turkic dialectal variation. Uighur *aram* 'first month of the year' only has cognates in one other Turkic language, Hunno-Bulgarian, which is today extinct. In Hunno-Bulgarian, *alem* not only means 'first month of the year', but also the ordinal numeral 'first' (Pritsak 1955: 51–52: *Nominalia of the Bulgarian khans*). Because of the narrow semantics, the Uighur and Hunno-Bulgarian words can hardly be separated from each other, although the former has no surface meaning and is regarded a loan from Sogdian *r'm* by Knüppel (2002).

All three Turkic lexemes mentioned—'barley', 'witchcraft' and 'first month of the year' display a phonological structure aR(V)C[+LAB]—-so perhaps **l* was the regular outcome before consonants in parts of Bolghar Turkic (possibly before labials specifically, though the motivation for such a conditioning would be less clear). In that case, the Balkan 'barley'-word and the Anatolian 'witchcraft'-word would represent borrowings from the Turkic subgroup confusingly (and for different reasons) called *r*-Turkic, as opposed to *z*-Turkic which comprises all living Turkic languages except Chuvash. Most of the nomadic tribes haunting Europe in ancient and medieval times are known to have been speakers of the previously more widespread *r*-Turkic languages.

(Dialectal) *r*-Turkic		***z*-Turkic**	
alem	'first month'	*aram*	'first month'
**alpa*	'barley'	*arpa*	'barley'
**alba-*	'witchcraft'	*arba*	'witchcraft'

When asserting a development of **-rC-* to **-lC-* in *r*-Turkic dialects, it is important to note that in the Old Bolghar languages *-r-* is already known to have been unstable when forming the first part of a cluster. Thus, it disappeared before a dental, cf., e.g., Donau Bolghar *σεκτεμ* ~ *шехтемь* '8th' < **sikərtəm*; Volga Bolghar *äti* < **ärti* 'he was'; and the personal name *Βασίχ* < **bars-siġ* 'feline-like' (Pritsak 1982).

The Iranian forms are ambiguous as to the original character of the liquid, since PIE **l* regularly yields Proto-Iranian **r*. The most likely explanation for the variation between Iranian **-p-* and Graeco-Albanian **-bʰ-* is that a folk-etymological reshaping took place in the latter on the basis of **álbʰos* 'white'; see section 6.

I would make the following conclusions on the 'barley'-word: While it is indeed theoretically possible, as proposed by Robbeets (2017), that the word was borrowed into Turkic from Iranian, it is notably not indigenous to Iranian in an Indo-European sense, and since it is reconstructible for Proto-Turkic with possible cognates in Mongolic and Tungusic, borrowing in the reverse direction—from Turkic into Iranian—appears much more likely.[9] Since 'barley' is a Eurasian culture-word in any case, it is also conceivable that the term entered into both language families from a third source—Robbeets allows for this possibility. At least it does not appear to be an Indo-European word, although secondary associations with the word for 'white' in Balkan Indo-European doubtlessly emerged (cf. Germanic **hwaitja-* 'wheat'; see also Blažek 2017).

6 How 'Barley' Came to Look Like 'Honey' in Greek

If the Balkan Indo-European 'barley'-word is really a Turkic loan, how did *ἄλφι* then acquire the same stem as **mél-it*? Greek *ἄλφι* may have acquired the morphology of **mélit-* 'honey' simply due to popular (and, in the latter case, perhaps etymologically correct) perception of these two terms as linked to the adjectives 'white' (**ἀλφος*) and 'dark' (*μέλας*), respectively:

**ἀλφος*	'white'	~ **ἀλφV-*	'barley'	→ *ἄλφι, -ιτ-*
μέλας	'dark'	~ *μέλι, -ιτ-*	'honey'	*μέλι, -ιτ-*

Alb. *elb* does not look like a loan from Greek (Alb. *-b-* vs. Gk. *-φ-* is regular in inherited words) so the analogy could have taken place in a common "Balkan Indo-European" precursor of Greek and Albanian:

**albʰ-*	'white'	~ **álpV-*[10]	'barley'	→ **álbʰ-it-*
**mel-*	'dark'	~ **mél-it-*	'honey'	**mél-it-*

However, as mentioned above, Albanian does not explicitly show a *-*t*- in *elp* as it does in *mjaltë* 'honey'. It cannot be excluded that this is due to the differences in the consonantal skeleton, but, more likely, *elb* continues the nom-

9 Aubaile-Sallenave (2012) further mentions how "the similarity of the [barley] terms and products among the speakers of Iranian languages (…) to those of Turkic speakers indicates the influence of both in diffusion of the terms and the products."

10 Or **albʰ-*, if **-bʰ-* arose already at the time of borrowing as a substitution for the foreign **p* (provided the latter was pronounced differently from the domestic **p*) rather than as a result of the folk-etymology involved.

inative *$\acute{a}lb^{h}$-it* while *mjaltë* derives from the secondary oblique stem **mélito-* (reshaped from PIE **mélno-*).

This relation might in itself justify a foreign word coming to look like a single inherited one. But a cultural motivation was probably in place as well. Barley-water or *Kykeon* (Gk. *κυκεών*) plays a ritual role in Homeric texts: it is famous for its use of rites of Demeter in the Eleusinian mysteries (Rinella 2010). Here, barley was mixed with wine, honey, water and herbs. A variant made with emmer, called *puls punica* 'Carthaginian porridge', is described in Cato's *De Agricultura*, and, curiously, several modern "Roman" cookbooks reproducing Cato's recipe (e.g., Dalby & Grainger 1996: 41) recommend using semolina instead. Some scholars have suggested that fungi were used to produce psychedelic effects in ritual barley products (see, e.g., Rinella 2010).

From the relevant passages of Homeric epics, it appears that the connection between 'barley' and 'white' is not particularly different from other color depictions, which simply form effective contrasts between the edible grains or groat and its container or other elements of a darker hue. Consider the following three passages (the translations are based on those at loebclassics.com):

a. Hecamede makes Kykeon, Iliad 11.628–641:[11]

628 *ἥ σφωϊν πρῶτον μὲν ἐπιπροΐηλε τράπεζαν*
629 *καλὴν κυανόπεζαν ἐΰξοον, αὐτὰρ ἐπ' αὐτῆς*
'... table with **dark-blue** feet ...'

631 *ἠδὲ 2μέλι χλωρόν, παρὰ δ' ἀλφίτου ἱεροῦ ἀκτήν*
'and **pale honey** ... holy **barley meal**'

640 *κνῆστι χαλκείῃ, ἐπὶ δ' ἄλφιτα λευκὰ πάλυνε*
'... with a bronze grater, and sprinkled **white barley** on it'

b. Circe makes Kykeon, Odyssey 10.234–235, 519–520 and 525–527:

234 *ἐν δέ σφιν τυρόν τε καὶ ἄλφιτα καὶ μέλι χλωρὸν*
'... a drink of cheese and **barley meal** and **yellow honey**'

235 *οἴνῳ Πραμνείῳ ἐκύκα: ἀνέμισγε δὲ σίτῳ*
'with Pramnian wine; ... in the food she mixed ...'

11 This scene is older than the Iliad (West 1998: 190–191).

519 *πρῶτα μελικρήτῳ, μετέπειτα δὲ ἡδέι οἴνῳ,*
'first with **honey**-milk, thereafter with sweet wine'

520 *τὸ τρίτον αὖθ' ὕδατι: ἐπὶ δ' ἄλφιτα λευκὰ παλύνειν.*
'thirdly with water, and sprinkle thereon **white barley** meal'

525 *παμμέλαν', ὅς μήλοισι μεταπρέπει ὑμετέροισιν.*
'a ram, wholly **black** …'

527 *ἔνθ' ὄιν ἀρνειὸν ῥέζειν θῆλύν τε μέλαιναν*
'sacrifice a young ram and a **black** ewe'

c. Homer's Hymn to Demeter, 206–208:

206 *τῇ δὲ δέπας Μετάνειρα δίδου μελιηδέος οἴνου*
207 *πλήσασ': ἡ δ' ἀνένευσ': οὐ γὰρ θεμιτόν οἱ ἔφασκε*
208 *πίνειν οἶνον ἐρυθρόν: ἄνωγε δ' ἄρ' ἄλφι καὶ ὕδωρ*
209 *δοῦναι μίξασαν πιέμεν γλήχωνι τερείνῃ.*
'Then Metaneira filled a cup with **honey-sweet wine**
and offered it to her; but she refused it, for she said it was not lawful for her
to drink **red wine**, but bade them mix **barley meal and water**
with soft mint and give her to drink.'

In Classical Persian, there was nonetheless a dichotomic relationship between a dark and white barley liquid in ritual contexts. Here, *kašk* signifies a kind of bread or curded milk, specifically mixed with or made from barley and most often fermented (first attested in Ferdowsi's *Shahnameh* from about 1000 AD; Aubaile-Sallenave 2012, retrieved from the online version 14 September 2017):

'white barley liquid'	'dark barley liquid'
kašk-e sefid	*kašk-e siāh*'[12]

The importance of distinguishing white and dark barley in a ritual context provides a good motivation for interpreting a loanword **albʰ-* 'barley' as connected to (or identical to) the domestic post-laryngeal **albʰ-* 'white', especially since

12 Pahlavi *ārd ī kaškēn* 'barley flour' has been borrowed into Armenian *kaškēn* 'barley bread' which may provide a parallel for Lat. *sibitillus*. It should be noted that Pers. *kašk* is unrelated to Gk. *κυκεών*.

**mél-it-* 'honey' which must have been associated with **mel-* 'dark' is used in the recipe for Kykeon.[13] From there, applying the same stem-formation, however rare, is only a small step.

7 PIE **-it* and Tocharian B *yap*

The above analysis leaves PIE **mélit* 'honey' as the only member of its stem-class. That the protolanguage possessed a suffix **-it* for 'foodstuffs' is thus highly dubitable. Instead, **-t* should be analyzed as a separate morphological element which could be added to different kinds of stems, in this case an original *i*-stem, thus **mél-i-t* 'honey'; and in a parallel fashion, e.g., **ál-u-t* 'beer' and **ĝlak-t* 'milk'. Olsen (1999: 169) categorizes **mélit* as a neutral *i/n*-stem with a supplementary **-t* in the nom.acc.sg. like **(h)i̯ékʷr̥-t* 'liver'. The genitive of **mél-i-t* would then have been **melnós* as reflected in Lat. *mellis*, not **mel-it-os*.

Pinault (2008: 371) explains Toch. B *yap* 'barley' (not 'millet', cf. Ching 2013 and Pinault 2017: 133, fn. 16) from **i̯éu̯-it*, remade from the original **i̯éu̯-om* on the model of **álbʰ-it* etc. According to Pinault, *yap* would count as a fourth noun of this type, constituting additional evidence for a suffix **-it*, even if not original in PIE. However, as pointed out to me by Michael Weiss (pers. comm., 25 Feb 2018), Toch B *yap* may just as well continue an inherited *i*-stem. Assuming the latter formation would in fact allow us to explain the otherwise obscure Gk. *ζεί-δωρος* 'grain-giving', an epithet of the earth.[14]

---

13 Remarkably in this context, a drink called *medos*, probably mead (i.e. made of honey, and in that case likely to be borrowed from some Indo-European language), and another drink called *kamon*, made of barley, are among only three Hunnic common nouns handed down to us from contemporary authors (the third being *strava* 'a kind of feast', perhaps from a Slavic word for 'food'); cf. Pronk-Tiethoff 2013: 58. It is conceivable that *kamon* was borrowed from Indo-European, too, and in that case, a definite contender is some cognate of the etymologically disputed Gk. *κῶμος* 'festival, often specifically to honor Dionysos'; cf. that Dionysos plays a significant role in the Eleusinian mysteries where barley drinks are of ritual importance (Riu 1999: 107; see also Charney 2005, vol. 2: 364–365).

14 In Weiss' current view, **i̯o/eu̯i-* (with reflexes in Greek and Tocharian B) and **i̯éu̯-o-m* (continued in Hittite) are two different substantivizations of an original deverbal adjective **i̯eu̯ó-* 'growing' *vel sim.*

8 Concluding Remarks

I venture to conclude that Hitt. *šeppit*(*t*)- is most likely a loan from Akkadian or another Semitic language, and that both the reconstructed lexeme **sép-it* and the suffix **-it* for 'foodstuffs' can be characterized as a phantom. PIE **mél-i-t* 'honey' rather constitutes its own subgroup of *-i-/-n-*heteroclitics. Balkan Indo-European **álbʰ-it* 'barley' is based on a loan from Turkic **arpa* 'barley', which is also the ultimate source of Iranian **arpucya-*, but acquired its ending from **mél-it* 'honey' because the two roots were interpreted as **albʰ-* 'white' and **mel-* 'black' respectively. Finally, Toch. B *yap* can easily reflect the same plain *i*-stem which we find (with divergent ablaut) in Gk. *ζεί-δωρος* 'grain-giving'.

There is thus no evidence for a term specifically meaning 'wheat' from Proto-Indo-European times. This is compatible with the fact that wheat seems to have been domesticated only by cultures that can be connected with speakers of Western Indo-European (such as Sredniy Stog; Michael Weiss, pers. comm.) but not by cultures on the Caspian steppe further to the East. It should, however, be noted that a very important crop may simply be designated with the generic term for 'grain' or 'crop', in this case **i̯éu̯om* (cf. also Tocharian B *ysāre* 'wheat' vs. Toch. A *wsār* 'heap of grain'; Ivanov 2003: 190).

The conclusions drawn here do not contradict Watkins' important observation that the sequence (1) WHEAT + (2) BARLEY makes up a PIE phrase as seen in

> Gk. *πυροὶ καὶ κριθαί*
> Hitt. *šeppit euwann-a=*
> Ved. *vrīhír yávaś ca* 'rice and barley'

—nor does it of course contradict any other evidence for Proto-Indo-European cereal rituals. But we can no longer be sure that the first cereal mentioned in the above formula was originally wheat (*pace* Mallory & Adams 2006: 170).

References

Aubaile-Sallenave, Françoise. 2012. Kašk. *Encyclopedia Iranica* 16(1). 70–74.

Bailey, Harold Walter. 1979. *Dictionary of Khotan Saka*. Cambridge: Cambridge University Press.

Blažek, Václav. 2017. On Indo-European 'barley'. In Bjarne Simmelkjær Sandgaard Hansen, Benedicte Nielsen Whitehead, Thomas Olander & Birgit Anette Olsen (eds.),

Etymology and the European lexicon. Proceedings of the 14th Fachtagung der Indogermanischen Gesellschaft, 17–22 September 2012, Copenhagen, 53–67. Wiesbaden: Reichert.

Campbell, Lyle. 1998. Nostratic: A personal assessment. In Brian Joseph & Joe Salmons (eds.), *Nostratic: Sifting the evidence*, 107–152. Amsterdam: Benjamins.

Charney, Maurice. 2005. *Comedy. A geographic and historical guide.* Westport, CT: Greenwood.

Ching Chao-jung. 2016. On the names of cereals in Tocharian B. *Tocharian and Indo-European Studies* 17. 29–64.

Clackson, James. 2017. Contamination and blending in Armenian etymology. In Bjarne Simmelkjær Sandgaard Hansen, Adam Hyllested, Anders Richardt Jørgensen, Guus Kroonen, Jenny Helena Larsson, Benedicte Nielsen Whitehead, Thomas Olander & Tobias Mosbæk Søborg (eds.): *Usque ad radices: Indo-European studies in honour of Birgit Anette Olsen*, 99–115. Copenhagen: Museum Tusculanum.

Dalby, Andrew, & Sally Grainger. 1996. *The classical cookbook*. London: British Museum Press.

Fortson, Benjamin W., IV. 2005. *Indo-European language and culture: An introduction.* 2nd ed., 2010. Malden, MA, Oxford & Carlton: Blackwell.

Hyllested, Adam. 2011. Stealing the thunder of *alpaš*: The fate of PIE *-*bʰo*- in Anatolian. Paper read at the colloquium of the Indogermanische Gesellschaft "Das Nomen im Indogermanischen", Erlangen, 15 September 2011.

Hyllested, Adam. 2016. European terms for 'oats', 'barley' and 'millet' in the light of Central Asiatic evidence. Paper read at the workshop "The language of the first farmers" at the 49th Annual Meeting of the Societas Linguistica Europaea, Naples, 3 September 2016.

Ivanov, Vyacheslav V. 2003. On the origin of Tocharian terms for GRAIN. In Brigitte L.M. Bauer & Georges-Jean Pinault (eds.), *Language in time and space, a festschrift for Werner Winter on the occasion of his 80th birthday*, 189–210. Berlin & New York: Mouton de Gruyter.

Jokl, Norbert. 1926. Griechisch-albanische Studien. In *Festschrift für Universitäts-Professor Hofrat Dr. Paul Kretschmer: Beiträge zur griechischen und lateinischen Sprachforschung*, 78–95. Vienna & New York: Deutscher Verlag für Jugend und Volk.

Joseph, Brian. 2017. Expanding the methodology of lexical examination in the investigation of the intersection of early agriculture and language dispersal. In Martine Robbeets & Alexander Savelyev (eds.), *Language dispersal beyond farming*, 259–274. Amsterdam & Philadelphia: Benjamins.

Kloekhorst, Alwin. 2008. *Etymological dictionary of the Hittite inherited lexicon.* Leiden & Boston: Brill.

Knüppel, Michael. 2002. Zur Herkunft von Uigurisch *aram* ~ *ram*. *Ural-Altaische Jahrbücher* 17. 156–163.

Kümmel, Martin J. 2017. Agricultural terms in Indo-Iranian. In Martine Robbeets & Alexander Savelyev (eds.), *Language dispersal beyond farming*, 275–290. Amsterdam & Philadelphia: Benjamins.

Mallory, James P., & Douglas Q. Adams. 2006. *The Oxford introduction to Proto-Indo-European and the Proto-Indo-European world.* Oxford: Oxford University Press.

Manzelli, Gianguido. 2013. Il nome di Árpád nell'onomastica antico ungherese: "granellino d'orzo" oppure "orzaiolo"? In Giulio Paulis & Immacolata Pinto (eds.). *Etimologia fra testi e culture*, 39–105. Milano: FrancoAngeli.

Oettinger, Norbert. 2017. Die Wechsel -*Ø*/*n*- und -*i*/*n*- im Rahmen der indogermanischen Heteroklisie. In Bjarne Simmelkjær Sandgaard Hansen, Benedicte Nielsen Whitehead, Thomas Olander & Birgit Anette Olsen (eds.), *Etymology and the European Lexicon. Proceedings of the 14th Fachtagung der Indogermanischen Gesellschaft, 17–22 September 2012, Copenhagen*, 319–326. Wiesbaden: Reichert.

Olsen, Birgit Anette. 1999. *The noun in Biblical Armenian.* Berlin & New York: Mouton de Gruyter.

Pinault, Georges-Jean. 2008. *Chrestomathie tokharienne: Textes et grammaire.* Leuven & Paris: Peeters.

Pinault, Georges-Jean. 2017. Current issues in Tocharian etymology and phonology. *Tocharian and Indo-European Studies* 18. 127–164.

Pritsak, Omeljan. 1955. *Die bulgarische Fürstenliste und die Sprache der Protobulgaren.* Wiesbaden: Harassowitz.

Pritsak, Omeljan. 1982. The Hunnic language of the Attila clan. *Harvard Ukrainian Studies 1982*. 428–476.

Pronk-Tiethoff, Saskia. 2013. *The Germanic loanwords in Proto-Slavic.* Amsterdam: Rodopi.

Rédei, Károly. 1988. *Uralisches etymologisches Wörterbuch.* Budapest: Akadémiai Kiadó.

Rieken, Elisabeth. 1999. *Untersuchungen zur nominalen Stammbildung des Hethitischen.* Wiesbaden: Harrasowitz.

Rinella, Michael A. 2010. *Pharmakon: Plato, drug culture, and identity in ancient Athens.* Lanham, ML: Rowman & Littlefield.

Riu, Xavier. 1999. *Dionysism and comedy.* Lanham, ML: Rowman & Littlefield.

Robbeets, Martine. 2017. Proto-Trans-Eurasian: Where and when? *Man in India* 97(1). 19–46.

Sallares, Roberto. 1991. *The ecology of the ancient Greek world.* Ithaca: Cornell University Press.

Schmidt, Klaus T. 2002. Beobachtungen zur tocharischen Landschaftsterminologie. *Die Sprache* 41(1). 1–23.

Sevelyev, Alexander. 2017. Farming-related terms in Proto-Turkic and Proto-Altaic. In Martine Robbeets & Alexander Savelyev (eds.), *Language dispersal beyond farming*, 123–154. Amsterdam & Philadelphia: Benjamins.

Stachowski, Kamil. 2008. *Names of cereals in the Turkic languages*. Kraków: Księgarnia Akademicka.

Vasmer, Max. 1921. *Studien zur albanesischen Wortforschung*. Dorpat: Universität Derpt.

Watkins, Calvert. 1978. "Let us now praise famous grains". *Proceedings of the American Philosophical Society* 122(1). 9–17.

Watkins, Calvert. 1998. Proto-Indo-European: Comparison and reconstruction. In Paolo Ramat & Anna Giacalone Ramat (eds.), *The Indo-European languages*, 25–73. London & New York: Routledge. English version of "Il proto-indoeuropeo: Comparazione e ricostruzione", in *Le lingue indoeuropee*, Bologna: il Mulino, 1993, pp. 45–93. (2nd ed., 1997.)

West, Martin L. 1998: Grated cheese fit for heroes. *Journal of Hellenic Studies* 118. 190–191.

Witczak, Krzysztof T. 2003. *Indoeuropejskie nazwy zbóż*. Łódź: Wydawnictwo Uniwersytetu Łódźkiego.

Yakubovich, Ilya. 2008. The Luvian enemy. *Kadmos* 47. 1–19.

CHAPTER 6

And Now for Something Completely Different? Interrogating Culture and Social Change in Early Indo-European Studies

James A. Johnson

Recent developments in genetic (and isotopic) analyses of ancient human and animal remains have led to broad-scale reconsiderations of social change and mobility in archaeology and historical linguistics, along with culture as a bounded totality that expands and contracts even as it is reduced to homogeneity. Even the relatively few genetic studies conducted to this point strongly indicate ancestral admixture of ancient human populations, as well as varying scales and degrees of movement over time (Allentoft et al. 2015; Eisenmann et al. 2018; Haak et al. 2015; among others). More important (and problematic) for this chapter, is that the results of these recent genetic studies are typically (and conventionally) used to infer a different scale of population migrations; population migrations are too often equated with the movement of archaeological cultures.

As a result, there are a number of critiques levelled at how archaeologists make use of genetics. Most recently, Volker Heyd (2017) suggested we need to think carefully about the complex archaeological situation before us. Alexander Gramsch (2015) stated that we must rethink the concepts of culture and cultural change in light of the new genetic evidence. Before Heyd and Gramsch, Ben Roberts and Marc Vander Linden (2011: 6) pointed out:

> As demonstrated by research exploring the proposed global dispersal of languages and peoples through the spread of agriculture, there is immense potential in such collaborative projects; yet, there remains a very real need to be cautious in making assumptions concerning archaeological cultures.

1 Introduction

These cautions revolve around conceptualizations of culture as spatially-realized socio-economic entities who express their identity through shared styles

 | DOI:10.1163/9789004416192_008

of material goods such as pottery or lithics and sometimes other practices (burials, etc). This linking of spatial distributions and style of material practices with ethnicity, ultimately derived from Gustaf Kossinna (1911), is still commonly used by many archaeologists focused on prehistoric Europe and/or the Eurasian steppe, particularly those studying early Indo-European language speakers (Anthony 2007; Anthony and Ringe 2015; Heyd 2017; Kristiansen et al. 2017; Kuz'mina 2007; among many others). These purported linkages typically overlook variation between social groups comprising "cultures", even as archaeologists, as Heyd (2017: 348–349) notes, provide relatively few samples for genetic studies that in turn are used to issue proclamations about large-scale migrations and culture change.

As John Barrett (2004: 12) suggested, this may be because archaeologists are usually stuck on the idea that we are uniquely equipped to investigate broad-scale social phenomena and change. Yet, human social action, be it past or present, does not happen at a "single temporal scale" (ibid.), but rather is immersed in an admixture of asymmetrical temporal (past, present, and future) and spatial considerations (Geertz 1973; Johnson 2016, forthcoming; Touraine 1977). The problems with "archaeological culture" then are its conceptualization and application as a social totality fixed in space and time and not easily susceptible to change except as culture replacement. More troubling than its totalizing and fixed conception is culture's conflation with genetic identity. This despite the decades of ethnographic and archaeological research which suggests that culture is not genetically or biologically based. In this paper, I interrogate and dismantle culture as a socio-biological totality to better explore the theoretical and methodological possibilities for how ancient communities undertook social action, including change, and experienced socio-demographic breakdown and relocation. The ultimate goal is to find a better way to link human sociality and genetics; one that recognizes the inherently complex nature of culture through a critical, albeit brief, review of how culture is conceptualized and used anthropologically, while affirming the biological/genetic reality of people. Before I do this, however, I take a look at the presumed and (still) problematic relationships between culture, genetics, and archaeology.

2 Interrogating Archaeological Cultures as Socio-Biological Totalities

In a recent article, Eisenmann et al. (2018: 2) proposed, following a discussion of how genetic clusters are labelled in Haak et al. (2015) and other publications, a "mixed" system of classifications based on: (1) geography; (2) time period; (3)

geography and subsistence strategy; and (4) archaeological culture. Their suggestion is to combine at least two of these archaeogenetic groupings for the sake of brevity, coherence, accessibility, and stability. While I would argue that a fifth benefit, comparability, is useful for these studies, there is a much deeper, more pervasive problem to be dealt with; one that these (and other) authors mention explicitly but leave uninterrogated. The problem is the compression and use of "culture" as a tightly-packed, socio-biological totality that can be tracked through space, time, and matter, but which may have no actual basis in prehistory. Indeed, Eisenmann et al. (2018: 6–7), in their explanations of a more cautious approach to the admixture of history and archaeology/ archaeology and genetics, state that:

> If and how the historical records about a certain group of people and the archaeological record are connected with each other needs again to be investigated on a case-by-case basis. If geneticists use names originating from the field of archaeology for genetic clusters, an inevitable byproduct is to transfer at least part of the name's archaeological meaning into the genetic study. Giving groups that have been identified through a completely different line of evidence—in this case material culture and genomics—the same or related names result in their conflation and the archaeological designations risk becoming reified in genetic terms (and vice versa).

I am particularly interested in their comment (not cited above) that even if there are patterns of relatedness between culture and genetics, this does not indicate that the "archaeological culture" in mind was a meaningful entity in the past, which "invites further reflection and investigation." Despite these accurate points and criticisms, the authors admit "we do not feel it is appropriate to abandon the practice of comparing a genetic cluster and an archaeological culture." Interestingly, this "feeling" seems to be shared by other archaeologists. Before Eisenmann et al. (2018), Gramsch (2015: 341) stated that there is little agreement as to what culture and social (or cultural) change are. I suggest that we extend this a bit farther to say that there is also little, if any, agreement on what culture and social change mean to each other. Even with this clear lack of agreement, Gramsch does not offer a critical engagement with culture, but rather focuses almost exclusively on cultural change and the various small prompts for change that have an impact on identity formation and quotidian practice. This is interesting, as I think the problems facing archaeologists, historical linguists, and geneticists are caught between these conceptual and analytical scales—between the inter-regional scale of populations and the micro-scale of daily practice. Ulf Hannerz (1992: 19) suggested that "micro and macro may be terms out of place when culture is held to be merely replicated uniformity" or what can be understood as homogeneity. Gramsch (2015: 345) stated that the normative concept of culture as the homogenous set of common sets of norms, traditions, values, and symbols shared by participants in that culture poses problems as there is deviancy in the mortuary practices of various cultures. His proposal then is that we accept that there are alternatives to the homogenizing concept of culture, where cultural change is driven by agentive social actions and transformations in daily routine, or what Bourdieu (1977) termed *habitus*, i.e., our predispositions to act in certain ways and their relationship with broader social structures. Gramsch's proposal is convincing and, indeed, appealing as it offers a more nuanced way to understand cultural change.

That said, "cultural change" is a misnomer. Culture is always changing, sometimes in noticeable ways and other times in ways that go unnoticed (thus culture is never actually homogeneous, nor necessarily stable or static). Even in her often-cited critique of culture, Lila Abu-Lughod (1991: 470; drawing upon Clifford Geertz 1973: 44) indicates something similar—culture is learned and changes. Yet, the repercussions of using the term "cultural change" goes beyond semantics; it reflects, if not reifies, how we conceptualize and use culture as a static entity; how social change is equated with rupture (and/or denouement); and the conflation, if not essentialization, of culture as a biological and/or genetic totality. Thus, refusals to engage with how we conceptualize culture or how and why it is conflated with biological entities, no matter the potential for correlation, i.e., that an individual of a certain ancestry may share cultural symbolic practices, norms, values, and traditions, perpetuates a "still", homogeneous, and totalizing nature for culture (and biology) that may have little basis in reality. Ultimately, this needs to be investigated and not assumed (Eisenmann et al. 2018: 8).

At issue here is less that there may be correlations between how culture is expressed in various ancestral groups, than illuminating and interrogating the persistent tendency to totalize human sociality, reducing it to identifiable and trackable forms, cultural or otherwise. Our engagements with materials and/or languages should not be automatically reduced (nor expanded) to measurable, if not predictable, societal or cultural phenomena that benefit the scientist and her/his endeavour while remaining at best empty of meaning for the lived worlds that are the focus of our studies and at worst outright stripping past lived worlds of meaning and its potency. Hannerz (1992: 3–4) sees culture as having two loci where cultural processes interrelate or flow through, between, and beyond these loci (and their situated public practices), with these flows (and ebbs) consisting of externalizations of meaning produced through the arrangement of these practices. Hannerz (ibid. 4) summarizes cultural flow as "even as you perceive structure, it is entirely dependent on ongoing process." If culture is a process, one that ebbs and flows, then its treatment as a fixed socio-biological totality needs to be rethought.

Rather than treating culture as an entity subject to scales of analysis for assessing meaning in similar and/or different contexts, i.e., the creating and reification of difference, social totalities should be engaged as contingent fields of sometimes potent and meaningful social relations between people, things, knowledge, and discourses. Sociologist Alain Touraine's (1977: 2–9) Marxian conceptualization of post-industrial society as an entity of changing social relations that is self-produced and reproduced from the historically rich and interrelated roles of experience and social action offers a useful, though still somewhat problematic, model. For Touraine (1977: 4; emphasis as in original):

> Human society possesses a capacity of symbolic creation by means of which, between a "situation" and social conduct, there occurs the formation of meaning, *a[n open] system of orientation of conduct* ... This distance that society places between itself and its activity, and this action by which it determines the categories of its practice, I term historicity. *Society is not what it is but what it makes itself be.*

The point in this chapter is not to advocate the study of the totality itself as a cohesive entity (as Touraine ends up doing), but rather to investigate how social relations between people and materials are intertwined with the social, economic, and political conditions in which they are found, and how meaning comes to be made and expressed, including those shared between language and materiality. Where I move beyond Touraine is to see meaning as it relates to cultural ebbs and flows as caught up in different modes (and moments) of historical expression and signification, be they based in material or language. Methodologically, culture cannot, or at the very least should not, be reduced or essentialized to a few material items, settlement designs, or burial practices. As I see it the totalizing concept of culture as a spatially and socially delineated unit reifies assumed links between (equally problematic) notions of race, ethnicity, and material things, without addressing the externalization or expression of meaning. Totalities generally avoid or deny more active, if not agentive, roles for the tensions between emplacement and potential movements of people, places, things, and knowledge/practices. What I mean here is that by myopically focusing on, if not outright creating and highlighting, perceived emplaced similarities we may be: (1) assuming correlations between material culture use and genetic ancestry; (2) creating patterns where none exist; and/or (3) reifying alleged patterns instead of drawing attention to equally important, and informative, (mobile, moveable, or moved) processes and practices, not to mention their ebbs, flows, and historicities. Indeed, by totalizing social and biological entities, we reduce or essentialize their capacity for change as absolute, usually interpreted as rupture, replacement, or denouement. This denies the possibility that social actions associated with culture-as-process or -flow may change at different tempos than biological change, or that forms of sociality may continue even as populations experience genetic flow (or drift). These possibilities are crucial when exploring social breakdown in communities, and the potential for change and/or continuity in social practices.

3 Rethinking Social Breakdown as Denouement: An Archaeogenetic Epistemology

In a recent publication, I highlighted the fact that Eurasian prehistory is steeped in culture history and, as such, social change is too often treated as a form of rupture, *sensu* Dawdy (2010) (Johnson 2016: 61). I proposed that archaeologists consider the relationality of multiple temporalities in prehistoric Eurasian social action. As I finished that piece, I started to think about what it meant theoretically and methodologically to treat "culture" as a social totality, and in turn, what that meant for considerations of social change. With the recent influx of archaeo-genetic and -linguistic studies, such considerations have become increasingly important. The above section highlights some recent thoughts on this. In terms of what this volume is about—the split of the early Indo-European language families—reassessing social change and breakdown is highly relevant as archaeologically and genetically (maybe linguistically), the factors involved are usually assumed to be isolated and subsequently, monolithic rather than multivalent.

Genetically, social change is usually determined through the analysis of data gathered from the genome, or the sum total of an organism's DNA, and reduced to the presence of certain haplogroups. Undoubtedly, the ability to collect and analyze genome-wide data has transformed our approaches to prehistory. Without going into the specifics of aDNA data collection and analysis, as covered in Kaestle and Horsburgh (2002), Haak et al. 2015, and Allentoft et al (2015), aDNA studies have allowed some insights into the nature of "population transformation in Europe" (Haak et al. 2015: 1). For the sake of brevity, I use Haak et al. (2015) as my primary example when discussing socio-demographic change, as well as the conflation of culture and biology, as I believe it to be representative of the recent slate of archaeo- and linguistic-genetic studies. In Haak et al. (ibid.) there are sustained discussions of population transformations or turnovers, i.e., rupture or replacement, even as the authors indicate that for the Middle Neolithic in Europe, there was an increase in WHG (western European hunter-gatherers) ancestry, whereas in Russia there appears to have been a decrease in EHG (eastern European hunter-gatherers) ancestry (Haak et al. ibid. 2). Even more important for this chapter, is that Haak et al. (ibid.) suggest that "the Yamnaya" have ancestry derived from the Caucasus and South Asia, with this collective ancestry appearing in Central Europe, with the "Corded Ware" culture, around 2500 BC (ibid.).

While admitting that there were increases and decreases in ancestry among these prehistoric populations, Haak et al. (ibid. 3) suggest an "inferred degree of population turnover" or that "Corded Ware [people] who were formed by a mixture of Yamnaya and Middle Neolithic Europeans", this despite the fact that "the Yamnaya individuals sampled may not be directly ancestral to the Corded Ware individuals from Germany." In the supplementary information section (found only online), the authors state that the Yamnaya cultural complex, dated to around 3300 BC, actually consists of at least six regional groups or variants, which have at least two to four chronological phases (ibid. 28). Furthermore, the authors list the following "unifying" traits for the Yamnaya: (1) mobile pastoral economy; (2) new metallurgical practices (and techniques); (3) copper mining; (4) nearly exclusive burial of adult males (around 80% of those excavated); burial of wheels or wagons; deposition in burials of animal remains; and the use of stone stelae (in the Ukrainian/ Pontic steppe). As Anthony (2007: 303) has noted, there are few Yamnaya settlements known west of the Don River and none known of east of the Don. One is left with questions regarding the degree of homogeneity for the geographic distribution of Yamnaya populations.

What is abundantly clear is that early Bronze Age populations, commonly referred to as the Yamnaya cultural complex, underwent social change as they became increasingly mobile and, subsequently, geographically dispersed. However, with the presence of numerous distinct variants of the Yamnaya cultural complex, with two of the most obvious consisting of east of the Don and the other west of the Don, we might think of these variants as social groups that participated differently in a shared cultural process—one based at least initially on mobility and herding. David Anthony (2007: 304) suggested that beyond differences in lifestyle via the presence/absence of settlements, there is also a notable difference in the use and possible consumption of grains where in the west there is significant evidence for this, while east of the Don there is no evidence for reliance on grains. There seems to be sufficient evidence to demonstrate that the boundaries drawn to delimit (and totalize) the Yamnaya cultural area are poorly equipped to illustrate the variations in lifestyle, and indeed impose a sense of cultural homogeneity that borders on misleading for non-specialists. Even more so, and in the absence of systematic sampling and testing, there seems reason for skepticism regarding any claim of shared genetic ancestry among the Yamnaya variants.

The end of the Yamnaya cultural period, dated to *c.* 2200 cal BC (Koryakova and Epimakhov 2007: 52), saw many customs and traditions continue on into the Poltavka, Abashevo, and Sintashta periods, *c.* post-2200 BC to approximately 1700 BC, along with the emergence of new technologies, traditions, and customs, including the making and use of the chariot. In the supplementary information of Allentoft et al. (2015: 5), the Sintashta "culture" is listed as not archaeologically recognizable in terms of their origin. Genetically, however, the authors of this study highlight that there is a strong affinity between Corded Ware and Sintashta given that the individuals sampled and tested from each "culture" probably shared a genetic source since both have evidence of Neolithic farming ancestry, though they demonstrate stronger admixture of Mesolithic hunter-gatherer and Bronze Age steppe sources (Allentoft et al. 2015: 169). Interestingly, there is an even stronger affinity with what came afterwards—the Andronovo family of cultures. This is not surprising because what is at issue here is not colonization as is suggested in the supplementary materials (ibid. 5), but rather community breakdown by 1800/1700 BC, accompanied or followed by population dispersal (Johnson 2014, 2016; Sharapov 2017), which fits better with what we know of the genetic affinity between the Sintashta and later social groups. Given the evidence collected in the Uy River valley regarding this phenomenon, what came after the Sintashta period included both social change *and* continuity; of communities adopting a more mobile lifestyle even as populations relocated, built new settlements, and revived Sintashta-period socio-technological practices such as pottery traditions and chariot construction, while avoiding some original Sintashta-period settlements (Johnson 2016, forthcoming). What is evident from these archaeogenetic studies is that there are different kinds of social and biological action going on and that we need to develop better understandings of how social action, including change and continuity, are potentially and contingently related to human biology and/or genetic ancestry.

4 Conclusions: On Babies and Bandwagons—Theoretical and Methodological Musings

In the previous sections, I argued that culture, as a form of historically conditioned sociality or historicity, should not be conflated with genetic identity, i.e., haplogroups, and that the two even if used separately should not be totalized or essentialized—that what we see is all we need to see to understand human social action in prehistory. For the articles addressed in this chapter, I sought to highlight the dual nature of human social action (the co-presence of change *and* continuity) and culture, as used in social anthropology for over 30 years, and what this might mean for our use of terms like cultural change, cultural transformation, and population replacement or turnover. In essence, I argue for jettisoning *either/or* scenarios for more productive *and/and* scenarios (Johnson, forthcoming).

With this in mind, there are clear methodological implications for such scenarios. First of all, there is the matter of representation and scale. Drawing upon Bas Van Fraassen's (2008: 13–14) *Scientific Representation*, I pose the following questions: Have we separated resemblance from representation? How have our representations of culture and genetic groupings become distorted, if not conflated (with distortion considered as a departure from resemblance)? A logical starting point regarding representativeness is questioning if 69 individuals as found in Haak et al. (2015) or 101 individuals as found in Allentoft et al. (2015) can truly be representative of numerous prehistoric social groups, or "cultures"? Statistically speaking, the answer is a fairly emphatic no. Haak et al. (2015: 1 and methods section—pg. 2, respectively) state in the second sentence of the article:

> Realizing its (genome-wide analysis of ancient DNA) promise, however, requires collecting genome-wide data from an adequate number of individuals to characterize population changes over time, which means not only sampling a succession of archaeological cultures, but also multiple individuals per culture.
>
> **Sample Size.** No statistical methods were used to predetermine sample size.

If human populations of the geographic areas in question are not all being tested, then sampling (of one strategy or another) is absolutely crucial, as without it we can never be certain that the samples (individuals in this case) accurately represent the population under study (Drennan 2010: 85). Robert Drennan (ibid.) explores the notion and use of random sampling in archaeology, which he suggests some archaeologists misuse as they think that the use of random sampling guarantees accuracy in representativeness. Drennan states that while there is no guarantee, it is "our best chance at a representative sample." Furthermore, and I will quote him directly here as it is both his and my main point (italics in original): *"Most important of all, random sampling provides a basis for estimating how likely it is that our inferences about the population are wrong, and thus tells us how much confidence we should place in those inferences."*

In other words, our sampling strategies should be more rigorous and transparent. Instead of studies exploring the relationship between genetic populations, we should also discuss how confident we can be that the results are not due to the vagaries of sampling (Drennan 201: 151). For instance, given the nature of data collection for both Haak et al. (2015) and Allentoft et al. (2015), we cannot be certain that their results are not due to individuals chosen from various projects that were already determined to have connections—be they social or biological—to their ancestral populations. To put it another way, we might be answering questions that we already know the answers to. Whether this is true or not is impossible for the readers of these studies to determine, as there is no sampling strategy presented for either the genetic studies nor for the sampling of local or regional populations by archaeologists. What is suggested here then is that: (1) sampling strategies be undertaken by the archaeologists providing the individuals for analysis and (2) the geneticists need to determine sample size to provide representative accuracy. Until this happens, and given our data are derived from the level of the individual or small group (though again we don't know how or why such a group of individuals was submitted for analysis), we must seriously question representativeness and the idea of cultural replacement, population turnover, or even large-scale migration. In the current state of the field, we would do better not to over-interpret, as pointed out by Eske Willerslev at a recent inter-disciplinary workshop on the archaeology, genetics, and languages of the Indo-Europeans hosted by Kristian Kristensen and Guus Kroonen at the University of Gothenburg.

Along with the adoption of more rigorous sampling strategies for individuals submitted for genetic testing, we might use more carefully chosen and standardized nomenclature for identifying both social and biological groups in the past. I know we have all felt the push to jump on the bandwagon and publish these wide-reaching studies. But caution needs to be exercised in terms of questioning what we are comparing, how these things might be correlated, and establishing nomenclature that can be used widely. Eisenmann et al. (2018) offers just such a standardized set of references, though I would strongly suggest the designations of archaeological culture be abandoned when discussing genetic groupings and focus specifically on geographic region, time periodization, and economic base (agrarian, hunter-gatherer, pastoralist) when known. This can then be compared to the stylistic groupings of material culture often used to archaeologically identify "culture". At the same time, however, we might pay closer attention to Gramsch's (2015) suggestions of changes in daily practice and identity formation, though I would add the possibility for continuation even in the face of widespread changes such as social breakdown or disintegration. Finally, even though Heyd (2017) suggests that we might provoke a smile from Kossinna due to our turn back to "archaeological cultures", "ethnic identity", and large-scale migrations, I'd like to suggest we might be better off provoking a grimace from the spirit of Kossinna by more thoroughly interrogating and investigating the relationality of these concepts, their relationship with genetics, and undertaking more theoretically rigorous and methodologically transparent studies.

Acknowledgements

As so often seems to be the case when I write, I need to thank the editors, Matilde and Thomas, for their patience as I wrote and rewrote this chapter. I'd also like to thank the Roots of Europe program and the Department of Nordic Studies and Linguistics, both at the University of Copenhagen, where I was a postdoctoral scholar between 2016–2018. Finally, I need to thank the National Science Foundation and the Sintashta Collaborative Archaeological Research Project for the opportunity to conduct my fieldwork in the Uy River valley in the southern Urals region between 2009–2011.

References

Abu-Lughod, Lila. 1991. Writing against culture. In *Recapturing Anthropology: Working in the Present*, edited by Richard Fox, pp. 137–154. Santa Fe: School of American Research Press.

Allentoft, Morten E., Martin Sikora, Karl-Göran Sjögren, Simon Rasmussen, Morten Rasmussen, Jesper Stenderup, Peter B. Damgaard et al. 2015. Population genomics of Bronze Age Eurasia. *Nature* 522. 167–172. doi:10.1038/nature14507

Anthony, David W. 2007. *The Horse, the wheel, and language: How Bronze-Age riders from the Eurasian steppes shaped the modern world.* Princeton: Princeton University Press.

Anthony, David W., & Don Ringe. 2015. The Indo-European homeland from linguistic and archaeological perspectives. *Annual Review of Linguistics* 1. 199–219.

Barrett, John. 2004. Temporality and the study of prehistory. In Ralph Rosen (ed.), *Time and temporality in the ancient world*, 1–27. Philadelphia: University of Pennsylvania Museum of Archaeology and Anthropology.

Bourdieu, Pierre. 1977. *Outline of a theory of practice*. Cambridge: Cambridge University Press.

Dawdy, Shannon. 2010. Clockpunk anthropology and the ruins of modernity. *Current Anthropology* 51(6). 761–793.

Drennan, Robert. 2010. *Statistics for archaeologists: A common sense approach*. New York: Springer.

Eisenmann, Stefanie, Eszter Banffy, Peter van Dommelen, Kerstin Hofman, Joseph Maran, Iosif Lazaridis, Alissa Mittnik et al. 2018. Reconciling material cultures in archaeology with genetic data: The nomenclature of clusters emerging from archaeogenomic analysis. *Scientific Reports* 8. 1–12.

Geertz, Clifford. 1973. *The interpretation of cultures: Selected essays*. New York: Basic Books.

Gramsch, Alexander. 2015. Culture, change, identity—approaches to the interpretation of cultural change. *Anthropologie* 53(3). 341–349.

Haak, Wolfgang, I. Lazaridis, N. Patterson, N. Rohland, S. Mallick, B. Llamas, G. Brandt et al. 2015. Massive migration from the steppe was a source for Indo-European languages in Europe. *Nature* 522(7555): 207–211.

Hannerz, Ulf. 1992. *Cultural complexity: Studies in the social organization of meaning*. New York: Columbia University Press.

Heyd, Volker. 2017. *Kossinna's smile*. Antiquity 91(356). 348–359.

Johnson, James. 2014. Community matters? investigating social complexity through centralization and differentiation in Bronze Age pastoral societies of the Southern Urals, Russian Federation, 2100–900 BC. PhD Dissertation, Department of Anthropology, University of Pittsburgh.

Johnson, James. 2016. One eye forward, one eye back: Multiple temporalities, community, and social change in the culture history of the Southern Urals, Russian Federation (2100–1300 BC). In Kathryn Weber, Emma Hite, Lori Khatchadourian & Adam T. Smith (eds.), *Fitful histories and unruly publics: Rethinking temporality and community in Eurasian archaeology*, 56–79. Leiden: Brill.

Johnson, James. Forthcoming. Theorising "nomadic" betweenness: movement, contingency, and materiality in the pastoral societies of the Bronze Age Eurasian steppe. In Catriona Gibson, Kerri Cleary & Catherine Frieman (eds.), *Making journeys: Archaeologies of mobility*. Oxford: Oxbow Press.

Kaestle, Fredrika, & K. Ann Horsburgh. 2002. Ancient DNA in anthropology: Methods, applications, and ethics. *Yearbook of Physical Anthropology* 45. 92–130.

Koryakova, Ludmila, & Andrej Epimakhov. 2007. *The Urals and Western Siberia in the Bronze and Iron Ages*. Cambridge: Cambridge University Press.

Kossinna, Gustaf. 1911. *Die Herkunft der Germanen. Zur Methode der Siedlungsarchäologie.* Würzburg: Kabitzsch.

Kristiansen, Kristian, Morten E. Allentoft, Karin M. Frei, Rune Iversen, Niels N. Johannsen, Guus Kroonen, Łukasz Pospieszny et al. 2017. Re-theorising mobility and the formation of culture and language among the Corded Ware Culture in Europe. *Antiquity* 91. 334–347.

Kuz'mina, Elena. 2007. *The origin of the Indo-Europeans*. Leiden: Brill.

Roberts, Ben, & Marc Vander Linden. 2011. Investigating archaeological cultures: Material culture, variability, and transmission. In Ben Roberts & Marc Vander Linden (eds.), *Investigating archaeological cultures: Material culture, variability, and transmission*, 1–21. New York: Springer.

Sharapov, Denis. 2017. Bronze Age settlement patterns and the development of complex societies in the Southern Urals (3500–1400 BC). PhD Dissertation, Department of Anthropology, University of Pittsburgh.

Touraine, Alain. 1977. *The self-production of society*. Translated by Derek Coltman. Chicago: University of Chicago Press.

Van Fraassen, Bas. 2008. *Scientific representation.* Oxford: Oxford University Press.

CHAPTER 7

The Archaeology of Proto-Indo-European and Proto-Anatolian: Locating the Split

Kristian Kristiansen

1 Background

This is an archaeological investigation into the possible origin of Proto-Indo-Anatolian (PIA) and the first split into a non-Anatolian and an Anatolian branch. In historical linguistics it is generally accepted that Anatolian represents the oldest split, at a time when PIA was still in its early stage. Likewise, Tocharian represents the second and much later split (Anthony & Ringe 2015: Figure 2; Kortlandt 2018: 225). This second split can now be documented archaeologically and genetically, which may serve as a chronological and geographical boundary for locating the Anatolian split further back in time.

I start therefore with the archaeological, genetic, linguistic premise that Tocharian originally was brought east by the early Yamnaya migration from the western steppe directly to Altai (Kroonen, Barjamovic & Peyrot 2018: 10), there forming the Afanasievo Culture (Allentoft et al. 2015: Figure 1). It later expanded south towards Xinjang, where Tocharian is documented in written sources from the late 1st millennium AD (Li et al. 2015; Damgaard et al. 2018). This original Yamnaya migration to the east across the central steppe inhabited by Botai horse herders took place in the very beginning of the 3rd millennium BC, which implies that the Anatolian split should be placed well before that time, in the 4th millennium BC. Not least since we now know that Anatolian is documented in Near Eastern sources already around 2500 BC (Kroonen, Barjamovic & Peyrot 2018). Thus, Proto-Anatolian must be several hundred years older. These new findings correspond well with our premise that early Yamnaya groups in the western steppe already spoke a later version of PIE. The Yamnaya and later Corded Ware/Bell Beaker groups mostly belonged to the original *centum* group, while the slightly later Fatjanovo, and Abashevo groups to the north, between the Baltic Sea and the Urals, belonged to the *satem* group of pre-Baltic, before the Andronovo migrations into central Asia (Allentoft et al. 2015: Figure 1).

 | DOI:10.1163/9789004416192_009

2 Genetic Evidence

In addition to archaeological sources we now also have important genetic evidence from both the Caucasus and Anatolia from the Chalcolithic through the Bronze Age (Damgaard et al. 2018, Wang et al. 2018). From this we learn that Anatolian Bronze Age individuals, among them also some from a specifically Hittite settlement, harbored no steppe DNA. Instead they show admixture from Caucasian. As a Chalcolithic individual showed the same admixture we may assume that this admixture event or series of migratory events took place most likely during the 4th millennium BC. Recent genetic evidence from a 3000 year transect in the Caucasus revealed that during later prehistory this mountain ridge rather functioned as a bridge than a barrier (Wang et al. 2018). The genetic evidence clustered in two groups, termed "steppe" and "Caucasus". The characteristic "steppe" profile is a mixture of EHG and CHG/Iranian ancestry. The Caucasus genetic profile lasted from the Eneolithic until the Late Bronze Age, and is shared by groups belonging to both Maykop and Kura-Axes cultures. Interestingly, they also harbor Iranian Chalcolithic ancestry, which would seem to correspond to the cultural interaction zone leading to the formation of the Maykop culture at the transition between the 5th and 4th millennium BC. Also, the appearance of the "steppe" ancestry could be identified already during the Eneolithic in the Samara steppe.

We can thus observe genetic admixture processes between the Caucasus and Anatolia beginning in the Chalcolithic, and continuing into the early Bronze Age, similar to the transmission into the Caucasus and the Samara steppe of Caucasian/Iranian ancestry during the late 5th millennium BC. There existed a rather clear genetic borderline between Caucasus and steppe groups that had been established already during the Eneolithic. It would only be penetrated by the expansion of Maykop into the steppe during the later 4th millennium BC. It implies that the early "steppe" ancestry in Eneolithic Samara should come from another geographical region than the Caucasus.

3 Archaeological Evidence

How does that correspond to the archaeological evidence? Here the 4th millennium stands out as a period of large-scale interaction linked to the spread of innovations in metallurgy (copper tools and weapons) and transportation (wheel and wagon), both across the Caucasus from south to north and from north to south, and in a broad zone in the Black Sea region, including the Carpathians, the Balkans and the Aegean/Anatolia. This metallurgical koine was first identified by Evgeny Chernykh (summarized in 2008), and later detailed in works by Svend Hansen (2010 and 2014) and Lorenz Rahmstorf (2010; also Cultraro 2014 and 2016). As there is now genetic evidence of an early appearance of steppe ancestry in eastern Europe during this period (Mathieson et al. 2018), this would seem to confirm David Anthony's long held hypothesis of an early westward spread of Anatolian, which would enter Anatolia from the west (Anthony and Ringe 2015). However, with the new genetic evidence from Anatolia showing that there is no steppe admixture in individuals found in a Hittite context from the Chalcolithic through the Bronze Age, this hypothesis cannot be upheld. Rather the origin of Anatolian should be located in the Caucasus, at a time when it acted as a civilizational corridor between south and north.

Here the Maykop Culture of the northern Caucasus stands out as the most probable source for Proto-Anatolian, and perhaps even Proto-Indo-Anatolian (to be discussed below), as it encapsulated many of the traits/institutions that were later taken over by the Yamnaya Culture (Kohl & Trifonov 2014; Sagona 2017: Figure 4.1). This scenario is supported by a Maykop expansion into the steppe, forming the Steppe Maykop Culture (Rezepkin 2000; Chernykh 2008: Figure 5). It is far more difficult to pinpoint the southward influences into Anatolia except in more general terms (e.g. pottery types), and then they mostly follow a maritime route along the southern Black Sea coast (Bauer 2011). Recent evidence, however, suggests that Maykop kurgans also existed in the southern Caucasus (Lyonnet et al. 2008). Additionally, a break of continuity can be observed at Arslantepe around 3000 BC with the introduction of a Caucasian kurgan burial ritual of new elites, the so-called "royal kurgan" (Palumbi 2007). Thus, we may assume that earlier traditions were embraced by the Kura-Axes expansion, including southern Maykop.

The Maykop phenomenon with its rich burials and many imports from the south reflected influence from both the Uruk expansion (Pitskhelauri 2012) and Iran through a civilizational corridor stretching into Central Asia (Ivanova 2012). Mesopotamia and Anatolian city states such as Arslantepe needed the metals from the Caucasian mines (Frangipane 2017), some of which could have been controlled by Maykop and related groups. Shortly after, beginning in the mid 4th millennium BC, the southern Caucasus became the locus of the formation of the Kura-Axes Culture, which later expanded into eastern Anatolia and the Levant (Sagona 2017: Figure 5.1), although its early phase is debated (discussion Smith 2009). With a more Near Eastern-based village organization that concealed internal hierarchies (Stöllner 2016: Figure 1), it does not seem a likely candidate for Anatolian, but rather for Hurrian, even if we cannot exclude that this culture included more than one language group. Thus Kristiansen et al. 2018:

> The personal names borne by individuals coming from the state of Armi in southern Anatolia attested in the archives as early as the 25th century BCE at Ebla (Archi 2011; Bonechi 1990) constitute a mixture of Semitic, Anatolian IE, and unknown background (Kroonen et al. 2018). A possible interpretation is that multiple groups moved into Anatolia from the Caucasus during the late 4th and early 3rd millennia BCE, including groups of proto-Hurrian and early IE Anatolian speakers. Clear from the written record of Bronze Age Anatolia, however, is also that language was not considered an ethnic marker there and that the region is characterized by its high population mobility and plurality of languages and traditions.

Where does this take us with respect to the origin of Proto-Indo-European? In the words of Kroonen, Barjamovic & Peyrot (2018) (note that "Indo-Hittite" is synonymous with "Indo-Anatolian"):

> Since the onomastic evidence from Armi is contemporaneous with the Yamnaya culture (3000–2400 BCE), a scenario in which the Anatolian Indo-European language was linguistically derived from Indo-European speakers originating in this culture can be rejected. This important result offers new support for the Indo-Hittite Hypothesis, and strengthens the case for an Indo-Hittite-speaking ancestral population from which both Proto-Anatolian and residual Proto-Indo-European split off no later than the 4th millennium BCE.

As it stands the present evidence thus points towards the northern Caucasus as the cradle of Proto-Indo-Anatolian and Proto-Anatolian from where it diffused into Anatolia sometime during the 4th millennium BC. I cite from the conclusion of Kroonen, Barjamovic & Peyrot (2018):

> The period of Proto-Anatolian linguistic unity can now be placed in the 4th millennium BCE and may have been contemporaneous with e.g. the Maykop culture (3700–3000 BCE), which influenced the formation and apparent westward migration of the Yamnaya and maintained commercial and cultural contact with the Anatolian highlands (Kristiansen et al. 2018). Our findings corroborate the Indo-Anatolian Hypothesis, which claims that Anatolian Indo-European split off from Proto-Indo-European first and that Anatolian Indo-European represents a sister rather than a daughter language. Our findings call for the identification of the speakers of Proto-Indo-Anatolian as a population earlier than the Yamnaya and late Maykop cultures.

4 Conclusion: A Scenario for the Split

Let me therefore end with a possible scenario for the split from Maykop of Proto-Anatolian and slightly later Proto-Indo-European.

The *Proto-Anatolian split*: the early and middle Maykop Culture of the northern Caucasus, together with the Maykop of the southern Caucasus, represented an older Proto-Anatolian dialect before the invention of wheel and wagon. Groups from this culture moved south and west into Anatolia sometime during the early to mid 4th millennium BC. This movement was in all probability linked to the coastal regions of the Black Sea, with the Sinop province and Ikiztepe as an entry point into Anatolia (Bauer 2008 and 2011). It is therefore less visible than a land-based migration.[1] We may also hypothesize that the Kura-Araxes expansion of the mid to late 4th millennium BC unified several previous ethnic and linguistic groups under their umbrella. This, however, would only include eastern/central Anatolia. Around 3000 BC a "Royal Road" from the south Caucasus west through Anatolia towards northern Aegean can be observed (Cultraro 2016), which may account for the further westward expansion of Anatolian.

The *Proto-Indo-European split*: steppe Maykop groups introduced a superior cattle-based pastoral economy and transportation technology to the pre-Yamnaya groups living in the steppe in the mid to late 4th millennium BC. This is reflected in the earliest burials with nose rings to control the bulls, pairs of oxen in burials, while in the steppe the wagon is more often deposited (Reinholdt et al. 2017: Figure 8.7). Sabine Reinholdt and her team document and discuss this transmission of skills to the steppe environment that by the late 4th millennium BC led to the formation of the Yamnaya social formation. I suggest that this transmission also included a language transmission corresponding to the formation of Proto-Indo-European, as a sister language to Proto-Anatolian. Once the new economy and technology was adopted to the steppe environment it was followed by a fast demographic and geographic expansion, whose final manifestation was the Yamnaya Culture starting around 3000 BC. By this time the speakers of pre-Tocharian separated from the remaining groups.

This scenario implies that the mother language of both Proto-Indo-European and Proto-Indo-Anatolian should be pushed further back in time, perhaps into the mid to later 5th millennium. As stated in Wang et al. 2018: "Perceiving

1 The chronology of the cultural sequences has been redefined in recent years (originally proposed in Thissen 1993), suggesting that the Early Bronze Age cemetery starts around 3500 BC (Welton 2010). In her PhD thesis Welton defined two groups of non-locals: one coming in from long-distance, and another being linked to pastoral transhumance.

the Caucasus as an occasional bridge rather than a strict border during the Eneolithic and Bronze Age opens up the possibility of a homeland of PIE south of the Caucasus, which itself provides a parsimonious explanation for an early branching off of Anatolian languages." Here I would replace PIE with Proto-Indo-Anatolian, and I would locate it rather in the northern Caucasus, but with possible cultural links south of the Caucasus that did not have lasting linguistic effects.

Thus, the 4th millennium BC stands out as a period of increasing interaction between the Caucasus, Anatolia, the Levant and Greece, stimulated by movements of groups of people at land and sea, including the Black Sea coast (Bauer 2011), which had both genetic (Damgaard et al. 2018; Lazaridis et al. 2017; Wu et al. 2018), cultural and linguistic consequences, including Anatolian from the early to mid 4th millennium BC. After the middle of the 4th millennium steppe Maykop expanded north, leading to the formation of the Yamnaya Culture and Proto-Indo-European, which by the beginning of the 3rd millennium saw the development of ancient Tocharian and the first migrations towards the east/Altai and the west/Europe.

References

Allentoft, Morten E., Martin Sikora, Karl-Göran Sjögren, Simon Rasmussen, Morten Rasmussen, Jesper Stenderup, Peter B. Damgaard et al. 2015. Population genomics of Bronze Age Eurasia. *Nature* 522. 167–172. doi:10.1038/nature14507

Anthony, D., & D. Ringe. 2015. The Indo-European homeland from linguistic and archaeological perspectives. *Annual Review of Linguistics* 1. 199–219.

Bauer, A. 2008. Import, imitation or communication? Pottery style, technology and coastal contact in the Early Bronze Age Black Sea. In P.F. Biehl & Y.Y. Rassamakin (eds.), *Import and imitation in archaeology*, 89–104. Langenweißbach: Beier & Beran.

Bauer, A. 2011. The Near East, Europe and the "routes" of community in the Early Bronze Age Black Sea. In T.C. Wilkinson, S. Sherratt & J. Bennet (eds.), *Interweaving worlds. Systemic interactions, 7th to 1st millennia BC*, 175–188. Oxford & Oakville, CT: Oxbow.

Chernykh, E. 2008. The "Steppe Belt" of stockbreeding cultures in Eurasia during the Early Metal Age. *Trabajos de Prehistoria* 65(2). 73–93.

Cultraro, M. 2014. A Transcaucasian perspective: Searching for the Early Bronze Age North Aegean metallurgy. In M. Kvachadze, M. Puturidze, & N. Shanshashvili (eds.), *Problems of early Metal Age archaeology of Caucasus and Anatolia: Proceedings of International Conference*, 125–138. Tbilisi: Mtsignobari.

Cultraro, M. 2016. Undercurrents: Cultural interaction between Southern Caucasus and Northern Aegean during the Early and Middle Bronze Age. In M. Kvachadze

& N. Shanshashvili (eds.), *Aegean world and South Caucasus: Cultural relations in the Bronze Age. International Workshop, September 23–25, 2016*. Tbilisi: Mtsignobari.

Damgaard, Peter de Barros, Rui Martiniano, Jack Kamm, J. Víctor Moreno-Mayar, Guus Kroonen, Michaël Peyrot, Gojko Barjamovic et al. 2018. The first horse herders and the impact of Early Bronze Age steppe expansions into Asia. *Science*. doi:10.1126/science.aar7711

Frangipane, M. 2017. The role of metallurgy in different types of early hierarchical society in Mesopotamia and Eastern Anatolia. In J. Maran & P. Stockhammer (eds.), *Appropriating innovations. Entangled knowledge in Eurasia, 5000–1500 BCE*, 171–183. Oxford: Oxbow.

Hansen, S. 2010. Communication and exchange between the Northern Caucasus and Central Europe in the fourth millennium BC. In S. Hansen, A. Hauptmann, I. Motzenbäcker & E. Pernicka (eds.), *Von Maykop bis Trialeti. Gewinnung und Verbreitung von Metallen und Obsidian in Kaukasien im 4.–2. Jt. v. Chr.*, 297–316. Bonn: Habelt.

Hansen, S. 2014. The 4th millennium: A watershed in European prehistory. In B. Horejs & M. Mehofer (eds.), *Western Anatolia before Troy. Proto-urbanisation in the 4th millennium BC?*, 243–259. Vienna: Österreichische Akademie der Wissenschaften.

Ivanova, M. 2012. Kaukasus und Orient: Die Entstehung des "Maykop-Phänomens" im 4. Jahrtausend v. Chr. *Praehistorische Zeitschrift* 87(1). 1–28.

Kohl, P., & V. Trifonov. 2014. The prehistory of the Caucasus: Internal developments and external interactions. In C. Renfrew & P. Bahn (eds.), *The Cambridge world prehistory*, 1571–1595. New York: Cambridge University Press.

Kortlandt, F. 2018. The expansion of the Indo-European languages. *Journal of Indo-European Studies* 46(1–2). 219–231.

Kristiansen, K., Brian Hemphill, Gojko Barjamovic, Sachihiro Omura, Süleyman Yücel Senyurt, Vyacheslav Moiseyev, Andrey Gromov et al. 2018. Archaeological supplement A to Damgaard et al. 2018: Archaeology of the Caucasus, Anatolia, Central and South Asia 4000–1500 BCE. doi:10.5281/zenodo.1243933

Kroonen, G., G. Barjamovic & M. Peyrot. 2018. Linguistic supplement to Damgaard et al. 2018: Early Indo-European languages, Anatolian, Tocharian and Indo-Iranian. doi:10.5281/zenodo.1240523

Lazaridis, Iosif, Alissa Mittnik, Nick Patterson, Swapan Mallick, Nadin Rohland, Saskia Pfrengle, Anja Furtwängler et al. 2017. Genetic origin of the Minoans and Mycenaeans. *Nature* 548. 214–218. doi:10.1038/nature23310

Li, Chunxiang, Chao Ning, Erika Hagelberg, Hongjie Li, Yongbin Zhao, Wenying Li, Idelisi Abuduresule, Hong Zhu & Hui Zhou. 2015. Analysis of ancient human mitochondrial DNA from the Xiaohe cemetery: Insights into prehistoric population movements in the Tarim Basin, China. *BMC Genetics* 16(78). doi:10.1186/s12863-015-0237-5

Lyonnet, Bertille, T. Akhundow, Khagani Almamedow, L. Bouquet, Bakhtiyar Jellinov, F. Huseynov, S. Loute, Z. Makharadze & S. Reynard. 2008. Late Chalcolithic Kurgans in Transcaucasia. The cemetery of Soyuq Bulaq (Azerbaijan). *Archäologische Mitteilungen aus Iran und Turan* 40. 27–44.

Mathieson, I., Songül Alpaslan-Roodenberg, Cosimo Posth, Anna Szécsényi-Nagy, Nadin Rohland, Swapan Mallick, Iñigo Olalde et al. 2018. The genomic history of southeastern Europe. *Nature* 555. 197–203. doi:10.1038/nature25778

Palumbi, G. 2011. The Arslantepe royal tomb and the "manipulation" of the kurgan ideology in eastern Anatolia at the beginning of the third millennium. In E. Borgna & S.M. Celka (eds.), *Ancestral landscapes*, 47–59. Lyon: Maison de l'Orient et de la Méditerrannée.

Pitskhelauri, K. 2012. Uruk migrants in the Caucasus. *Bulletin of the Georgian National Academy of Sciences* 6(2). 153–161.

Rahmstorf, L. 2010. Indications of Aegean–Caucasian relations during the third millennium BC. In S. Hansen, A. Hauptmann, I. Motzenbäcker & E. Pernicka (eds.), *Von Maykop bis Trialeti. Gewinnung und Verbreitung von Metallen und Obsidian in Kaukasien im 4.–2. Jt. v. Chr.*, 263–295. Bonn: Habelt.

Sabine Reinhold, Julia Gresky, Natalia Berezina, Anatoly R. Kantorovich, Corina Knipper, Vladimir E. Maslov, Vladimira G. Petrenko, Kurt W. Alt & Andrey B. Belinsky. 2017. Contextualising innovation: Cattle owners and wagon drivers in the North Caucasus and beyond. In J. Maran & P. Stockhammer (eds.), *Appropriating innovation. Entangled knowledge in Eurasia, 5000–1500 BCE*, 78–97. Oxbow Books.

Rezepkin A.D. 2000. *Das frühbronzezeitliche Gräberfeld von Klady und die Majkop-Kultur in Nordwestkaukasien*. Rahden (Westf.): Leidorf.

Sagona, A. 2017 *The archaeology of the Caucasus: From earliest settlements to the Iron Age*. New York: Cambridge University Press.

Smith, Adam T. 2009. Historical and anthropological problems in the archaeology of southern Caucasia. In Adam T. Smith, Ruben S. Badalyan & Pavel Avetisyan (eds.), *The archaeology and geography of ancient Transcaucasian societies*. Vol. 1. *The foundations of research and regional survey in the Tsaghkahovit Plain, Armenia*, 21–32. Chicago: Oriental Institute of the Universtity of Chicago.

Stöllner, T. 2016. The beginnings of social inequality: Consumer and producer perspectives from Transcaucasia in the 4th and 3rd millennia BC. In M. Bartelheim, B. Horejs & R. Krauss (eds.), *Von Baden bis Troja: Ressourcesnutzung, Metallurgie und Wissenstransfer. Eine Jubiäumsschrift für Ernst Pernicka* (OREA 3), 209–234. Rahden (Westf.): Leidorf.

Thissen, L. 1993. New insights in Balkan–Anatolian connections in the Late Chalcolithic: Old Evidence from the Turkish Black Sea Littoral. *Anatolian Studies* 43. 207–237.

Wang, Chuan-Chao, Sabine Reinhold, Alexey Kalmykov, Antje Wissgott, Guido Brandt,

Choongwon Jeong, Olivia Cheronet et al. 2018. The genetic prehistory of Greater Caucasus. *bioRxiv*. doi:10.1101/322347

Welton, M.L. 2010 Mobility and social organization on the ancient Anatolian Black Sea coast: An archaeological, spatial and isotopic investigation of the cemetery at Ikiztepe, Turkey. PhD thesis, University of Toronto.

CHAPTER 8

Hittite *ḫandā*(*i*)- 'to Align, Arrange, etc.' and PIE Metaphors for '(Morally) Right'

H. Craig Melchert

1 Introduction

Ziegler (2014) has explained Hittite *ḫandā*(*i*)- 'to arrange, etc.' as a denominative verb from PIE *$*h_2$ent-o-* '(that which is) woven; start of weaving' to a root *$*h_2$ent-* 'to set the warp, begin to weave' attested in Greek *ἄττομαι* 'idem' and Albanian *end* 'to weave' < *$*h_2$n̥t-ye/o-*. Janda (2016) has adduced further support in Greek *ἀντίον* '(upper) loom beam'. Ziegler's etymology is highly illuminating for the Hittite verb, but many aspects of the handbook treatments of *ḫandā*(*i*)- (*HW*²: 3.163–167, Puhvel 1991: 96–107, Kloekhorst 2008: 289–291) are inaccurate. The true basic meaning of the word strongly reinforces Ziegler's account.

2 *ḫandā*(*i*)- as 'to Align (Oneself)'

The oldest and most fundamental sense of active and medio-passive *ḫandā*(*i*)- is 'to align', (m.-p.) 'to align oneself' in both a concrete and moral sense. Examples (1) and (2) illustrate the concrete use:

1 KBo XVII 21 + Ro 9 (KI.LAM Festival; OH/OS):
[LÚ ᴳᴵˢB]ANŠUR ᴺᴵᴺᴰᴬ*zippulašne* ᴳᴵˢ*arimpi ḫantāizzi*
"The tab[le-man] aligns/arranges the *z.*-bread on the *a.*"

See the correct translation (*HW*²: 3.163), whose basic meaning 'ordnen' is close to the mark.

2 KUB 17.10 iv 22 (Myth of Telipinu; OH/MS):
ištananiš DINGIR.MEŠ-*naš ḫandantati*
"The altars of the gods were put in order/alignment' or 'The altars were put in order for the gods."

 | DOI:10.1163/9789004416192_010

It is important to note that in this text *ḫandantati* expresses the opposite of *we/išuriyantat(i)* "became twisted, disordered" (Melchert 2016: 215 with multiple references).

The verb is also used metaphorically to refer to the state of the mind or soul. In the following example the metaphor is made explicit:

3 KUB 17.10 ii 31–32 (Myth of Telipinu; OH/MS):
GI-*az lazzaiš māḫḫan ḫandānza zik* ᵈ*Telipinuš QATAMMA ḫandaḫḫut*
"As a/the *l.* reed is well-aligned (i.e., straight), so may you, Telipinu, become well-aligned!"

The outstanding characteristic of a reed is that it is *straight* because its individual sections are all *aligned* in a straight line. Likewise the out-of-sorts soul of the angry Telipinu is to again become well aligned and hence also order in the world restored (see further Melchert 2016: 216–219).

The medio-passive is also used to mean 'to draw even with, line up with':

4 KBo 25.31 ii 8–12 and duplicates (Festival with the NIN.DINGIR-priestess; OH/OS)
NIN.DINGIR-*aš* LÚ ᴳᴵˢGIDRU-*aš pēran ḫuwāi* N[(IN.DINGIR-*aš uezzi* 2 DUMU.MEŠ É.GAL ŠÀ-*BA kētt=a*)] 1-*iš kētt=a* 1-*iš ḫarzi* 15 ᴸᵁ́.ᴹᴱˢ*ḫā*[(*piēš* ᵁᴿᵁ*Ḫatti* EGIR=*ŠU*)] *išgaranteš ḫaššan=kan* 1-*ŠU* [(*ḫuwāi*)] § *mān=ašta* LUGAL-*i* NIN.DINGIR-*aš ḫandāētta* L[Ú x (LÚ ᴳᴵˢGIDRU)] *āppianzi ta* A.ŠAR=*ŠUNU appanzi*
"The staff-bearer of the NIN.DINGIR-priestess precedes. The NIN.DINGIR-priestess comes. There are two palace officials of whom one keeps to one side, one keeps to the other. Fifteen *hapiya*-men are lined up behind her. She proceeds (around) the hearth once. When the NIN.DINGIR-priestess draws even with the king, the [ ] (and) the staff-bearer step back and take their places."

Puhvel (1991: 97) and Goedegebuure (2014: 281–282) understand the passage correctly (against *HW*²: 3.163–164).[1]

1 Correct, however, and very important is the finding (*HW*²: 3.805) that contrary to a widespread misconception *ḫuwai-* means simply 'to move, proceed', with *no* implication of speed or haste. The Hittite verb 'to run' is *piddai-*ᵇᵇⁱ.

5 IBoT 1.36 ii 29 (Royal Bodyguard Instructions; MH/MS)
nu=šši=kan māḫ[ḫa]n LÚ.MEŠ *MEŠEDI* DUMU.MEŠ.É.GAL*=ya ḫandāntari*
"And when the bodyguards and palace officials draw even/are lined up with him ..."

The context of a procession assures this meaning (Güterbock and van den Hout 1991,17 and *passim*). The older medio-passive is already replaced in this sense by the active intransitive ibid. iii 45 and 48, and becomes normal in New Hittite:[2]

6 KBo 14.3 iv 29–30 (Deeds of Suppiluliuma; NH)
nu=kan edani pangawi LÚ.[(KÚR 1-*anki=pat anda ḫ*)]*andaizzi*
"And he (my father) drew even/caught up with that entire enemy all at once."

(compare similarly Güterbock 1956: 76). The duplicate KUB 19.18 i 24–25 has a present plural: *anda ḫandānzi* "they caught up" (historical present).

Intransitive *ḫandā*(*i*)- may also mean 'to align oneself with' in the sense of 'to ally oneself with':

7 KBo 4.14 ii 75 (Treaty/Protocol of Suppiluliuma II; NH)
zik=ma=šmaš=kan anda ḫandāši
(Or some lords desert/defect on me,) "and *you* align yourself with them."

Likewise ibid. ii 49. This usage is equivalent to 'to join (up with)' (thus Puhvel 1991: 96).

3 Other Meanings of *ḫandā*(*i*)-

All other genuine senses of *ḫandā*(*i*)- are also derivable from 'to align'. It may be used to mean 'to equate/compare with' (compare German 'gleichstellen, vergleichen'):

2 This is also the sense in KUB 28.99:5 (against Puhvel 1991: 97): "When the king draws even with the huwaši-stone ...", where we cannot tell whether the incomplete verb is active or medio-passive.

8 KUB 21.38 Ro 13 (Puduhepa Letter to Ramses II; NH)
n=an=kan kuedani ḫandami ANA DUMU.MUNUS KUR [URU]*Kara-*[d]*duniya*[*š* KUR] [URU]*Zulapi* KUR [URU]*Āššur ḫandam*[*i*]
(The daughter of heaven and earth that I give to [my] brother,) "to whom shall I equate/compare her? Shall I equate/compare her to the daughter of the land of Babylon, of the [land] of Zulapi, of the land of Assur?"

This is clearly the correct interpretation (Edel 1994: 217, Hoffner 2009: 283, et al.). A meaning 'to betroth' for *ḫandā*(*i*)- does not exist (against Puhvel 1991: 97).

We also find the verb used to mean 'to match up', first in a physical sense:

9 KUB 55.20+9.4 i 2–3 ("Ritual of the Ox"; ?/NS)
12 [UZU]ÚR.ḪI.A=*ya anda ḫandāmi* SAG.DU-*aš=kan* SAG.DU-*i ḫandanza* …
(Now I am treating him throughout this day.) "I also match the twelve body parts: the head is matched with the head …". (that is, that of the patient and that of the ram serving as ritual substitute)

Puhvel (1991: 96) thus renders the ritual usage optimally. Beckman (1990: 45) less accurately translates "arrange together." We find likewise ibid. i 19 *ḫandanun* "I have (also) matched up."

Better attested is 'to make a match' or 'to be a match' in the sense of spiritual or psychological compatibility, like-thinking, or harmony:

10 KUB 1.1 iii 2–3 ("Apology" of Hattusili III; NH)
nu ḫandāwen [(*nu=nn*)]*aš* DINGIR-*LUM ŠA* [LÚ]*MUDI* D[A]/M *āššiyatar pešta*
(I took as my wife the daughter of the priest Pentipšarri, Puduhepa, at the word of the deity,) "and we were a match/compatible, and the deity gave us the love of a husband and wife."

Otten (1981: 17) renders the example freely "wir hielten zusammen", glossing the verb (ibid. 86) as '(sich) fügen'. Güterbock (1983: 160) likewise translates correctly "we were in harmony." Puhvel (1991: 100) again falsely invents a nonexistent "we got married."[3] The same sense is found at KUB 24.7 i 19–21 (Güterbock 1983: 156 and 160 against Puhvel 1991: 100).

3 Puhvel's repeated understanding of the verb as expressing 'to get married' is quite impossible, for among other reasons because we know that, as expected in an ancient society, marriage

11 KUB 21.38 Ro 58 (Puduhepa Letter to Ramses II; NH)
nu=mu ITTI ŠEŠ=*KA ḫandait nu=za* DUMU.NITA.MEŠ DUMU.MUNUS .MEŠ DÙ-*nun*
(My personal deity, who had also done that, when the Sun-goddess of Arinna, the Storm-god, Hebat, and Šaušga made me queen,) "made me compatible with your brother, and I produced sons and daughters."

Much less likely is the interpretation of "hat mich gleichgestellt" (Edel 1994: 221). Certainly false is "married me off to your brother" (Puhvel 1991: 99). Puduhepa's entire line of argument to Ramses is to boast of how she and her husband Hattusili are soul-mates, thanks to divine arrangement—and to assure him that the same will be true for him and his Hittite bride.

12 KUB 30.56 iii 10–11 (Tablet Inventory; NH)
Mān ÙKU-*ši* ARAD.MEŠ=*ŠU* GÉME.ME[Š=*ŠU=ya ŪL*] SIxSÀ-*anzi našma* LÚ-*LUM* MUNUS-*TUM=ya ŪL ḫandanzi*
"If a man's male and female slaves do not get along, or a man and woman/ husband and wife do not get along ..."

Dardano (2006: 213) properly translates "übereinstimmen" (likewise *HW*²: 3.165). False once again is "marry" (Puhvel 1991: 98). The same objection applies as that given in footnote 3 regarding example (10).

The participle *ḫandānt-* is used predicatively in the technical sense 'in alignment with' (a model/archetype), hence 'corresponding/true to':

13 KUB 31.143 ii 17 (Invocation of Hattic Deities; OH/OS) (and *passim*)
[ ]x ᵈ*Inaraš maltešnaš ḫandān*
"[This is] true to/corresponds with the recitations/ritual of/for Inara."

14 KUB 2.6 vi 3–4 (Winter Festival; OH/NS)
ANA GIŠ.ḪUR *ḫandān*
"True to/corresponding with an archetype."

This expression is often found in colophons. It is surely from this usage that the attributive use 'true, accurate' developed: hence KBo 3.23 iv 12 (OH/NS) *ḫandān memian* "true word" (Puhvel 1991: 102), "mot juste" (Archi 1979: 42). Likewise

for the Hittites was not a joint act of a man and woman. A man married a woman, who became his wife.

probably also EME-*aš ḫandanza* and EME-*an ḫandan* 'true speech', literally 'true tongue' (Güterbock & Hoffner 1980: 23).[4]

The final step is that the participle acquires the *moral* sense of 'just, loyal':

15 KUB 24.8 iv 4 (Tale of Appu; pre-NH/NS)
[^{LÚ}Ḫ]UL-*aš* ŠEŠ-*aš* ^{LÚ}NÍG.SIxSÁ ŠEŠ=*ši mem*[*iškewan dāiš*]
"Brother Bad [began to sp]eak to his brother Just."

The righteous brother is thus consistently characterized throughout this text (Siegelová 1971: 12, 18, and 24 with references). See also ibid. iii 14–15: NÍG.SIxSÁ-*an* KASKAL-*an* "the right/just path/way."

16 KUB 31.127 i 51 (Prayer/Hymn to Sun-god; pre-NH/NS)
n=an ḫantantan ARAD=*KA* ^{d}UTU-*uš kišar*[*t*]*a ēp*
"And may you, Sun-god, take him, your just/loyal servant, by the hand!"

Compare "your just servant" (Singer 2002: 37) and "deinen treuen Diener" (Rieken et al. 2016). Puhvel (1991: 103) offers further examples of the moral usage.

That the fundamental meaning of *ḫandā*(*i*)- is 'to align' should by now be clear. It is also not difficult to derive from it two uses of the verb that have often wrongly been taken to be basic. It is a short step from 'to align, arrange' physical objects to 'to arrange' events, hence 'to ordain, determine'. This sense is seen especially in *parā ḫandānt*- and *parā ḫandantātar*, freely translatable respectively as 'providential' (of deities and humans) and 'providence', but literally '(favorably) pre-ordaining' (of a deity), '(favorably) pre-ordained, blessed' (of a human) and '(favorable) preordination, predetermination' (well treated by Puhvel 1991: 105). Note the archaic use of *p*(*a*)*rā* < **pró* in a locatival temporal sense 'before', not the synchronic directional 'forth, out' (Melchert 2008: 202).

For the further development from 'to determine, fix, ordain' to 'to determine, ascertain' one may compare English 'to determine' and French *determiner*. Due to the nature of our extant texts, this last use is prominently attested in the specific sense 'to determine by an oracular inquiry' (Puhvel 1991: 98–100, *HW*²: 3.164–165).

4 While "just/loyal speech" cannot be excluded (see immediately below), that seems less likely than 'true' in the sense 'accurate, honest'.

4 Hittite [GIŠ]*ḫanzan-* '(Upper) Loom Beam'

The true fundamental meaning of *ḫandā*(*i*)- 'to align' clearly strengthens Ziegler's derivation of the word. Further support comes from a rare Hittite noun whose genuine sense has also not been fully appreciated. As shown by Tanaka (2008), [GIŠ]*ḫanzan-* (a neuter *n*-stem) does not refer to a cutting tool (against Hoffner 1997: 119–120), but to some type of beam, as in the following ritual passage:

17 KUB 7.13 Ro 5–8 (purification ritual; ?/NS)
andurzi=ya=kan [...] [GIŠ]*kattal*[*uz*]*ziyaš* [GIŠ]ÙR.MEŠ [GIŠ]*ḫanza* GIŠ-*ru*[(-) ...] *arḫa* [*ḫašḫ*]*aššanzi ANA* É.MEŠ.ŠÀ=*ya=kan da*[*pia*(*nt*)- [GIŠ]] ÙR.MEŠ [GIŠ]AB.ḪI.A=*ya arḫa ḫašḫaššanzi*
"Also inside [...] they scrape off the beams of the lintel(s), the *hanzan* (pl.), the wood[en? ...]. Also inside the house they scrape off a[ll] the beams and the windows."

This example shows that the better-known passage in the Hittite Laws refers to unlawful removal of a partially woven cloth from a loom beam:

18 KBo 6.10 iii 11–13 (Laws § 144; OH/NS; restored after KUB 29.29 ii 4; OS)
takku TÚG.SIG [GIŠ]*ḫanzan*[*i ku*(*iški tuḫšari*)] 10 GÍN.GÍN KÙ.BABBAR *pāi t*[*akku* ...] *kuiški tuḫšari* [(5 GÍN.GÍN KÙ.BABBAR *pāi*)]
"If someone cuts off/removes fine cloth from a *hanzan*, he shall pay ten shekels of silver. If someone cuts off/removes [...], he shall pay five shekels of silver."

Hoffner (1997: 119–120) restores an instrumental [GIŠ]*ḫanzan*[*it*] and assumes that the reference is to a tool with which cloth is cut. However, as argued by Tanaka (2008: 740), it would be odd to have a provision against cutting cloth with a particular instrument. Furthermore, as she correctly emphasizes, Hittite *tuḫš-* means not merely 'to cut', but implies 'to cut off, separate', suggesting that [GIŠ]*ḫanzan-* in the Laws refers to that from which the fine cloth is cut off.[5] Based

5 The traces of the broken sign at the end of the word show a clear ⟨ni⟩, not ⟨na⟩, so restoration of an ablative [GIŠ]*ḫanzan*[*az*] is excluded (against Tanaka 2008: 742). However, a dative–locative [GIŠ]*ḫanzan*[*i*] is entirely in order. Although it is still not fully acknowledged, use of the dative–locative to express the place from which something is taken (in competition with the ablative) is already attested in Old Hittite texts in Old Script (Hoffner and Melchert 2008: 259, § 16.69).

on the evidence from example (17) that ^{GIŠ}*ḫanzan*- referred to a kind of interior house beam, Tanaka (2008: 742–744) convincingly argues that in the Laws the reference is either to an interior house beam used to support a vertical warp-weighted loom or by extension to a freestanding warp-weighted loom. In any case, ^{GIŠ}*ḫanzan*- confirms that Hittite did inherit a base *$h_2$ent- 'to set the warp, begin to weave' in the context of weaving.

5 Tentative Morphological Analysis[6]

As argued by Kloekhorst (2008: 132–135), Old Hittite still distinguishes between denominative verbs in **-o-ye/o-* (reflected as *mi*-conjugation verbs with present third singulars in *-āizzi* beside third plurals in *-ānzi*) and those in **-eh_2-ye/o-* (reflected as *mi*-conjugation verbs with present third singulars in *-āyezzi* and third plurals in *-āyanzi*). Within the history of Hittite the latter class is merged into the former.[7] The evidence presented by Kloekhorst precludes derivation of all verbs of the *-āizzi. -ānzi* class from a single source, either **-o-ye/o-* (Oettinger 1979: 357–358) or **-eh_2-ye/o-* (Melchert 1994: 122 and 130). However, the very limited evidence from Old Script and the productivity of the class make it hard to determine the prehistorical source of a given stem.

In the case of our verb the Old Script evidence is in fact conflicting. The neuter nominative-accusative participle *ḫandān* (attested eleven times in four manuscripts, but all belonging to a *single* composition) argues for derivation from a **$h_2$ento-*, but the present third singular medio-passive *ḫa-an-da-a-e-et-ta* (KBo 25.31 ii 11, cited in example (4) above) can hardly be read other than as /xanda:yet:a/, thus pointing to derivation from a collective **$h_2$enteh$_2$*.[8] The fact that elsewhere in Old Script the medio-passive present third singular appears as *ḫa-an-da-a-it-ta* (KBo 20.26 (iii) 22, 17.9 i 8, and 25.33 i 13)[9] and the active present third singular as *ḫa-an-ta-a-iz-zi* (KBo 20.33 Ro 9) plus the absence of any spellings †*ḫa-an-d/ta-(a)-i-e-^{o}* together suggest that *ḫa-an-da-a-e-et-ta* is a

6 I am much indebted to Alan Nussbaum for invaluable references and discussion of the issues treated in this section, but responsibility for the analysis presented here is entirely mine.

7 For example, in the Old Script version of the Hittite Laws 'looks at' consistently appears as *šu-wa-i-ez-zi* (four syllables), but in the New Script copies one finds contracted *šu-wa-a-iz-zi* (three syllables). This reading of the latter and new inflection in the *-āizzi, -ānzi* class is confirmed by examples like imperative second plural *šuwātten* (OH/NS).

8 For my interpretation of *-a-e-et-ta* as /-a:yet:a/ with a glide see the arguments of Kloekhorst (2014: 158–159) regarding similar spellings, with extensive preceding documentation.

9 The last two examples are partially restored, but context and spacing make the restorations secure.

nonce form and thus favor derivation from *$h_2$ento-*, but it is hard to be certain. In any case, since *$h_2$enteh$_2$* may easily be taken as the plural of a neuter noun *$h_2$ento-*, the ambiguity has no serious impact on the further prehistoric analysis.

As a minimalist scenario we may, slightly modifying previous accounts (Ziegler 2014: 212 and *LIV*²: 269), assume a primary PIE root *$h_2$ent-* 'to align', already with a specialized use 'to set the warp threads, (begin) to weave', attested in a primary present *h_2n̥t-ye/o-* in Greek ἄττομαι 'idem' and Albanian *end* 'to weave'. We may derive Hittite *ḫandā(i)-* 'to align' (originally in the context of weaving) from an adjective *$h_2$ent-o-* or *h_2n̥t-o-* 'aligned (like the warp threads)' (compare *kappā(i)-* 'to diminish' from *kappi-* 'small' or *šarlā(i)-* 'to exalt' from *šarla-* 'exalted') or from a substantivized *$h_2$ent-o-* '(the vertically aligned) warp threads, (start of) a woven fabric' (Ziegler 2014: 213)—or less likely from the plural thereof. From the same *$h_2$ent-o-* Greek derived a secondary noun *$h_2$antí(y)on* 'that pertaining to aligning the warp threads' > ἀντίον '(upper) loom beam' (compare formally πέδον 'ground' → πεδίον 'plain').

From an original adjective *$h_2$ent-o-* 'aligned (like the warp threads)' Hittite may have derived a substantive *$h_2$ent-i-* 'the aligned warp threads/fabric on the loom' (compare arguably Latin *antēs, antium* 'rows' < *'aligned things'), whence *$h_2$enty-o-* 'of alignment' > *$h_2$entyo-Hon-* 'the aligning thing' > ^{GIŠ}*ḫanzan-* '(upper) loom beam'. The productivity of the Hittite type in *-anzan-* makes it likely that not all the supposed steps of this idealized derivational chain actually existed (cp. Melchert 2003: 136).

One fact raises at least some doubt about the derivation just presented. It is far from assured, based on example (17), that Hittite ^{GIŠ}*ḫanzan-* referring to an interior house beam took its name from its use in weaving. One might instead suppose for *$h_2$ent-* a primary meaning 'to fix (in a position)', a suitable source for Latin *antae* (feminine plurale tantum) 'rectangular columns, wall posts of a temple' and/or Sanskrit *ánta-* (masculine) 'end, border, edge' and Germanic *andija-* 'end' (Old Norse *endir* etc.). The usual assignment of the latter to *$h_2$ent-* 'front, face' hardly imposes itself semantically. Under this account, the sense 'to align' would have arisen specifically in the context of weaving, where aligning the warp threads by fixing/attaching them to an existing horizontal beam would have been carried over to a free-standing warp loom.[10] At least Hittite ^{GIŠ}*ḫanzan-* and probably Greek ἀντίον would thus reflect 'fixed thing'.

10 I forgo here an extended discussion of the prehistory of such a putative *$h_2$ent-* 'to fix (in position)', in part because, as some readers will have already seen, it raises the very complex issue of whether one should in fact posit a root *$h_2$en(H)-*, from which a series of

What matters for our immediate purposes is that by either scenario regarding the presumed PIE root *$h_2$ent-* (or even *$h_2$en(H)-*), the demonstrated basic sense 'to align' for Hittite *ḫandā(i)-* (not 'to fix in position'!) and the existence of [GIŠ]*ḫanzan-* fully vindicate Ziegler's immediate etymology of the Hittite verb, which makes sense only in the context of weaving terminology.

6 Indo-European Metaphors for Moral Order/Propriety

The interest of this finding for our overarching theme concerns the dialectal distribution and relative chronology of various Indo-European metaphors expressing morality or propriety. The two most widespread metaphors are based either on the idea of fitting together in a harmonious fashion or on the notion of what is aligned and thus straight (versus crooked or twisted).

The first metaphor '(what is) fitting, proper' < 'to fit together' (transitive or intransitive) is multiply attested. One instance is illustrated by Hittite *āra* '*moral* order' < PIE *(h_1)ar-* 'to fit together' (Puhvel 1984: 120, following already Hrozný), cognate with the adverb seen in Sanskrit *áram* = Avestan *arəm* 'fittingly', Sanskrit *ṛtá-* 'universal Order' and other Indo-Iranian reflexes.[11] An exhaustive treatment of Hittite *āra* (Cohen, 2002) has reaffirmed its clear sense of universal morality versus mere local custom. The matching moral sense in Hittite and Indo-Iranian plus the very weak attestation of the verbal root in Indo-Iranian and its apparent complete absence in Hittite suggests that the metaphor is an inheritance. Based on the derivatives for 'joint (of the body)', the root was probably intransitive (*LIV*^{2}: 269).

Weiss (2015, especially 190–194) has argued that PIE *(h_x)reith$_2$-* 'to join, blend, unite' (transitive) is the source of Latin *rīte* 'correctly, properly' and Tocharian AB *rittwatär/rittetär*, which in Tocharian B also has the sense 'is fitting'. The Tocharian verb also preserves the sense 'to attach, blend'. Whether the moral sense is in this instance an archaism (Randerscheinung) or reflects independent developments is hard to determine. There is no trace of the base verb in Latin or Italic, but the frequency of the metaphor (compare, e.g., the moral sense of English 'fitting' or German *mit Fug* (*und Recht*) 'justly, rightly') easily allows for the Latin and Tocharian B uses to be independent developments.

---

t-stem nominals were derived. A reasoned consideration of just how and how far such an analysis should be pursued is not possible in the present context.

11 See also the demonstration of Massetti (2013–2014) that various collocations and figurae confirm that Greek ἀρετή 'excellence' reflects the same metaphor of 'proper order' from 'fitting together'. I thank Matilde Serangeli for this reference.

The second metaphor deriving '(morally) proper' from 'aligned, straight' is famously attested in the PIE adjective **$h_3$reĝ-to-* '(physically) straight' < **$h_3$reĝ-* 'stretch out straight, draw straight', which has the moral sense 'aligned, in proper order', hence 'right, proper' in Latin *rēctus* and Germanic **rehta-*. Other derivatives of the root show the same moral sense in multiple branches (Pokorny 1959: 854–857), and the metaphor is surely in this instance inherited.

Ziegler (2014: 213–214) cogently cites from the specific context of weaving the case of Proto-Italic **ord-ye/o-* 'to set the warp, begin to weave', that is 'to align the warp threads', whose derivative **ord-n-* comes to be used in Latin *ordō, ordinis* both for 'order, alignment' in various physical senses and 'proper order, morality'.

As we have seen, whatever the ultimate derivation of PIE **$h_2$ent-* 'to set the warp, begin to weave' may be, the true basic sense of Hittite *ḫandā(i)-* 'to align' confirms her derivation of it from a **$h_2$ent-o-* 'the aligned threads of the warp'. The noun ^{GIŠ}*ḫanzan-* 'upper loom beam' strongly suggests that the weaving sense of **$h_2$ent-o-* was inherited into Anatolian. Like the moral sense of Latin *ordō*, so also that of the Hittite participle *ḫandānt-* 'just, moral, right(eous)' is surely a specific Hittite development. What we cannot know is whether at least the Latin and Hittite extension of 'to align' from weaving to other contexts, non-physical as well as physical, reflects an already PIE usage that has undergone lexical renewal.[12]

References

Archi, Alfonso. 1979. L'humanité des hittites. In *Florilegium anatolicum: mélanges offerts à Emmanuel Laroche*, 37–48. Paris: Bocard.

Beckman, Gary. 1990. The Hittite "Ritual of the Ox" (*CTH* 760 I.2–3). *Orientalia NS* 59. 34–55.

Cohen, Yoram. 2002. *Taboos and prohibitions in Hittite society*. Heidelberg: Winter.

Dardano, Paola. 2006. *Die hethitischen Tontafelkataloge aus Ḫattuša* (*CTH* 276–282). Wiesbaden: Harrassowitz.

12 Ziegler (2014: 213) also cites Hittite *takšeššar* 'arrangement, constellation' as an example of 'order, alignment' that arose in a weaving context. However, as shown by Olsen (2017: 192), Armenian *tˤekˤem* means 'to forge, hammer into shape, whet' in the context of metallurgy and has nothing to with weaving (despite the misleading translations found in many handbooks). Likewise, all attested uses of Hittite *takš-* are derivable from a core meaning 'to *fit* together, unite', but none of these involve weaving (Melchert 2018). It is thus very unlikely that the specific sense 'to weave' of Latin *texō* is inherited from PIE.

Edel, Elmar. 1994. *Die ägyptisch-hethitische Korrespondenz aus Boghazköi in babylonischer und hethitischer Sprache.* Band I. *Umschriften und Übersetzungen.* Opladen: Westdeutscher Verlag.

Goedegebuure, Petra. 2014. *The Hittite demonstratives: studies in deixis, topics and focus.* Wiesbaden: Harrassowitz.

Güterbock, Hans G. 1956. The deeds of Šuppiluliuma I as told by his son, Muršili II. *Journal of Cuneiform Studies* 10. 41–68, 75–98, 107–130.

Güterbock, Hans G. 1983. A Hurro-Hittite hymn to Ishtar. *Journal of the American Oriental Society* 103. 155–164.

Güterbock, Hans G. & Harry A. Hoffner. 1980. *The Hittite dictionary of the Oriental Institute of the University of Chicago.* Vol. 1. Fascicle 1. Chicago: The Oriental Institute.

Güterbock, Hans G. & Theo P.J. van den Hout. 1991. *The Hittite instruction for the royal bodyguard.* Chicago: The Oriental Institute.

Hoffner, Harry Angier Jr. 1997. *The laws of the Hittites: A critical edition.* Leiden: Brill.

Hoffner, Harry A. Jr. 2009. *Letters from the Hittite kingdom.* Atlanta: Society of Biblical Literature.

Hoffner, Harry A. Jr. & H. Craig Melchert. 2008. *A grammar of the Hittite language.* Vol. 1. *Reference grammar.* Winona Lake: Eisenbrauns.

HW^2 = Johannes Friedrich & Annelies Kammenhuber. 1975–. *Hethitisches Wörterbuch.* Zweite, neubearbeitete Auflage auf der Grundlage der edierten hethitischen Texte. Heidelberg: Winter.

Janda, Michael. 2016. Indogermanisch *$^*h_2ant$-* 'anzetteln'. In Henning Marquardt, Silvio Reichmuth & José Virgilio García Trabazo (eds.), *In honorem Johannis Tischler septuagenarii dedicata,* 121–126. Innsbruck: Institut für Sprachen und Literaturen der Universität Innsbruck.

Kloekhorst, Alwin. 2008. *Etymological dictionary of the Hittite inherited lexicon.* Leiden: Brill.

Kloekhorst, Alwin. 2014. *Accent in Hittite: A study in plene spelling, consonant gradation, clitics, and metrics.* Wiesbaden: Harrassowitz.

LIV^2 = Martin Kümmel & Helmut Rix. 2001. *Lexikon der indogermanischen Verben.* Zweite, erweiterte und verbesserte Auflage. Wiesbaden: Reichert.

Massetti, Laura. 2013–2014. Gr. *ἀρετή*, ved. *ṛtá-*, av. *aṣ̌a* e l'eccellenza come ordine aggiustato. *Münchener Studien zur Sprachwissenschaft* 67(2): 123–148.

Melchert, H. Craig. 1994. *Anatolian historical phonology.* Amsterdam: Rodopi.

Melchert, H. Craig. 2003. Hittite nominal stems in *-anzan-*. In Eva Tichy, Dagmar S. Wodtko & Britta Irslinger (eds.), *Indogermanisches Nomen: Derivation, Flexion und Ablaut. Akten der Arbeitstagung der Indogermanischen Gesellschaft / Society for Indo-European Studies / Société des Études Indo-Européennes, Freiburg 19. bis 22. September 2001,* 129–139. Bremen: Hempen.

Melchert, H. Craig. 2008. Hittite *duwān (parā)*. In Claire Bowern, Bethwyn Evans &

Luisa Miceli (eds.), *Morphology and language history in honour of Harold Koch*, 201–209. Amsterdam: Benjamins.

Melchert, H. Craig. 2016. Marginalia to the myth of Telipinu. In Šárka Velharticá (ed.), *Audias fabulas veteres. Anatolian studies in honor of Jana Součková-Siegelová*, 210–220. Leiden: Brill.

Melchert, H. Craig. 2018. Semantics and etymology of Hittite *takš*-. In Lucien van Beek, Alwin Kloekhorst, Guus Kroonen, Michaël Peyrot, Tijmen Pronk & Michiel de Vaan (eds.), *Farnah. Indo-Iranian and its Indo-European origins: in honor of Sasha Lubotsky*, 209–216. Ann Arbor: Beech Stave.

Oettinger, Norbert. 1979. *Die Stammbildung des hethitischen Verbums*. Nürnberg: Carl.

Olsen, Birgit. 2017. Armenian textile terminology. In Salvatore Gaspa, Cécile Michel & Marie-Louise Nosch (eds.), *Textile terminologies from the Orient to the Mediterranean and Europe, 1000 BC to 1000 AD*, 188–201. DigitalCommons@University of Nebraska—Lincoln.

Otten, Heinrich. 1981. *Die Apologie Hattusilis III. Das Bild der Überlieferung*. Wiesbaden: Harrassowitz.

Pokorny, Julius. 1959. *Indogermanisches etymologisches Wörterbuch*. Bern: Francke.

Puhvel, Jaan. 1984. *Hittite etymological dictionary*. Vol. 1. *Words beginning with A*; Vol. 2. *Words beginning with E and I*. Berlin: Mouton.

Puhvel, Jaan. 1991. *Hittite etymological dictionary*. Vol. 3. *Words beginning with H*. Berlin: Mouton de Gruyter.

Rieken, Elisabeth et al. 2016. CTH 372—Hymne und Gebet an die Sonne (Šamaš). Accessed May 13, 2018. E. Rieken et al. (ed.), hethiter.net/: CTH 372 (INTR 2016-01-18).

Siegelová, Jana. 1971. *Appu-Märchen und Ḫedammu-Mythus*. Wiesbaden: Harrassowitz.

Singer, Itamar. 2002. *Hittite prayers*. Atlanta: Society of Biblical Literature.

Tanaka, Terri. 2008. GIŠ*ḫanza(n)*- in the Hittite laws. In Alfonso Archi & Rita Francia (eds.), *VI Congresso Internazionale di Ittitologia: Roma, 5–9 settembre* 2005, 739–744. Rome: CNR.

Weiss, Michael. 2015. The rite stuff: Lat. *rīte, rītus*, TB *rittetär*, TA *ritwatär*, and Av. *raēϑβa*-. *Tocharian and Indo-European Studies* 16. 181–198.

Ziegler, Sabine. 2014. Die Ordnung als Gewebe: Kann eine andere etymologische Erklärung für heth. *ḫandai*-*zi* "(durch Semantik) festgestellt werden"? In Cyril Brosch & Annick Payne (eds.), *Na-wa/i*-VIR.*ZI/A* MAGNUS.SCRIBA: *Festschrift für Helmut Nowicki zum 70. Geburtstag*, 211–215. Wiesbaden: Harrassowitz.

CHAPTER 9

Cognacy and Computational Cladistics: Issues in Determining Lexical Cognacy for Indo-European Cladistic Research

Matthew Scarborough

1 Introduction[1]

The use of computational cladistics as a tool to investigate the phylogeny of the Indo-European languages has garnered much attention in recent years. In many studies cognacy judgements from comparative word lists form the basis for the computational analysis either partially or entirely.[2] The added extensions of potential chronological and phylogeographical analysis have recently further stoked wider debates over the time-depth of the Indo-European language family and the question of the location of the Indo-European homeland.[3] Nevertheless, it is frequently held that lexical data from comparative word lists form the least reliable evidence for subgrouping arguments.[4] In this

1 Standard bibliographical abbreviations used in this paper include: *ÈSSJa* (Trubačev et al. 1974–), *EWAia* (Mayrhofer 1992–2001), *EWAhd* (Lloyd et al. eds. 1988–), *IE-CoR* (Heggarty et al., eds.), *IELex* (Dunn et al.), *IEW* (Pokorny 1959–1969), *LIPP* (Dunkel 2014), *LIV*² (Rix et al. 2001). Linguistic abbreviations include: AGk. (Attic Greek), Alb. (Albanian), Arm. (Armenian), Av. (Avestan), Bulg. (Bulgarian), Capp. (Cappadocian [Greek]), Cz. (Czech), Goth. (Gothic), Hitt. (Hittite), It. (Italian), Khot. (Khotanese), Lat. (Latin), Latgal. (Latgalian), Latv. (Latvian), Lith. (Lithuanian), Luw. (Luwian), Lyc. (Lycian), Maced. (Macedonian), MIA (Middle Indo-Aryan), MW (Middle Welsh), Myc. (Myceanaean), NHG (New High German), NIA (New Indo-Aryan), NT (New Testament [Greek]), OAv. (Old Avestan), OBret. (Old Breton), OCS (Old Church Slavonic), OE (Old English), OIr. (Old Irish), ON (Old Norse), OPr. (Old Prussian), OS (Old Saxon), Osc. (Oscan), PIE (Proto-Indo-European), Pol. (Polish), Russ. (Russian), SCr. (Serbo-Croatian), Skt. (Sanskrit), Slk. (Slovak), SMG (Standard Modern Greek), Sogd. (Sogdian), Sp. (Spanish), TochA (Tocharian A), TochB (Tocharian B), Tsak. (Tsakonian), Ukr. (Ukrainian), Ved. (Vedic), YAv. (Young Avestan).

2 Ringe et al. (2002) uses data points coded from phonological and morphological as well as lexical characters, Gray & Atkinson (2003), Bouckaert et al. (2012), Chang et al. (2015) are based solely on lexical data.

3 In this regard, cf. especially Bouckaert et al. (2012) and Chang et al. (2015).

4 Cf. Ringe et al. (2002: 69). The question of the position of Tocharian as the second branch to split off from Proto-Indo-European is primarily supported by lexical correspondences according to Ringe et al. (2002: 99–100). Note, however, Malzahn (2016) recently doubting the value

 | DOI:10.1163/9789004416192_011

paper I will not be strictly engaging with the methodology of cognacy-based phylogenetic methods and their further applications, but instead will be focusing on methodological problems arising with the encoding of lexical cognacy judgements in the first instance.

For Bayesian phylogenetic analyses comparative word lists are only the starting point. For comparative word lists to be useful in determining genetic relationships, cognate relations need to be indexed between lexemes. These cognate judgements are made on the basis of our knowledge of the comparative phonology and morphology of the individual daughter languages. In turn these cognate judgements, once made, can then be used as data points representing shared linguistic history that can be used for phylogenetic analyses. In determining lexical cognacy judgements the standard handbooks can be used as references, and in a large proportion of cases etymologies *are* straightforward. Nevertheless, as we are well aware, not all etymological proposals are equally certain and agreed upon, either through differences in scholarly opinion over formal reconstruction or via uncertainties where a given proposed etymology may happen to be simply a conjecture. Computational cladistics ideally requires very clear-cut, preferably binary data input. In many cases a cognate vs. non-cognate decision may be straightforward, but in others there may be, for many reasons, uncertainties where it is not easy to reduce a given proposed cognate relationship to such a binary decision. For this reason, establishing reliable and consistent cognacy judgements in a machine-readable format is not always a straightforward task.

In order to address some of these issues, in this paper I will discuss methodological and practical problems in establishing lexical cognacy, based on work undertaken as part of the *Indo-European Cognate Relationships* (*IE-CoR*) database project at the Max Planck Institute for the Science of Human History. I will first introduce the background of the *IE-CoR* project and its approach and guiding principles to establishing cognacy in the lexica of Indo-European languages. I will then discuss some practical problems that have commonly arisen in establishing lexical cognacy judgements and some proposed solutions to these problems within the *IE-CoR* framework in order to minimise the amount of inconsistent data. Finally, I will discuss some issues pertaining to the limits of lexical cognacy for phylogenetic analyses.

---

of the lexical correspondences between Anatolian and Tocharian for characterising an early split vis-à-vis the rest of Indo-European.

2 Research Context: The *IE-CoR* Project

The *IE-CoR* database represents a fresh break from the old *IELex* database developed by Michael Dunn and used as the basis for high-profile but controversial phylogenetic studies such as Bouckaert et al. (2012), and Chang et al. (2015).[5] The *IELex* database was designed to host the lexicostatistical dataset of Dyen et al. (1992), combined with the lexical cognacy data from the Swadesh meanings used in Ringe et al. (2002), and to output those data on cognacy relationships in the NEXUS file format required as the input to many quantitative and phylogenetic analysis algorithms. While one of the functions of the *IE-CoR* database is likewise to export cognacy judgement data in the same NEXUS file format, the comparative language data themselves are entirely new, and indeed the approach to coding cognacy has been thoroughly revised. The *IE-CoR* database has been ambitiously conceived to cover a large representative sample of Indo-European languages with the comparative lexical data provided by experts in the individual languages based on a new reference list of comparison meanings that have been carefully defined to ensure a consistent medium of semantic comparison. In addition to the lexical data being elicited anew, the cognacy judgements have been thoroughly revised by specialists in Indo-European comparative linguistics and specialists in individual branches of Indo-European with a cognacy policy explicitly rooted in phylogenetic systematics.[6]

2.1 *The Jena 200 Concept List*

The *IE-CoR* database project developed a new concept list in order to reduce the amount of inconsistent data in cognacy-based phylogenetic analyses. The basis for this was the Swadesh 207 list (itself the combination of his 100 and 200-meaning lists) combined with the Leipzig-Jakarta 100 list that originated

5 Studies based on IELex data have been heavily criticised (cf. Pereltsvaig & Lewis 2015). The recognition of problems in the consistency of both the source data and cognacy of IELex was the impetus for a radical re-conceptualisation of a new database of Indo-European Cognate judgements.

6 The main editor of the Indo-European cognacy judgements and cognacy metadata for IE-CoR is Matthew Scarborough, but important contributions to the cognate coding have also been made at various points in the revision process by Cormac Anderson (Celtic, Iranic, Italic & Romance), Erik Anonby (Iranic), Alexander Falileyev (Celtic), Cassandra Freiburg (Indo-European), Ulrich Geupel (Albanian), Geoffrey Haig (Iranic), Britta Irslinger (Indo-European and Celtic), Lechosław Jocz (Slavic), Thomas Jügel (Iranic), Ron Kim (Tocharian), Martin Kümmel (Indo-European, Indo-Iranic), Martin Macak (Armenian) and Roland Pooth (Indo-Iranic). Regarding the IE-CoR cognacy policy, see § 2.2 below.

with the *World Loanword Database* project (in turn showing considerable overlap with the Swadesh 207).[7] These meanings added from the Leipzig-Jakarta list include:

- ANT, BITTER, TO CARRY, CLAW, TO CRY/WEEP, TO DO/MAKE, FLY (NOUN), TO GO, TO GRIND/CRUSH, HARD, TO HIDE, HOUSE, NAVEL, RUN, SHADE/SHADOW, SWEET, THIGH, YESTERDAY

An attempt was made at a close semantic specification of the combined list of 227 concepts in several workshops held in Jena between October and November 2015.[8] From these, the twenty-seven most problematic concepts were removed on the basis of various criteria such as ease of elicitation, fuzziness of meaning, difficulty in coding, and linguistic and cultural universals, resulting in the Jena 200 concept list.[9] From the combined 227 list the following meanings were rejected:

- Adpositional meanings, conjunctions, pronouns, grammatical words:
  - ALL, AND, AT, BECAUSE, HE/SHE/IT, IF, IN, OTHER
- Quantifiers too fuzzy for closer semantic specification:
  - FEW, MANY, SOME
- Meanings problematic in terms of cultural universals:
  - HUSBAND, ROAD, ROPE, WIFE
- Meanings semantically vague, difficult for consistent elicitation, or "non-basic":
  - ANIMAL, DULL (BLUNT), FLOAT, FLOW, HOLD, RUB, SPLIT, SQUEEZE, STAB, SUCK, WIPE

This pruning of meanings that are difficult to identify and encode has been a part of an effort to minimise the amount of unreliable and bad data that was a typical criticism of the reliability of the *IELex* dataset. The final Jena 200 list is given in Table 9.1.[10]

---

7 Cf. Tadmor (2009). The Swadesh 207 list used by Ringe et al. (2002) and IELex specified the meaning claw of the Swadesh 207 (cf. Comrie & Smith 1977) as (finger)nail, so the original Swadesh 207 comparison meaning claw was reintroduced from the Leipzig-Jakarta list. Dyen et al. (1992) used only the Swadesh 200 list of comparison meanings.

8 Similarly, cf. Kassian et al. (2010). The definitions used for the final Jena 200 list can be found on the IE-CoR public wiki on GitHub: https://github.com/lingdb/CoBL-public/wiki.

9 For the complete list of meanings determined for the Jena 200 list, see http://concepticon.clld.org/contributions/Heggarty-2017-200.

10 The Jena 200 list was finalised at a workshop held at the Max Planck Institute for the Science of Human History 27–29 November 2015, whose attendees included Cormac Anderson, Oleg Belyaev, Harald Bichlmeier, Tonya Dewey-Findell, Martin Findell, Robert Forkel, Andrew Gargett, Paul Heggarty, Steve Hewitt, Britta Irslinger, Lechosław Jocz, Martin Kümmel, Martin Macak, Sergio Neri, Roland Pooth, Tijmen Pronk, Jakob Runge, Matthew Scarborough, Kim Schulte, Matilde Serangeli, Aviva Shimelman, and Ariel Silva.

TABLE 9.1 The Jena 200 concept list

ANT	FLOWER	MOTHER	STAND
ASH	FLY (NOUN)	MOUNTAIN	STAR
BACK (BODY PART)	FLY (VERB)	MOUTH	STICK
BAD	FOG	NAIL	STONE
(TREE) BARK	FOOT	NAME	STRAIGHT
BELLY	FOREST	NARROW	SUN
BIG	FOUR	NAVEL	SWEET
BIRD	FREEZE	NEAR	SWELL
BITE	FRUIT	NECK	SWIM
BITTER	FULL	NEW	TAIL
BLACK	GIVE	NIGHT	TAKE
BLOOD	GO	NOSE	THAT
BLOW	GOOD	NOT	THERE
BONE	GRASS	OLD	THEY
BREATHE	GREEN	ONE	THICK
BURN	GRIND	PERSON	THIGH
CARRY	GUTS	PLAY	THIN
CHEST	HAIR	PULL	THINK
CHILD	HAND	PUSH	THIS
CLAW	HARD	RAIN	THREE
CLOUD	HEAD	RED	THROW
COLD	HEAR	RIGHT	TIE
COME	HEART	RIVER	TONGUE
COUNT	HEAVY	ROOT	TOOTH
CRY	HERE	ROTTEN	TREE
CUT	HIDE	ROUND	TRUE
DAY	HIT	RUN	TURN
DIE	HORN	SALT	TWO
DIG	HOT	SAND	VOMIT
DIRTY	HOUSE	SAY	WALK
DO	HOW	SCRATCH	WASH
DOG	HUNT	SEA	WATER
DRINK	I	SEE	WE
DRY	ICE	SEED	WET
DUST	KILL	SEW	WHAT
EAR	KNEE	SHADOW	WHEN
EARTH	KNOW	SHARP	WHERE
EAT	LAKE	SHORT	WHITE

TABLE 9.1 The Jena 200 concept list (*cont.*)

EGG	LAUGH	SING	WHO
EYE	LEAF	SIT	WIDE
FALL	LEFT	SKIN	WIND
FAR	LEG	SKY	WING
FAT	LIE	SLEEP	WITH
FATHER	LIVE	SMALL	WOMAN
FEAR	LIVER	SMELL	WORM
FEATHER	LONG	SMOKE	YEAR
FIGHT	LOUSE	SMOOTH	YELLOW
FIRE	MAN	SNAKE	YESTERDAY
FISH	MEAT	SNOW	YOU (PL.)
FIVE	MOON	SPIT	YOU (SG.)

2.2 *Practical and Methodological Issues in Determining Cognacy in* IE-CoR

The main methodological problem of preparing lexical cognacy data is determining which lexemes (within a given comparison meaning) are cognate with one another, and rendering those cognate relations into a machine-readable format consisting of a binary cognate or non-cognate decision. As we are well aware, not all proposed etymologies are as certain as others, and we may have varying levels of confidence about the reliability of a given etymological proposal. If one is overly trusting of more conjectural etymologies, one runs the risk of introducing inaccurate data into analyses. As Don Ringe frequently reminds us, "if we are to maintain scientific rigor, we must reject etymologies that are attractive but flawed".[11] At the same time, however, if we are completely hypercritical of the comparative evidence, this often leads to postulating excessive differences between branches, undermining the whole enterprise of phylogenetic analysis in the first place. An additional problem is that of variable degrees of cognacy. In the Indo-European context, one can speak of root cognacy as the most basic and fundamental cognate relationship, or closer cognate relationship through a shared derived stem.[12] In the context of *IE-CoR*, it

11 Ringe (2017: 2), cf. Ringe (1996: xvi–xvii).

12 This is actually even more complex in many cases where finite verbs have been replaced by light-verb constructions. In such cases the nominal elements are coded for cognacy. For example, in the meaning FEAR Bulgarian *straxuvam se*, Rusyn *strašitɪ s'a* 'to fear' continue finite verbs derived from Proto-Slavic *strax-, while Kashubian *miec strach*, Upper

was decided that the basic criterion for cognacy was the Indo-European root, with the possibility left open for introducing cognate subsets to reflect different morphological derivations within a given cognate set in potential database expansions at a later date.[13] In order to deal with the problem of maintaining a balance of scientific rigor and being too hypercritical of proposed etymologies, the following solutions were implemented.

2.2.1 Hypercriticism over Forms in Closely Related Varieties

A practical problem that frequently occurs with closely related linguistic varieties is the question of the cognacy of lookalikes, especially among closely related dialects. At what point can one be justified in postulating a dialectal loanword from, e.g., Standard Italian into Friulian, or from Persian into modern West Iranian varieties, when the regular reflexes may be expected to look exactly or nearly the same as the loanword source? In practice, some effects of otherwise unrecognised loanwords are partly mitigated by having the language experts authoring the datasets of individual languages indicate all known loanwords, but it is an inevitability that some unrecognised loanwords will slip through. A solution for these cases comes from the theoretical underpinnings of phylogenetic systematics, where the principle followed is that in absence of clear evidence to the contrary, by default we assume common inheritance from a more recent shared ancestor rather than independent innovation (in this case, lexical replacement via an inter-dialect loanword).[14]

2.2.2 Encoding Proposed but Uncertain Cognate Relations: Some BAD Etymologies

While this principle works well at the microscopic level within an individual recognised branch of the Indo-European languages, it is more difficult to maintain it when considering less certain etymological proposals between

Sorbian *měć strach* 'to have fear' are calques on Standard German *Angst haben*, and based instead upon nominal derivatives of Proto-Slavic **strax-*. In this case the Slavic lexemes are technically cognate but represent quite different morphosyntactic constructions.

13 For cases where an Indo-European etymology is lacking the policy is to take an etymology as far back within its individual clade as possible. Loanword classes are rooted at the event of their borrowing and form their own cognacy classes based on these "loan events".

14 This principle is known in biological phylogenetic systematics as Hennig's Auxiliary Principle (cf. Hennig 1966: 121–122) and is based on Hennig's conviction that if the burden of proof is required to be given in each individual case that a feature is not convergent or a parallel independent innovation, the entire practice of phylogeny would lose all the ground on which it stands.

two or more branches of Indo-European. Such cases are the most critical for Indo-European phylogeny, since accepting or rejecting etymologies between Indo-European branches directly impacts the output results for subgrouping hypotheses. To illustrate my point, I will examine a couple of BAD examples for what Ringe (2017: 2) might perhaps consider attractive but ultimately flawed etymologies. The first example is the proposed cognacy of Hittite and Tocharian lexemes in the comparison meaning BAD:

1 Hitt. *idālu-* 'bad, evil, evilness' Luw. *ādduu̯āli-*, TochB *yolo* 'bad, evil' < ?**$h_1$ed-u̯ol-*.[15]

According to Kloekhorst (2008: 420–422), Hittite *idālu-*, Luwian *ādduu̯āli-* may go back to an original Proto-Anatolian stem *(*ʔ*)*eduo-*. These Anatolian lexemes were further connected by Watkins (1982) to the complex of words consisting of Armenian *erkn* 'pain, labour pains', Ancient Greek *ὀδύνη* 'pain, grief', Old Irish *idu* 'pain', which Schindler (1975) attempted to bring together from putative Indo-European **$h_1$ed-u̯ol/n-*. While the root etymology to **$h_1$ed-* 'bite; eat' (*LIV*^{2} 230–231) is doubted by Kloekhorst, he does not explicitly reject a possible connection to Tocharian B *yolo* 'bad, evil' which had been proposed as an additional cognate to this complex by Rasmussen (1984: 144–145).[16] If this etymology connecting the Anatolian and Tocharian lexemes is correct, this formation would be a unique Anatolian–Tocharian isogloss in this particular comparison meaning. As it stands, however, Michaël Peyrot has given sufficient reason that this etymology may bc doubted, as it is also quite possible that Tocharian B *yolo* is a loanword ultimately from Old Turkic *yavlak* 'bad, evil' (via Khotanese *yola* 'falsehood, lies').[17] One may observe from all this that while there is a reasonable amount of support for a possible proto-form **$h_1$ed-u̯ol/n-* which can account for all these forms, there exists sufficient doubt surrounding the etymologies of the Tocharian and Anatolian forms that it is difficult to say with complete certainty whether or not these forms are definitely cognate to each other.

A second BAD etymology where much uncertainty exists is the question of Greek and Albanian lexemes in this comparison meaning:

15 Cf. Schindler (1975), Rasmussen (1984: 144–145), Puhvel (1984: 487–493), Kloekhorst (2008: 420–422), Adams (2013: 555–556).

16 Cf. also Adams (2013: 555–556), accepting Rasmussen's etymology.

17 Peyrot (2016). I thank Michael Weiss for alerting me to this reference.

2 AGk. *κακός* 'bad' < Proto-Greek **kako/ā-*, Alb. *keq* 'bad' < Proto-Albanian **kaki̯a/ā-*.

The standard handbooks for Greek regard *κακός* as without a secure etymology.[18] By contrast, in the Albanological literature an etymology with Greek *κακός* for Albanian *keq* is frequently assumed from a common base **kak-* albeit with different derivational morphology.[19] If this is correct, this would qualify as a root etymology and might be a Greek-Albanian isogloss which could serve as a small piece of evidence in the question of a *Balkanindogermanisch* subgrouping within Indo-European.[20] One admits that Albanian *keq* certainly looks old and does not so easily appear to be the result of an early loan from Greek, but at the same time, the phonological and derivational uncertainties over the Albanian material and its great chronological remove from the earliest attested Greek make this etymology far from certain.[21]

Further cases like these two BAD examples could be easily assembled. The point is, the decisions made in cases such as these are critical for the subgrouping of individual branches of Indo-European. However, in trying to come to some sort of compromise over the etymological disputes, we are caught between our two methodological principles: We don't want to be hypercritical towards proposed etymologies since hypercriticism may lead to dismissing potentially relevant data for subgrouping. On the other hand, as with Ringe, we want to avoid introducing etymologies that are not fully secure since that risks introducing false-positive data into the analyses. When we make cladistic

18 Cf. Frisk (1960–1972, 1: 758–759), Chantraine (1968–1980: 482), Beekes (2010: 619–620). Willi (2016: 505–507) has recently argued that the irregular comparative and superlative forms *κακίων* and *κάκιστος* may be best accounted for by assuming an original *u*-stem adjective **κακύς*, but the further etymology is not easily decided. The best candidates are either the proposal of Hübschmann (1885: 154) to OAv. *kasu-* 'small, mediocre' (which formally accounted for via a zero-grade root **kn̥ḱ-* or **kaḱ-*, cf. also de Lamberterie 1990: 821–830), or a zero-grade *u*-stem noun derived to the verbal root **ḱenk-* 'to hang' (cf. *LIV*² 325) in the sense of *'hanging' > *'hesitant, wavering' > 'cowardly, bad' vel sim. (Willi 2016: 506–507). Proposed connections with AGk. *κάκκη* 'shit' remain unconvincing (Willi 2016: 505).

19 Cf. Huld (1984: 79–80), Demiraj (1997: 216–217), Orel (1998: 175), Schumacher & Matzinger (2013: 223, 239).

20 Cf. Klingenschmitt (1994: 244–245) for some proposed isoglosses.

21 Cf. Huld (1984: 79–80). Demiraj (1997: 217) has healthy scepticism, admitting that the possibility of a Greek loan cannot be ruled out, as "[d]ie paradigmatischen Verhältnisse, insbesondere der Akzentwechsel zwischen Singular- und Pluralstamm sprechen jedenfalls für eine uralte Formation (evtl. *i*-Stamm oder als solcher empfunden), die auf gr. (Komp.) *κακίων* bezogen werden kann".

arguments on the basis of qualitative arguments, we can simply ignore these cases, but when doing cognate coding with Swadesh-style comparison lists for phylogenetic analyses, it is not feasible to simply omit an entire concept meaning because one or two etymologies within that meaning set are difficult to decide.[22]

A significant weakness of the *IELex* database was its inability to code a cognacy relationship beyond a binary cognate/non-cognate decision. Within the *IE-CoR* framework an intermediate solution is proposed: In situations like these BAD examples where there is sufficient uncertainty over a proposed etymology or several competing proposals outside of a single branch of Indo-European, these cognate sets are split into separate classes. As split classes, this would be the hypercritical approach. However, built into the database framework is a *proposed cognacy* system, which allows uncertain or disputed cognacy proposals between branches to be cross-linked in the database and assigned scores equivalent to the varying levels of consensus over the etymology in the standard handbooks (cf. Fig. 9.1).

This proposed solution eliminates the need to have to settle on an absolute cognate/not-cognate decision process by encoding varying degrees of uncertainty in difficult cases of cross-branch etymologies. By encoding the data in this way the database system can easily generate different outputs depending on how permissive or restrictive one wishes to be in accepting more conjectural etymological comparisons.

22 It is worth observing, as Cormac Anderson points out to me, that while selectively ignoring data from certain comparison meanings may well be useful, doing so is potentially open to abuse by pre-selecting what meanings are considered to be more diagnostic than others. The opposite situation, stacking the list of comparison meanings to favour a given analysis is likewise true: if one wishes to use cognacy-based methods to test, e.g., the Greco-Armenian hypothesis, one could preselect the list of comparison meanings used to include meanings with exclusive Greek and Armenian isoglosses that could bias the sample towards a result that could make Greek and Armenian appear closer to each other with respect to the rest of Indo-European. Similarly, in traditional subgrouping much depends on deciding what features (phonological, morphological, etc.) are decided to be the most probative for classification in a given situation. Competing analyses may disagree what these features are, and—perhaps unconsciously—select the features that favour one analysis over another. This has in the past been a criticism regarding the testability of the comparative method (cf. McMahon & McMahon 2005: 69). In any case, the potential for pre-selecting meanings that favour a given analysis is a strong argument for a standardised list of comparison meanings.

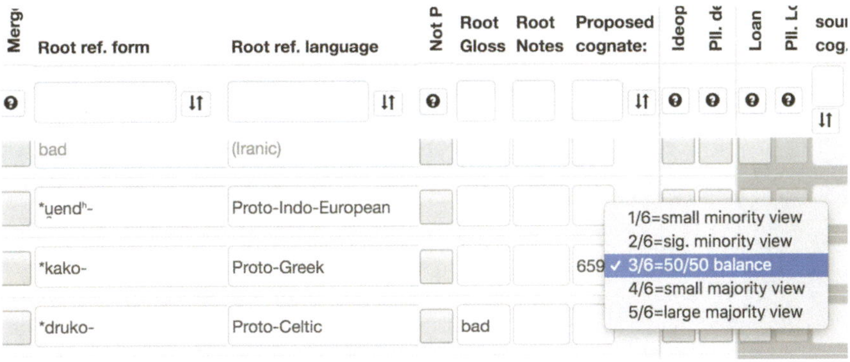

Merg	Root ref. form	Root ref. language	Not P	Root Gloss	Root Notes	Proposed cognate:	Ideop	Pll. d	Loan	Pll. L	sour cog.
	bad	(Iranic)									
	*uendʰ-	Proto-Indo-European									
	*kako-	Proto-Greek				659					
	*druko-	Proto-Celtic		bad							

1/6=small minority view
2/6=sig. minority view
✓ 3/6=50/50 balance
4/6=small majority view
5/6=large majority view

FIGURE 9.1 The *IE-CoR* proposed cognacy system in the data-entry website

2.2.3 A Proposed Decision-Making Framework for Encoding Lexical Cognacy Judgements

With the introduction of the proposed cognacy system in the *IE-CoR* database, I have devised the following framework as a set of guidelines for systematising cognate judgement decisions (Fig. 9.2). The purpose of these guidelines is to streamline the decision-making process in order to ensure as much consistency as possible and to make explicit the degree of confidence in the scholarly consensus regarding any given cognate set in the database.

The starting point for this decision-making process is the assessment of any given lexeme in a single meaning (e.g. BAD, BACK, BARK, etc.). The etymology of an individual lexeme is assessed within its own individual branch of Indo-European, typically by consulting the standard reference works for that language or branch. If there is no etymology within its own sub-branch of Indo-European elsewhere in that comparison meaning, then the lexeme is treated as etymologically isolated (although there may be uncertain proposals which can be indexed using the proposed cognacy system). If, alternatively, there is an established etymology within the clade to, e.g. Proto-Germanic, Proto-Celtic, etc., then the lexeme is to be added to that set. Further decisions in the guidelines concern the multi-branch etymologies: If there is no certain etymology outside of a given branch of Indo-European, then a set of decisions is followed parallel to the assessment whether an individual lexeme is isolated within its own branch. If the two or more-branch etymology is widely accepted, then the cognate sets are to be merged into a multiple-clade set. At all stages, references are added into the database metadata in order to provide justification for the cognacy decisions.

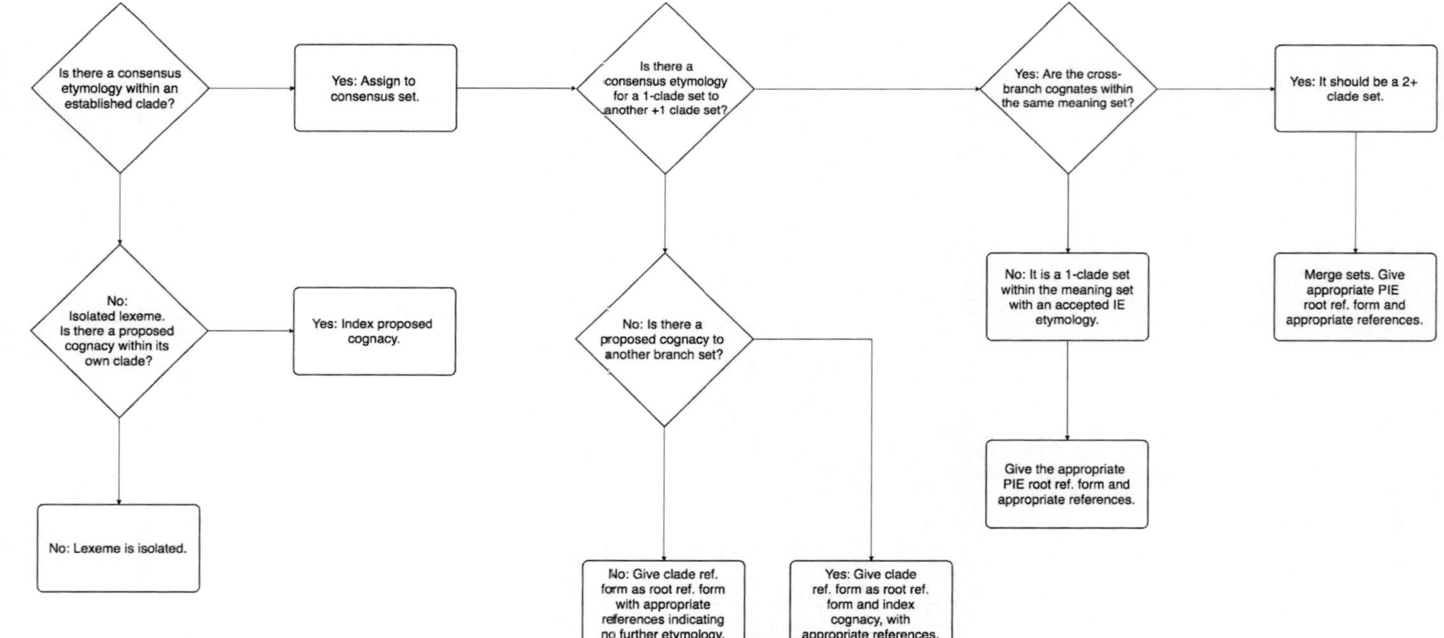

FIGURE 9.2 Systemised Guidelines for Cognate Judgements in the *IE-CoR* Database

3 Practical Problems of Cognacy Coding in Comparative Wordlists

3.1 *An Indo-European Specific Problem: What is a Root Etymology Anyway?*

A perhaps not so obvious problem is the definition of an Indo-European root etymology in itself. As Indo-Europeanists we operate with established theories of root structure, but if we consider root etymologies as our basic criterion of Indo-European cognacy then difficulties in assigning cognacy arise in assessing whether individually reconstructed Indo-European roots may be cognate with others. In practice, this primarily concerns cases whether s-mobile roots and roots that exhibit root extensions are to be considered the same root or lexically distinct roots etymologically. Consider the roots in the meaning CUT in (3) and (4):

3 2. *(*s*)*ker*- 'scheren, kratzen, abschneiden' (*LIV*[2] 556–557, *IEW* 938–940): ON *skera*, OE *scieran* (but possibly extended *(*s*)*kerH*- (*LIV*[2] 558, cf. Lith. *skìrti* 'trennen, teilen, unterscheiden'), so Kroonen 2013: 443–444).

4 *(*s*)*kert*- '(zer)schneiden' (*LIV*[2] 559–560, *IEW* 941–942): YAv. *kərəṇtaiti*, OPers. **kart*-, Ved. *kr̥t*-

In *IE-CoR* we have followed the practice of *LIV*[2] which splits up lemmata from their potentially root-extended variants, but lumps together s-mobile variants.[23] Certainly this is a reasonable pre-established policy following the practice of a standard reference work, but perhaps it requires some further methodological justification. On the one hand, the function of s-mobile is not fully understood, but it is certainly well documented.[24] The role of root-extensions in Proto-Indo-European and/or pre-Proto-Indo-European derivational morphology is likewise not well understood, but given the large number of morphemes that have been claimed as root extensions (but are functionally unclear), it is difficult to determine whether roots with extensions were derived forms within Indo-European, or near homophonous forms of independent origin. For the purposes of establishing cognacy, I would therefore argue that extended roots should be split into separate classes in the database and be

23 For the justification of *LIV*[2] on this practice, cf. *LIV*[2] 6–7.

24 One standard view on the origins of s-mobile variants is in sandhi, i.e. *-s # # C-* → *-sC-*, in which case one would not expect any *functional* distribution of s-mobile forms at all as they would have arisen via *ad hoc* reanalyses as part of PIE phonotactics (cf. Mayrhofer 1986: 119–120). I thank the anonymous reviewer for alerting me to this reference.

indexed as potentially related to each other. Methodologically, this approach also has the advantage that sets with root extensions that have been indexed for proposed cognacy (cf. § 2.2.2 above) can easily be automatically merged if one wishes to run an analysis that does take potentially extended roots as cognates. Thus systematically splitting and indexing proposed cognacy in these cases allows for greater flexibility at the level of the phylogenetic analysis.[25]

3.2 *Taboo Deformation*

Taboo deformation is a general problem in etymology that obscures the identification of true cognates.[26] By its nature, taboo deformation introduces irregular sound correspondences into lexical comparisons, and consequently obscures etymological relationships. In some cases the invocation of taboo distortions is justifiable, in others it may be used to prop up attractive but flawed etymologies. We cannot eliminate a whole meaning from the concept list simply because taboo distortions are exhibited in that meaning, therefore proposals of taboo distortions in etymologies need to be carefully evaluated on a case-by-case basis. I would like to illustrate this through three examples drawn from the *IE-CoR* database in (5), (6), and (7).

5 TONGUE from PIE **dn̥ĝ*^{h}*u̯éh*$_2$*-* : TochA *käntu*, TochB *kantwo*, Arm. *lezow*, Av. *hizuua*, Ved. *jihvā́*, OCS *językъ*, Lith. *liežùvis*, OPr. *insuwis*, Goth. *tuggō*, Osc. **fangvam**, Lat. *lingua*, OIr. *tengae*.

The standard post-Anatolian word for TONGUE is notorious for exhibiting extensive taboo-deformation in most of the daughter branches that attest it. The individual deformations, however, are generally well explained, even if their specific motivations are unclear, and we can generally be confident of this etymology.[27]

---

25 It is worth observing that the practice of splitting roots with enlargements offers a degree of further resolution in the analysis of subgrouping, i.e. two branches that might show the same enlarged root in contrast to other branches that exhibit only the unenlarged root may be potential evidence for a shared morphological innovation in the former group. If both unenlarged and enlarged variants were merged into, e.g. **(s)ker(t)-*, no further subgrouping information could be extracted from this lexical cognacy data point.

26 On taboo distortion in general, cf. Hock (1991: 303–305). On taboo distortion specifically in Indo-European, cf. the discussion in Mallory & Adams (1997: 493–494), Mallory & Adams (2006: 89).

27 For this cognate judgement, cf. the discussion of Mallory & Adams (2006: 175), Martirosyan (2010: 307–308), Adams (2013: 147), *EWAia* 1: 591–593, de Vaan (2008: 343), Derksen (2008: 159), Derksen (2015: 285), Lehmann (1986: 349), Matasović (2009: 368).

6 ANT from PIE ?*moru̯i- : TochB *warme**, AGk. *μύρμηξ*, Arm. *mrǰiwn*, YAv. *maoiri-*, Ved. *vamrá-*, OCS *mravii*, ON *maurr*, Lat. *formīca*, OBret. *morion*

ANT, a meaning on our comparison list taken over from the Leipzig-Jakarta list, is difficult to fully account for in all the branches, but a proto-form is generally reconstructed from the many variants, and we can be more or less confident of an Indo-European etymology although the exact shape of the reconstruction remains uncertain.[28]

7 LOUSE (*IEW* 692: **lū̆s* (gen. **lu̯u̯-ós*) 'Laus')
  a Germanic and Celtic ?**lū̆-* : ON *lús*, OE *lūs*, OS *lûs*; MW *lleuen*, OBret. *louenn* (Orel 2003: 252, Seebold & Kluge 2011: 563, Matasović 2009: 250)
  b Ved. *yūka-* (> MIA, NIA forms, e.g. Pāli *ūkā*, Hindi *jūm̐*, Bengali *ukun*, Nepali *jumro*, etc., cf. *EWAia* 2: 415, Turner 1962–1966: 608, no. 10512).
  c Proto-Slavic **vŭš-* (SCr. *uš*, Maced. *voška*, Russ. *vošʹ*, Ukr. *voša*, Pol. *wesz*, Cz. *veš*, Slk. *voš*, cf. Derksen 2008: 532).
  d Baltic forms: Lith. *utėlė̃*, Latv. *uts*, Latgal. *vuts* (to be connected with Slavic forms: Fraenkel 1962–1965: 1173; against connection with Slavic forms cf. Derksen 2008: 532).

Indo-European LOUSE, however, is a most difficult case for which to securely establish cognacy. The reconstructed etymon in *IEW* is simply not large enough in terms of reconstructed segments for us to be fully confident that the deviant forms ascribed to it go back to the same source. It is attractive to posit a single IE etymon for LOUSE, as Pokorny does, but given the difficulties in reconstruction the only principled solution, as I see it, is to reject the attractive etymology and to split the different forms postulated to **lū̆s* in *IEW* into the most plausible individual cognate sets. It is probably worth observing that Kassian, Zhivlov & Starostin (2015: 311) have recently given up on using LOUSE in their list of comparison meanings for a lexicostatistical assessment of Indo-Uralic because of the difficulty of reliably reconciling these lexemes to a single original PIE protoform.

3.3 *Contamination and Blending*

Similar to taboo deformation is the question of *contamination* and *blending* of two distinct lexical roots, where a given word may not have a single root

28 For this cognate judgement and further discussion of these lexemes, cf. Matasović (2009: 278), Beekes (2010: 982), *EWAia* 2: 507, *ÈSSJa* 19: 248–249, Martirosyan (2010: 482–483), Adams (2013: 630), de Vries (1977: 380).

etymology. True blends are where two lexemes in closely associated semantic spheres have merged, creating a new lexeme in the process that takes on semantic aspects of both original lexemes. A contamination, by contrast, is where the phonetic form of a lexeme is altered due to close association with another lexeme in a related semantic field (Hock 1991: 198, Clackson 2017: 101–102). An example of simple contamination has been plausibly suggested for the reflexes of the IE word for TONGUE, where Latin *lingua* and Armenian *lezow* are not actually taboo distortions but are the result of an associative contamination with the PIE root **leu̯ĝʰ-* 'to lick', which could well have occurred independently in both branches (cf. Lat. *lingō* 'I lick', Arm. *lizem* 'id.').[29] In such examples, the semantics of the original lexeme remain intact. By contrast, for a prototypical example of a true blend one may consider English *brunch* which is a blending of the words *breakfast* and *lunch*, where the semantics have also blended to indicate a late morning meal that is not-quite breakfast, nor entirely lunch.[30]

A concrete example of a family of lexemes arising from an original blending might be attested in the case of Armenian *tesanem* 'I see', proposed since Meillet (1936: 135) to have originally been a blend of reflexes from the PIE roots **spek̑-* 'to see' and **derk̑-* 'to see' which formed a suppletive pair elsewhere in Indo-European (cf. Skt. pres. *paśyati* vs. aor. *adarśat*).[31] Such examples are problematic for establishing a single root etymology, since the result is not fully cognate with lexemes from either of the two roots. In such cases a principled solution, and the one that has been adopted in *IE-CoR*, could be to consider true blends as the creation of an entirely new lexeme, not directly cognate to either of the source lexemes that were originally blended. There is no clear way, however, to acknowledge the sources of the blending other than in the metadata for the new cognate set.

3.4 *Meanings in Grammatical Words and Pronominal Stems*

High-frequency grammatical words that are subject to increased wear-and-tear in the lexicon are not straightforward to code for cognacy. Initially some of these concepts were eliminated from the comparison list because lexical cognacy was not straightforward due to the lack of a single clearly identifiable

29 Cf. de Vaan (2008: 343), Martirosyan (2010: 307–308).

30 Hock (1991: 198), cf. "brunch, n." in OED Online http://www.oed.com (accessed June 12th 2018).

31 For further discussion of this example cf. Clackson (2017: 105–106) and see there *passim* for further proposed examples of blends in Armenian etymology. An alternative possibility for an etymology of Armenian *tesanem* may be a backformation from a root aorist **dek̑-* ~ **dk̑-* > Arm. *etes* 'saw' with a semantic development 'receive' > 'take in' > 'see' (accepted by *LIV*² 109–110, cf. Klingenschmitt 1982: 228, Schmitt 2007: 146, 190).

lexical root. This can be observed in (8) and (9) for various lexical elicitations in the comparison meaning BECAUSE, with examples in Slavic and Hellenic. In these cases, single root etymologies are impossible because there is no one single morpheme; these are all periphrases of different prepositions, pronouns and particles. As such they are difficult to encode consistently and are consequently more than likely to be a source of bad data.

8 BECAUSE in Slavic: OCS *zanje(že)*, *ponje(že)*; Bulg. *zaščoto*; Maced. *zatoa što*; Russ. *potomu čto*; Ukr. *tomu ščo*, Cz., Slk. *pretože*

9 BECAUSE in Greek: AGk. *διότι* (= *διά* + *ὅ* + *τι*), *ἕνεκα*; SMG *γιατί* (*για* + *τί*), *επειδή* (*ἐπεί* + *δή*), SMG *διότι*; Pontic *επειδήσκαι* (*επει* + *δη* + (*σ*?) + *και*), Capp. *ασο* (*ας* + *το*), Cypriot *επειδή* (*επει* + *δη*), Tsakonian *γιατσί* (= SMG *γιατί*), Italiot *τι*.

For this reason, the comparison meaning BECAUSE was rejected from the Jena 200 list, but as work proceeded other grammatical words that are otherwise generally more stable also transpired not to be exempt from difficulties in cognacy coding. To demonstrate this, I will discuss examples in the concept NOT (verbal negation, indicative) in (10) and (11). It may be observed that the majority of Indo-European languages use an indicative negation particle based on PIE **ne* which has been generally stable in most branches (10).

10 **ne* 'not' : Hitt. *natta*, Alb. *nuk*, Av. *nōit̰*, Ved. *ná*, OCS *не*, Lith. *ne-*, Goth. *ni*, Lat. *nōn*, OIr. *ní* (cf. *LIPP* Vol. 2 530–549 s.v. 1. **né* 'nicht')

A characteristic lexical innovation of Hellenic is a different negation particle *οὐ*(*κ*) with no certain etymology outside of its branch, with the possible exception of Armenian *oč'*.[32]

11 NOT in Hellenic:
a Ancient: Myc. *o-u-*, AGk. *οὐ*(*κ*), NT *οὐ*(*κ*)
b Modern: SMG *δεν*, Tsak. *δε*(*ν*), *ο-*, *ου-* (prefix), Capp. *δεν*

32 Against the interpretation of Cowgill (1960) as a putative **ne* h_2*oi̯u* (*kʷid*) 'not (ever) in life' I follow the reserved judgement of Clackson (1994: 158), Clackson (2004/2005: 155–156), and Martirosyan (2010: 531), who see Arm. *oč'* as more likely to be an inner-Armenian creation based on the simple pronoun *o-* (cf. *o-k'* and *o-mn* 'someone') + simple negative *č'* < **kʷid*.

The Modern Greek dialects present continuity issues with the cognacy from Ancient Greek *οὐ(κ)*. Standard Modern Greek and several modern dialects show a reflex *δεν*, which is historically accounted for via Ancient Greek *οὐδέν* (*οὐ* 'not' univerbated with *δέ* 'and' and *ἕν* 'one' = 'and not one'), which had been simplified to *δεν* following the tendency of Modern Greek to delete unstressed initial vowels.[33] In the case of Modern Greek *δεν* the original semantic-bearing morpheme that forms the basis for a cognate class, Ancient Greek *οὐ(κ)*, has been entirely lost. Should then, Modern Greek *δεν* be considered the same as Ancient Greek *οὐ(κ)* for the purposes of establishing a cognate judgement relationship? The answer to this question is difficult to decide. Strictly from the point of view of historical morphology, the original elements from which Modern Greek *δεν* were formed do not have anything to do with Ancient Greek *οὐ(κ)*. On the other hand there has not been any total lexical replacement, since the loss of *οὐ-* is the result of a regular sound change in the development of Modern Greek and there has been no break in functional continuity of the morpheme(s) used for indicative negation. Any cognacy coding decision implemented in this case, either to keep *οὐ(κ)* and *δεν* together as cognates or to split them as non-cognate, is ultimately an arbitrary decision. An alternative solution would be to assign cognate classes to each of *οὐ(κ)*, *δέ*, and *ἕν*, but consistently implementing multiple cognate-codes solutions across the entire Indo-European language family becomes increasingly fraught as time progresses and additional deictic markers or adpositional elements are grammaticalised (as in the example of BECAUSE above). Additionally, as the same inherited deictic and pronominal elements may well be independently re-used, it is not certain whether such a solution will necessarily improve the quality of output data to be used in lexicon-based phylogenetic analyses. In short, this example illustrates that in certain cases, coding lexical cognacy judgements can be occasionally arbitrary, especially in cases with compounded morphemes and other pleonastic elements, as frequently is the case in comparison meanings that are grammatical words or pronouns.[34]

33 Cf. Babiniotis (2010: 338).

34 This case from Hellenic was selected because it is one of the clearest examples of arbitrariness in the cognacy coding of pronominal and grammatical elements. The same difficulties are regularly found in pronominal elements. Further levels of absurdity in coding ghost morphemes could be reached in the Hellenic example if one accepts the etymology of Cowgill (1960), cf. n. 32 above, where the semantic-bearing morpheme **ne* 'not' is not even attested as part of the proposed collocation at all in the history of Greek.

3.5 *Sound Symbolism, Onomatopoeia, and Child Language*

Another set of problems comes from trying to consistently encode comparison meanings that are prone to frequent lexical renewal and distortion from other inherent semantic qualities of the comparison meanings themselves. I would focus on two examples:

12 SPIT from PIE **sptie̯u̯H-* 'spucken, speien' (*LIV*^{2} 583–584) : Lat. *spuī* (pf.), Lith. *spiáuti*, OCS *pljьvati*, Goth. *speiwan*, AGk. *πτῡ́ω*, Ved. *aṣṭhaviṣam* (aor.) 'habe gespuckt'

In (12) we have many phonologically similar lexemes in the comparison meaning SPIT, which, if one follows *LIV*^{2}, may to go back to an original Indo-European root **sptie̯u̯H-* 'to spit'.[35] Presumably Proto-Indo-European speakers did have a verb 'to spit' that was inherited by its daughter languages, but like the taboo deformation examples, presumably these underwent occasional deformations in individual branches; perhaps to maintain an imitative sounding verbal stem that complies with changes in phonological inventory, syllable structure, etc. Because the various *sp-*, or *pt-* reflexes of the daughter languages from the reconstructed initial cluster **spt-* appears to be imitative of the act of spitting, I find it is hard, at least in principle, to rule out new imitative forms being independently re-created among the daughter languages.[36] It is consequently difficult to be completely confident of the cognacy of such forms.

35 *IEW* 999–1000 reconstructs **(s)p(h)i̯ēu-* : **(s)pi̯ū-*, **(s)pīu-*.

36 Another possible candidate for sound-symbolism interfering with etymology is the case of lexemes for the meaning scratch, for which there are no less than seven roots reconstructed with phonetic elements **s*, **k*, and **r* in various permutations which could well be (partly) influenced by imitation of a scraping noise: PIE 2. **(s)ker-* 'scheren, kratzen, abschneiden' : Arm. *k'erem* (*LIV*^{2} 556–557, Martirosyan 2010: 662–663); PIE **kes-* 'ordnen' : OCS *česati*, Latv. *kasît* (*LIV*^{2} 357, Derksen 2008: 86, Derksen 2015: 231); PIE **kseu̯-* 'schaben, schliefen': SMG *ξύνω* (< AGk. *ξύω*), Hindi *khuracanā* (cf. Skt. *kṣuráti*) (*LIV*^{2} 372, Beekes 2010: 1039–1040, Turner 1962–1966: 194, no. 3729, *EWAia* 1: 435–436.); PIE **ksneu-* 'schärfen' : Ved. *kṣṇav-* (*LIV*^{2} 373, *EWAia* 1: 441, cf. Lat. *novācula* 'Rasiermesser'); PIE **skab*^{h}*-* 'kratzen, schaben' : Lat. *scabere*, OS *skaƀan* (*LIV*^{2} 549, de Vaan 2008: 541, Kroonen 2013: 438, cf. Lith. *skõbti* 'to plane'); PIE **(s)kreb-* 'schaben, kratzen' : OE *screpan*, MW *crauu* (*LIV*^{2} 562, cf. Orel 2003: 344); PIE **(s)kerp-* 'abschneiden, abrufen' : Lith. *krapštýti* (*LIV*^{2} 559). Cf. also Germanic **krat-* > NHG *kratzen*, etc. (*EWAhd* 5: 762–764) without secure etymology outside of Germanic. Not all of these root etymologies need be dismissed outright, but potential influence from onomatopoeia or sound symbolism in these cases should perhaps not be entirely ruled out.

Similarly, when target lexemes arise in child language they are difficult to reliably assign cognacy. Consider the following phonetically similar words in the target meaning FATHER in Anatolian, Germanic, and Slavic (13):

13 Hitt. *attaš*, Goth. *atta*, OCS *otьcь*

To these lexemes we may also compare Ancient Greek *ἄττα* 'father', Latin *atta* 'father', Old Irish *aite* 'foster father'. Considering an original Indo-European nursery word **atta-* ancestral to all of these forms is tempting, although it is remarkable that we do not have, e.g., Hitt. †*az-za* or Gk. †*ἄστα* which might be expected due to the well-known PIE phonological rule where epenthesis of **s* occurs in dental + dental clusters.[37] Furthermore, similar formations attested in unrelated languages (e.g. Dravidian **attan* 'father, elder', Turkish *ata* 'father', Hungarian *atya* 'father'), also rather make it appear more likely that the forms found among the various Indo-European branches are independent creations.[38] Consequently, in such a set, cognacy cannot be reliably assigned between these three forms, and similar arguments could be made in cases of other familiar kinship terms of the same nature.

3.6 *Proposed Solutions: Further Emendations to the Jena 200 Concept List*

Some of the problems that we have encountered here, such as those with grammatical words in §3.4, were known at the time of the compilation of the Jena 200 concept list. The pervasive difficulties in consistently encoding cognacy for pronouns, deictic elements, and concepts prone to onomatopoeia and sound-symbolism became much more apparent through the cognacy revision process. It is not particularly problematic to identify the best target lexeme for these

37 Cf. Mayrhofer (1986: 110–111) and examples like Hitt. *ez-za-zi* /ed-t^{s}i/ > [et^{s}-t^{s}i] '(s)he eats' from PIE **h₁ed-ti* '(s)he eats', Gk. *ἴσθι* 'know!' (2.sg.imptv.) < **u̯id-dʰi*. One could possibly speculate, however, that the very nature of the putative **atta* as a lexeme rooted in child language has inoculated it against the normal phonological rules, but I feel such an assumption unwarranted.

38 For a survey of opinions in standard handbooks, cf. Kloekhorst (2008: 225–226) "clearly onomatopoeic", Chantraine (1968–1980: 135) "le terme a une origine indo-européenne", Beekes (2010: 165) "A nursery word found in several IE languages, and may be inherited", de Vaan (2008: 60) [reconstructs **h₂et-o-*], Lehmann (1986: 46) "nursery word [...] [n]o need to assume borrowing in spite of earlier attestations, such as Hitt *attas*", Kroonen (2013: 39) "A cross-linguistically uniform nursery word", Derksen (2008: 383) "must be considered a nursery word", *ÈSSJa* 39: 168–173 "Слав. **otьcь* через и.-е. **att-iko-s* связано с и.-е. **ătta*". For Dravidian, cf. Burrow & Emeneau (1984: 15).

comparison meanings, but as I have attempted to demonstrate through various examples, these are not always the meanings for which it is easiest to encode cognate relations reliably or consistently. Consequently, although these elements could be considered basic vocabulary, I would argue that concepts of these types should be avoided in comparative lexical word lists altogether. In *IE-CoR* a further twenty most problematic concepts were removed from the project's comparison list for these reasons. These include:

- Pronominal and Deictic Meanings
  - HERE, HOW, I, THAT, THERE, THEY, THIS, WE, WHAT, WHEN, WHERE, WHO, YOU_PL., YOU_SG.
- Miscellaneous grammatical words
  - NOT, WITH
- Meanings frequently prone to onomatopoeia
  - BLOW, SPIT
- Meanings prone to independently recurring child-language variants:
  - FATHER, MOTHER

The further emendation of the Jena 200 list has addressed a few of the most obvious data problems outlined here, although not all of them. Possible examples of taboo deformation in § 3.2 and blending in § 3.3 still need to be carefully weighed on a case-by-case basis, and just because some of the most onomatopoeia-prone meanings have been omitted does not mean that cases of onomatopoeia will not occur in other meaning sets.[39]

4 The Limits of Cognacy

Before I conclude, I would like to briefly address two issues where lexical cognacy methods, strictly followed, have the potential to produce misleading results: independent parallel semantic shifts in distantly related linguistic varieties, and semantic calquing among closely related linguistic varieties.

4.1 *Parallel Semantic Shift*

In some cases, it appears that strict adherence to the principles of a root etymology leads to some cognate sets that are parallelisms not inherited from a more

39 Within the framework IE-CoR it is additionally possible to mark individual problematic cases as "ideophonic" if it cannot be ruled out that all the lexemes in a given cognate set are not independent parallel creations. In such marked cases these individual cognate sets are simply removed from the dataset in a data export.

recent ancestor. Observe CHILD in Lycian and Modern Romance varieties in (14) and GIVE in Middle Iranian and Old Irish in (15).

14 CHILD derivations from PIE *$*d^{h}eh_{1}$(i̯)-* ‘(Muttermilch) saugen’ : Lyc. *tideimi-* ‘child’; Sp. *hijo*, It. *figlio* ‘child’, etc. < Lat. *filius* ‘son’ (*LIV*[2] 138–139, Kloekhorst 2008: 875–877, Neumann 2007: 359–360, de Vaan 2008: 219).

15 GIVE from PIE *$*b^{h}er$-* ‘tragen’ : Khot. *heḍä*, Sogd. *ϑbr-* from **fră̌-bar-*; OIr. *do·beir* (Bailey 1979: 499, Cheung 2007: 6–10, Matasović 2009: 62).[40]

Descriptively, these cases are lexically cognate at the Indo-European root level, and strictly are to be connected together according to the *IE-CoR* cognacy policy. Nonetheless, the derivations are secondary formations, and one cannot use the coincidence of these forms to claim that the language branches in these examples are more closely related to each other because they share a root etymology in these sets. Perhaps these cases of parallel semantic shift may be few enough that the noise they bring to the phylogenetic signal could be minimal, but strictly speaking these cases—if sufficiently numerous—may potentially add false-positive data for closer genetic relationships between individual branches of Indo-European. In the *IE-CoR* database we have explicitly introduced a system to indicate such cases.[41] It is also worth emphasizing that Bayesian methods are probabilistic, not absolute, and are designed to handle occasional independent parallel derivations at different points within a tree, but such examples are less capably handled by traditional lexicostatistical analyses.

4.2 *Semantic Calquing and Convergence in Lexical Semantics: The Case of Tsakonian*

Since the criterion of comparison in lexical cognacy judgements is cognacy across semantic identities, a major problem for these methods is semantic

---

40 The anonymous reviewer rightly pointed out that OIr. *do·beir* is part of a suppletive paradigm in Old Irish and wondered how verbal suppletion is handled in IE-CoR. This is a very good question given the ubiquity of root suppletion between derived aspect stems found among the Indo-European languages. In general, the IE-CoR policy on this point is to encode the root of the present stem as the comparison form. In exceptional cases where root/stem suppletion occurs *within* a present stem paradigm, the root cognacy is coded for the third person singular indicative active, e.g. Hittite SAY root cognacy is coded for 3.sg. *tēzzi* < *$*d^{h}eh_{1}$-ti* rather than *ter-/tar-* < **ter-* / **tr̥-*, Modern French GO is cognacy coded for 3.sg. *va* (cf. Latin *vādere*) rather than infinitive *aller*.

41 These cases marked in IE-CoR as “parallel derivations” are treated as cases in n. 39 above.

TABLE 9.2 Percentages of shared cognates in target meanings across Greek varieties on the Jena 180 comparison list

	Ancient (Attic)	New Testament	Modern Std	Tsakonian
Ancient (Attic)		158/167 = 94.6%	103/180 = 57.2%	95/180 = 52.8%
New Testament	158/167 = 94.6%		97/167 = 58.1%	89/167 = 53.3%
Modern Std	103/180 = 57.2%	97/167 = 58.1%		131/180 = 72.8%
Tsakonian	95/180 = 52.8%	89/167 = 53.3%	131/180 = 72.8%	

calquing and lexical convergence between dialects. Where lexical semantics have converged within a given clade, one runs the risk of misrepresenting the actual historical relationships between individual varieties. Tsakonian, a modern Hellenic variety, provides a case where purely lexical methods can, depending on one's point of view, either completely fail, or at least illustrate that conventional historical linguistic narratives may be more nuanced than formerly assumed.

On the basis of phonological and morphological isoglosses it is generally agreed that Tsakonian is descended from a Doric or West Greek dialect of Ancient Greek, as opposed to all other Modern Greek dialects, which stem from a form of the East Greek Attic-Ionic *koiné*.[42] Consequently, in a traditional phylogenetic analysis of Tsakonian *vis-à-vis* the other Modern Greek dialects, the split between them is quite ancient, predating the first attestation of the Ancient Greek dialects.[43] A lexicostatistical analysis of Tsakonian with respect to Ancient Greek and Modern Standard Greek, however, tells a somewhat different story. Percentages of cognate vocabulary in the targeted concept meanings of the Jena 180 list (cf. § 3.6 above) shared between the *IE-CoR* Attic Greek, New Testament Greek, Modern Standard Greek, and Peloponnese Tsakonian varieties of Hellenic have been compiled in Table 9.2.[44]

A lexicostatistical analysis of these percentages based on absolute distances would subgroup Tsakonian with Standard Modern Greek instead of placing it on a branch separate to all three of the Attic / Attic-Ionic *koiné* derived varieties as one would expect from the analysis based on the comparative

42 For further discussion on Tsakonian, cf. Horrocks (2010: 87–88), Liosis (2014), Liosis (2016).

43 For a conventional discussion of Ancient Greek dialectal phylogeny, cf. Horrocks (2010: 13–24).

44 Cf. Scarborough (forthcoming a), Scarborough (forthcoming b), Scarborough (forthcoming c), Liosis (forthcoming).

method. This is, perhaps, unsurprising considering that Tsakonian did not develop in isolation of other Modern Greek dialects, and the reasons for this are almost certainly contacts and convergence with other Medieval Greek superstrates.[45]

How, then, are we to interpret this situation? It is clear that the picture from lexicostatistical comparison is at odds with the one obtained from the more rigorous methodologies of comparative reconstruction. On the one hand we could consider that the limits of lexical-cognacy based methods are reached where long-term convergence in lexical semantics has occurred.[46] On the other hand, perhaps we need not be so dismissive here since the picture obtained from cognacy-based methods and that of comparative reconstruction are illustrating two different but important aspects of the linguistic history of Tsakonian. The inability of lexical methods to reproduce a deep phylogeny that is predicted by comparative reconstruction does illustrate their limits and that they cannot fully be a replacement for phylogenies reconstructed on the basis of more reliable criteria. Nevertheless, the unexpected result of Tsakonian being *lexically* closer to Modern Greek varieties rather than being more divergent illustrates the problematic aspects of the narrative of a deep phylogenetic split. The West Greek dialectal varieties ancestral to Tsakonian have never been out of contact with other East Greek and *koiné* dialects, and the fact that these dialects have been in contact is reflected in the lexicon-based results. Both analyses are complementary to our understanding of the evolution of Tsakonian. One must bear the caveat in mind, however, for one would misinterpret the dialectal history of Greek here on the basis of the comparative lexical analysis alone.

5 Conclusions

In this paper I have attempted to outline some of the issues in determining lexical cognacy judgements for the Indo-European language family within the framework of the *IE-CoR* database project. Throughout this paper I have attempted to emphasise the difficulty of encoding lexical cognacy judgements in terms of all-or-nothing binary data. Of course, in very many cases cognacy

45 Liosis (2014: 886–887).

46 I have used absolute lexicostatistical distances for the sake of simplification in this example. Probabilistic Bayesian phylogenetic methods also fail in this case, but perhaps not so overtly because of the built-in ability to handle occasional independent parallel innovations (cf. § 4.1 above).

judgements are straightforward and recognisable, especially at the level within a given sub-clade of Indo-European. This paper has focused on a selection of the more difficult cases where uncertainties cannot be easily reduced to such binary clarity. I have sought to illustrate these through various case studies drawn from the examples encountered during the cognacy revision process of the *IE-CoR* database. I have also attempted to outline some proposed solutions to these methodological and practical problems of determining lexical cognacy judgements implemented in *IE-CoR*. I would emphasise that cases such as these are generally the exception across the entire dataset, and the recognition of problems such as those discussed in this paper is what motivated a complete re-think of how a database of cognate relations for computational cladistics can be more reliably and consistently realised. As studies in computational historical linguistics continue to proliferate, I hope the discussion offered in this work will provide not only some theoretical justification for the cognacy decisions made within the *IE-CoR* database, but also stimulate further fruitful discussion on ways to improve the quality and usefulness of lexical cognacy datasets more generally.

Acknowledgements

The present paper is based on work carried out on the *Indo-European Cognate Relationships* (*IE-CoR*) database (formerly *Cognacy in Basic Lexicon* [*CoBL-IE*]), a project based at the Max Planck Institute for the Science of Human History. Much of the content of this paper on problems of encoding lexical cognacy has been born out of practical work undertaken on this project, and many of the problems and proposed solutions presented have been worked out with the co-editors of the database Cormac Anderson and Paul Heggarty, as well as with our many database co-authors and collaborators. A full list of authors in the *IE-CoR* database can be found at http://iecor.clld.org/contributors/. I would like to specifically thank my fellow Indo-Europeanist colleagues and individual branch specialists who have collaborated on the cognacy coding aspects of the *IE-CoR* project at various phases and with whom I have discussed many individual cases and methodological problems of etymology: Cormac Anderson, Erik Anonby, Cassandra Freiberg, Ulrich Geupel, Geoffrey Haig, Britta Irslinger, Lechosław Jocz, Martin Kümmel, Martin Macak, and Roland Pooth. I also specifically wish to thank the conference attendees for comments on the original version of this paper, and my colleagues Paul Heggarty and Cormac Anderson for many helpful comments which considerably improved this paper. I would also like to thank the anonymous reviewer for constructive criticisms and helpful suggestions. All remaining errors and other deficiencies, of course, remain my responsibility alone.

References

Adams, Douglas Q. 2013. *A dictionary of Tocharian B*. Second edition, revised and greatly enlarged. Amsterdam: Rodopi.

Babiniotis, Georgios. 2010. *Ετυμολογικό λεξικό της νέας ελληνικής γλώσσας*. Αθήνα: Κέντρο λεξικογραφίας.

Bailey, Harold W. 1979. *A dictionary of Khotan Saka*. Cambridge: Cambridge University Press.

Beekes, Robert S.P. 2010. *An etymological dictionary of Greek*. Leiden: Brill.

Bouckaert, Remco, Philippe Lemey, Michael Dunn, Simon J. Greenhill, Alexander V. Alekseyenko, Alexei J. Drummond, Russell D. Gray, Marc A. Suchard & Quentin D. Atkinson. 2012. Mapping the origins and expansion of the Indo-European language family. *Science* 337. 957–960.

Burrow, Thomas, & Murray B. Emeneau. 1984. *A Dravidian etymological dictionary*. Second Edition. Oxford: Clarendon Press.

Chang, Will, Chundra Cathcart, David Hall & Andrew Garrett. 2015. Ancestry-constrained phylogenetic analysis supports the Indo-European Steppe Hypothesis. *Language* 91. 194–244.

Chantraine, Pierre. 1968–1980. *Dictionnaire étymologique de la langue grecque*. Paris: Klinksieck.

Cheung, Johnny. 2007. *Etymological dictionary of the Iranian verb*. Leiden: Brill.

Clackson, James. 1994. *The linguistic relationship between Armenian and Greek*. Oxford: Blackwell.

Clackson, James. 2005. Review of Frederik Kortlandt. 2003. *Armeniaca: Comparative notes, with an appendix on the historical phonology of Classical Armenian by Robert Beekes* (Ann Arbor: Caravan Books). *Annual of Armenian Linguistics* 24–25. 153–158.

Clackson, James. 2017. Contamination and blending in Armenian etymology. In B.S.S. Hansen, A. Hyllested, A.R. Jørgensen, G. Kroonen, J.H. Larsson, B. Nielsen Whitehead, T. Olander & T.M. Søborg (eds.), *Usque ad radices: Indo-European studies in honour of Birgit Anette Olsen*, 99–115. Copenhagen: Museum Tusculanum.

Comrie, Bernard, & Norval Smith. 1977. Lingua Descriptive Series: Questionnaire. *Lingua* 42. 1–72.

Cowgill, Warren. 1960. Greek *ou* and Armenian *oč'*. *Language* 36. 347–350.

Demiraj, Bardhyl. 1997. *Albanische Etymologien*. Amsterdam: Rodopi.

Derksen, Rick. 2008. *Etymological dictionary of the Slavic inherited lexicon*. Leiden: Brill.

Derksen, Rick. 2015. *Etymological dictionary of the Baltic inherited lexicon*. Leiden: Brill.

Dunkel, George. 2014. *Lexikon der indogermanischen Partikeln und Pronominalstämme.* Band 1. *Einleitung, Terminologie, Lautgesetze, Adverbialendungen, Nominalsuffixe, Anhänge und Indices.* Band 2. *Lexikon.* Heidelberg: Winter.

Dunn, Michael, et al. Indo-European Lexical Cognacy Database. Nijmegen: Max Planck Institute for Psycholinguistics. http://ielex.mpi.nl/

Dyen, Isidore, Joseph B. Kruskal & Paul Black. 1992. An Indoeuropean classification: A lexicostatistical experiment. *Transactions of the American Philosophical Society* 82. iii–iv, 1–132.

Fraenkel, Ernst. 1962–1965. *Litauisches etymologisches Wörterbuch.* Heidelberg: Winter.

Frisk, Hjalmar. 1960–1972. *Griechisches etymologisches Wörterbuch.* Heidelberg: Winter.

Gray, Russell D., & Quentin D. Atkinson. 2003. Language-tree divergence times support the Anatolian theory of Indo-European origin. *Nature* 426. 435–439.

Heggarty, Paul, Cormac Anderson & Matthew Scarborough (eds.). Forthcoming. *Indo-European Cognate Relationships Database (IE-CoR).* Jena: Max Planck Institute for the Science of Human History. http://iecor.clld.org

Hennig, Willi. 1966. *Phylogenetic systematics.* Urbana: University of Illinois Press.

Hock, Hans Heinrich. 1991. *Principles of historical linguistics.* Second edition, revised and updated. Berlin & New York: Mouton de Gruyter.

Horrocks, Geoffrey. 2010. *Greek: A history of the language and its speakers.* Chichester: Wiley-Blackwell.

Hübschmann, Heinrich. 1885. *Das indogermanische Vocalsystem.* Strassburg: Karl J. Trübner.

Huld, Martin. 1984. *Basic Albanian etymologies.* Columbus, OH: Slavica.

Kassian, Alexei, George Starostin, Anna Dybo & Vasiliy Chernov. 2010. The Swadesh List: An attempt at semantic specification. *Journal of Language Relationship* 4. 46–89.

Kassian, Alexei, Mikhail Zhivlov & George Starostin. 2015. Proto-Indo-European–Uralic comparison from the probabilistic point of view. *Journal of Indo-European Studies* 43. 301–347.

Klingenschmitt, Gert. 1982. *Das altarmenische Verbum.* Wiesbaden: Reichert.

Klingenschmitt, Gert. 1994. Die Verwandschaftverhältnisse der indogermanischen Sprachen. In J.E. Rasmussen (ed.), *In honorem Holger Pedersen: Kolloquium der Indogermanischen Gesellschaft vom 26. bis 28. März 1993 in Kopenhagen,* 235–251. Wiesbaden: Reichert.

Kloekhorst, Alwin. 2008. *Etymological dictionary of the Hittite inherited lexicon.* Leiden: Brill.

Kroonen, Guus. 2013. *Etymological dictionary of Proto-Germanic.* Leiden: Brill.

de Lamberterie, Charles. 1990. *Les adjectifs grecs en -υς: Sémantique et comparaison.* Louvain-la-Neuve: Peeters.

Lehmann, Winfred P. 1986. *Gothic etymological dictionary.* Leiden: Brill.

Liosis, Nikos. 2014. Language varieties of the Peloponnese: Contact in diachrony. In G. Kotzoglou et al. (eds.), *11th International Conference on Greek Linguistics (Rhodes, 26–29 September 2013): Selected Papers/Πρακτικά*, 884–894. Rhodes: Department of Mediterranean Studies, University of the Aegean.

Liosis, Nikos. 2016. Tsakonian studies: The state-of-the-art. *Μελέτες για την ελληνική γλώσσα* [*Studies in Greek Linguistics*] 36. 205–217.

Liosis, Nikos. Forthcoming. Tsakonian: Peloponnese. In Cormac Anderson, Paul Heggarty & Matthew Scarborough (eds.), *Indo-European Cognate Relationships Database (IE-CoR)*. Jena: Max Planck Institute for the Science of Human History.

Lloyd, Albert L., Otto Springer, Rosemarie Lühr, Harald Bichlmeier, Maria Kozianka & Roland Schuhmann (eds.). 1988–. *Etymologisches Wörterbuch des Althochdeutschen*. 6 vols. Göttingen: Vandenhoeck & Ruprecht.

Mallory, James Patrick, & Douglas Q. Adams. 1997. *Encyclopedia of Indo-European culture*. London: Fitzroy Dearborn.

Mallory, James Patrick, & Douglas Q. Adams. 2006. *The Oxford introduction to Proto-Indo-European and the Proto-Indo-European world*. Oxford: Oxford University Press.

Malzahn, Melanie. 2016. The second one to branch off? The Tocharian lexicon revisited. In Bjarne Simmelkjær Sandgaard Hansen, Benedicte Nielsen Whitehead, Thomas Olander & Birgit Anette Olsen (eds.), *Etymology and the European lexicon. Proceedings of the 14th Fachtagung der indogermanischen Gesellschaft, 17–22 September, Copenhagen*, 281–292. Wiesbaden: Reichert.

Martirosyan, Hrach K. 2010. *Etymological dictionary of the Armenian inherited lexicon*. Leiden: Brill.

Matasović, Ranko. 2009. *Etymological dictionary of Proto-Celtic*. Leiden: Brill.

Mayrhofer, Manfred. 1986. *Lautlehre: Segmentale Phonologie des Indogermanischen*. In *Indogermanische Grammatik*. Band 1, 73–177. Heidelberg: Winter

Mayrhofer, Manfred. 1992–2001. *Etymologisches Wörterbuch des Altindoarischen*. 3 vols. Heidelberg: Winter.

McMahon, April, & Robert McMahon. 2005. Language classification by numbers. Oxford: Oxford University Press.

Meillet, Antoine. 1936. *Esquisse d'une grammaire comparée de l'arménien classique*. Vienne: Imprimerie des pp. Mekhitharistes.

Neumann, Günter. 2007. *Glossar des Lykischen (Überarbeitet und zum Druck gebracht von Johann Tischler)*. Wiesbaden: Harrassowitz.

Orel, Vladimir. 1998. *Albanian etymological dictionary*. Leiden: Brill.

Orel, Vladimir. 2003. *A handbook of Germanic etymology*. Leiden: Brill.

Pereltsvaig, Asya, & Martin D. Lewis. 2015. *The Indo-European controversy: Facts and fallacies in historical linguistics*. Cambridge: Cambridge University Press.

Peyrot, Michaël. 2016. Language contact in Central Asia: On the etymology of Tocharian B *yolo* 'bad'. In Bjarne Simmelkjær Sandgaard Hansen, Benedicte Nielsen Whitehead, Thomas Olander & Birgit Anette Olsen (eds.), *Etymology and the European lexicon. Proceedings of the 14th Fachtagung der indogermanischen Gesellschaft, 17–22 September, Copenhagen*, 327–335. Wiesbaden: Reichert.

Pokorny, Julius. 1959–1969. *Indogermanisches etymologisches Wörterbuch.* 3 vols. Bern & München: Francke.

Puhvel, Jaan. 1984. *Hittite etymological dictionary.* Vol. 1. *Words beginning with A*; vol. 2: *Words beginning with E and I.* Berlin: Mouton.

Rasmussen, Jens Elmegård. 1989. *Studien zur Morphophonemik der indogermanischen Grundsprache* (Innsbrucker Beiträge zur Spachwissenschaftt 55). Innsbruck: Institut für Sprachwissenschaft der Universität Innsbruck.

Ringe, Donald A. 1996. *On the chronology of sound changes in Tocharian.* Vol. 1. *From Proto-Indo-European to Proto-Tocharian.* New Haven: American Oriental Society.

Ringe, Donald A. 2017. *From Proto-Indo-European to Proto-Germanic.* 2nd ed. Oxford: Oxford University Press.

Ringe, Donald A., Tandy Warnow & Ann Taylor. 2002. Indo-European and computational cladistics. *Transactions of the Philological Society* 100. 59–129.

Rix, Helmut, Martin Joachim Kümmel, Thomas Zehnder, Reiner Lipp & Brigitte Schirmer. 2001. *Lexikon der indogermanischen Verben: Die Wurzeln und ihre Primärstammbildungen.* 2. Aufl. Wiesbaden: Reichert.

Scarborough, Matthew J.C. Forthcoming a. Greek: Ancient (Attic). In Cormac Anderson, Paul Heggarty & Matthew Scarborough (eds.), *Indo-European Cognate Relationships Database (IE-CoR)*. Jena: Max Planck Institute for the Science of Human History.

Scarborough, Matthew J.C. Forthcoming b. Greek: New Testament. In Cormac Anderson, Paul Heggarty & Matthew Scarborough (eds.), *Indo-European Cognate Relationships Database (IE-CoR)*. Jena: Max Planck Institute for the Science of Human History.

Scarborough, Matthew J.C. Forthcoming c. Greek: Modern Std. In Cormac Anderson, Paul Heggarty & Matthew Scarborough (eds.), *Indo-European Cognate Relationships Database (IE-CoR)*. Jena: Max Planck Institute for the Science of Human History.

Schindler, Jochem. 1975. Armenisch *erkn*, griechisch *ὀδύνη*, irisch *idu*. *Zeitschrift für vergleichende Sprachforschung* 89. 53–65.

Schmitt, Rüdiger. 2007. *Grammatik des Klassisch-Armenischen mit sprachvergleichenden Erläuterungen.* 2., durchgesehene Auflage. Innbruck: Institut für Sprachen und Literaturen der Universität Innsbruck.

Schumacher, Stefan, & Joachim Matzinger. 2013. *Die Verben des Altalbanischen: Belegwörterbuch, Vorgeschichte und Etymologie.* Wiesbaden: Harrassowitz.

Seebold, Elmar, & Friederich Kluge. 2011. *Etymologisches Wörterbuch der deutschen Sprache.* 25., durchgesehene und erweiterte Auflage. Berlin: de Gruyter.

Simpson, J., & E. Weiner (eds.). *The Oxford English dictionary*. 2nd ed. Oxford: Oxford University Press.

Tadmor, Uri. 2009. Loanwords in the world's languages: Findings and results. In M. Haspelmath & U. Tadmor (eds.), *Loanwords in the world's languages: A comparative handbook*, 55–75. Berlin: de Gruyter.

Trubačev, O.N. et al. 1974–. *Этимологический словарь славянских языков*. 40 vols. Москва: Наука.

Turner, Ralph Lilley, Sir. 1962–1966. *A comparative dictionary of the Indo-Aryan languages*. London: Oxford University Press.

de Vries, Jan. 1977. *Altnordisches etymologisches Wörterbuch*. Leiden: Brill.

Watkins, Calvert. 1982. Notes on the formations of the Hittite neuter. In E. Neu, *Investigationes Philologicae et Comparativae. Gedenkschrift für Heinz Kronasser*, 250–262. Wiesbaden: Harrassowitz.

Willi, Andreas. 2016. *κακός* and *καλός*. In Bjarne Simmelkjær Sandgaard Hansen, Benedicte Nielsen Whitehead, Thomas Olander & Birgit Anette Olsen (eds.), *Etymology and the European lexicon. Proceedings of the 14th Fachtagung der indogermanischen Gesellschaft, 17–22 September, Copenhagen*, 505–513. Wiesbaden: Reichert.

CHAPTER 10

Italo-Celtic and the Inflection of **es-* 'be'

Peter Schrijver

1 Introduction

In light of the recent revival of the notion that Celtic and Italic once formed a common node on the Indo-European family tree (e.g. Weiss 2011: 465–466, Weiss 2012, Schrijver 2015: 196–197, Schrijver 2016), this contribution aims to provide a revised reconstruction of the inflection of **es-* 'be', which is based on a step by step reconstruction of the Italic and the Celtic material, first independently of one another: section 2 on Italic and sections 3–5 on the complex Celtic material; this is followed by a reconstruction of the Italo-Celtic paradigm in sections 6–7. Underlying this article is the supposition that if Italo-Celtic existed, it needs to be taken into serious account when reconstructing Celtic or Italic and when assessing the contribution of either to the reconstruction of Proto-Indo-European, in two senses:

- Celtic material is more directly relevant to the reconstruction of Italic than material from any other branch of Indo-European, and vice versa.
- Although absolute dating of prehistoric stages in the development of languages is problematic in principle, it seems safe to posit that the Italo-Celtic linguistic unity belongs to the second millennium BCE, which in chronological terms means that it is on a par with Mycenaean Greek, Indo-Iranian and early Anatolian. Italo-Celtic reconstructions offer a valuable control of reconstructions arrived at on the basis of Indo-Iranian and Greek (which are rather similar to one another) and on the basis of Anatolian (which is eccentric in many ways).

True to the first principle, I intend to reconstruct the present tense paradigm of **es-* for Italo-Celtic by concentrating entirely on the Italic and Celtic material and by excluding almost all possible preconceptions about its further Indo-European pedigree, apart from the rather basic assumptions that Proto-Indo-European possessed athematic presents beside thematic presents and subjunctives (in verbs in general rather than in **es-*, which is the subject of this enquiry), and that it possessed primary (expressing *hic et nunc*) beside secondary (not expressing this) verbal endings.

 | DOI:10.1163/9789004416192_012

2 Thematic Forms in the Italic Present of *es-

Latin possesses a number of well-known verbs that in their present tense inflexion show what looks like thematic beside athematic forms (e.g. Weiss 2011: 425–435). Among them is the verb 'to be'. In this particular case, the Sabellian branch of Italic provides corroborative evidence:

	Athematic	Thematic
1sg.		*sum* < Old Latin *esom*;[1] Hercynian, Umbrian *esu*, South Picene, Presamnitic *esum* < **es-o-m* (beside Campanian *sim*)
2sg.	*es* < **es-si*	
3sg.	*est* < **es-ti* (Oscan *est, íst*)	
1pl.		*sumus* < **(e)s-o-mos*
2pl.	*estis* < **es-tes* (replacing **s-tes*)	
3pl.	Oscan, Umbrian *sent* < **s-enti*	*sunt*, Oscan *sú[nt]* < **(e)s-o-nti*[2]

The usual approach to explaining this amalgam is informed by the observation that other older Indo-European languages, such as Greek and Indo-Iranian, point to an originally athematic paradigm. Hence the thematic forms must have arisen secondarily, by analogy (Szemerényi 1964: 191–195, Wallace & Joseph 1987, Meiser 1998: 221, Weiss 2011: 425–426). The starting point of the thematicization is supposed to be the 1sg. *sum* < Old Latin *esom* < Common or Proto-Italic **esom*. The expected athematic 1sg. form was **esmi*. As a result of apocope of **-i* (which also affected the 2nd and 3rd person singular and the 3rd person plural),[3] this should have become **esm̥*. Subsequently, it is proposed, syllabic **m̥* yielded **om*. Since **esom*, although athematic in origin, now looked like a thematic form with secondary endings, other forms in the paradigm modelled themselves on it and became thematic as well: Proto-Italic 1pl. **es-o-mos* and 3pl. **es-o-nt(i)*. A slightly different explanation of the 1pl. *sumus* states that

1 Attested on the Garigliano Bowl, see Vine 1998.

2 There is no evidence for the full grade root in **esomos*, **esonti* (rather than **somos*, **sonti*) but in view of the presence (and subsequent loss) of **e-* in 1sg. **esom*, its reconstruction is possible. If, as argued in this paper, these thematic forms originally represented a subjunctive with secondary endings, full-grade root would be expected throughout the paradigm.

3 On apocope of **-i*, see e.g. Weiss 2011: 146–147.

it may have arisen from *_somos_ < *_sm̥os_, in which *_m̥_ was analogically introduced from 1sg. *_esm̥_ (Weiss 2011: 426).

The problem with this account is that *_esom_ (and *_somos_ in Weiss' account) is the only example of the sound change *_m̥_ > *_om_, which therefore is unconvincing (Dunkel 1998). Proto-Indo-European syllabic *_m̥_, *_n̥_ yielded *_em_, *_en_ in Latin (e.g. *_septm̥_ > Latin _septem_ 'seven') and *_am_, *_an_ (first syllable) or *_em_, *_en_ (elsewhere) in Sabellian. Syllabic *_m̥_, *_n̥_ that arose secondarily in Latin at a much later date became _im_, _in_ (Greek _mnā_ > Latin _mina_ 'unit of weight'; *_skafnelom_ > *_skabn̥lom_ by syncope > _scabillum_ 'bench'). It is true that in unstressed position Latin _im_ and _um_ interchanged (e.g. _maximus_, _maxumus_) and that this may account for the rise of Latin _simus_ beside _sumus_ (Weiss 2011: 426 footnote 5), but this is evidently not comparable with stable, pan-Italic and therefore probably Proto-Italic *_o_ in 1sg. *_esom_.

The reason that most Indo-Europeanists take this account of the rise of Latin _sum_ for granted in spite of the evident problem is, presumably, that it is a small price to pay for avoiding the alternative, which is to take *_esom_ at face value and to analyse it as an inherited thematic form with a secondary ending (Proto-Indo-European *_-m_). One of reasons why this alternative may be so hard to accept is that it would make Italic rather different from the other Indo-European languages, in particular Greek and Indo-Iranian, which point to a pervasively athematic present of 'to be'. In classical Indo-Europeanist terms, *_esom_ would be a subjunctive with a secondary ending, which presents us with the problem that it is hard to think of a semantic pathway that would turn that modal, non-present form into an indicative present form of the verb 'to be'. By contrast, it is much easier to understand that the subjunctive with primary ending, *_esō_ etc., which originally expressed the expectation of the speaker that the verbal action or state would come to pass, became the Latin future (_erō_). No Indo-European language preserves a semantic contrast between the subjunctive with primary and secondary endings (Indo-Iranian possesses them side by side but apparently without functional difference), and accepting that Latin does would make it unique. Accepting the problematic sound change *_m̥_ > *_om_ means that we no longer have to deal with those morphological and semantic problems. In spite of this, however, other Indo-Europeanists took the other route and did assume that *_esom_ is an old thematic form (e.g. Watkins 1969: 148, Dunkel 1998).

In light of the evidence for a common Italo-Celtic node on the Indo-European family tree, it is relevant to the Italic problem that Celtic, too, has extensive evidence for a thematic beside an athematic inflection of the present tense of 'to be'.

3 The Old Irish Present of the Copula

The Old Irish present tense paradigm of the copula (i.e. verbal forms based on the Indo-European root **es-*) is characterized by unusual differences between the absolute and conjunct series. The absolute inflection, which the verb takes on if it stands at the head of its clause, and the conjunct inflexion, which is used if the verb follows a limited series of so-called conjunct particles (mostly negations, preverbs and a number of conjunctions), historically differ from one another only by the fact that a particle followed (absolute) or preceded (conjunct) the verb. For instance, Proto-Celtic **bereti* 'carries' underlies both the absolute, OIr. *beirid*, and conjunct, OIr. *-beir*. In the absolute form, the particle **(e)ti*[4] followed the verb and protected its right-hand side, both from the early apocope of *i*[5] and the main Primitive Irish apocope of the fifth century AD.[6]

- Absolute: **bereti-(e)ti* > early i-apocope **bereti-t* > lenition, palatalization, apocope /ˈb'er'əð'/ *beirid*
- Conjunct: **nī-(e)ti bereti* > early i-apocope **nī-t beret* > lenition, palatalization, apocope /nī ˈb'er'/ *ní-beir*

In the case of the present tense of the copula, however, the difference between the absolute and conjunct forms is in many cases not amenable to this or a similar explanation. This requires an elaborate discussion, which is based on the excellent reconstructions in Schumacher 2004: 295–317. Schumacher, like many before him, starts from a single athematic paradigm in Proto-Celtic, which subsequently, in Insular Celtic, split into an absolute paradigm which by and large retained its athematic character, and a conjunct paradigm that contained a number of forms that appear to be thematic.

Before we go into the details, it may be useful to point out that reconstructing the copula is even more complex than reconstructing other verbs because the Old Irish copula is an unstressed proclitic, which means that attritions occur that are typical of proclitics and which destroy some of the phonologi-

---

4 This is the Proto-Indo-European conjunction **$h_1$eti* 'and, further', which became a clitic in Celtic and obeyed Wackernagel's law. See Schrijver 1994, 1997: 147–158, Schumacher 2004: 97–114. Readers who accept a different reconstruction of the particle and readers who are persuaded by different accounts of the origins of the absolute-conjunct distinction (e.g. McCone 2006) may substitute their favorite reconstructions. The argument concerning the thematic and athematic forms of 'to be' presented here does not depend on one's position in this matter.

5 Early i-apocope affected Irish, British Celtic and probably also Gaulish as well as, during the historical period, Celtiberian; the available evidence suggests that it affected final **-i* after voiceless consonants only (Schrijver 2007; based on crucial earlier work by McCone 1978).

6 Primitive Irish apocope deleted final syllables of the type -V̄, -V̆, -V̆C(C) and turned -V̄C into -V̆.

cal oppositions that are normally preserved, directly or indirectly, in stressed and post-tonic syllables: long vowels are shortened; palatalized consonants are depalatalized; vowel oppositions are reduced (_e_ and _a_ merge as _a_; _o_ and _u_ merge as a vowel that could be spelled either as 'o' or as a 'u'); initial _sV-_ is reduced to _V-_. A consequence of all this is that reconstructions are always ambiguous: if we start reconstructing backwards by making an inventory of all phonologically possible reconstructions of the attested Old Irish forms, we are confronted with a host of competing reconstructions, only a few of which make etymological and morphological sense. I have therefore adopted the procedure of reconstructing forward, from Proto-Celtic to Old Irish. Starting from both an uncontroversial athematic present _*es-mi_, etc., and a controversial thematic present _*es-ō_ (with primary ending) or _*es-om_ (with secondary ending), I attempt to establish to which of these candidates an Old Irish form can and cannot go back, taking into account the rules of Old Irish historical phonology.

3.1 _The Old Irish Absolute Present_ (_Reconstructed with Particle_ *(e)t < *eti)

		Athematic	Thematic	
			1	2
1sg.	_amm < *eḿḿ < *emmi-t <_	_*es-mi_	~~_*es-ō_~~	~~_*es-om_~~
2sg.	_at_[7] _< *e + t < *ē <_	_*es-si_	_*es-esi_	_*es-es_
3sg.	_is < *iś < *eśś < *etsi-t < *esti-t <_	_*es-ti_	~~_*es-eti_~~	~~_*es-ed_~~
1pl.	_ammi < *emmi < *emmī-t < *emmosi-t <_	_*(e)s-mosi_	~~_*es-omosi_~~	~~_*es-omos_~~
2pl.	_adib_[8] _< *eϑ'e + β' < *ētēt < *esetes-et <_	?~~_*(e)s-tes_~~	?_*es-etes_[9]	?_*es-ete(s)_
3pl.	_it < *id'_ for _*ed' < *henti-t < *senti-t <_	_*s-enti_	~~_*es-onti_~~	~~_*es-ond_~~

7 The alternative form _it_, which occurs in the Milan glosses, probably arose in the collocation _air it_ 'for you are' (Ml. 55d11), whence once _it_ in absolute clause-initial position (Ml. 108d2; Schumacher 2004: 306; differently McCone 2006: 112–113, 120–121, who assumes that _it_ is original and _at_ analogical).

8 18 occurrences in the Old Irish glosses, beside _adi_ (2×), _ada(b)_ (1×). The basic form is _*adab_ /aðəβ/, while _ad(a)ib_ introduced palatalization that is normally lost in proclitics from the posttonic 2pl. suffixed pronoun. The short form _adi_ probably underwent influence from 1pl. _ammi_ beside _ammin_. See Schumacher 2004: 307–308. Differently McCone 2006: 112, 120–122, who takes _adi_ as the most archaic form.

9 Schumacher (2004: 301–302) and McCone (1995: 127) reconstruct basic _*e-tes(i)_, on which see the main text below.

One of the striking innovations concerns the influence of clitic (suffixed and infixed) pronouns on the absolute paradigm. This probably started in the 1sg. *amm*, which could be reanalysed as *a* + clitic pronoun of the 1st person singular *-mm*. This provided the model for the analogical spread of clitic pronouns to other absolute forms. The 2sg., Primitive Irish **e* > *a*, was remodelled to *a-t*, which contains the clitic pronoun of the 2nd person singular, *-t*. Similarly, alternative forms arose for the plural: 1pl. *ammi-n* (beside widespread *ammi*), 2pl. *adi-b* (beside very rare *adi*, on which see below).

The explanation of the vocalism of 2sg. *at* is not straightforward. Schumacher (2004: 139–140) seems to suggest that **esi-t* > **ehi-t* > **e.ih* contracted to **ēh* before apocope, whence proclitic shortening to **e* and proclitic vowel change to *a*, but this would be the only example of a contraction **e.i* > **ē* (as pointed out by McCone 2006: 112). Alternatively, hiatus was retained in **e.ih* until apocope, by which **-ih* was lost, leaving **e* > *a*. McCone, who takes the 2sg. *it* to be the most conservative form, proposed a rule according to which unstressed **es* before vowel became **is*, hence the unstressed 2sg. of the copula **esi-* became **isi-* > Old Irish *i-* + 2sg. pronoun *-t*. See McCone 1995: 125, 2006: 111 ff. on this rule. Schrijver 1995: 387–388 and Schumacher 2004: 138–153 discussed material that strongly suggests there was no such development, however.

Similarly problematic is the reconstruction of the 2pl., where McCone 1995: 127 and Schumacher 2004: 307–308 reconstruct **e-tes(i)* with a stem **e-* rather than any of the reconstructions provided above: see two paragraphs below for the remodelling that may have led to this stem. They disagree on the status and reconstruction of the second syllable, however (cf. footnote 8).

The *i* of Old Irish 3sg. *is* and, probably, 3pl. *it* did not receive a plausible explanation until Griffith 2016 (see p. 50 for his discussion of previous proposals). Primitive Irish raising does not affect unstressed syllables and the Irish copula is unstressed, so **esti* and **enti* could not have become **issi*, **iddi* > *is, it* as a result of that rule. The British Celtic rule **e* > *i* /_NT does not affect Irish, so it does not help to explain *it* (Schrijver 1993). Since all those rules fail, the 3sg. should have become **es'* > **as* and the 3pl. **ed'* > **at*. Griffith proposes that raising of unstressed **e* to **i* (and **o* to **u*) occurred regularly before Primitive Irish palatalized **s*, hence **esti-t* > **es'* > **is'*> (depalatalization of proclitics) *is*. Thence *i* may have spread analogically to the 3pl. according to the following proportional analogy: Archaic Old Irish 3sg. relative **es* : absolute **is'* = 3pl. relative **ed'e* : absolute *ed'*, where **ed'* is then replaced by **id'* > OIr. *it*; the idea is that the vowel contrast *e* : *i* of the 3sg. was interpreted as carrying the semantic contrast relative : non-relative and thence spread to the 3pl. (thus Schumacher 2004: 310).

As stated earlier, Schumacher (2004, esp. 301–302) and McCone (1995: 127) explain all forms on the basis of a Proto-Celtic athematic inflexion. According to this explanation, the crucial stage, intermediate between Proto-Celtic and Old Irish, possessed forms in which various sound changes had obliterated the fact that the root was **es-* rather than **e-*:

1sg. **emmi-t(i)* as a result of *-*sm-* > *-*mm-*
2 sg. **esi-t(i)* as a result of the (probably already Indo-European) simplification of **es-si* to **esi*
3sg. **etsi-t(i)* > **essi-t*, as a result of early Celtic intervocalic *-*st-* to *-*ts-* > *-*ss-*
3pl. **enti-t(i)* as a result of the loss of initial **s-* > **h-* in proclitics

According to Schumacher, who by and large follows McCone (1995: 227), morphological reanalysis of the 2sg. and 3pl. led to the interpretation that they contained a root **e* followed by the regular athematic endings *-*si* and *-*(e)nti*. Application of this reanalysis to the 1sg. led to **e-mmi-t*, which reanalysis is confirmed by the fact that on the basis of this form, *-*mmi-t* spread to the athematic nasal presents, e.g. 1sg. **sernaimm* 'spread' < **ster-na-mmi-t*, where it replaces the inherited form *-*mi* with single *-m-*, as in inherited **ster-na-mi-t*. In a second step, the inherited 1pl. **s-mosi* and 2pl. **s-tes* were replaced by the forms created on the basis of a stem **e-* followed by the endings of the regular verb. For the 2pl., this resulted in **e-tes-et*, which regularly yielded *adi-* in *adib*. For the 1pl., the analogy should have given rise to **e-mosi-t* > OIr. **ami* /aṽi/ rather than attested *ammi* /ami/. Schumacher explains the latter by analogy to the 1sg., which had double *-*mm-* < *-*sm-*.

All of this is plausible rather than compelling, but that is enough for present purposes. Returning to the diagram, we may note that indeed all absolute forms except the 2pl. can be arrived at on the basis of a Proto-Celtic athematic paradigm, and one could say that McCone's and Schumacher's account takes care of the 2pl. By contrast, thematic reconstructions are impossible for all absolute forms except the 2sg. and 2pl. There are indeed still problems facing some reconstructions, but these cannot be solved by considering that they may have reflected thematic forms. To conclude, there is no compelling evidence so far for thematic forms of **es-*, let alone for the Proto-Celtic reconstruction of such forms. But things are more complex when we turn to the Old Irish conjunct forms.

3.2 *The Old Irish Conjunct Present*

		Athematic	Thematic	
			1	**2**
1sg.	*-a* + lenition < **eu* < **esū*	~~**es-mi*~~	**es-ō*	~~**es-om*~~
2sg.	*-a* < **eh* < **ēh* < **eheh* < **eses*(*i*) <	~~**es-si*~~	**es-esi*	**es-es*
3sg.	*-Ø* + *h*-pref. < **eh* < **est*(*i*)	**es-ti*	~~**es-eti*~~	**es-ed*
1pl.	*-am* < *-em* < **eaṽ* < **esomos*(*i*) <	?~~*(*e*)*s-mosi*~~	**es-omosi*	**es-omos*
2pl.	*-ad* < *-ed* < **eeϑ'* < **esetes*	~~*(*e*)*s-tes*~~	**es-etes*	?**es-ete*(*s*)
3pl.	*-at* < *-et* < **eod* < **esont*(*i*) or *-at* < *-et* < *(*h*)*ent* < **senti*	**s-enti*	**es-onti*	~~**es-ond*~~

Conjunct forms of the present tense of the copula are always preceded by *t, d* /d/ except in the 3rd sg. after the main clause negation *ní* (3sg. *ní* 'is not' but 1sg. *nita* 'am not', 3pl. *nitat* 'are not') and after the subclause negations *nád, nach*. The origin of this /d/ is unknown.[10]

The reconstructions that are presented in the diagram above call for a number of comments.

The 1sg., *-a* + lenition, probably reflects thematic **eū* < **ehū* < **esū* (which would be its Proto-Celtic form if it existed at the time): compare the 1sg. subjunctive of stressed verbum substantivum *beu* < **beū*, the unstressed counterpart of which can be found in the 1sg. subjunctive of copula *ba* < **beu* < **beū* (McCone 1991: 122, 2006: 113). Neither **esmi* nor **esom* are capable of yielding OIr. *-a* + lenition.

The 2sg. *-a* may reflect **esesi*, which became **eses* by early *i*-apocope and then **eheh* > **ēh* > **e* > proclitic *a*. It may also reflect **eses*, with identical developments except for early *i*-apocope (Schumacher 2004: 311). The only form it may not reflect, at least directly, is athematic **essi*, which via **ehi* > **eh* would have yielded zero in Old Irish. We will return to the 2sg. form later on because

10 A comparison with equally anomalous Middle Breton *nend-eu* 'is not' strongly suggests that Old Irish *-t-* reflects **-nt-*. The **-t-* may conceal the 'absolute' particle **eti* or the adverb **ita* which underlies the particle Middle Welsh *yd-*, Middle Breton *ed-* that often precede present and imperfect forms of 'to be' (Schumacher 2013–2014). The **-n-* is more difficult to explain, but in light of the fact that Middle Welsh *yw* 'is' occurs in syntagmas whose Old Irish counterparts are nasalizing relative clauses (see 5.2 below), it is tempting to connect the **-n-* with the clitic particle or pronoun that underlies relative nasalization in Irish (i.e. **jom* or **em*; cf. e.g. Schrijver 1997: 91–113, with references).

it is a crucial form for Schumacher's derivation of the conjunct forms from an athematic paradigm.

The 3sg. is non-leniting zero, which prefixes an *h*- to a following vowel in Middle Irish. This is traditionally derived from athematic **esti* > (early *i*-apocope) **est* > **ets* > **ess* > **eh* > (regular apocope) zero + *h*- (thus also Schumacher 2004: 311). Strictly speaking, a thematic 3sg. with secondary ending, **esed*, would have yielded the same result: **esed* > early (but not Proto-) Celtic **ese* > **esɪ* > (early *i*-apocope) **es* > **eh* > zero + *h*-. For the chronology of the loss of final **d* and for **e* taking part in early *i*-apocope, see Schrijver 2007, especially 366–369. This reconstruction has never been seriously entertained because the alternative, **esti*, performs just as well in terms of historical phonology and is morphologically straightforward (in contrast to **esed*).

In Archaic Old Irish, the 1pl. is attested as *-em* (Cambrai Homily) and *-am* (Würzburg glosses, prima manus) before it is replaced by the pronominally inspired *-an* (the clitic 1pl. pronoun is *-n*; Schumacher 2004: 312). Schumacher (ibid.) assumes that the earlier form is phonologically /em, am/, with unlenited *m* from athematic 1pl. **emmos* < **emmosi*. Considered in isolation, this is quite possible, but in the wider context of the Old Irish verb, it seems more likely that the form was /eṽ, aṽ/, with lenited *m*. We have seen that the 1pl. absolute of the copula influenced the ending of the 1pl. absolute of the regular verb, where inherited *-ṽ- < single *-m- was replaced by *-m- < double *-mm-. If the copula had a 1pl. conjunct **emmos* > *-*amm* beside the (unproblematic) 1pl. absolute **emmosi-t* > *ammi*, as Schumacher supposes, and if the copula influenced the 1pl. ending of the regular verb, which it did, we would surely expect to find an unlenited *-m- < *-mm- in the 1 pl. conjunct ending of the regular verb too, but that ending has retained lenited *-ṽ* (1pl. conjunct ending /-əṽ/ *-am* < Proto-Celtic *-*omosi*). However, if the copula had 1pl. absolute *ammi* /ami/ beside conjunct *-am* /aṽ/, as I argue, it is easy to understand that its influence on the regular verb led to the analogically changed Old Irish 1pl. endings absolute /-(ə)mi/ *-ammi, -mmai* beside retained conjunct /-əṽ/ *-am*. Old Irish *-em* > *-am*, with /ṽ/, may reflect thematic **esomos*(*i*) > **ehaṽ* > **eəṽ* > **ēṽ* > *eṽ* (spelled *em*).

The 2pl. *-ad* < *-ed* presupposes the same protoform **esetes* as the 2pl. absolute (or, if one prefers, the analogical **etes*(*i*)).

The athematic form, **senti*, which probably cannot account for the 3pl. absolute *it* directly (see above), can account for the vocalism of the 3pl. conjunct: **senti* > *(*h*)*ent* > **ε̄d*[11] > (proclitic shortening) *-et* > *-at* (Schumacher 2004:

11 McCone (e.g. 1995: 125) assumes that lengthening of **e* to **ε̄* before **nt* > *d* was limited to stressed syllables so did not affect the (unstressed) copula; if one follows this assumption, *(*h*)*ent* became **ed* = OIr. *-et* immediately.

312). So, however, can a thematic form **esonti* > **ehod* > **eəd* > **ēd* > *ed* (spelled *et*) > *at*.[12]

We may conclude that all conjunct forms look as if they require a thematic reconstruction, except 3sg. and 3pl., which allow both athematic and thematic reconstructions. We may add that a thematic reconstruction of the 3sg. is possible only on the basis of a form with secondary ending, **esed*, but that this reconstruction is implausible because primary endings were generalized in the prehistory of Irish.[13] This leaves us with the conclusion that the Irish conjunct forms probably reflect athematic beside thematic forms.

4 The British Celtic Present of 'To Be'

Before we turn to the Proto-Celtic reconstruction in more detail, it is important to take stock of the fact that British Celtic supports the conclusion reached on the basis of Irish, that roughly speaking the absolute paradigm of the copula presupposes athematic and the conjunct paradigm presupposes thematic beside athematic forms. The absolute—conjunct distinction survived into the 12th century in Middle Welsh (Rodway 2013: 85–116), but in the case of 'to be' this is true only for the 3rd person singular present.[14] In the following diagram, Middle Welsh is representative of all three British languages:

MWelsh			**Athematic**	**Thematic**	
				1	**2**
1sg.		*wyf*	~~**es-mi*~~	**es-ō*	~~**es-om*~~
2sg.		*wyt*	**es-si*	**es-esi*	~~**es-es*~~
3sg.	abs.	*ys*	**es-ti*	~~**es-eti*~~	~~**es-ed*~~
	cj.	*nyt-Ø*	(**nī-eti-*) **es-ti*	~~**es-eti*~~	?**es-ed*
		wy > *yw*[15]	~~**es-ti*~~	**es-eti*	~~**es-ed*~~

12 If stressed, conjunct **esont(i)* would have become disyllabic **iät*. The 3pl. of the conjunct future of the stressed substantive verb is *biät*, its proclitic counterpart, the 3pl. of the copula, is *-bat*.

13 See section 2.5 above.

14 For instance in the Black Book of Carmarthen (ed. Jarman 1982), the 1sg. *wyf* appears clause-initially (*oef* 27.40, *viw* 53.37) and non-initially (*vif* 27.59, *wiff* 52.2, *wif* 53.36, *viw* 76.27; references are to page numbers and line numbers in Jarman's edition).

15 The earlier form *wy* is attested in Old Welsh *hittoi*, which contains a conjunction *hitt-* + *-ui*

(*cont.*)

MWelsh		Athematic	Thematic	
			1	2
1pl.	*ym*	**es-mosi*	~~**es-omosi*~~	~~**es-omos*~~
2pl.	*ywch* (innovation)	~~**es-tes*~~	?**es-etes*	?~~**es-ete(s)*~~
3pl.	*ynt*	**s-enti*	~~**es-onti*~~	~~**es-ond*~~

The historical phonology that is relevant to assessing the prehistory of these forms centres around the complex British Celtic developments undergone by **es-* before vowel (Schrijver 1995: 385–399; Schumacher 2004: 138–153). This became **ehV*, and subsequently **h* was lost and **e* was lengthened in hiatus:

1 to **ɛ̄* > **ɔɨ* before a Proto-British front vowel (e.g. Proto-Celtic **swesūr* 'sister' > **hwe(h)īr* > **hwɛ̄īr* > Late Proto-British **hwɔɨr* > Middle Welsh *chwaer*, Middle Breton *choar*)

2 to **ī* > **i* before a Proto-British back vowel (e.g. Proto-Celtic s-stem plural **tegesā* 'houses' > **teγe(h)ā* > **teγīa* > Late Proto-British **teγi* > Middle Welsh *tei*).

The forms of the British Celtic present tense of 'to be' do not seem to follow these rules, however. The exceptions involve rule 1 and come in two phonologically defined categories, which strongly suggests that they are amenable to an explanation in terms of regular sound change:

1a The 1sg. in Middle Welsh is *wyf* rather than expected *oef*:[16] **esū* + 1sg. athematic ending **-mi* or affixed 1sg. personal pronoun **me* > **ehīṽi* > **ɛ̄īṽ* > **ɔɨiṽ* > **oef*. The complication in this case is that *wy* does not go back to **ɔɨ* but to *ɔɨi*, with non-apocopated and non-syncopated **-i-*. It is conceivable that the additional closed front vowel was responsible for the result *wy* rather than *oe*.[17]

1b The 3sg. in Old and Early Middle Welsh is *wy* (> Middle Welsh *yw*) instead of expected **oe*: **eseti* > (early *i*-apocope) **eset* > **ehed* > **ɛ̄ed* > (British

spelled *-oi* (Schumacher 2013–2014: 204 with footnote 47), and in Middle Welsh *ny-hu-wy* 'is not so', *and-wy* 'is (from)' (Schumacher 2004: 296–297, with references to the sources).

16 The latter is perhaps attested once in the Black Book: see previous footnote. Alternatively and more simply, *oef* is a relic of Old Welsh orthography, where the diphthong /uɨ/ can be spelled with both *o* (as *oi*) and *u* (as *ui*) (Schrijver 2011: 28).

17 If **ɔɨ* was followed by **e*, the result was Middle Welsh *oe*, cf. *oes* 'there is' < **ɔɨes* < **ɛ̄ ess* < **e(d) est(i)* (Schrijver 1997: 173, where incorrect **iss* was reconstructed, following McCone 1995).

apocope) _*ɛ̄_ > _*oe_. In this particular case, the loss of _*-h-_ resulted in the adjacency of two _identical_ vowels, _*ee_. It is possible to assume that in this particular case hiatus was not preserved and contraction to _*ē_ took place before lengthening in hiatus could occur. Contracted _*ee_ merged with already existing _*ē_ (< Proto-Celtic _*ei_), which regularly became Late Proto-British _*uɨ_, whence Welsh _wy_ (> _yw_). This development is supported by OIr. _teimel_ 'darkness' < _*temeselo-_, Middle Welsh _tywyll_, Middle Breton _teffoal_ 'dark' < _*temesel-(j)o/ā_ (Schumacher 2004: 142, 303–304).[18]

Explanation 1a may be used in order to account for the 2sg., Middle Welsh _wyt_, if this reflects the old absolute 2sg., Proto-Celtic (_*es-si_ >) _*esi_ + 2sg. affixed pronoun _*te_ or _*tū_ > _*ehi-de/dī_ > _*ɛ̄id_ > _*ɔɨid_ > _wyt_ rather than _*oet_. Schumacher (2004: 302) reconstructs the 2sg. as a thematicized absolute _*esesi-t(i)_, however, which may work out phonologically on the basis of explanation 1b: _*esesi-t(i)_ > _*ehehid_ > _*ee(h)id_ > _*ēhid_ > (apocope) _*ē(h)_ > _*uɨ_ + 2sg. pronoun _-d_ > Welsh _wy-t_.

The 3sg. _wy_ > _yw_ is a thematic conjunct form, as explained under 1b (_*eseti_), but there is also an old 3sg. conjunct that reflects an athematic form: the existential 'there is' in Middle Welsh _nyt oes_ 'there is not' < < _*nī-d ɛ̄ ess_ < _*nī-d e ess_ (with lengthening of _*e_ in hiatus) < _*nī-(e)t(i) e(d) est(i)_, literally 'there is not to it' (Schrijver 1997: 175–176, Schumacher 2004: 314; its counterpart in Middle Cornish is _us, ues_, in Middle Breton it is _eux_; the absolute counterpart survives in Welsh _yssit_ < _*esti-(e)t(i) ed_). When cliticized, the unstressed 3sg. _*est(i)_ > _*ess_ was simplified to _*es_, which can be found in the negative Middle Welsh _nyt_ 'is not' < _*nid-es_ < _*nī (e)t(i) est(i)_ (Schumacher 2004: 302). It is conceivable (as in the case of Irish _ní_ 'is not') that _nyt_ 'is not' originally contained the 3sg. thematic with secondary ending, _*esed_ > _*eh_ rather than _*esti_, but that runs into the problem that the British 3sg. present of 'to be' is the only locus that would presuppose all three reconstructed forms: _*esti_ (absolute _ys_, conjunct _oes_), _*eseti_ (conjunct _wy_ > _yw_) and _*esed_ (conjunct _nyt_), while at the same time two, _*esti_ and _*eseti_, are enough to formally account for the attestations. We noticed earlier (3.2) that _*esed_, with its retained secondary ending, is an unlikely reconstruction to begin with.

The Welsh 1pl. _ym_ reflects athematic conjunct _*ɨmmoh_ < _*emmoh_ (by raising of _*e_ to _*ɨ_ before nasal; see in general Schrijver 1995: 30–44) < _*esmosi_ (by _i_-apocope; Schumacher 2004: 305). Absolute _*esmosi-t(i)_ should have yielded

18 Compare also the development of _*tepes-mo-_ > _*teemmo-_ > _*tēmm_ > Middle Welsh _twym_ (Schrijver 2011: 68–69).

Welsh *ymmo (for the historical phonology involved, cf. 3sg. masculine of the prepositional pronoun *-o* in Old Welsh *trui-o, truss-o*, Old Southwest British *hepd-o em*, Middle Cornish *gans-o*, all from **-sosom*; Schrijver 1997: 35). Its Breton counterpart is *omp, oump* instead of expected **emp*. Schumacher (2004: 315) explains the *o, ou* by assuming that it arose by analogy to the 1pl. verbal ending of the present of the regular verb *-omp*, but it is difficult to understand how that analogy would have worked, given that all other forms of 'to be' differ from the present endings of the regular verb (e.g. Breton 3pl. *int* 'they are' versus 3pl. ending *-ont*).[19] It seems more likely that the Late Proto-British stem **ui-*, which arose regularly in the 1st, 2nd and 3rd person singular, spread to the 1st person plural. In both Breton and Cornish, the resulting 1pl. **uim* regularly became **um, *om*, resulting in Breton *omp, oump* and Middle Cornish *on* (with *-n* replacing *-m* under the influence of the 1pl. affixed pronoun *-n*). The development is conditioned by the following labial nasal and may be compared to Late Proto-British **tuim* > Middle Breton *toem, tom* 'warm' (Jackson 1967: 220–221; see footnote 18 on the origin of this word). The same development was responsible for the Late Proto-British 1sg. **uiṽ* turning into Middle Breton *ouff, off*, Middle Cornish *of(f)* 'I am'. In the 2sg., Late Proto-British **uid* became Middle Breton *out* rather than expected **oued*, probably as a result of regular developments in unstressed position (cf. place-names beginning with **pluiv* 'parish' becoming *Plou-*, Jackson 1967: 221–222).

As in Irish, the 1pl. **esmosi* > **immoh* was responsible for the replacement of the 1pl. ending of the regular verb in the British languages, **-V-mosi* > **-V-ṽ*, by **-V-m*, with unlenited *-m*. The *-p* of Breton *-omp* probably arose in the collocation with an emphatic pronoun, **-om ni* > **-omp ni*. There is no British evidence for a thematic form **esomosi*.

The Welsh 2pl. *ywch* is an innovation based on the affixed pronoun of the 2pl, *-wch*; similarly Breton 2pl. *och, ouch*, Middle Cornish *ough* (Schumacher 2004: 315–316). It is possible that the original 2pl. was identical to its Irish counterpart, so **esetes*, which yielded **ehedeh* > **ēdeh* (as per 1b above) > **ēd* > **uid*, and that this was replaced because it had merged with the 2sg. The innovated 2pl. form modelled itself on the affixed pronoun by replacing **-d* by **-xw*: 2sg. **ui-d*, with its affixed 2sg. pronoun, created the model for 2pl. **ui-xw* > **uiwx*, with a triphthong **uiw* that developed as it did in the only other word that had it, Proto-Celtic **deiwos* > Late Proto-British **duiw* 'god' > Middle Welsh *dyw*,

19 The only exception is the Middle Breton *och* 'you are' and the 2pl. ending of the regular verb, *-och*, but in this case both are innovations based on the 2pl. affixed pronoun *-ch*.

duw (hence also 2pl. *ywch*)[20] and Middle Breton *doue* (whence **ouech* > *ouch* with the same reduction in unstressed position as in the 2sg., **oued* > *out*).

The Welsh 3pl. *ynt* straightforwardly reflects athematic **senti*. Middle Cornish *yns* may reflect the same form, or it may be identical to Middle Breton *int*. The latter cannot directly reflect **senti*, which should have become **ent*. *Int* probably arose in the collocation with the 3pl. affixed pronoun *i*: **ent-i* > Middle Breton *ind-y* by secondary *i*-affection (Schrijver 2011: 30, 2011a: 378). There is no evidence for a thematic form **esonti*.

5 Discussion

5.1 *Insular Celtic Reconstruction*

After the presentation of the relatively shallow reconstructions of the Irish and British paradigms of the present tense of the root **es*-, which was undertaken in the preceding sections, it is possible to attempt a reconstruction of the paradigm before British Celtic and Irish split up, a stage that is labelled Insular Celtic.

1sg. athematic **esmi* (Irish) occurs beside thematic **esū* (Irish and British), where only Irish supports that the former was absolute and the latter conjunct.

2sg. is open to many reconstructions. Athematic **essi* > **esi* is one (in the Irish absolute and the general British form), but this fails to account for the Irish conjunct form, which presupposes thematic **eses*(*i*). If we apply Occam's razor, thematic **eses*(*i*) is the only secure form, because it is capable of generating the Irish absolute and the general British form as well.

1pl. athematic **esmosi*, which develops into the absolute form in Irish but into the general 1pl. form in British. Irish provides plausible (but not certain) evidence for a conjunct form with lenited **ṽ* that could only have arisen in thematic **esomosi*. In light of the better preservation of archaic verbal morphology in Irish than in British, it seems likely that Irish retains the original distribution while British introduced unlenited *-m* from the absolute into the conjunct 1pl. Accordingly, Insular Celtic probably had absolute **esmosi* versus conjunct **esomosi*.

20 The absence of a Middle Welsh spelling *uwch*, comparable to *duw* 'god', is remarkable, however (as was pointed out by an anonymous reviewer).

2pl. thematic **esetes* appears to have been the only Insular Celtic form, which is directly attested in Irish (unless one prefers to reconstruct analogical **etes*(*i*)) and indirectly in British, where its phonological merger with the 2sg. provided the trigger for its replacement by an innovation based on the 2pl. of the pronoun. Why athematic **estes* did not leave a trace in Irish is not clear.

3pl. athematic **senti* is capable of providing the conjunct form in Irish: it certainly did the only attested British form. It may also account for the Irish absolute form, as discussed earlier. The Irish conjunct form alternatively allows—but does not independently support—a thematic reconstruction **esonti*.

5.2 *Athematic and Thematic 3sg. in British Celtic*

The 3sg. is key to a proper understanding of the prehistory of the athematic and thematic forms and therefore requires a more elaborate discussion. Athematic **esti* is the only form underlying the 3sg. absolute in Irish and British. As a rule, the absolute form occurs in absolute clause-initial position. The Irish conjunct form, which is always preceded by some element, is -∅ and can be explained on the basis of **esti* as well. So it is reasonable that previous scholarship reconstructed only **esti* for all attested 3sg. present forms.

But the British evidence is more complex, as we saw earlier. A conjunct form **esti* is definitely required by the existential 3sg., Welsh (*nyt*) *oes* 'there is not' < **nī-*(*e*)*t*(*i*)*-e*(*d*)*-est*(*i*), literally 'it is not to it', and this supports the reconstruction of the ambiguous Irish conjunct form as **esti*. So does the negative copula *nyt* 'is not' < **nī-*(*e*)*t*(*i*)*-est*(*i*).

Welsh *yw* and its cognates in Breton and Cornish, on the other hand, presuppose thematic **eseti*. Although a detailed investigation of the Middle Welsh syntax of *yw* remains a task for the future, the preliminary conclusion seems warranted that **esti* and **eseti*, both of which are used in positions in which Irish would use a conjunct form, originally appeared in complementary distribution. While athematic **esti* occurs clause-initially (Welsh *ys*) and clause-initially after the negation (Welsh *nyt*), thematic **eseti* > *yw* never occurs clause-initially or directly after the negation. In Middle Welsh, *yw* has three main syntactic uses:[21]

Type 1. In *copula constructions* of the structure 'noun phrase (noun, pronoun, adjective) + *yw*'. Syntactically, determining whether the noun phrase is subject

21 See Charles-Edwards 2005: 162. I am indebted to Aaron Griffith for providing me with this reference and for discussion, from which this section benefited greatly. Needless to say, the responsibility remains mine.

or predicate is not straightforward, but agreement rules strongly suggest that it is the predicate. There are three subtypes.

Subtype 1a. Predicate + *yw* + subject, e.g.

> (Peniarth 44 p. 22) *Enweu y uerchet yw er rey hyn*: … 'the names of his daughters are these: …'. This appears to be 'subject (i.e. old information/topic) + *yw* + predicate (i.e. new/salient information)' but a well-known Welsh agreement rule shows otherwise: if the *subject* is a plural noun which immediately follows the verb, the verb is in the third person singular rather than plural. Since this rule obtains here, the syntactic structure is 'predicate + *yw* + subject'.
>
> (Peniarth 44 p. 53) *Edyuar yw kennyf ryuelu a thyty* 'it is regrettable to me to wage war with you'; word for word: 'regrettable is to me waging war with you'. This must be 'predicate + *yw* + subject' because the adjective cannot be subject.
>
> According to Schumacher 2011: 207, *miui yw Llwyt uab Kil Coet* 'I am Llwyt fab Kil Coet' (Peniarth 4, 79 l. 17–18) has the structure 'subject + *yw* + predicate', but the agreement pattern (*yw* agrees with *Llwyt* rather than *miui* 'me') rather suggests 'predicate + *yw* + subject'. A translation 'Llwyt fab Kil Coet, that's me' would bring this out.

The examples indicate (rather than constitute proof, which would require a more thorough investigation of the material) that *yw* is used in the type 'predicate + *yw* + subject'. By contrast, if the *subject* precedes the copula, Middle Welsh uses a different form of the copula, viz. *yssyd*. Diachronically, *yssyd* originated as a subclause-initial relative form consisting of the athematic 3sg. **esti* + the relative particle **jo*. The original syntagm was: 'it is X which is Y', where X is predicate of the main clause but coreferential with the subject of the subclause.[22]

Subtype 1b. Noun phrase + *yw* + prepositional or adverbial phrase. This subtype is used in a strongly restricted context: if the noun phrase is subject and expresses a place that is identified with the prepositional or adverbial phrase which expresses a place as well. E.g.

> (Cotton Titus D.ii. f. 1v) *E le yn y llys yw y rvg yr osp a'r penhebogyd* 'his place in court is between the guest and the chief falconer'

22 Charles-Edwards (2005: 162) assumed that 'subject + *yw* + predicate' did exist, which

Intuition suggests that the word order of this example is 'subject + *yw* + predicate (in the form of a prepositional phrase)', but intuition about what is subject and predicate has turned out to be of little use in the previous examples. It is impossible to rule out the possibility that the prepositional phrase is subject, although this may be counterintuitive (but think of an English clause such as *In bed is where you'll find him* in order to dispell the preconception that a subject must be a noun phrase). The agreement pattern is of no help in settling this matter either.

Subtype 1c. Conjunction + noun phrase + *yw* + noun phrase. The conjunctions involved are: *canys* 'for', *os* 'if' (which consist of the conjunctions *can* and *o* + the 3sg. absolute of the copula, *ys* 'is' < **esti-*(*e*)*t*(*i*)); *canyt* 'for not', *onyt* 'if not' (the same conjunctions followed by the negation *ny* and the 3sg. conjunct of the copula, *-t* < **-et*(*i*)*-est*(*i*)).

> (Llanstephan 1 p. 1) *kanys annyan pob kaeth yw ucheneydyau ar y rydyt* 'for yearning for his freedom is the nature of every captive'

As the historical analysis of the conjunctions shows, the origin of this type lies in cleft constructions of the type 'for it is X that is Y'. Whether Y is subject or predicate, and therefore whether Y is coreferential with predicate or subject of 'is' in the subclause, cannot be established beyond reasonable doubt.

Type 2. In *copula constructions* of the type 'conjunction *pan* + *yw* + noun phrase'. This type is limited to subclauses. There are two subtypes:

Subtype 2a. is the main type, e.g.

> (Peniarth 30 col. 149) *pan yw kyhyt a'r gur hwyaf en y tref* 'when he is as tall as the tallest man in the village'
>
> Old Welsh: *bichet paniu petguarid did di aries* 'until (*bichet pan*) it is (*iu*) the fourth day (*petguarid did*) to *aries*' (Computus fragment; edited by Williams 1926–1927)

Subtype 2b: *pan yw* with the specialized meaning 'that is', introducing cleft constructions in subclauses that are preceded by a verb of saying, thinking, supposing (here *pan yw* is interchangeable with *y mae*),[23] e.g.

---

means that for him there is no functional difference between this and 'subject + *yssyd* + predicate'.

23 Schumacher 2011: 216.

(Llanstephan 1, p. 115) ... *rey* ... *a tebygassant panyw Gortheyrn a gwnathoed e brat hunnu* '... some ... supposed that it is Gortheyrn who committed that treason'

Type 3. In *non-copula constructions* of the type 'element X + *yd* + *yw* + prepositional or adverbial phrase'. The combination *yd* (a particle or, as argued by Schumacher 2011: 210, 2013–2014: 163 fn. 13, a preverb) + *yw* ('is') comes out in Middle Welsh as *ydiw, yttiw*. *Yw* 'is' can usually be paraphrased as 'is situated'. The element X can be any of the following: the negations *nyt* (main clause), *nat* (subclause); the conjunctions *pan* 'when', *o*(*t*) 'if', *can* 'for', *canys* 'for', *cany*(*t*) 'for not', *tra* 'while'; the question particle *a*; and the particle *neu*(*t*), which expresses surprise or horror on the part of the speaker,[24] e.g.

nit ydiw ema 'he is not here'
ot ydiw yg karchar 'if he is in prison'
a yttiw Kei yn llys Arthur 'whether Kei is at Arthur's court'

The clause *nit ydiw ema* can be reconstructed as **ne* 'not' + particle *(*e*)*t*(*i*) + 3sg. conjunct of the copula **est*(*i*) + **ita* 'thus' + **eset*(*i*) + adverb, hence word for word: 'it is not so that he is here'. The reason for reconstructing the invisible copula is the presence of the visible particle *(*e*)*t*(*i*), which in Irish and British only occurs in connection with a verb.[25] A similar cleft construction underlies the other examples of this type.

While it is clear that conjunct **eseti* (> *yw*) occurs in contexts that are different from those in which conjunct **esti* (> ∅) occurs, it is less straightforward to define how the syntax of the former differed *systematically* from the syntax of the latter. The material presented above is suggestive, however.

Some conjunctions that introduce subclauses are followed by absolute *ys* < athematic **esti*-(*e*)*t*(*i*) (*can-ys, o-s,* see type 3), while the conjunction *pan* is followed by conjunct thematic **eseti* (*pan yw,* type 2). This is reminiscent of

24 Evans 1976: 143, but more extensively Schumacher 2011: 210, who demonstrated that in these cases *yw* is always preceded by *yd* /əd/; examples are taken from both publications.

25 An anonymous reviewer correctly points to the fact that if the copula were present, one should expect the question particle *a* (in e.g. the example *a yttiw Kei yn llys Arthur*) to have been **ae*. If that reasoning is correct, *nyt, ot, neut,* etc. must be analogical (since -*t* < **eti* regularly combines only with a verb) and in that case it was introduced on the basis of the synchronic Welsh rule that such forms in *t* regularly appear before vowel. Alternatively, it is the question particle *a* (instead of expected *ae*) that is analogical, because of the synchronic opacity of the copula construction.

Irish, where some conjunctions are followed by absolute forms (e.g. *ar* 'for', *resíu* 'before') and others (e.g. *co n-*, *ara n-* '(so) that') by conjunct forms.

Leaving aside these syntagms for a moment, we may consider the following analysis of the other syntactic uses of *yw*. The material suggests that **eseti* (> *yw*) occurs in conjunct position, if the predicate noun (rather than the subject: see type 1) or the adverb **ita* 'thus' (> *yd*; type 3) precedes it. Now it is not entirely clear what the prehistory of these instances of verb-second syntax is. In general, verb-second syntax in Welsh (as well as in Breton and Cornish) resulted from the semantic bleaching of original cleft constructions of the type 'it is X who/which does Y', where the initial copula was lost (e.g. Schrijver 1997: 165–172, with references). Accordingly, Middle Welsh *ef a dywawt* 'he said' originated as *ys ef a dywawt* 'it is he that said', with optional and in the course of Middle Welsh regular suppression of the initial unstressed *ys*. This scenario is possible for type 1a–1b as well: *gwir yw hynny* 'that is true' may have started life as **ys gwir yw hynny* 'it is true that that is'. If so, this would bridge the gap between British Celtic and Irish copula syntax: Irish lacks type 1a–1b but has plenty of examples of the cleft construction (with and without suppressed initial copula). The hypothesis that a cleft construction underlies *gwir yw hynny* receives support from type 1c: as soon as 1a–1b is placed in a subclause after a conjunction, the clause-initial copula must appear: *canys gwir yw hynny* 'for that is true', word for word 'for it is true that that is'. So it may well be that *yw* < **eseti* was originally limited to the head position of subclauses. That would resonate well with the fact that *yw* in *pan yw* (type 2) occurs in a subclause, too.

Athematic **esti* occurs in conjunct position only if the negation precedes it (e.g. *nyt* < **nī-*(*e*)*t*(*i*)*-est*(*i*)). In absolute clause-initial position, **esti* occurs in the following syntagms:

a absolute *ys* < **esti-*(*e*)*t*(*i*) in main clauses and after certain conjunctions (*can-ys*, *o-s*)

b relative *yssyd* < **esti-jo* in the subclause of cleft sentences of the type 'it is X which is Y'

But athematic **esti* in *yssyd* only occurs, it seems, if X is coreferential with the *subject* (rather than predicate noun) of 'is' in the subclause (the so-called subject antecedent, see the discussion above under subtype 1a). If on the other hand X is coreferential with the *predicate noun* of 'is' in the subclause (predicate antecedent), **eseti* > *yw* appears. If, as argued just before, **eseti* > *yw* originally occurred only at the head of subclauses in cleft sentences, then that should now be modified to: at the head of subclauses other than those with a subject antecedent (which use **esti* + the relative particle **jo* > *yssyd*).

Many details of British copula syntax and its relation to Irish copula syntax remain to be investigated, so these considerations on British copula syntax must remain preliminary. The essential point that I am making in this section and which is relevant to the overarching argumentation is that in British Celtic (as opposed to Irish) there are two different forms of the third person singular present of the copula, one thematic (*yw* < **eseti*) and the other athematic (∅ < **esti*), and that those forms are syntactically complementary rather than synonymous.

5.3 *Proto-Celtic Reconstruction*

This functional distinction is relevant to the history of the thematic forms of **es-* in general: if, as is traditionally assumed, the thematic forms in Celtic arose by a relatively recent reanalysis of originally athematic forms, as McCone (1995) and Schumacher (2004: 302) argue, it would be necessary to provide a plausible account for the rise of the functional distinction between the two in the 3sg., which seems to me hard to accomplish. Until such time, then, it is more plausible that the thematic and athematic forms together with their different functions (whatever those may have been exactly at an earlier stage of Celtic or even Indo-European) were inherited.

These considerations, therefore, render unlikely the accounts by McCone (1995) and Schumacher (2004: 302), who derive all forms from a Proto-Celtic athematic paradigm. Let us nonetheless have a closer look at the details of Schumacher's explanation. He starts from the observation that at some point in the prehistory of the athematic paradigm, the conjunct 2sg. **esi* and the conjunct 3sg. **esti* would have fallen together: after *i*-apocope and the development of **-st* > **-ts* > **-ss*, these forms had become 2sg. **es* and 3sg. **ess*, respectively. When cliticized, the unstressed 3sg. **ess* was simplified to **es* and thus merged with the 2sg. **es*.[26] Schumacher states that this homonymy was eliminated by adding the thematic ending **-es* (< **-esi*) of the regular verb to the 2sg., whence **eses*. This provided the basis for the creation of thematic forms in other persons, e.g. 1sg. **esū*, 3sg. **eset*(*i*). While perhaps not impossible if considered in isolation, this scenario lacks plausibility: given the fact that the absolute forms do not show a merger of 2sg. **esi-t*(*i*) and 3sg. **essi-t*(*i*), and the non-clitic conjunct forms remain separate as well, surely the easiest solution to the homonymy would have been to restore **ess* for **es* in the clitic 3sg. conjunct. The crucial counterargument against Schumacher's proposal, however, is that on the evidence of British Celtic thematic **eseti* occurred alongside rather than

---

26 The stressed form of the 3sg. probably did not undergo this merger, cf. Middle Welsh *nyt oes* 'there is not' < **nī-t-e-ess* < **nī-eti ed esti*, literally 'there is not to it' (Schrijver 1997: 175–176, Schumacher 2004: 314). Contrast Proto-Celtic **xdes* 'yesterday' > **des* > **deh* > Middle Breton *dech* (Schrijver 1995: 390).

instead of athematic **esti* (why would analogy create a superfluous form?), and that they had different syntactical functions (what would have exerted the pressure for analogy to have created this functional innovation?).

I conclude that the existence of a thematic beside athematic inflection of **es-* in Celtic has a respectable pedigree and that the original locus of the thematic forms was possibly a particular type of subclauses and in any event clauses in which **es-* was preceded by anything other than the subject (or rather subject antecedent) or the negation. This distribution of the thematic forms is indirectly supported by the absence of certified instances of thematic absolute forms in Celtic (absolute forms are clause-initial) and the predominance of thematic forms, beside athematic ones, in the conjunct inflection (conjunct forms are non-clause-initial): compare athematic 1sg. **esmi*, 1pl. **esmosi* underlying the Irish absolute paradigm, with thematic 1sg. **esō* and probably 1pl. **esomosi* underlying the conjunct paradigm.

6 Italo-Celtic

Since the thematic inflection of **es-* 'be' cannot be understood as an innovation in either Italic or Celtic, it stands to reason that the distinction between a thematic and an athematic present of **es-* must go back to Italo-Celtic. Two issues remain to be resolved: did the Italo-Celtic thematic paradigm have secondary endings (as in Italic) or primary endings (as in Celtic)? And what may have been the functional difference between the two paradigms?

6.1 *Secondary or Primary Endings?*

Celtic has primary endings in the thematic paradigm, while Italic has secondary endings. The secondary endings clearly must be more original, for two reasons:

- Italic has preserved an opposition between **es-om*, with present indicative function, and **es-ō* > Latin *erō*, with future function, which arises from a Proto-Indo-European subjunctive with primary endings. It is interesting that Celtic, too, may well preserve this old subjunctive with primary endings in the fossilized subjunctive forms 3sg. *-d* < **eseti-t*, 3pl. *-t* < **esonti-t* that are attested in 3sg. *mad* 'if is' *ced* 'although is', 3pl. *mat, cet* 'if are, although are' (i.e. the conjunctions *má* 'if', *cía, cé* 'although' + 'to be'; Schumacher 2004: 312, following Thurneysen 1946: 489).[27]

27 The corresponding 3sg. form with secondary ending, **esed*, if it had survived in Celtic,

– As noted earlier, Celtic generally replaces old secondary endings by primary endings, except in a few 3sg. forms.[28] One of those exceptions is the 3sg. of the suffixless preterite, which partly reflects the old perfect *_-e_ and partly the old thematic aorist *_-ed_ (e.g. in Old Irish _-luid_ 'went' < *h_1lud^h_-e-d_); the latter was definitely not replaced by primary *_-eti_. The other exception probably is the Irish _s_-subjunctive: the Proto-Indo-European and Proto-Celtic 3sg. *_-s-ed_ became *_-sɪ_ in early Celtic > *_-s_ (early _i_-apocope), which survives in OIr. (Schrijver 2007: 367–368); the other persons in that paradigm introduced primary endings, e.g. 1sg. *g^w_ed-s-ū_, 2sg. *g^w_ed-s-esi_ versus 3sg. *g^w_ed-s-ed_ > Old Irish conjunct 1sg. _-gess_, 2sg. _-geiss_, 3sg. _-gé_ (of _guidid_ 'prays'). In all other forms of all other inflectional categories, including the _s_- and _t_-preterites that reflect the Proto-Indo-European _s_-aorist with secondary endings, Insular Celtic generalized primary endings (e.g. _s_-preterite 1sg. *_gabassū_, 2sg. *_gabassesi_, 3sg. *_gabass(i)_, all based on a stem _gabass-_ that reflects the 3sg. _s_-aorist *_-s-t_, yield Old Irish conjunct 1sg. _-gabus_, 2sg. _-gabais_, 3sg. _-gab_).

Hence, thematic forms with secondary endings and with indicative, present-tense function can be reconstructed for Italo-Celtic:

1sg.	*_es-om_	1pl.	*_es-omos_
2sg.	*_es-es_	2pl.	*_es-etes_
3sg.	*_es-ed_	3pl.	*_es-ond_

6.2 _Functional Difference between the Thematic and Athematic Present_

The Italo-Celtic thematic forms *_esom_, *_eses_, *_esed_ etc. look like a subjunctive with secondary endings, but they lack the semantics of a subjunctive. Subjunctive function does underlie the paradigm with primary endings *_esō_, *_esesi_, *_eseti_, etc., as this became the Latin future and probably the petrified subjunctive of the copula in Irish after _cía_ and _má_ (as discussed in 6.1).

It is possible to speculate about the original functional difference between the thematic and athematic paradigms in spite of the fact that in Italic they merged into one paradigm. In Latin, word order can be manipulated freely in order to serve pragmatic needs. As Adams (2014) argued, it is a syntactic property of the verb 'to be' to follow a focused constituent. Many lexemes by their

would have lost its final *_-d_ very early (see Schrijver 2007: 357–360), so it would not come out in Irish as _-d_.

28 For reasons of historical phonology, the 3sg. of the Irish _s_- and _t_-preterites are ambiguous in this respect (secondary *_-s-t_, as in Proto-Indo-European, and primary *_-s-ti_, which could have been the innovated Celtic form, would both have yielded the attested Old Irish forms).

nature are often or always focused, so the verb 'to be' often or always follows them. Examples are the negation, interrogative pronouns, and polar adjectives (good/bad, big/small, etc.). If the verb 'to be' is itself focused, it takes first position in the clause. Since Latin gave up the functional distinction between the thematic and athematic present of **es-*, this placement rule obviously governs both old thematic and old athematic forms.

In Insular Celtic, word order is fixed to a large extent. Since Irish and Old Welsh have verb-initial word order, this is probably the ancestral state as well. The commonest mechanism that is employed in order to focus a constituent is by using a cleft construction with an initial copula. So the Insular Celtic equivalent of English *I'm travelling to Róme* (rather than any other place) would be (*it*) *is to Rome* (*that*) *I'm travelling*. Taking Old Irish as the model for ancestral Insular Celtic, there is only a limited set of word classes that may precede the verb, among them negations, conjunctions, interrogatives and question particles. Some trigger conjunct inflection, others (mainly a small set of conjunctions) are followed by absolute verbal forms. We have seen in section 6.2 that British Celtic preserves a functional (syntactic) difference between the 3sg. thematic **eseti* and athematic **esti*. The Middle Welsh reflex of the former is found in non-sentence-initial position, if what precedes is neither the subject (or subject antecedent) nor the negation, but, in the attested instances, a predicative (pro)noun, certain conjunctions, and **ita* 'thus, so' in the structure 'it is so (that) X is ...'. On the basis of a comparison with Old Irish, it is possible that the British construction 'predicative (pro)noun + **eseti* + subject' reflects an earlier cleft sentence of the type 'it is X that is ...', in which case one could say that **eseti* was originally limited to certain subclauses (viz. those that do not have a subject antecedent), but whether one accepts this conclusion depends on whether one believes that Irish word order syntax is always more archaic than British word order syntax.

It is conceivable that the Latin property of the copula to follow a left-dislocated, focused constituent, and the Welsh property of the reflex of thematic 3sg. **eseti* to follow a left-dislocated, focused predicative (pro)noun or adverb (**ita* 'so') are historically connected. If so, it is possible to speculate that in Italo-Celtic the thematic forms of **es-* occurred after focused constituents. It is an open question whether this originally included all focused constituents or (as in Welsh) only some of them. This hypothesis is perhaps supported by the evidence of one of the oldest Latin inscriptions, *CIL* I^2, 1, the *cippus* found on the Forum Romanum. The beginning of this fifth century BC text reads 1 *quoi ho*[ ] 2 [ ] *sakros esed* 'whoever [...] thi[s ...] is (will be) cursed'. The usual interpretations of *esed* as an early form of the past subjunctive *esset* or the future *erit* meet with the problem that a past subjunctive is difficult to accommodate semantically and with the problem that *erit* goes back to a paradigm with primary endings, so that one would expect to find *eset* in this archaic text. If we take *esed* as the 3sg. counterpart of 1sg. *esom*, in other words, as a thematic form with secondary endings, both the semantic and the formal problems disappear. The fact that in *sakros esed* the thematic 3sg. follows a focused predicative adjective may well be significant in light of the fact that this is exactly the position in which Welsh **eseti* > *yw* is at home (the primary ending of **eseti* is of course an innovation, as explained in the preceding section).

What remains to be explained is the place of these thematic presents with secondary endings within the wider scheme of Indo-European. It is possible to speculate along the following lines. The Latin syntax of the copula suggests that a clause-initial copula, with or without negation, is a focused copula and that focus on the copula means that the assertive and veridical use of 'be' is foregrounded. That particular use calls for the use of an indicative of **es-*, which is athematic. The British Celtic evidence suggests that thematic forms of the present of **es-* occurred if the copula was preceded by certain constituents: nominal predicate, adverb of manner, adverb of time, which because they precede the copula probably carried focus. It is conceivable that those focused verbal adjuncts played a role in turning a present indicative (factual, *hic et nunc*) into a subjunctive with secondary endings. By foregrounding a verbal adjunct, which modifies the applicability of verbal state, the speaker draws attention away from the factuality of the verbal state (hence the preference of subjunctive to indicative) as well as from the time frame of the verbal state (hence the preference of a timeless secondary ending to the *hic-et-nunc* primary ending). Needless to say, this account is hypothetical as well as abstract (i.e. I cannot provide examples in which foregrounding of verbal adjuncts has the described effect).

7 The Italo-Celtic Imperfect of **es-*

A possible confirmation of the Italo-Celtic date of the thematic beside athematic presents of **es-* can be found in the imperfect of **es-*. The Latin imperfect, *eram*, etc., reflects **es-ā-*, while the Welsh 3sg. imperfect, *oedd*, reflects **es-ē-d* (Schrijver 1999, Schumacher 2004: 316–317). The suffixes may well be identical to the suffixes **-ā-* and **-ē-* that are used in Italic as markers of the subjunctive and future. Many suggestions have been made in order to account for the prehistory of these suffixes (Meiser 2003: 50 ff.) but there is no consensus. I have attempted to argue on the basis of the distribution of the suffixes *-ā-* and *-ē-* in the Latin subjunctive and future that the former was originally (i.e. in Proto-Italic) limited to thematic stems and the latter to athematic stems (2006: 58–59). If this is correct and if we assume that the Italo-Celtic situation was identical, it is possible to understand how **es-ā-* and **es-ē-* came to exist side by side, the one derived from the thematic and the other from the athematic present stem:

Italo-Celtic athematic **es-ti* ⇒ **es-ē-* (> Welsh *oedd* 'was')
Italo-Celtic thematic **es-ed* ⇒ **es-ā-* (> Latin *erat* 'was')

8 Concluding Remarks

The reconstruction of a double present of **es-* in Italo-Celtic is rather different from the traditional reconstruction of a single, athematic present for Proto-Indo-European. While the reconstruction of a single, athematic present is based on the input of the other Indo-European branches towards reconstructing the Proto-Indo-European paradigm, the Italo-Celtic double paradigm is the product of a step by step reconstruction of the Italic and Celtic data on their own. I claim that in reconstructing Italo-Celtic, the latter has precedence over the former. The next step, which will not be undertaken here, consists of bridging the gap between Italo-Celtic and the other Indo-European languages, in particular Indo-Iranian and Greek. This endeavour probably centres around the question whether the present tense function of what looks like a subjunctive with full grade of the root and secondary thematic endings (**es-om*, **es-es*, **es-ed*) can be squared with an origin as a subjunctive, or whether the Italo-Celtic reconstruction provides yet another argument in support of the idea that the subjunctive started out as a present, which could acquire modal functions (see especially Bozzone 2012).[29]

References

Adams, J.N. 1994. *Wackernagel's Law and the placement of the copula* esse *in Classical Latin*. Cambridge: Cambridge Philological Society.

Bozzone, Chiara. 2012. The PIE subjunctive: function and development. In H.C. Melchert (ed.), *The Indo-European verb*, 7–18. Wiesbaden: Reichert.

Charles-Edwards, Thomas. 2005. Middle Welsh *mae* 'is'. In B. Smelik et al. (eds.), *A com-*

29 I am indebted to Aaron Griffith for providing me with this reference.

panion in linguistics. A festschrift for Anders Ahlqvist on the occasion of his sixtieth birthday, 161–170. Nijmegen: De Keltische Draak.

Dunkel, George. 1998. On the 'thematicization' of Latin *sum, volo, eo* and *edo*. In J. Jasanoff et al. (eds.), *Mír Curad. Studies in honor of Calvert Watkins*, 83–100. Innsbruck: Institut für Sprachwissenschaft der Universität Innsbruck.

Griffith, Aaron. 2016. On the Old Irish third palatalisation and the 3sg. present of the copula. *Ériu* 66. 39–62.

Jackson, Kenneth. 1967. *A historical phonology of Breton*. Dublin: Dublin Institute for Advanced Studies.

Jarman, A.O.H. 1982. *Llyfr Du Caerfyrddin*. Cardiff: University of Wales Press.

McCone, Kim. 1978. The dative singular of Old Irish consonant stems. *Ériu* 29. 26–38.

McCone, Kim. 1991. *The Indo-European origins of the Old Irish nasal presents, subjunctives and futures*. Innsbruck: Institut für Sprachwissenschaft der Universität Innsbruck.

McCone, Kim. 1995. Der Präsens Indikativ der Kopula und die Relativendung *-s* im Altirischen. In H. Hettrich et al. (eds.), *Verba et structurae. Festschrift für Klaus Strunk zum 65. Geburtstag*, 123–133. Innsbruck: Institut für Sprachwissenschaft der Universität Innsbruck.

McCone, Kim. 2006. *The origins and development of the Insular Celtic verbal complex*. Maynooth: Department of Old Irish, National University of Ireland, Maynooth.

Meiser, Gerhard. 1998. *Historische Laut- und Formenlehre der lateinischen Sprache*. Darmstadt: Wissenschaftliche Buchgesellschaft.

Rodway, Simon. 2013. *Dating medieval Welsh literature, evidence from the verbal system*. Aberystwyth: CMCS.

Schrijver, Peter. 1993. On the development of vowels before tautosyllabic nasals in Primitive Irish. *Ériu* 44. 33–52.

Schrijver, Peter. 1994. The Celtic adverbs for 'against' and 'with' and the early apocope of **-i*. *Ériu* 45. 151–189.

Schrijver, Peter. 1997. *Studies in the history of the Celtic pronouns and particles*. Maynooth: Department of Old Irish, National University of Ireland, Maynooth.

Schrijver, Peter. 1999. Griechisch *ᾔδη* 'er wußte'. *Historische Sprachforschung* 112. 264–272.

Schrijver, Peter. 2006. Review of G. Meiser, *Veni Vidi Vici. Die Vorgeschichte des lateinischen Perfektsystems*, München: Beck, 2003. *Kratylos* 51. 56–64.

Schrijver, Peter. 2007. Some common developments of Continental and Insular Celtic. In P.-Y. Lambert & G.-J. Pinault (eds.), *Gaulois et Celtique continental*, 355–371. Geneva: Droz.

Schrijver, Peter. 2011. Old British. In E. Ternes (ed.), *Brythonic Celtic—Britannisches Keltisch*, 1–84. Bremen: Hempen.

Schrijver, Peter 2011a. Middle and Early Modern Breton. In E. Ternes (ed.), *Brythonic Celtic—Britannisches Keltisch*, 359–429. Bremen: Hempen.

Schrijver, Peter. 2015. Pruners and trainers of the Celtic family tree: the rise and development of Celtic in the light of language contact. In Liam Breatnach et al (eds.), *Proceedings of the XIV International Congress of Celtic Studies*, 191–219. Dublin: Dublin Institute for Advanced Studies.

Schrijver, Peter. 2016. Sound change, the Italo-Celtic linguistic unity, and the Italian homeland of Celtic. In J.T. Koch & B. Cunliffe (eds.), *Celtic from the West.* Vol. 3. *Atlantic Europe in the Metal Ages: questions of shared language*, 489–502. Oxford: Oxbow Books.

Schumacher, Stefan. 2004. *Die keltischen Primärverben.* Innsbruck: Institut für Sprachen und Literaturen der Universität Innsbruck.

Schumacher, Stefan. 2011. Mittel- und Frühneukymrisch. In E. Ternes (ed.), *Brythonic Celtic—Britannisches Keltisch*, 85–235. Bremen: Hempen.

Schumacher, Stefan. 2013–2014. *y*(*d*) und *yt*: Zur Syntax zweier 'Partikeln' des Mittelkymrischen. *Keltische Forschungen* 6. 159–217.

Szemerényi, Oswald. 1964. *Syncope in Greek and Indo-European and the nature of Indo-European accent.* Naples: Istituto universitario orientale di Napoli.

Thurneysen, Rudolf. 1946. *A grammar of Old Irish.* Dublin: Dublin Institute for Advanced Studies.

Vine, Brent. 1998. Remarks on the Archaic Latin 'Garigliano Bowl inscription', *Zeitschrift für Papyrologie und Epigraphik* 121. 257–262.

Wallace, Rex & Brian Joseph. 1987. Latin *sum*/Oscan **súm, sim,** ***esum***. *American Journal of Philology* 108. 675–693.

Watkins, Calvert. 1969. *Indogermanische Grammatik.* Band 3. *Formenlehre*, erster Teil: *Geschichte der indogermanischen Verbalflexion.* Heidelberg: Winter.

Weiss, Michael. 2011. *Outline of the historical and comparative grammar of Latin.* 2nd edition. Ann Arbor & New York: Beech Stave.

Weiss, Michael. 2012. Italo-Celtica: Linguistic and cultural points of contact between Italic and Celtic. In S.W. Jamison et al. (eds.), *Proceedings of the 23rd Annual UCLA Indo-European Conference*, 151–173. Bremen: Hempen.

Williams, Ifor. 1926–1927. The Computus Fragment. *Bulletin of the Board of Celtic Studies* 3. 245–272.

CHAPTER 11

The Anatolian Stop System and the Indo-Hittite Hypothesis—Revisited

Zsolt Simon

1 Kloekhorst's Hypothesis and His Arguments

Alwin Kloekhorst has recently argued in several contributions, especially in his 2016 paper (cf. also 2008: 21–25 and 2014: 546–547), that the contrast of the Anatolian stops was not one of voice, but one of length, and that this contrast was inherited from Proto-Indo-European. Accordingly, the contrast in voice would be an innovation of the non-Anatolian Indo-European languages, which, if correct, would represent a robust argument for a non-Anatolian node of the Indo-European *Stammbaum*. However, this proposal depends entirely on the synchronic phonetic and phonological interpretation of the stops of the 2nd-millennium Anatolian languages preserved in cuneiform, which is one of the classical unsolved problems of Hittitology. In this paper I do not intend to settle this issue; my goal is only to investigate if the reinterpretation in terms of length by Kloekhorst is necessary and whether it is consistent with the linguistic material; in other words, if the contrast in voice really represents a diagnostic innovation of the non-Anatolian Indo-European languages.

1.1 *Kloekhorst's Arguments against the Contrast in Voice*

1. The Hittites did not use the distinction in voice available in the cuneiform script; instead simple and geminate spelling was used (simple spelling reflecting etymologically voiced consonants, geminate spelling reflecting etymologically voiceless consonants, as described by Sturtevant's Law). According to Kloekhorst, it remains unexplained why the Hittites would have invented a much more complicated system (Kloekhorst 2016: 214, cf. also 2014: 544–554).

While this is certainly correct, nowadays we have a much more nuanced view of this spelling practice, mainly due to the investigations of Kloekhorst himself, since it was Kloekhorst who, in a paper from 2010, demonstrated that the voiced and voiceless series represent phonologically distinct sounds in initial position in Hittite cuneiform—irrespective of their exact phonetic value

 | DOI:10.1163/9789004416192_013

(TA vs. DA, KE/I vs. GE/I, KA vs. GA). Moreover, as Pascual Coello demonstrated in his dissertation (2014), the use of voiced vs. voiceless signs in their expected value is highly consistent in internal position in several verbal endings, pronominal forms and words (again, this was supported by Kloekhorst's own investigations [2013]). One can thus conclude that Hittite scribes were aware of the phonetic distinction between the voiced and voiceless series and even of their original voiced and voiceless value.

Moreover, the precise origins of the Hittite cuneiform are still unclear (surely not Alalaḫ VII, see Weeden 2011: 65–70 and Popova 2016, esp. 89, *contra* Kloekhorst 2010, 2013) and thus it is still not possible to exclude that the orthographical practice of single/geminate spelling is inherited; in other words, the Hittites did not invent this system themselves, but rather adopted it (for the most recent critical overview see Weeden 2011: 370–375).

2. On the basis of forms such as *e-ku-ut-ta* and *e-uk-ta* or *e-ku-ud-du* which unambiguously point to /egʷta/ '(s)he drank' and /egʷtu/ '(s)he shall drink', i.e. a cluster of a voiced and a voiceless stops, Kloekhorst argues that one expects either regressive or progressive voice assimilation, as its lack is "extremely unlikely", but since neither happens, the two stops were apparently not distinct in voice (Kloekhorst 2008: 23; 2014: 545; 2016: 214–215).

This argument is, however, based on the misunderstanding that voice assimilation is a universal feature, which it is not. It is well-known that not all languages have this sort of assimilation. A perfect analogy of the Hittite example is provided, for instance, by Georgian *vaḳetebt* 'we do' from the 1st plural circumfix *v-* … *-t* and the verb *ḳet-eb-* 'to do'. Exactly like in Hittite verbs, here we are dealing with a consonant cluster resulting from a morphological process and without voice assimilation.[1] Note that the lack of voice assimilation is well-attested in Hittite within a single syllable too (see e.g. *nekuz* (*mēḫur*) /negʷts/ 'at night'), and Eichner 2015: 13–14 thus cautiously suggested that it is the voice assimilation which is a non-Anatolian innovation (cf. also Kloekhorst 2008: 602).[2]

In other words, Kloekhorst's arguments do not exclude the possibility of contrast in voice.

1 I have tested this claim with native speakers of Georgian.

2 The (modern) name of the capital of Georgia, Tbilisi, is another perfect parallel. On the lack of voice assimilation and the so-called non-harmonic clusters in Modern Georgian see e.g. Aronson 1990: 19; 1991: 223; 1997: 934, 937.

1.2 *Kloekhorst's Arguments for the Contrast in Terms of Length*

As Kloekhorst (2008: 22; 2014: 546–547, 2016: 216 n. 12, with critical remarks) mentions, Melchert has already suggested a synchronic system similar to his own, at least in the sense that voiceless stops were geminates, cf. Melchert 1994: 20:

> inherited voiceless/voiced stops would thus contrast only in intervocalic position, where the distinction is realized as geminate vs. simple [...] *-TT-* [...] vs. *-D-* [...] Note that there is no longer *any* contrast of simple *T* vs. *D*. The operative contrast is one of long vs. short internally. (emphasis as in original).

Accordingly, Melchert's arguments will also be taken into account.

1. Kloekhorst rightly points out that in the prehistory of Hittite */ī/ was shortened in closed syllables but not in open ones (cognate words in Palaic and Luwian show that this was a development after Proto-Anatolian, cf. Hitt. *ki-*, but Pal. *kī-*, Luw. *zī-* 'to lie'). Cf. the following cases:

	pre-Hittite	Old Hittite
**Kéis-o*	**kīša*	*kīša* '(s)he becomes'
**Kéis-h₂e*	**kīsḫa*	*kišḫa* 'I become'
**ḱéi-to*	**kītta*	*kitta* '(s)he lies'

In other words, the *-tt-* of the ending in **kītta* was a closing element, thus it must have been a geminate (Kloekhorst 2014: 418–420, 545–546; 2016: 215; similarly in 2008: 23).

This is, however, not necessarily so. If we look at the prehistory of the paradigm of *kitta*, we will immediately see that there were other forms, too, with an */ī/ standing in a closed syllable (the same distribution applies to the past forms as well, besides the 3rd pl. imperative):

pre-Hittite	Old Hittite (pres. midd.)
**ḱéi-h₂a*	**kiḫḫa*
***ḱéi-th₂o** > ***ḱītHa**[3] > ***kita**	**kitta*

3 The survival of the post-consonantal laryngeal into pre-Hittite in **ḱéi-th₂o* > **ḱītHa* > **kita* is

(*cont.*)

pre-Hittite	Old Hittite (pres. midd.)
**ḱéi-to*	*kitta*
**ḱéi-wosd*^{h}*h*$_2$*o*	**kiwašta*
**ḱéi-d*^{h}*h*$_2$*we* > **ḱī-tuwo*	**kittuma*
ḱéi-nto** >ḱīnta** > ***kinta**	(*ki*(*y*)*anda*)[4]

In other words, */i/ already existed in the paradigm of **kitta* independently from the *-tta*-ending and thus one cannot exclude that it simply spread through the entire paradigm by levelling out the alternation **kī-*/*ki-* (similarly to *kīš-*/*kiš-* 'to become', where the allomorph *kiš-* ousted *kīš-* in New Hittite: Kloekhorst 2008: 480). One may object that the majority of the forms had */ī/ and one would not expect the 2nd sg. and the 3rd pl. as starting points for paradigmatic levelling. However, nothing excludes that analogy starts from the minority of the forms or from the forms just mentioned. As an example one can quote the paradigm of *dā-*/*d-* 'to take' to be discussed below, where /ā/ was ousted by /a/, which was originally in minority and restricted to the 2nd and 3rd plural forms. Thus one must conclude that nothing requires a 3rd sg. form /kitta/.

2. Kloekhorst observes that Old Hittite /ā/ was later shortened to /a/ in closed, non-final syllables (2008: 98; 2014: 256–307). He claims, however, that this happened before stops spelled with geminate as well, which in turn means that the stops that were spelled in this way were real geminates (2016: 215–216). He quotes the cases of *dātten* > *datten* 'you shall take', *dātti* > *datti* 'you take' as well as *šākki* > *šakki* '(s)he knows'.

However, his examples are not probative, since both are ablauting verbs from Old Hittite onwards, having both /ā/ and /a/ in their paradigms (*šākk*/*šakk-* belongs to the *ā*/*a*-ablauting verbs, Kloekhorst 2008: 695[5]), and thus one can-

shown by the following relative chronology (Kloekhorst 2010: 205–206): (1) pre-Hitt. **di-* > *š-* and **ti-* > *z-*; (2) pre-Hitt. **dHi-*, **tHi-* > *ti-* (cf. *tiye*/*a-* 'to step' <*(*s*)*th*$_2$*-ye*/*o-*; *tiyanzi* 'they place' < **d*^{h}*h*$_1$*-i-énti*).

4 The ending is analogically renewed.

5 Kloekhorst himself interprets the spelling of the word as /sāk-/, /sk-/, although this is not possible, since initial /sk-/ automatically led to [isk-]. He admits this problem by claiming that the only similar case is *šākan*, *šakn-* 'oil', which he interprets as /ságn/, /sgnás/ (2008: 697). However, the latter interpretation is based exclusively on the mechanical forcing of a specific PIE paradigm type on the attested spellings, which is methodologically doubtful, especially

not exclude that we are dealing with paradigmatic levelling of the short /a/. See, for instance, the Old Script paradigm of *dā-/d-* 'to take' in present active (and cf. also OS *daške/a-*, data following Kloekhorst 2008: 803):[6]

dāḫḫe *dāweni/tumeni*
dātti *dattēni*
dāi *danzi*

This assumption is not only illustrated but also demonstrated by this verb, since its New Hittite spellings show a short /a/ also in those cases where Kloekhorst's sound law does not apply, i.e. the shortening of /ā/ in these cases and in this verb in general was independent from this sound change (data following Kloekhorst 2008: 803): 3sg. pres. act. *dai*; 3sg. pret. act. *taš* (Middle Script); 1pl. pret. act. *dawēn*; 1sg. imp. act. *talit*; 3sg. imp. act. *dau*.

3. According to Kloekhorst, resonants and laryngeals, too, were spelled as single and geminate, i.e. had short and long variants, which is a further support for reinterpreting the stops as long and short phonemes (2016: 216–217, cf. 2014: 547). However, this is not the case. First, the phonemic contrast in resonants is irrelevant for the phonemic contrast in stops. For instance, there is a phonemic distinction in Hungarian between single and geminate continuants (*kassza* 'cash desk, counter'/*kasza* 'scythe', *hal* 'fish'/*hall* 'to hear'), and yet Hungarian stops do show a contrast between voiced and voiceless ones (that can occur both as single and geminate).[7] Second, the difference between single and geminate spelling of the laryngeals is not and cannot be the length, as was shown in detail by Simon 2014b (not quoted by Kloekhorst 2016).[8]

4. Kloekhorst 2016: 219–220 also suggests that the different outcomes of the Hittite assibilation of **di-* and **ti-* (*š-* and *z-*, respectively) "can only be

because no assured cognates are known; and Kloekhorst himself admits that it cannot be excluded that the first vowel was real in the oblique cases, being an analogically introduced vowel (2008: 698–699). In other words, there is no need to assume irregular phonology in any of these cases.

6 The ongoing discussion about whether there was an Old Script distinct from a Middle Script has no relevance here, since the point is the change itself between the earlier and later paradigms.

7 Note furthermore that it is exactly for this reason that the assumed shortening of **-ss-* in PIE **$h_2$ómsei* > pre-PAnat. **hṓssē* > PAnat. *hṓsē* > Hitt. *ḫāši* 'she gives birth' (if this reconstruction is correct) is not relevant for the question of whether Proto-Anatolian stops contrasted in length or in voice (*contra* Kloekhorst 2016: 223–224).

8 Kloekhorst 2018 now provides a phonetic interpretation different from that of Simon 2014b, but the difference is still not based on length.

explained by assuming" that they were different in consonantal length (i.e. *ttj > ts and *tj > s); otherwise one would expect a symmetrical outcome, *ts* vs. *dz* or *s* vs *z*.

There are two problems with this view. First, the exact phonetic nature of the signs with ⟨z⟩ is undetermined: one cannot exclude that they represented a [z] in specific cases (Hoffner & Melchert 2008: 47). However, the methodological issue is more problematic: the direction of phonological changes is neither obligatory nor necessarily parallel. Thus nothing excludes that the reflexes of *di and *ti in the same language will be different in terms of voice; cf. e.g. the different reflexes of *diV-* and *tiV-* in Italian: *giorno* vs. *zio*.

5. Finally, as mentioned above, Melchert also assumes that geminate voiceless stops were indeed geminates. He quotes two examples, where accented /a/ remained short; thus they had to stand in closed syllables. Since the vowels were followed by voiceless stops in these cases, he concludes that these voiceless stops were geminates (Melchert 1994: 147):

a *Hwápo- > *ḫ(u)wappa-* 'evil';

b *$h_2$éto- > *Háto- > *ḫatta-* 'cut';

However, these examples are not probative. As admitted by Melchert himself, the etymology of *ḫatta-* 'cut' is actually not known (cf. also Kloekhorst 2008: 331), and thus this word cannot be used as an argument. As for *ḫ(u)wappa-*, its consonant can be attributed to the analogy of its verbal base *ḫuwapp-*/*ḫupp-* 'to do evil'. Nevertheless, this verb does not show the expected lengthening either. However, we are dealing with a *ḫi*-conjugated verb (see the detailed discussion in Kloekhorst 2008: 369–371), and due to the endings, the stem vowel thus stood mostly in a closed syllable in the paradigm, where lengthening is not expected. The resulting allomorphy with long and short stem vowels was levelled paradigmatically in favour of the majority (i.e. the short /a/) already in Pre-Hittite (one may surmise that a similar scenario applies to *ḫatta-* as well).[9] In other words, the accented /a/ did stand in a closed syllable in this case, but this was caused by a consonant cluster and not by a geminate stop.

Thus the arguments presented until now do not necessarily require a contrast in length. Moreover, there is a type of evidence, completely neglected by

9 Kloekhorst 2008: 371 reconstructs *$h_2$wóph_1-, since the verbal base *$h_2$wóp- would have given †*ḫ(u)wāp-* (instead of the attested *ḫuwapp-*/*ḫupp-*) with lenition of *p due to *ó, which would refute Melchert's example. However, Melchert 2012 (esp. 175) rightly pointed out that its Sanskrit cognate, *vap-* 'to strew (out), to scatter (seed)', is an aniṭ-root (cf. its participle *uptá-*) and convincingly restricted this lenition effect to laryngeals. For the only case he could not explain (*sh_3ók^w-eh_2 > Hitt. *šākuwa-* 'eye'), see the critical remarks of Rieken 2010: 129–130.

Kloekhorst, that excludes the interpretation of these consonants as voiceless short and long stops. This evidence consists of contemporary transcriptions of Hittite and Luwian words and names as well as borrowings from these languages.

2 Arguments against the Contrast in Length: The Evidence of Transcriptions and Borrowings

Before turning to the evidence, we have to define precisely what we are looking for in this material. As we could see above, the key issue is the intervocalic position: in Melchert's system the contrast appears in intervocalic position as geminate voiceless and single voiced stops. In Kloekhorst's system we have geminate voiceless and single voiceless stops. Note that his position is not entirely clear. Earlier he assumed that a single voiceless stop was allophonically voiced in intervocalic position, which is, in fact, Melchert's position (Kloekhorst 2013: 139–140), but later Kloekhorst abandoned this view in favour of absence of voicing and maintained his purely voiceless system throughout his 2016 paper. However, in a footnote in this paper he claims that "I maintain that this voicing is sub-phonemic only, and that the real phonemic distinction between fortis and lenis stops is not one in voice, but in consonantal length" (2016: 216 n. 12), which is in fact the description of his 2013 position. Either way, we have two competing systems, -TT- : -D- (Melchert 1994; Kloekhorst 2013) and -TT- : -T- (Kloekhorst 2016). However,

a both systems have to be rejected if intervocalic voiceless stops (in the traditional sense) are not reflected as geminate stops in the languages that can express gemination (not all languages in question did so in writing, and thus their data are not helpful);
b the system of Kloekhorst 2016 has to be rejected if intervocalic voiced stops (in the traditional sense) are reflected as voiced stops in the languages that can mark voice.

In the following I have tried to compile all possible material from all relevant languages, although I have included only those examples in which the transcription or loanword status is relatively assured. In other words, although one can find many more suggested loanwords, many of them have not been included here, because their loanword status cannot be maintained (see below for references). Unfortunately while proposals regarding loanwords and transcriptions are abundant, critical investigations are few and still ongoing.

As for the evidence, Egyptian (lack of contrastive voice in the investigated period) and Old Assyrian (lack of contrastive spelling) material was excluded (*contra* Patri 2009a),[10] and no relevant examples were found among the loanwords in Armenian and Hebrew (for excluded cases see Simon 2013 and Simon 2014b: 882 n. 21[11]).

However, Aramaic, Greek, Neo-Assyrian, Neo-Babylonian, Phrygian, Phoenician, Ugaritic and Urartian transcriptions and loanwords do provide relevant data. Due to the fact that we need specific cases and specific phonemes only, the evidence is limited; nevertheless it is varied and ample enough to show a consistent and clear picture.

2.1 *Voiceless Stops: Consistent Single Reflexes instead of Geminates*

The voiceless status of the stops spelled with geminate is clear also from the languages that do not express geminate stops in writing; cf. the Ugaritic transcription *ṯpll* of *Šuppiluliuma* and the Ugaritic loanword *ảkl* from Hitt. *akkala-* 'furrow, plough' (Watson 2004; for the critique of some of the further assumed loanwords that would belong here see Simon 2014b: 878 n. 11[12]) and the Aramaic name KTMW borrowed from Luwian, whichever Luwian word is the underlying one (for the most recent discussion see Younger 2009: 159–166 with refs.).[13] Thus the only question is whether they were perceived as geminates.

Before turning to the data, the methodological problem of the lack of an orthographic distinction between single and geminate voiceless consonants in Hittite cuneiform must be mentioned: Data with geminate spelling are not probative *if* we do not know their origin, since we cannot exclude that they are

10 The same lack of contrastive spelling applies to the East-Semitic language of Eblaite, too, if the hypothesis of Eblaite transcription of Anatolian names most recently proposed by Kroonen, Barjamovic & Peyrot 2018 turns out to be correct. The probable Hittite loanword in Eblaite, *zeri* (Watson 2008), is not helpful either.

11 Hebrew *lappid* 'torch, lightning' was not discussed in that paper, but it can hardly be from Hittite or Luwian *lappiya-* (*contra* Rabin 1963: 128–129) not only due to different morphology (Rabin's idea of borrowing of the form in the instrumental case is hardly probable), but also because of semantic problems: the uncertain meaning of the Hittite word 'embers?, resinous wood?, kindling?' is based exclusively on the homonymy of its stem with the verb for 'to glow, to flash' (CHD s.v.), and the meaning of the Luwian word is unknown (Melchert 1993: 126 with ref.; cf. also below). For excluded Neo-Babylonian cases see Simon forthcoming.

12 Numerous further Hittite/Luwian loanwords have been proposed by Watson (e.g. 2007: 118–124), but still need to be critically examined. Since, however, gemination is not marked in Ugaritic spelling, they would have only limited value in this discussion and thus their critical investigation is postponed to another occasion.

13 Possibly also the Phoenician transcriptions 'WRK (of Awarikus) and MTŠ, if they reflect Luwian names (on Awarikus see Simon 2017c, on MTŠ see Mosca and Russell 1987: 12).

originally geminates. These include the toponyms Ḫatti and Ḫattuša. All other remaining cases show single spelling:

Language	Transcription/borrowing	Anatolian source	References
Ugaritic	*pwt*/*puwatu* (RS Akkad.)/ *puwati* (syll. Ug.) 'madder (*bot.*)'	Hitt./Luw. *puwatti-* 'madder (*bot.*)'?	Watson 1998: 757; 2006: 723; 2010: 837[14]
Neo-Assyrian	*Mut(t)alli*/*u* (kings of Gurgum and Kummuh);[15]	CLuw. *muwattalla*/*i-*	Simon 2018b: 127
	Urik(ki)/*Urayaikki* (kings in Hiyawa)[16]	HLuw. /Wrayka-/	Simon 2018b: 128 with refs. (also transcribed in Phoenician as WRYK, Simon 2014a: 93 with refs.)
Greek[17]	τολύπη 'a clew of wool or yarn'	CLuw. (Kizzuwatna Luwian[18]) *taluppa*/*i-* 'lump, clod (of clay and dough)'	Furnée 1972: 35 n. 33, 340; for a full list of references and discussion see Simon 2018a: 406[19]

14 Note that a Semitic loan is not probable, since the Anatolian word has a plausible etymology; see Tischler 2001: 679 and Puhvel 2013: 148.

15 The geminate spelling appears only later and inconsistently, and is due to internal Neo-Assyrian factors: either a stressed syllable was expressed by the geminate consonant or a closed syllable replaced the long vowel (here contracted from *-uwa-*) in an open syllable; see Simon 2018b: 127 based on Luukko 2004: 98–101, 126–128.

16 On the geminate spelling see n. 15.

17 A critical overview of all supposed Anatolian borrowings in Greek is still missing; for a first attempt see Simon 2018a. Note that the word δέπας (Myc. *di-pa-*) 'goblet' widely held to be borrowed from Luwian cannot be used as an argument here, since it is a borrowing from another Luwic language at best, if not a common borrowing from a third source; see the detailed discussion in Simon 2017a with refs.

18 This word is attested only in this dialect of Luwian; for the attestations see Melchert 1993: 203, for the dialectological classification of Cuneiform Luwian texts see Yakubovich 2010a: 15–74 and Melchert 2013: 168.

19 One may, of course, attempt to provide alternative explanations; in this case there are basically two possibilities: First, τολύπη is inherited from PIE together with its Luwian equivalent (suggested by De Decker 2015: 13). Although this is possible formally, their restricted distribution to a neighbouring area militates against this assumption. Second, τολύπη was borrowed together with the Luwian word from a third, substrate or neighbouring, language (cf. Beekes 2010, xv–xvi, 1492). While this cannot be excluded *a priori*, this is not a real explanation, just an *obscurum per obscurius*. Note that due to their quasi-identical form and meaning and their geographical closeness it is hardly probable that τολύπη has nothing to do with the Luwian word. Finally, τολύπη cannot be a Greek loanword in Kizzuwatna Luwian due to obvious chronological and geographical reasons.

This table shows that voiceless stops were always and consistently perceived as voiceless consonants and in the languages which could mark geminate pronunciation they were not perceived as geminate consonants. This can be further supported by cases like the following where the Luwian name was spelled in other systems by a single voiceless stop (and not by a geminate voiceless stop assumed by the hypothesis of Melchert 1994 and Kloekhorst 2013), even though the Luwian spelling is ambiguous (since these names were written in Luwian hieroglyphs):[20]

- Neo-Assyrian *Hili/a/ukku* (Bagg 2007: 105–107)/Neo-Babylonian *Hilik*(*k*)*u** (Zadok 1985: 162)/Greek *Kilikia* (cf. HLuw. *Hil/rika-*, ACLT s.v.)
- Neo-Assyrian *Ki*(*a*)*kki* 'PN' (Simon 2018b: 127)/Neo-Babylonian *Kikî* (Zadok 1979: 167) (cf. HLuw. *Kiyakiya*, ACLT s.v.)
- Neo-Assyrian *Sapa-lulme* 'king of Patin' (cf. HLuw. *Sapa-ziti*, Simon 2018b)
- Neo-Assyrian *Tuatti* 'king in Tabal' (Simon 2018b: 127–128)/Phrygian *Tuvatis* (G-133, Brixhe and Lejeune 1984: 122; cf. also HLuw. *Tuwati*, ACLT s.v., as well as its Urartian transcription *Tuate*, Laroche 1966: 194 No. 1406)

Although one may want to dismiss the Ugaritic and Greek loanwords in favour of other solutions (see the relevant footnotes), a dismissal is not possible in the cases of the Neo-Assyrian, Neo-Babylonian, Phrygian and Greek spellings of the onomastic material. Thus it must be concluded that the geminate theory of Melchert and Kloekhorst cannot explain the Akkadian, Greek, Phrygian, and Ugaritic spellings of Hittite and Luwian forms.

2.2 *Voiced Stops: Consistent Voiced Spelling instead of Voiceless Spelling*

The data are as follows:[21]

Language	Transcription/borrowing	Anatolian source	References/remarks
Ugaritic	*ủbdît/ủbdy* (once *updt*) '±leased land'	Hitt. *upāti-* 'land grant'/ Luw. *upātit-*	Watson 1995: 542; 1996: 704; 1999: 786; 2006: 717; 2007: 118; 2010: 833, with refs.
	pdģb 'PN'	*Puduḫepa*	Zehnder 2010: 257
Neo-Assyrian	*Lubarna* (kings of Patin)	*Labarna*	Simon 2018b: 127–128
	Melid(*d*)*u* 'GN'	*Malidiya*	also in MAss/NBab/Elam. (Bagg 2007: 172–174; Zadok 1985: 228–229)[22]

20 On the geminate spelling in Neo-Assyrian forms see n. 15.

21 Aramaic QRPDL of the KTMW stele may also reflect a Luwian word with a dental, see Yakubovich 2010b, 396.

22 On the occasional geminate spelling in Neo-Assyrian see n. 15.

(*cont.*)

Language	Transcription/borrowing	Anatolian source	References/remarks
Phoenician	?ZTWD 'PN'	Azatiwada	Röllig 1999
	?DN 'GN'	Adana	Röllig 1999[23]
Phrygian[24]	*Midas*	Hitt./Luw. *Mīta-*	Laroche 1966: 119 (No. 808)

This table does not require specific comments. It shows unambiguously that the consonants traditionally assumed to be intervocalic voiced stops in Hittite and Luwian were indeed perceived consistently as voiced stops throughout different languages, regions and periods. This excludes the interpretation as a single voiceless consonant suggested by Kloekhorst. However, it fits Melchert's description of them as voiced stops as well as Kloekhorst's alternative description, where he assumes voiced stops. Nevertheless, as the previous table shows, these voiced stops are contrasted with single voiceless stops intervocalically, and thus the evidence of loanwords and transcriptions exclude both the system of Melchert–Kloekhorst and that of Kloekhorst (and just for the record: also the entirely *ad hoc* system of Patri 2009b). In fact, all evidence is consistent with the traditional voiced/voiceless opposition, except the orthography, which is, however, on the one hand, only a partial exception (demonstrated by Kloekhorst and Pascual Coello, as per above), and, on the other, may have its reasons in the still unclear prehistory of Hittite cuneiform.

3 Conclusions

Kloekhorst's arguments against the traditional voiced/voiceless contrast in Anatolian stops are not probative. None of his arguments necessarily require a contrast in length. Moreover, transcriptions and loanwords from half a dozen languages equivocally and unambiguously show that Hittite and Luwian stops were always perceived as voiceless and voiced stops and never as geminates, *pace* Melchert and Kloekhorst. One cannot reject this evidence since the perception was consistent across many languages and many centuries (almost one millennium) involving both Hittite and Luwian. In other words, there is no reason to assume that the contrast in Anatolian stops was in length; and con-

23 Perhaps also in Hassan Beyli line 3 ⌜DN⌝ (Lemaire 1983: 11–12).

24 Phrygian *tubeti*(*v*) is not a loanword from Luwian: see the detailed discussion in Simon 2017b with references.

sequently the contrast in voice is neither a shared innovation nor a defining feature of the non-Anatolian Indo-European languages.

Acknowledgements

This paper was written within the framework of the "Digitales philologisch-etymologisches Wörterbuch der altkleinasiatischen Kleinkorpussprachen" financed by the DFG. I am very grateful to: Alwin Kloekhorst for his critical remarks after my talk, Ola Wikander for reminding me of an important issue and Gabriella Juhász for correcting my English. Needless to say, all responsibilities are mine.

References

ACLT = Ilya Yakubovich. *Annotated corpus of Luwian texts.* http://web-corpora.net/LuwianCorpus (last accessed: 11 July 2018)

Aronson, Howard I. 1990. *Georgian. A reading grammar.* Corrected edition. Bloomington: Slavica.

Aronson, Howard I. 1991. Modern Georgian. In Alice C. Harris (ed.), *The indigenous languages of the Caucasus.* Vol. 1. *The Kartvelian languages,* 219–312. Delmar: Caravan.

Aronson, Howard I. 1997. Georgian phonology. In Alan S. Kaye (ed.), *Phonologies of Asia and Africa (including the Caucasus),* 929–939. Winona Lake: Eisenbrauns.

Bagg, Ariel M. 2007. *Die Orts- und Gewässernamen der neuassyrischen Zeit.* Band 1. *Die Levante.* Wiesbaden: Reichert.

Beekes, Robert. 2010. *Etymological dictionary of Greek.* Leiden & Boston: Brill.

Brixhe, Claude & Michel Lejeune. 1984. *Corpus des inscriptions paléo-phrygiennes,* Vol. 1. Paris: ADPF.

CHD = Hans G. Güterbock, Harry A. Hoffner & Theo P.J. van den Hout (eds.). 1980–. *The Hittite dictionary of the Oriental Institute of the University of Chicago.* Chicago: The Oriental Institute.

De Decker, Filip. 2015. A new book on Pre-Greek. *International Journal of Diachronic Linguistics and Linguistic Reconstruction* 12. 1–21.

Eichner, Heiner. 2015. Das Anatolische in seinem Verhältnis zu den anderen Gliedern der indoeuropäischen Sprachfamilie aus aktueller Sicht. In Thomas Krisch & Stefan Niederreiter (eds.), *Diachronie und Sprachvergleich. Beiträge aus der Arbeitsgruppe "Historisch-vergleichende Sprachwissenschaft" bei der 40. Österreichischen Linguistiktagung 2013 in Salzburg,* 11–24. Innsbruck: Institut für Sprachen und Literaturen der Universität Innsbruck.

Furnée, Edzard J. 1972. *Die wichtigsten konsonantischen Erscheinungen des Vorgriechischen. Mit einem Appendix über den Vokalismus*. Den Haag: Mouton.

Hoffner, Harry A. & H. Craig Melchert. 2008. *A grammar of the Hittite language*. Vol. 1. *Reference grammar*. Winona Lake: Eisenbrauns.

Kloekhorst, Alwin. 2008. *Etymological dictionary of the Hittite inherited lexicon*. Leiden & Boston: Brill.

Kloekhorst, Alwin. 2010. Initial stops in Hittite (with an excursus on the spelling of stops in Alalaḫ Akkadian). *Zeitschrift für Assyriologie* 100. 197–241.

Kloekhorst, Alwin. 2013. The signs TA and DA in Old Hittite: Evidence for a phonetic difference. *Altorientalische Forschungen* 40. 125–141.

Kloekhorst, Alwin. 2014. *Accent in Hittite: A study in plene spelling, consonant gradation, clitics, and metrics*. Wiesbaden: Harrassowitz.

Kloekhorst, Alwin. 2016. The Anatolian stop system and the Indo-Hittite hypothesis. *Indogermanische Forschungen* 121. 213–247.

Kloekhorst, Alwin. 2018. Anatolian evidence suggests that the Indo-European laryngeals **h2* and **h3* were uvular stops. *Indo-European Linguistics* 6. 69–94.

Kroonen, Guus, Gojko Barjamovic & Michaël Peyrot. 2018. Linguistic supplement to Damgaard et al. 2018: Early Indo-European languages, Anatolian, Tocharian and Indo-Iranian. doi:10.5281/zenodo.1240524

Laroche, Emmanuel. 1966. *Les noms des hittites*. Paris: Klincksieck.

Lemaire, André. 1983. L'inscription phénicienne de Hassan-Beyli reconsidérée. *Rivista di studi fenici* 11. 9–19.

Luukko, Mikko. 2004. *Grammatical variation in Neo-Assyrian*. Helsinki: Neo-Assyrian Text Corpus Project.

Melchert, H. Craig. 1993. *Cuneiform Luvian lexicon*. Chapel Hill: self-published.

Melchert, H. Craig. 1994. *Anatolian historical phonology*. Amsterdam & Atlanta: Rodopi.

Melchert, H. Craig. 2012. Hittite *ḫi*-verbs of the type *-āC₁i, -aC₁C₁anzi*. *Indogermanische Forschungen* 117. 173–185.

Melchert, H. Craig. 2013. Luvian language in "Luvian" rituals in Hattuša. In Billie Jean Collins and Piotr Michalowski (eds.), *Beyond Hatti. A tribute to Gary Beckman*, 159–172. Atlanta: Lockwood.

Mosca, Paul G. & James Russell. 1987. A Phoenician inscription from Cebel İres Dağı in Rough Cilicia. *Epigraphica Anatolica* 9. 1–28.

Pascual Coello, David. 2014. *Valor y uso de los signos CV-oclusivos en interior de palabra en hitita*. PhD dissertation, Universidad Complutense de Madrid.

Patri, Sylvain. 2009a. La perception des consonnes hittites dans les langues étrangères au XIIIe siècle. *Zeitschrift für Assyriologie* 99: 87–126.

Patri, Sylvain. 2009b. Problèmes de phonologie louvite et d'isoglosses anatoliennes. *Historische Sprachforschung* 122. 67–95.

Popova, Olga V. 2016. Cuneiform orthography of the stops in Alalaḫ VII Akkadian. *Zeitschrift für Assyriologie* 106. 62–90.

Puhvel, Jaan. 2013. *Hittite etymological dictionary*. Vol. 9. *Words beginning with PE, PI, PU*. Berlin & New York: Mouton de Gruyter.

Rabin, Chaim. 1963. Hittite words in Hebrew. *Orientalia* 32. 113–139.

Rieken, Elisabeth. 2010. Review of A. Kloekhorst, *Etymological dictionary of the Hittite inherited lexicon*. *Kratylos* 55. 125–133.

Röllig, Wolfgang. 1999. Appendix I—The Phoenician inscriptions. In Halet Çambel. *Corpus of Hieroglyphic Luwian inscriptions*. Vol. 2. *Karatepe-Aslantaş. The inscriptions: Facsimile edition*, 50–81. Berlin & New York: Walter de Gruyter.

Simon, Zsolt. 2013. Die These der hethitisch-luwischen Lehnwörter im Armenischen. Eine kritische Neubetrachtung. *International Journal of Diachronic Linguistics and Linguistic Reconstruction* 10. 97–135.

Simon, Zsolt. 2014a. Awarikus und Warikas. Zwei Könige von Hiyawa. *Zeitschrift für Assyriologie* 104. 91–103.

Simon, Zsolt. 2014b. Der phonetische Wert der luwischen Laryngale. In Piotr Taracha (ed.), *Proceedings of the Eighth International Congress of Hittitology. Warsaw, 5–9 September 2011*, 873–895. Warsaw: Agade.

Simon, Zsolt. 2017a. *δέπας* und die anderen: Spuren eines verschollenen luw(o)iden Dialekts? *Wékʷos: Revue d'études indoeuropéennes* 3. 245–259.

Simon, Zsolt. 2017b. Etruscan *tupi*, Armenian *topᶜem*, Phrygian *tubeti*. In Olav Hackstein, Jared L. Miller & Elisabeth Rieken (eds.), *Digital philological–etymological dictionary of the minor ancient Anatolian corpus languages*. München & Marburg. http://www.ediana.gwi.uni-muenchen.de/dictionary.php?lemma=289

Simon, Zsolt. 2017c. Der luwische Name Awarikus. *Beiträge zur Namenforschung* 52. 115–122.

Simon, Zsolt. 2018a. Anatolian influences on Greek. In Łukasz Niesiołowski-Spanò & Marek Węcowski (eds.), *Change, Continuity, and Connectivity. North-eastern Mediterranean at the turn of the Bronze Age and in the early Iron Age*, 376–418. Wiesbaden, Harrassowitz.

Simon, Zsolt. 2018b. Sapaziti, Sapalulme und die Suppiluliumas von W/Pal(a)stin(a/i). *Altorientalische Forschungen* 45. 122–132.

Simon, Zsolt. Forthcoming. Anatolian names in Neo-Babylonian transmission.

Tischler, Johann. 2001. *Hethitisches etymologisches Glossar*. Band 2(11–12): *P*. Innsbruck: Institut für Sprachen und Literaturen der Universität Innsbruck.

Watson, Wilfred G.E. 1998. Non-Semitic words in the Ugaritic lexicon (3). *Ugarit-Forschungen* 30. 751–760.

Watson, Wilfred G.E. 2004. A Hittite loanword in Ugaritic? *Ugarit-Forschungen* 36. 533–538.

Watson, Wilfred G.E. 2006. Non-Semitic words in the Ugaritic lexicon (6). *Ugarit-Forschungen* 38. 717–728.

Watson, Wilfred G.E. 2007. *Lexical studies in Ugaritic*. Barcelona: Ausa.

Watson, Wilfred G.E. 2008. Some Akkadian and Hittite equivalences. *Nouvelles Assyriologiques Brèves et Utilitaires* 2008(68): 95–96.

Watson, Wilfred G.E. 2010. Non-Semitic words in the Ugaritic lexicon (8). *Ugarit-Forschungen* 42. 831–845.

Weeden, Mark. 2011. *Hittite logograms and Hittite scholarship*. Wiesbaden: Harrassowitz.

Yakubovich, Ilya. 2010a. *Sociolinguistics of the Luvian language*. Leiden & Boston: Brill.

Yakubovich, Ilya. 2010b. The West Semitic god El in Anatolian hieroglyphic transmission. In Yoram Cohen, Amir Gilan & Jared L. Miller (eds.), *Pax Hethitica. Studies on Hittites and their neighbours in honour of Itamar Singer*, 385–398. Wiesbaden: Harrassowitz.

Younger, K. Lawson. 2009. Two epigraphic notes on the new Katumuwa inscription from Zincirli. *Maarav* 16. 159–179.

Zadok, Ran. 1979. On some foreign population groups in first millennium Babylonia. *Tel Aviv* 6. 164–181.

Zadok, Ran. 1985. *Geographical names according to New- and Late-Babylonian texts*. Wiesbaden: Reichert.

Zehnder, Thomas. 2010. *Die hethitischen Frauennamen. Katalog und Interpretation*. Wiesbaden: Harrassowitz.

CHAPTER 12

Two Balkan Indo-European Loanwords

Rasmus Thorsø

1 Loanwords and Cladistics

All languages frequently borrow elements—roots, derivational morphemes and, more rarely, inflectional morphemes—from other languages that they are in contact with. It is only reasonable to assume that this has been the case ever since human language emerged. When a loanword has been fully integrated into the lexicon of a language, it generally behaves like any other word, being susceptible to the same phonological and morphological changes as inherited words. As a consequence, there are certain comparisons for which it is impossible to establish a direct ancestor form, and which display features that make a borrowing scenario more likely, or the only one possible. Such features may include a phonological make-up offending the phonotactics of the ancestral language, a very limited distribution, or extralinguistically, an incompatibility between the semantics and the established theories about the material culture and subsistence strategies typical of the speakers of the ancestral language. Sometimes, related forms in two or more branches may be traced to a common proto-form which at the same time cannot be reconstructed for the older parent language. When this is the case, and especially when similar, but incomparable forms are found among the other branches of the family, we can reasonably infer that the etymon was borrowed at a common pre-stage of these branches. This article examines two examples of such a situation in the hypothetical common pre-stage of Greek, Armenian, and Albanian.

Borrowing is a type of lexical innovation, but the probative value of loanwords is frequently understated when discussing the cladistics of a language family.[1] Thus, while shared innovations in the core linguistic structure (phonol-

1 Cf. e.g. Clackson (1994: 23–24) who distinguishes four basic types of lexical innovation: replacement of a root (e.g. through borrowing), innovation of form and meaning, of form only, and of meaning only. Clackson does not explicitly assign more weight to one over the other, however. In his summary (1994: 190), isolated roots which are borrowings are assigned to a special category, but no distinction is made between those lexemes that show regular sound correspondences, such as Arm. *siwn* = Gk. *κίων* 'pillar', and those that do not, such as Arm. *kamowrǰ* ~ Gk. *γέφυρα* 'bridge'.

 | DOI:10.1163/9789004416192_014

ogy and morphology) are rightly considered key evidence, shared innovations that take the form of borrowed lexical material are often disqualified or disregarded. Shared innovations in (inflectional) morphology are surely still the pillar of cladistic evidence because they are often less easily repeatable; however, one may argue that also lexical borrowings represent unique, significant innovations when they can be traced to a common form for which there is no evidence in the previous clade. In such cases, borrowings are even more significant than lexical innovations based on inherited material, including lexemes that are completely isolated, but otherwise show no signs of being loanwords, thus still having a chance of being shared archaisms.

2 Evidence for Balkan Indo-European

The so-called Balkan Indo-European languages[2] have been shown to relate to each other in various ways. A common pre-stage of Greek, Armenian, Albanian, and Phrygian is primarily hypothesized on the basis of lexical evidence, but some morphological innovations like the analogical transfer of **m-* to the 1. person active middle ending, i.e. PIE **-$h_2$ai̯* → **-mai̯* > Gk. *-μαι*, Arm. *-m*, Alb. *-m* (Klingenschmitt 1994: 245), may also be noted. The hypothesis is corroborated by shared innovations that can be established for only two of the constituent languages, e.g. the productive agent noun suffix **-ikʷi̯o-* > Arm. *-ičʿ*, Alb. *-ës* (Matzinger 2016: 167). For an overview of isoglosses, see Matzinger 2005c: 381–382. On some points, Albanian and Armenian may show a similar treatment of the PIE gutturals (Kortlandt 1986), but their exact development is highly debated. At the same time, Armenian and Greek share a larger number of isoglosses, most famously the vocalization of initial, pre-consonantal laryngeals in e.g. Gk. *ἀνήρ*, Arm. *ayr* 'man' < **$h_2$ner-*, also seen in Phrygian *αναρ* 'husband'. Chiefly, Greek and Armenian show a relatively large set of lexical correspondences which caused them to be closely connected by many scholars since Pedersen (1924), who also noted a number of lexical isoglosses with Albanian.[3]

Based on a number of important isoglosses shared with Greek (Neumann 1988, Brixhe 2008: 72) and to a lesser degree, with Armenian (de Lamberterie

2 This widely used term is admittedly somewhat misleading. There is no direct evidence placing all of these languages or their hypothetical common ancestor on the Balkan peninsula itself. A discussion of the geographical circumstances is beyond the scope of this paper, however.

3 An exhaustive discussion of the Greek–Armenian isoglosses is given by Clackson (1994) who is sceptical about the idea of a subgroup. The hypothesis is even more explicitly rejected by Kim (2018).

2013, Kortlandt 2016), it seems sensible to include Phrygian in the Balkan IE subgroup.[4] However, the exact classification of Phrygian will not be given further attention here, where it suffices to repeat the received opinion that its closest known relative is Greek (Brixhe l.c., Ligorio & Lubotsky 2018: 1816–1817).

The establishment of the Balkan IE subgroup is frequently considered highly uncertain or unlikely. Many thus seek to explain the notable shared innovations through a period of intense contact alone, assuming an ancient *Balkansprachbund* which like the modern one may have encompassed a large area (Hajnal 2003). Especially the fact that the earliest attestations of Armenian and Albanian are relatively late (respectively 5th and 16th century CE) and highly deviant from PIE makes it challenging to judge the evidence these languages provide and lowers the amount of extant evidence. The judgement of the few key items is therefore of great importance. The following sections give a discussion of two loanwords which in their exact form are confined to Greek, Armenian, and Albanian, and may represent borrowings at the common pre-stage of these languages. Neither of these etymologies is new, but the chronology of borrowing relative to the dissolution of PIE does not seem to have been sufficiently stressed.

3 **ai̯ĝ(i)*- 'Goat'

The comparison of Gk. *αἴξ* 'goat' (gen. *αἰγός*) and Arm. *ayc* '(nanny)goat', (gen.-dat.-abl.pl. *aycicᶜ*) has been recognized for nearly two centuries (cf. NHB s.v.) and has never really been questioned, even if there are in fact morphological difficulties. Thus, while the Greek noun shows root inflection with nominative **ai̯ĝ-s*, many Armenian forms have an underlying suffixed stem **ayci-*, i.e. nom.pl. *aycikᶜ* (beside less frequent *ayckᶜ*) and gen.-dat.pl. *ayceacᶜ*, (beside less frequent *aycicᶜ*). Consequently, the Armenian nominative with its primarily feminine semantics is commonly analysed as an **ih₂*-derivative (Meillet 1936: 76; Martirosyan 2010: 58), but such a form is not likely to be reflected in the primary (non-collective) nominative *ayc*—it would probably yield †*ayč̣*[5] con-

4 Other *Trümmersprachen* of the Balkans and Italy may also belong to the group, e.g. Messapian, for which a particular affinity with Albanian has been suggested (Matzinger 2005b). Finally, some shared innovations with Tocharian may be noted (Klingenschmitt 1994: 245).

5 There is admittedly no certain example of the cluster *-*ĝi̯*- in Armenian (but see e.g. Martirosyan 2010: 370 s.v. **koč-*). However, considering the development of other clusters with a stop and a semivowel, it is unlikely that the reflex was simply -*c*-. Cf. the recent discussion and references in Kocharov 2019: 30–31.

sidering the regular development[6] of final *-ih_2 > *-i̯a seen in *sterǰ* 'sterile', cf. Gk. *στεῖρα*, Lat. *sterīlis*, and in *verǰ* 'end', derived by Olsen (1999: 84) from **uperih*$_2$-. It is sensible to assume the coexistence of a root noun *ayc-* and a derivative **ayci-* in Proto-Armenian, perhaps with an original singulative and collective function respectively.

Outside Greek and Armenian, the only potential match, also showing the pattern of root noun versus feminine/collective derivative, is Alb. *edh* 'goat kid' and *dhi* 'nanny goat', reflecting PAlb. **aidza*, **aidzijā* respectively (Orel 1998: 85).

No true cognates are found in other Indo-European languages. Skt *ajá-* 'goat' and Lith. *ožỹs*, *ožkà* 'goat' are, despite the identical semantics, not related etymologically with the form underlying the Greek, Armenian, and Albanian words. Rather, they formally presuppose *(h_2)*aĝ*-. The derivation of Skt *eḍa-* 'kind of sheep, ewe' from **aiĝ-* (Mayrhofer 1992: 264) is very implausible considering the phonological and semantic incompatibilities. So is the frequent comparison of Av. *īzaena-* 'made of leather', purportedly from a zero grade *(h_2)*iĝ*-; We do not know whether this term originally referred to goatskin, and more importantly, we do find the expected reflex of *(h_2)*aĝ*- in YAv. *aza-* 'billy goat', clearly identical with Skt. *ajá-*, showing no *-i̯-. There is also no clear evidence for a zero grade elsewhere, despite Martirosyan's quite complicated suggestion that *ayc* derives from "*h_2*iĝ*- > *Hyĝ*, with *y* analogically after NSg *h_2*eiĝ*-" (2010: 58), seemingly in order to explain the absence of initial *h-* from *#h_2-. The implied, rather controversial sound law (PIE *#h_2- > Armenian #*h*-) is probably valid after all,[7] but it seems far simpler to explain the lack of this reflex by assigning **aiĝ-* to a post-PIE stage.

6 This development of *-ih_2# could well have been morphologically conditioned, i.e. the result of analogical leveling on basis of the oblique cases (cf. de Lamberterie 1990: 490), but that does not change the fact that its absence here would be unexpected. Based on its apparent presence in Tocharian as well (cf. Toch. B *lāntsa* 'queen' < **ulh*$_2$*ntih*$_2$), this development may be assigned to a very old stage, but the alleged Albanian evidence, *zonjë* 'lady' < **desi̯ās potnih*$_2$ according to Klingenschmitt (1994: 244) is very uncertain. We can therefore assume that the change of *-ih_2# > *-*ya*# was not a change common to Balkan IE but rather to Graeco-Armenian only; we may even be dealing with completely independent developments.

7 See e.g. Polomé 1980, Martirosyan 2010: 712 with literature. Clearly, the most problematic counterexample, adduced by e.g. Olsen (2017: 430), is *acem* 'lead' < *h_2*eĝ-e/o-*, cf. Gk. *ἄγω* etc. The alternative etymology comparing Lat. *gerō* 'carry' < *h_2*ĝ-es-* leads to new problems such as the Arm. aorist *aci*. We may thus have to explain *acem* as influenced by compounds ending in *-ac* (Clackson 2005: 155). It is likely that initial *h-* in Armenian became an unstable phoneme which could sometimes appear and disappear irregularly, much like the situation in Albanian. In this light, the number of examples where Arm. *ha-* still seems to correspond to *h_2*e-* is noteworthy.

Consequently, the root *h_2eịĝ- 'goat' that frequently appears in Indo-European handbooks (e.g. Mallory & Adams 1997: 229) should be eliminated. One could of course try to salvage the PIE heritage by deriving the Baltic and Indo-Iranian word for 'goat' from the well-known root *h_2eĝ- 'drive' (Gk. ἄγω) and abandon the connection with *h_2eịĝ-. The semantics of this derivation is not quite convincing. Furthermore, the theory of a substrate borrowing may in fact be corroborated by areal words for 'goat' in other IE languages. Lat. *haedus* 'kid' and Got. *gaits* 'goat' reflect *g^haịd(-o)-, a substrate etymon frequently connected with Semitic, cf. Akkadian *gadû*, Aramaic *gaδịā* 'kid'. The source of borrowing was most likely not Semitic directly, but a European substrate language which had borrowed the word from a third, common source (see Kroonen 2012: 246–247 with references). It is difficult to regard the vague similarity to *a(ị)ĝ- and another limited, non-IE synonym, viz. OCS *koza* 'nanny-goat' < *kaĝ^h-, as completely coincidental. In fact, as Kroonen (2012: 245) notes, none of the alleged roots with a meaning 'goat' are likely to be PIE but may all originate from the substrate languages spoken by the settled agriculturalists who were encountered by immigrating Indo-European pastoralists. It fits the data well to think of *aịĝ- and *aĝ- as relatively early, post-PIE borrowings (thus already Specht 1939: 13; Solta 1960: 405). During the independent borrowings into Balkan IE on the one hand, and Balto-Slavic and Indo-Iranian on the other, the final consonant of the root, possibly some sort of palatovelar obstruent, was interpreted in various ways.

All this draws a picture of an old cultural word that slowly passed through various European languages, later to be adopted by the intrusive Indo-European speakers. In this scenario, it is indeed significant that Greek, Albanian, and Armenian exclusively share a common proto-form that could have been borrowed at a common pre-stage. Additionally, these three languages could have jointly formed a feminine/collective derivative. To take this thought a step further, we may speculate whether *-i-* was an element originally belonging to the donor form (cf. "*aịdị-" in Kroonen 2012: 247) In turn, this may provide an explanation for the unusual compositional vowel *-ι-* in clearly old compounds like αἰγίβοτος 'grazed by goats' (Od.) that existed next to compounds with the consonant stem, e.g. αἰπόλος 'goatherd'—cf. Myc. a_3-]*ki-pa-ta*, interpreted as *aịgipa(s)tās* 'goatherd' (DMic I: 135, Duhoux 2008: 295). A segmentation *aigipa(s)t-* would in any case be clearer than that of Heubeck (1963: 15–16), i.e. *aig-iptās* 'he who forces the sheep together'.

4 *$\hat{g}^h r\bar{\imath}t^h$- 'Barley'

No PIE word for 'barley' can be securely reconstructed. Mallory & Adams (2006: 164 s.v. 'barley') list three reconstructions:[8] *h_2*élbʰit* (Gk. *ἄλφι*, Alb. *elb*), **meiĝ*(*h*)- (Lith. *miežỹs*, less likely Khot. *mäṣṣa*- 'field'), and finally *$\hat{g}^h$*résd*^{h}(*i*) (OHG *gersta*, Lat. *hordeum*, and Gk. *κρῑθή*, Hom. *κρῖ*, Myc. *ki-ri-ta*[9]). But the distribution of the former two is very limited, and the latter cannot directly underlie any of the attested forms. OHG *gersta* thus presupposes *g^h*ersd*-, Lat. *hordeum* is from *g^h*ord-ei̯o*-, and Homeric *κρῖ*, already to be internally reconstructed as **κρῖϑ*, must reflect something like *$g^h r\bar{\imath}d^h$ or *$g^h r\bar{\imath}t^h$-[10] with no reflex of *-*s*. These discrepancies alone are strongly suggestive of a substrate origin.[11]

Alb. *drithë* 'cereal, grain', a neuter since the earliest attestations (Demiraj 1997: 145), is frequently traced to the zero grade of a root nearly identical to the one reflected in OHG *gersta*, i.e. *$\hat{g}^h r̥(s/z)d^h$-, (cf. Demiraj 1997: 145–146, Orel 1998: 75 with references). But the missing aspiration of **d* in Lat. *hordeum* remains a significant obstacle, leading to the assumption of a *Wanderwort*. It may then be preferable to derive *drithë* from a form identical to *κριϑή*, i.e. PAlb. **ðriϑā*[12] < *$\hat{g}^h r\bar{\imath}t^h\bar{a}$. Some phonological issues with this etymology may be raised. Firstly, the lack of depalatalization, which has been explained by the assumption of a vocalic **r̥*, could also be caused by the fact that this rule was no longer fully effective at the time of borrowing (though see fn. 13 below). Secondly, the development *T^h > Alb. *th* is perhaps not regular, though it may be seen in *djathë* 'cheese', compared with Skt. *dádhi* 'sour milk' (cf. Demiraj 1997: 135–136). According to Orel (1998: 67), *djathë* is a diminutive with the suf-

---

8 See also Blažek 2017 where most relevant material is presented.

9 Hapax legomenon on a tablet from Knossos, probably to be read as an acc. [kritʰan] or [kritʰans], the direct object of *e-ko-si* 'they have' (Ventris & Chadwick 1959: 215). It betrays a certain age for the thematic (collective) formation.

10 Although the reconstruction of a voiceless aspirated series for PIE can rightly be considered unsustained, it is probably fair to assume its monophonemic existence in later IE dialects, primarily as the outcome of **TH* clusters. See also Rasmussen 1987.

11 Rasmussen (1989: 91–92) offered an original alternative, instead analysing the root as an "*eRi*/*Rī*-type", i.e. having an original nom.-acc.sg. *$\hat{g}^h$*érHi̯-sd*^{h}-, gen.sg. *$\hat{g}^h$*r̥hi̯-sd*^{h}-*ós*, which later yielded *$\hat{g}^h$*érsd*^{h}-, *$\hat{g}^h$*rihsd*^{h}*ós*. For Arm. *gari*, explained as a Sievers–Lindeman variant *g^h*r̥hisd*^{h}-, it implies that the spread of the oblique stem to the nom.sg. happened quite early. Unfortunately, such discrepancies as the vacillation of **d* in Germanic and Latin, versus *T^h in the Balkan forms, and the apparent lack of **s* in at least Greek and Armenian remain unexplained. For the depalatalization of *$\hat{g}^h r$- > *$g^h r$, see fn. 13.

12 The dissimilation of initial **ð*- > *d*- was perhaps caused by the following sibilant, as in *dorë* 'hand' < *$\hat{g}^h$*esr*- (Orel 2000: 70), but it also seems to have occurred in other environments, as shown by *dimër* 'winter' < *$\hat{g}^h$*eimōn*, Gk. *χειμών*.

fix *-th*, but Demiraj (l.c.) more plausibly assumes either dissimilation with the voiced anlaut or devoicing in auslaut. Devoicing can also be seen in *mb-ath* 'to put on shoes' and *z(b)-ath* 'to take off shoes' < *(h_2)Vu-d^h-* (cf. Arm. *awd* 'shoe'), where it later spread to the entire paradigm, e.g. *zbathur* 'barefoot' (B.D. Joseph apud Hyllested 2016: 74). This explanation is conceivable for *drithë* too.

Arm. *gari* 'barley' is sometimes compared to the Greek forms, but their formal relationship is not fully established (cf. Martirosyan 2010: 199). However, it is possible that they reflect the same root. In Classical Armenian, *gari* follows the "mixed", polysyllabic *ea*-inflection: gen.sg. *garwoy*, loc.sg. *garwoǰ*, gen.-dat.-abl.pl. *gareacᶜ*. This class most likely arose from old neuters with the suffix **-i̯o*, collective plural **-i̯$ə_2$* (Olsen 1999: 113; Matzinger 2005a: 65). The closely related *wo*-class (gen.-dat.-abl.pl. *-wocᶜ*) contains masculines with the same suffix. Assuming that Gk. *κρῑθή* reflects an original collective, we may thus easily understand why the Armenian reflex ended up in this class. In this case, however, the sequence **-i̯a* did not necessarily arise from the suffix. From a collective **ĝʰrītʰā* we may expect a regular development to **gʰriϑa*[13] > **griya* > **gri*.

A morphophonological parallel is provided by Arm. *eri* 'shoulder, side' (gen.-dat.-abl.pl. *ereacᶜ*) if this is compared with Lith. *ríetas* 'thigh, loin', Cz. *řit'* 'buttocks' (Olsen 1999: 444). Alternatively, one could of course presume a (possibly diminutive) derivation in **-i̯o-*, cf. Gk. *κριθίον*. In the oblique *o*-stem forms where **-i̯ó-* eventually yielded *-wó-*, the cluster **gru̯-* would possibly have been dissolved by a svarabhakti vowel at a stage sufficiently early for it to yield *a*, i.e. **grii̯óhyo* > **g(ə)ru̯óyo* > *garwoy*, which was later generalized in the paradigm.[14]

Formally, **ĝʰrītʰ-* may have been borrowed jointly by Greek, Armenian, and Albanian, who formed a neuter collective **ĝʰrītʰā*. In a larger perspective, this etymon could have been very widespread across non-IE languages early on,

13 The depalatalization of palatovelar stops before **r* is not universally accepted for Armenian. However, it is at least seen in internal position in *mawrowkᶜ* (pl.) 'beard' < **smoḱru-*, Skt. *smaśru-*, and perhaps in *garšim* 'to loathe' besides *jaṙ* 'curved, ugly' (see Martirosyan 2010: 199–200). Possibly depalatalization, also observed in Balto-Slavic, Albanian, and Indo-Iranian, occurred in several waves with slightly different conditions in extra-Anatolian IE, cf. Kloekhorst 2011. The fact that depalatalization in this word seems to have affected Armenian, but not Albanian, in turn requires the assumption of a later, perhaps analogical, application of this rule in Armenian.

14 Admittedly, the relative chronology in the development of the *wo-* and *ea*-stems is uncertain. A development **-i̯o-* > **-iu̯o-* with subsequent regular loss of unstressed *i* could also be assumed (cf. Pedersen 1905: 199).

judging from forms with a similar consonantal shape in mutually unrelated languages, cf. Georgian *kʰeri*, Basque *gari* 'wheat', *garagar* 'barley', Burushaski *gur* 'wheat' (Berger 1998: 161), Dargwa (NE Caucasian) *q̇ar* 'grass', and perhaps even Tibetan *k're* 'millet'.

5 Discussion

Despite the quite limited evidence, the analyses given above support a scenario in which Greek, Armenian, and Albanian descend from a common prestage posterior to PIE. This is in line with other isoglosses, of which some were mentioned in the beginning of this article. There is admittedly a great deal of insecurity involved, especially concerning the position of Albanian. Due to the larger number of possible shared innovations between Armenian and Greek, it thus seems reasonable to assume, at least tentatively, that Albanian was the first of the Balkan IE languages to branch off. Probably, this and the subsequent splits were very close in time (cf. Pereltsvaig & Lewis 2015: 85) leaving only a narrow chronological window for shared innovations. In this light, the findings that can after all be made should be considered significant.

The so-called Graeco-Armenian hypothesis (excluding Albanian) remains quite strong despite the criticism of Clackson (1994) and, recently, Kim (2018). Aside from the phonological correspondences, perfect, exclusive agreements like Arm. *kałin*, Gk. *βάλανος* < *$*g^{w}l̥h_2$-no-* and the more clearly innovated Arm. (*amis*) *ara-c'* 'month of harvest', Gk. *ὀπ-ώρα* < *$*h_1$os-r-eh_2* (Martirosyan 2013: 110) must be considered in light of the general scarcity and late attestation of the Armenian data. However, a popular opinion seems to be that Greek, Armenian and Indo-Iranian all branched out from the same PIE dialect, while the Greek–Armenian agreements all developed through subsequent, long-lasting contact (Martirosyan 2013: 126). This scenario seems to imply that these branches split off almost simultaneously—something that is a priori rather implausible, as language splits are most often binary (cf. Gąsiorowski 1999: 41–42). In other words, Armenian cannot be equally close to Indo-Iranian and Greek genetically, although it may be reasonable to maintain this scenario as an agnostic position. Without doubt, Greek, Armenian, and partly Albanian also underwent a longer period of contact (shortly) after they had diverged from one another, as betrayed by irregular correspondences like Gk. *σκόρ(ο)δον*, Arm. *sxtor, xstor*, Alb. *hudhër, hurdhë* 'garlic'. Later, there were certainly intense Greek–Albanian contacts, all things that potentially distort the picture. However, subsequent contact naturally does not exclude genetic affinity, which is the tentative conclusion that we may draw from this limited material. Furthermore, the distribution of forms in the two examples given here seem to suggest an early dialectal division of extra-Anatolian IE into Germanic–Italo-Celtic, Balto-Slavic–Indo-Iranian, and Balkan IE, of which the latter two in turn seem to be more closely related. However, this is an extremely complex issue that should be judged in the light of more possible evidence.

The two etymological analyses presented in this article are admittedly burdened with some uncertainty, especially that of part 4 (*$\hat{g}^h r\bar{\imath}t^h$-). However, if it ultimately has to be rejected, the central point of this paper remains; the attempt to reconstruct intermediate, post-PIE stages and clarify their particular innovations, whether internally or externally conditioned, should be an important objective of Indo-European linguistics and can indeed be aided by utilising loanwords as evidence.

The study of post-PIE loanwords has become increasingly popular in the last few decades, and more scholars are aware of its usefulness in reconstructing prehistoric contact interfaces and migrations, especially when combined with the still accumulating evidence from archaeology and ancient DNA. At the same time, loanwords may constitute significant evidence for language cladistics when combined with the stronger cladistic evidence of morphological innovations.

References

Berger, Hermann. 1998. *Die Burushaski-Sprache von Hunza und Nager*. Teil III: Wörterbuch. Wiesbaden: Harrassowitz.

Blažek, Václav. 2017. On Indo-European 'barley'. In Bjarne S.S. Hansen, Benedicte Nielsen Whitehead, Thomas Olander & Birgit A. Olsen (eds.), *Etymology and the European lexicon: Proceedings of the 14th Fachtagung der indogermanischen Gesellschaft, 17–22 September 2012, Copenhagen*, 53–67. Copenhagen: Museum Tusculanum.

Brixhe, Claude. 2008. Phrygian. In Roger D. Woodard (ed.), *The ancient languages of Asia Minor*, 69–80. Cambridge: Cambridge University Press.

Clackson, James. 1994. *The linguistic relationship between Armenian and Greek*. Oxford & Cambridge: Blackwell.

Clackson, James. 2005. Review of Kortlandt, *Armeniaca*. *Annual of Armenian Linguistics* 24–25. 153–158.

Demiraj, Bardhyl. 1997. *Albanische Etymologien: Untersuchungen zum albanischen Erbwortschatz*. Amsterdam & Atlanta: Rodopi.

DMic I = Francisco Aura Jorro (ed.). 1985. *Diccionario micénico*. Vol. 1. Madrid: Consejo Superior de Investigaciones Científicas, Instituto de Filología.

Duhoux, Yves. 2008. Mycenaean anthology. In Y. Duhoux & A. Morpurgo Davies (eds.), *A companion to Linear B: Mycenaean Greek texts and their world*. Vol. 1, 243–393. Leuven: Peeters.

Gąsiorowski, Piotr. 1999. The tree of language: A cladistic look at the genetic classification of languages. *Dialectologia et geolinguistica* 7. 39–57.

Hajnal, Ivo. 2003. Methodische Vorbemerkungen zu einer Paleolinguistik des Balkanraums. In A. Bammesberger & T. Vennemann (eds.), *Languages in prehistoric Europe*, 117–145. Heidelberg: Winter.

Heubeck, Alfred. 1963. Myk. *a_3-ki-pa-ta* 'Ziegenhirt'. *Indogermanische Forschungen* 68. 13–21.

Hyllested, Adam. 2016. Proto-Indo-European reconstruction and Albanian phonotactics. In Stephanie W. Jamison, H. Craig Melchert & Brent Vine (eds.), *Proceedings of the 26th Annual UCLA Indo-European Conference*, 63–81. Bremen: Hempen.

Kim, Ronald I. 2018. Greco-Armenian: the persistence of a myth. *Indogermanische Forschungen* 123. 247–272.

Klingenschmitt, Gert. 1994. Die Verwandtschaftsverhältnisse der indogermanischen Sprachen. In Jens E. Rasmussen (ed.), *In honorem Holger Pedersen*, 235–251. Wiesbaden: Reichert.

Kloekhorst, Alwin. 2011. Weise's Law: Depalatalization of palatovelars before *r in Sanskrit. In T. Krisch & T. Lindner (eds.), *Indogermanistik und Linguistik im Dialog: Akten der XII. Fachtagung der Indogermanischen Gesellschaft vom 21. bis 27. September 2008 in Salzburg*, 261–270. Wiesbaden: Reichert.

Kocharov, Petr. 2019. *Old Armenian nasal verbs. Archaisms and innovations*. PhD thesis, Leiden University.

Kortlandt, Frederik. 1986. Armenian and Albanian. In Maurice Leroy & Francine Mawet (eds.), *La place de l'arménien dans les langues indo-européennes*, 38–47. Leuven: Peeters.

Kortlandt, Frederik. 2016. Phrygian between Greek and Armenian. *Linguistique Balkanique* 55(2). 249–255.

Kroonen, Guus. 2012. Non-Indo-European root nouns in Germanic: evidence in support of the Agricultural Substrate Hypothesis. In Riho Grünthal & Petri Kallio (eds.), *A linguistic map of prehistoric northern Europe*, 239–260. Helsinki: Suomalais-Ugralainen Seura / Finno-Ugrian Society.

de Lamberterie, Charles. 1990. *Les adjectifs grecs en -υς*. 2 vols. Leuven: Peeters.

de Lamberterie, Charles. 2013. Grec, phrygien, arménien: des anciens aux modernes. *Journal des savants* 2013(1). 3–69.

Ligorio, Orsat, & Alexander Lubotsky. 2018. Phrygian. In J. Klein, B. Joseph & M. Fritz (eds.), *Handbook of comparative and historical Indo-European linguistics*. Vol. 3, 1816–1831. Berlin & Boston: De Gruyter Mouton.

Mallory, James P., & Douglas Q. Adams. 1997. *Encyclopedia of Indo-European culture*. London: Fitzroy Dearbourn.

Martirosyan, Hrach K. 2010. *Etymological dictionary of the Armenian inherited lexicon.* Leiden & Boston: Brill.

Martirosyan, Hrach K. 2013. The place of Armenian in the Indo-European language family: the relationship with Greek and Indo-Iranian. *Вопросы языкового родства* 10. 85–137.

Matzinger, Joachim. 2005a. *Untersuchungen zum altarmenischen Nomen: Die Flexion des Substantivs* (Münchener Studien zur Sprachwissenschaft. Beiheft, n.F. 22). Dettelbach: Röll.

Matzinger, Joachim. 2005b. Messapisch und Albanisch. *International Journal of Diachronic Linguistics and Linguistic Reconstruction* 2. 29–54.

Matzinger, Joachim. 2005c. Phrygisch und Armenisch. In G. Meiser & O. Hackstein (eds.), *Sprachkontakt und Sprachwandel: Akten der XI. Fachtagung der Indogermanischen Gesellschaft, 17.–23. September, Halle an der Saale*, 375–394. Wiesbaden: Reichert.

Matzinger, Joachim. 2016. *Die sekundären nominalen Wortbildungsmuster im Altalbanischen bei Gjon Buzuku: Ein Beitrag zur altalbanischen Lexikographie* (Albanische Forschungen 38). Wiesbaden: Harrassowitz.

Mayrhofer, Manfred. 1992. *Etymologisches Wörterbuch des Altindoarischen.* Vol. 1. Heidelberg: Winter.

Meillet, Antoine. 1936. *Esquisse d'une grammaire comparée de l'arménien classique.* 2nd revised ed. Vienna: Mekhitaristes.

Neumann, Günter. 1988. *Phrygisch und Griechisch. Ein Überblick über die Geschichte der phrygischen Sprache von vorgeschichtlicher Zeit bis zum Erlöschen des Phrygischen im frühen Mittelalter.* Wien: Verlag der Österreichischen Akademie der Wissenschaften.

NHB = Gabriēl Awetikᶜean, Xačᶜatowr Siwrmēlean & Mkrtičᶜ Awgerean. 1836–1837. *Nor baṙgirkᶜ haykazean lezowi.* 2 vols. Venice: St. Lazar.

Olsen, Birgit A. 1999. *The noun in Biblical Armenian: origin and word-formation—with special emphasis on the Indo-European heritage.* Berlin & New York: Mouton de Gruyter.

Olsen, Birgit A. 2017. Armenian. In Mate Kapović, Anna G. Ramat & Paolo Ramat (eds.), *The Indo-European languages*, 420–451. 2nd ed. London: Routledge.

Orel, Vladimir. 1998. *Albanian etymological dictionary.* Leiden: Brill.

Orel, Vladimir. 2000. *A concise historical grammar of the Albanian language: reconstruction of Proto-Albanian.* Leiden, Boston & Cologne: Brill.

Pedersen, Holger. 1905. Zur armenischen sprachgeschichte. *Zeitschrift für vergleichende Sprachforschung* 38(2). 194–240.

Pedersen, Holger. 1924. Armenier. B. Sprache. In Max Ebert (ed.), *Reallexikon der Vorgeschichte.* Vol. 1, 219–226. Berlin: Walter de Gruyter.

Pereltsvaig, Asya, & Martin W. Lewis. 2015. *The Indo-European controversy. Facts and fallacies in historical linguistics.* Cambridge: Cambridge University Press.

Polomé, Edgar C. 1980. Armenian and the Proto-Indo-European laryngeals. In John A.C. Greppin (ed.), *First International Conference on Armenian Linguistics: Proceedings*, 17–34. New York: Caravan Books.

Rasmussen, Jens E. 1987. Aspirated tenues and the Indo-European phonation series. *Acta linguistica Hafniensia* 20. 81–109.

Rasmussen, Jens E. 1989. *Studien zur Morphophonemik der indogermanischen Grundsprache*. Innsbruck: Institut für Sprachwissenschaft der Universität Innsbruck.

Solta, Georg Renatus. 1960. *Die Stellung des Armenischen im Kreise der indogermanischen Sprachen*. Vienna: Mekhitharistes.

Specht, Franz. 1939. Sprachliches zur Urheimat der Indogermanen. *Zeitschrift für vergleichende Sprachforschung* 66. 1–74.

Ventris, Michael, & John Chadwick. 1959. *Documents in Mycenaean Greek*. 2nd ed. Cambridge: Cambridge University Press.

CHAPTER 13

The Inner Revolution: Old but Not That Old

Michael Weiss

Mariae Lvdovicae Portiae Gerniae
egregiae investigatrici lingvarvm Italicarvm

∵

1 Introduction

If two genetically related languages share a trait, this trait might be (a) inherited, (b) the result of a common shared innovation, (c) diffused from one to the other, or (d) independently innovated. If these two languages are not adjacent, then the shared innovation and diffusion hypotheses become more costly, but not impossible. The Gallo-Italian dialects of southern Italy and Sicily, for example, share many features with Lombard.[1] These situations result from migration.

If the shared trait is lexical, then the hypothesis of independent innovation becomes more costly. That two languages would create the same lexical item *ex nihilo* independently is only likely to happen rarely by chance. But that a precursor meaning would independently develop in parallel fashion is quite plausible and well exemplified, e.g. 'human' > 'man'; 'cause to die' > 'kill'.[2] Another complication is the creation of identical lexical material from inherited roots and inherited derivational processes.

Thus the question of lexical matches between nonadjacent languages involving formally identical or nearly identical items is of some theoretical interest. If we observe such items, they may result from the retention of shared archaisms once common to the ancestors of all the daughter languages that converge at the same parent node. On the other hand, such items might be evidence that the geography of the ancestors was once other than is found at the earliest date of attestation.

1 Rohlfs 1931.
2 Chang et al. 2015: 203 call this process "derivational drift".

 | DOI:10.1163/9789004416192_015

Another theoretical issue: if we observe shared lexical items between two nonadjacent languages, what is significant? Presumably chance will lead to the situation that two languages descended from a common ancestor will occasionally preserve an item that survives nowhere else in the language family. This question can only be answered by the number, quality, and semantic distribution of the matches. Are they more numerous and of better quality than those found between any two random non-adjacent languages not belonging to the same subgroup? Do the items concentrate in a particular lexical field or are they randomly distributed? If the answers to these questions point to the existence of a significant phenomenon, how do we decide between archaism and migration? If we can show that a given lexical item must once have been present in intermediate languages, then we have proof, for at least this one item, that the archaism hypothesis must be correct. If the shared lexical features are archaic and have been lost in intermediate languages in such a way as to leave a distinctive profile of archaism and innovation, what either permitted the survival or encouraged the replacement? The explanation must be historical and/or sociological.

Some cautions from the study of Romance are in order. I recently had the opportunity to review a volume of the *Dictionnaire étymologique roman,*[3] which seeks to reconstruct Proto-Romance without reference to the evidence of written Latin, but by strict application of the Comparative Method alone. This work regards Sardinian and Romanian as the first and second offshoots of the Proto-Romance family, the "Proto-Anatolian" and "Proto-Tocharian" of Romance, so to speak. By the policies of the *DÉRom,* if an item is not found in Sardinian it can, strictly speaking, only be reconstructed for Proto-Continental Romance. For example, */ˈbrum-a/ 'winter' does not have a Sardinian reflex and hence "ne peut être reconstruit de façon sure que pour l'époque d'après la séparation du protoroman continental du protosarde".[4] In this instance, it is likely that the procedure has produced a correct result. The Central Sardinian word for 'winter' is *iverru* < *hībernum,* no doubt an older term. The innovation hitting Proto-Continental Romance was the semantic change from 'winter solstice' to 'winter season'. Sardinian, on the other hand, has simply lost the word */ˈbrum-a/ in any sense. In contrast, although */ˈaud-i-/ 'hear' likewise has no direct reflex in Sardinian, the authors of the article for *this* word show no hesitation about reconstructing it for Proto-Romance. Why? In this case the innovation lies on the Sardinian side where the word for 'hear' is *intendere,*

3 Buchi and Schweickard 2014.

4 Birrer, Reinhardt, Chambon s.v. pp. 385–386 apud *DÉRom.*

the cognates of which show the meaning 'extend' (Rom. *întinde*), or 'understand' (Sp. *entender* etc.). The semantic development 'extend' → 'direct (one's mind, attention)' → 'listen/hear' is obvious and the familiar Spanish meaning probably derives from an earlier 'hear'. So the Sardinian meaning, in fact, is intermediate between Spanish and Romanian.

Items shared exclusively by Ibero-Romance and Proto-Romanian, of which there are quite a few (e.g. Sp. *angosto*, Rom. *îngust* 'narrow', Sp. *hervir*, Rom. *fierbe* 'boil'),[5] are certainly old, but are, in my subjective view, scattered pretty evenly throughout the lexicon and many can be shown once to have existed in earlier forms of Romance where they are now missing (Sp. *yegua*, Rom. *iapă*, but OFr. *ive* 'mare' replaced in Modern French by *jument*).[6] These distributions result from what J.N. Adams called "lexical shrinkage."[7]

In this paper I will continue an examination of East–West lexical isoglosses, specifically items found only in Indo-Iranian and Italic and/or Celtic that are concentrated in the religious and legal spheres. I call this set of data "the Vendryes Phenomenon".[8] I hope to show that these items indeed are archaisms from the point of view of Inner Indo-European but also that the Vendryes Phenomenon is actually an innovative stratum of lexicon that does not go back to highest-node Proto-Indo-European. This can be shown not only by the absence of these items in Tocharian and Anatolian—which of course is not conclusive—but also in some cases by internal arguments that show how these items arose. In some instances it is possible to show that the current distribution results from lexical shrinkage, not contact, but in the case I will examine in detail in this paper, I can find no argument to decide this issue.

2 East–West Lexical Isoglosses. Some Questions

Following the lead of Kretschmer 1896, Vendryes 1918 pointed out some lexical correspondences between Italo-Celtic[9] and Indo-Iranian. While Kretschmer explained these as the result of prehistoric migrations, Vendryes chose to explain them as archaisms preserved by the priestly organizations continued

5 See Dworkin 2012: 51–53.
6 In fact, *equa* has reflexes in most forms of Romance except Italian and even in Italy the word is continued as *eka* in the dialect of Valsugana. What gives the false impression of a gap is the fact that the two central literary languages, Italian and French, have replaced the word.
7 Adams 2007: 13.
8 The treatment of the case of *śraddhā́* ~ *crēdere* in this paper may be regarded as a thematic continuation of Weiss 2017b.
9 I'm using Italo-Celtic loosely here to mean either Italic or Celtic or both.

at the edges of the Indo-European world. Thus he stressed the legal/religious nature of the archaisms. But are lexical correspondences between Italo-Celtic and Indo-Iranian really more impressive than those between other nonadjacent branches?[10] Do these correspondences skew toward the legal/religious lexicon? How well do the specific examples hold up? Some may be incorrect. Some may now be known from other branches. How do these corrections and clarifications affect the overall picture that Vendryes sketched? Now that we have two apparently higher nodes of the PIE family tree we have to ask if these alleged archaisms appear in Tocharian (and thus at NPIE) or Anatolian and (thus at PIE).[11] If they don't appear and, if we are convinced that they are archaisms at the Inner-PIE level, then can we decide whether they have been lost in the first branches off? On the other hand, if this is not the case, then can we make an inference about the date of this supposed priestly organization, which Vendryes posits was the main channel for transmission and preservation of the forms in question? These are far too many questions to answer within the short scope of this paper. A brief sketch of the history of the question and a case study follow.

3 History of the Question

Johannes Schmidt, one of the first Indo-Europeanists to address the issue of lexical matches between noncontiguous languages, listed only twenty exclusive Italo-Indo-Iranian lexical isoglosses in his work *Die Verwantschaftsverhältnisse der indogermanischen Sprachen*.[12] He included no Celtic data at all.[13] Most of Schmidt's examples are now dubious and many are just wrong.[14] In 1896

10 Polomé 1988, for example, was skeptical of the whole concept.

11 In this paper I take for granted the idea that Proto-Anatolian was the first branch to split off from Proto-Indo-European and the Proto-Tocharian was the second. The post-Anatolian group I call Nuclear Proto-Indo-European (NPIE). The post-Tocharian group I call Inner Proto-Indo-European (IPIE).

12 Schmidt 1872: 65–66.

13 Schmidt wrote on pp. 33–34: "Leider bin ich in den keltischen sprachen nicht bewandert, was ich hier als eine mögliche quelle von felern in meinen verzeichnissen bekennen muss."

14 This is the breakdown of Schmidt's list. The following examples are incorrect: (3) *carmen* 'song' < **kanmn̥* does not match Ved. *śásman-* 'invocation'; (4) *ēbrius* 'drunk' does not match Skt. *ahraya-* 'bold', which is *a-hraya-* 'not bashful'; (5) Osc. **eís-** 'this' is independently created and not comparable to Ved. *eṣá-*, Av. *aēša-* 'this'; (8) *iūs* does not match Ved. *yóḥ*, Aves. *yaoš* (see Weiss 2018a); (9) *Mars* cannot be compared with Ved. *Marút-*; (11) *mundus* 'clean' does not go with Skt. *maṇḍayati* 'adorns'; (14) *Saeturnus* cannot be compared with Ved. *Savitár-*; (17) *tussis* has no Avestan cognate *tušən*; the obscure word

Paul Kretschmer offered a much-expanded list that included Celtic data for the first time.[15] Kretschmer (p. 147) explained these agreements as the result of the prehistoric migration of a western tribe to the east. Similarly, Specht 1939: 48 attributed these agreements to migrations of the Corded Ware Culture.[16] This hypothesis might find support in the recent genetic finding that unlike the Early Bronze Age steppe pastoralists represented by the Yamnaya and Afanasievo cultures, the Late Bronze Age Sintashta and Andronovo people (likely ancestors of the Indo-Iranians) had a significant genetic admixture from European Neolithic farmers. This would suggest that there was a secondary expansion from the west after the formation of the Corded Ware Culture.[17] Time will tell whether further evidence will strengthen or weaken the migration hypothesis. The topic was clearly in the air in Paris in the 1910s. Alfred Ernout, for example wrote in 1911 "ils témoignent d'une communauté de vocabulaire italo-celtique et indo-iranienne, dont l'existence, pour déconcertante qu'elle soit, ne constitue pas un des faits les moins curieux de la linguistique indo-européenne."[18] But the whole question was given its clas-

transmitted at v. 3.32 is *tusən*; (18) *torus* is not cognate with Skt. *stara-* 'layer, stratum' since the oldest meaning of *torus* is 'bulge'. The following examples are dubious: (1) *cacūmen* 'peak' ~ Ved. *kakúbh-* 'peak'; (2) *caesariēs* 'long hair' ~ Ved. *késara-*. (16) *tumultus* 'noise, uproar' ~ Skt. *tumula-* 'noise' may be iconic. The following matches are now joined by cognates from other branches: (6) *ēnsis* 'sword' ~ Ved. *así-* 'knife' may have a cognate in Pal. *ḫašira-* 'dagger', although all the connections are dubious; (12) *Neptūnus* ~ Av. *napta-* 'moist' are probably part of the widespread family of **nebʰ-* 'moist, wet' (Gk. *νέφος* 'cloud' etc.); Ved. *apā́m nápāt-* 'grandson of the waters' and its Avestan match are better left aside; (15) *socius* 'comrade' is a closer formal match with ON *seggr* 'man' than with Ved. *sákhā*, YAv. *haxa* 'friend'. The remaining good and exclusive (or also including Celtic) shared lexical items are (7) Lat. *gliscere* 'grow up' ~ Ved. *jri-* 'take up space', Av. *zraiiō*, OP *drayah-* 'lake' (see Forsmann 2014 for a defense); (10) *menda* 'blemish' might match Ved. *mindā́* 'blemish' on the assumption that the vowel of the latter has been remade on the noun *nindā́* 'blame'. Related forms may also be continued in OIr. *mennar* 'spot' (but see. eDIL s.v. for doubts) and MW *mann* 'spot, blemish' (GPC *man²*). Hitt. *mant-* mentioned by de Vaan 2008: 372 is an uncertain hapax; (13) Lat. *opus* 'work', Umb. *ose* 'opere' ~ Ved. *ápas-* 'work', Av. *huuāpah-* 'doing good work'; the root is known from elsewhere (OHG *uoben* etc.), but the isolated *s*-stem is only Indo-Iranian and Latin; (19) *Venus* ~ Ved. *vánas-* 'desire', a RVic hapax (10.172.1); the root is widely attested but the *s*-stem again is just Latin or Italic (if Osc. *ϝενζει* is not borrowed from Latin) and Indic; (20) *uolua* which has the meaning (1) 'womb' (2) 'seed covering' and seems like a close match for Ved. *úlva~ úlba* which means (1) 'membrane around an embryo' or (2) 'womb'; the root is probably a *-u*-extended from of **u̯el-* 'to wind' (Lat. *uoluere* etc.).

15 Kretschmer 1896: 126–147.

16 Most recently Koncha 2015 has revived this approach.

17 See Damgaard et al. 2018: 5.

18 Ernout 1911: 89.

sic formulation by Joseph Vendryes in his 1918 article "Les correspondances de vocabulaire entre l'indo-iranien et l'italo-celtique." The findings of this work, which inspired the entire career of Georges Dumézil,[19] certainly passed for communis opinio when I first entered the field, but, to my knowledge, there has been no systematic evaluation of the question in the century since the initial publication of Vendryes' article. We can now recognize that Vendryes included some wrong etymologies. For example,

> Lat. *lēx* 'law' does not match OAv. *rāzarə̄/rāzan-* 'rule' but instead belongs with Lat. *legō* 'collect'. Note the same lengthened grade in *collēga* 'colleague'.[20] The Avestan forms cannot be separated from YAv. *rāzaiieiti* 'directs' and the *rēx* family.[21]
>
> Lat. *rītus* 'customary way' cannot be compared with Ved. *r̥tám* 'order', Av. *aṣ̌əm*. Instead the Latin form goes with TB *rittetär* 'is fitting', TA *ritwatär*, Av. *raēϑuua-*.[22] In this case, if the analysis offered in Weiss 2015 is correct, we would substitute an even more archaic East–West match for the one Vendryes suggested, but the religious normative specialization is independent in Italic and Tocharian.
>
> Lat. *erus* 'master' goes not with Ved. *ásura-* 'lord' etc., but with Hitt. *išḫāš* 'master', both from *$*h_1esh_2ós$*.[23] So this match would be another case of an even older layer of vocabulary.
>
> OIr. *orcaid, -oirg* 'kills', OBr. *treorgam* 'I pierce', *orgiat* 'murderer' does not belong with YAv. *ərəza-* 'combat' but with Hitt. *ḫark-* 'perish', Arm. *harkanem* 'strike' < *$*h_3erg$-*.

---

19 Dumézil wrote 1958: 91: "Une circonstance, sur laquelle un article de J. Vendryes avait attiré l'attention dès 1918, a commandé la démarche de beaucoup de ces recherches: le vocabulaire religieux des Indo-Iraniens d'une part, ceux des Celtes et des Italiotes d'autre part, présentent un grand nombre de concordances précises, et qui leur sont propres."

20 Kaczyńska 2013 argues that root in question was properly **sleĝ-* and that Lat. *lēx* has a near match in Ved. *sráj-* 'garland', the original meaning of the root noun having been 'collection'. But the reconstruction with an immobile initial **s* is difficult since initial **sl-* was retained in Latin into the historical period. Cf. SL(ITIBVS) ILLRP 316 (epitaph of Scipio Hispanus, praetor peregrinus, 139 BCE) and CIL 1^2.583, par. 8, 123/122 BCE for Classical Latin *litibus*. If the VOL form of *lēx* was really **slēks* it is surprising that we find no trace of such a spelling epigraphically or any discussion of such a form in the antiquarian literature. The earliest epigraphical attestation of a form of *lēx* is LEGED (CIL 1^2.3152, Paestum) dated between 250 and 200 BCE. Only if one is prepared to accept an *s*-mobile for this root, can the comparison between *lēx and sráj-* be maintained.

21 On the Iranian verbal forms descended from *$*h_3$reĝ-* see Cheung 2007 s.v. *Hraz-*.

22 See Weiss 2015.

23 See Kloekhorst 2008 s.v. *išḫāš* and de Vaan 2008 s.v. *erus*.

Lat. *flāmen* 'priest' is still an attractive comparandum for Ved. *brahmán-* 'priest' and the match is phonologically workable if we start from **bʰlaĝʰmḗn*, but this comparison presupposes an otherwise unattested root **bʰlaĝʰ-* or **bʰleĝʰ-*. Given that *brahmán-* is synchronically an internal derivative of *bráhma* 'sacred formula' it is hard to separate the Vedic forms from Gaul. *brictom* 'magical formula', OIr. *bricht* 'charm', ON *bragr* 'poetic talent', Lat. *fōrma*.[24] If that connection is correct, then Lat. *flāmen* would obviously have to be separated and instead compared with Go. *blōtan* 'sacrifice'.[25]

Some items are now identified in other branches:

Lat. *āra*, Osc. **aasaí** loc. sg., Umb. *asa* 'altar' ~ Ved. *ā́sa-* 'ashes' (AV), Hitt. *ḫāššā-* 'hearth', *ḫāšš-* 'soap', pl. 'ashes'. In fact the semantic and formal match between Hitt. *ḫāššā-* 'hearth' and Italic **āsā* is superior.[26]

4 A Case Study[27]

In this paper I will examine in detail the Indo-Iranian~Italo-Celtic isogloss constituted by Ved. *śraddhā́* f. 'trust', *śrád … dhatta* 'trust!', OAv. *zrazdā-* 'trusting'

24 Osthoff 1899: 131–134. The connection of *fōrma* with *bráhma* is phonologically possible.

25 See Schaffner 2010 for a recent defense of the *blōtan* connection.

26 See Kloekhorst 2008 s.v. *ḫāššā-*. Eichner 1982: 27–28 has suggested that Hitt. *šēša-* c. 'fruit' (see CHD s.v. for attestations) should be compared to Ved. *sasá-* 'food' < **sesh₁ó-* 'what is sown'← **seh₁-*. If this is correct then Anatolian would be added to the Celtic-Indo-Iranian lexical isogloss represented by MW *heid*, MBr. *heiz* 'barley' < **sesi̯o-* (or **sasii̯o-*, see Schrijver 1995: 318–319), Ved. *sasyám* 'grain in the field' (AV), YAv. *hahiia-* 'related to grain', cf. *paitiš.hahiia-* 'bringing in grain' (name of a deity of the third season). Kloekhorst 2008 doesn't discuss the word at all, though he does treat *šēšan(n)aš* under the lemma *šēšatar*. It is clear that the Hittite word doesn't mean 'grain' but 'fruit' (Akk. *INBU* including dates, olives, and other tree fruit). The specialization of a form originally meaning 'what is sown' for 'fruit' is possible but uncertain, so this Celtic-Indo-Iranian match may still exclusive.

27 In Weiss 2017b, which this paper continues, I argued that the Inner-IE word for 'king' resulted from the personification of an abstract noun **h₃rēĝ-s* 'rule' (Ved. *rā́ṭ* fem.) by way of the PIE analogue of the Ved. *idám bhū-* construction and further that feminine suffix **-nih₂* could only be explained on the model of the unique pair **h₃rēĝs* 'king' ~ **h₃rēĝnih₂* 'queen'. Thus wherever we find evidence for this suffix we can infer the quondam existence of the **h₃rēĝs* 'king' ~ **h₃rēĝnih₂* pair. Here I would add one additional point. David Stifter has kindly called my attention to a 2012 article of his which identifies a compound name *Volturex* 'ruling at will' (cf. YAv. *vasō.xšaϑrō* 'ruling at will') found at Laibach (Emona) and Ig as evidence for the 'king' word in "Northern Adriatic". Thus we see that the loss of the **h₃rēĝs* word is indeed the result of lexical shrinkage.

(Y. 31.1), with the superlatives YAv. *zrazdišta-* (Y. 53.7), and *zrazdātəma-* (Yt. 13.25), YAv. *zrazdāiti-* 'trust', YAv. *zras-ca dāṯ* 'and has believed' (Yt. 9.26), OP **drazdā-* (*adrazdā* 'faithfully' in the Aramaic "Letter of Artaxerxes" in Ezra 7.23 and *ādrazda-*, a personal name),[28] Lat. *crēdere* 'to believe', OIr. *creitid* 'believes', MW *credaf* 'I believe', OBr. *critim* 'belief' < **kred-dī-mā*, MCorn. *crys* 'believes' < **kred-dīt*.[29] There can be no doubt about the excellence and (so far) exclusiveness of this comparison,[30] but there are a few issues that call for some comment.

The first member of the collocation and compound **ḱred-* is a form of the word for 'heart'[31] and not some unknown element meaning perhaps 'stake' vel sim., as was the official doctrine of Meillet and his followers.[32] A positive

28 For the Aramaic see Nober 1958 and for the personal name Tavernier 2007 s.v.

29 Schulze-Thulin 2001: 38.

30 Already noted by Kretschmer 1896: 140.

31 First suggested by Darmesteter 1878: 120.

32 Ernout 1911: 85 doubted the connection of *śrád* with **ḱ(e)rd-* because of the Schwebeablaut. I address this question below in the text. Meillet 1913: 60 argued: (1) if *śrád* was always felt as a form of 'heart' how could it escape remodeling after *hṛ́d-*? (2) the heart in Indo-Iranian is nothing but an organ; (3) the synchronic meaning of *śraddhā́* is a matter of ritual practice, i.e. belief in the efficacy of sacrifice, not an "affaire de coeur". The answers to these questions are: (1) Even if **ćrád* was synchronically identified as a word meaning 'heart' in Proto-Indo-Iranian, a fixed collocation need not be updated to match the innovations of its constituent free forms. For example, the archaic accusative **mans* was retained in **mans *dhā-* 'think' even though as a free form **mans* was replaced by **mánas-*. (2) The heart is not just an organ. The compound *durhárd-* (AV), for example, means 'evil minded, malevolent' not 'in bad cardiovascular shape'. There are numerous instances of *hṛ́d-* in the RV as the seat of the emotions of joy and fear. The instrumental *hṛdā́* means 'gladly or willingly'. See Sellmer 2004 for a survey of the Vedic evidence. Of course, the actually relevant issue is whether PIE **ḱ(e)rd-* was also conceived of as a seat of various emotions and mental states and all evidences suggests that it was. Cf. Pl. *Am.* 1054 *neque ullast confidentia iam in corde quin amiserim* "There's no trust now in my heart that I haven't lost." and Hitt. (KUB I 16 III 63) *kuit kardi nu-za apāt ešši* "what is in your heart do that!". It seems pointless to multiply examples. (3) As argued below, the ritual meaning of *śraddhā́* is only one piece of the overall picture. Vendryes 1918: 266 claims that Meillet "a définitivement montré l'inanité de cette interprétation." but it should now be clear that this is not the case. Benveniste 1969 [English version 1973: 144] elaborates on Ernout and Meillet's original points. He admits that indeed the heart is a seat of emotions, not just an organ, but claims that the idiom "put one's heart into somebody" is "only an illusion born of modern metaphors" and completely excluded for the ancients. But if at least Inner Indo-European had a collocation **mens* d^heh_1- 'put mind' > 'think', which is indisputable, then is 'put heart' really so strange? We may also note Lat. *mandere* 'to entrust' < **man(u)* d^heh_1- 'put hand'. Cf. also the Biblical Hebrew idiom *śām lēb* 'to put heart' which means 'to pay heed', as noted by Orel 1995: 117. Further in Vedic at least the heart is not just any inner organ but the essence of the self. The first part of the sacri-

argument for the ancient association of the first part of the *$\hat{k}$red- d^heh_1- collocation and heart can be derived from the Proto-Iranian remodeling of the reflex of *$\hat{k}$red- under the influence of the transformed reflex of the word for 'heart'. As is well known, the Proto-Indo-Iranian word for 'heart' was remade from *ćr̥d- to *$ȷ́^h$r̥d- (Ved. *hr̥d-*, Av. *zərəd-*, Kati *ziri*). The standard explanation of this unexpected initial consonant is that it resulted from a contamination with a Proto-Indo-Iranian form cognate with Gk. χορδή 'guts'.[33] But we can make this hypothesis more precise. Hittite attests a *d*-stem. *karāt-* 'guts', often written with ŠÀ, the same Sumerogram used for *kēr* 'heart', < *$\hat{g}^h$r̥h_1-od-.[34] Such a proto-form would have yielded a PIIr. *$ȷ́^h$r̥Had- which would have overlapped semantically and phonologically to a notable degree with PIIr. *ćr̥d-. If this protoform were continued into Young Avestan the result would be *zaraδ-. Just such a form, I hesitantly suggest, is continued in the Young Avestan compound *zaraδāγniiāi* (V.1.14) The first part *zaraδ-* is unanimously transmitted according to Geldner,[35] and the meaning 'to strike the guts' rather than 'heart' seems equally possible.[36] The transformation of the element *ćrad- in Proto-Iranian to *ȷ́rad- under the influence of the free form for 'heart' *ȷ́r̥d- (cf. OP *ādrazda-) shows that the speakers of Proto-Iranian, at least, made a synchronic connection between 'heart' and 'believe'.[37]

The one formal problem in connecting *$\hat{k}$red- and the paradigm of *$\hat{k}$erd- ~ *$\hat{k}$r̥d- 'heart' is the unparalleled location of the full grade: why does the *e*-grade appear between *r and *d and not between *$\hat{k}$ and *r which is its normal full-grade locus in the heart word? Jochem Schindler suggested this could be

---

ficed animal basted with ghee is the heart because, as the *Śatapatha Brāhmaṇa* explains (3.8.3.8) *ātmā vai mano hr̥dayam* "the heart truly is the self, the mind." See Olivelle 2006: 53.

33 See Szemerényi 1970: 530 n. 32 for the history of this suggestion. Szemerényi appears to be the first to state the contamination hypothesis in unambiguous terms.

34 Kloekhorst 2008 s.v. *karāt-*.

35 Dr. Velizar Sadovski has kindly assembled the readings of the manuscripts available at the Avestan Digital Archive for me and has uncovered no significant variation. One Indian Vīdēvdād Sāde from the Bhandarkar Oriental Research Institute, Poona (Sig. 4504/Bh3/ fol. 51r) reads *zarəδāγniiāi*. If these forms have been corrupted from **zərədāγniiāi*, the corruption must be very old.

36 A trace of the quondam existence of this word in Indic may be seen in the meaning 'belly' (of Indra) in RV book 9, as shown by Renou 1961: 56.

37 Jacques 2017 suggests as an alternative conflation with the root of *hr̥ṇīte* 'gets angry', a possibility mentioned in passing by Meillet 1894: 298. Meillet's idea (1913) that in Iranian *ćradd^{h}ā underwent the last iteration of a pre-PIE assimilation of aspirates to become *$ȷ́^h$radd^{h}ā is implausible, especially since these elements are still separable even in Avestan.

explained by positing a phonotactically motivated Schwebeablaut induced by an *s*-stem ** *ḱerd-s* → **ḱred-s*.[38] The problem with this idea is the complete absence of evidence for an *s*-stem form of 'heart' as NIL p. 423 point out. But this otherwise unattested *s*-stem could be explained as an analogical creation on the model of the archaic *s*-stem **mens* also combined with *d^heh_1-*. (OAv. *mə̄n̦ dadē* 'I think', Ved. *mandhātár-* 'thinker'). Cf. the collocation 'with heart and mind' *utá hr̥dótá mánasā* (RV 8.98.2) *zərədācā manaŋhācā* (Y. 31.12). Thus there is no need to posit the existence of an *s*-stem outside of the collocation.

Such a **ḱred-s* would be indistinguishable in Indo-Iranian from **ḱred* in the forms in which it occurs, and the length of Lat. *crēdō* positively requires an *s* of some sort.[39] OIr. *creitid* too might work starting from **ḱred-s-(d^he-)d^heh_1-*. Cf. MIr. *net* 'nest' /n^{j}ed/ < **nisdo-*, but MW *credaf* with *d* < **dd* does not at first sight match MW *nyth* 'nest'. But there is no independent evidence for the outcome of *-*dsd-* and that *-*dsd-* should have a different outcome from *-*sd-* is not unlikely. One way or the other the Brittonic forms of 'nest' have undergone a devoicing and it is plausible that the preceding voiced consonant prevented this from happening. **ḱred-s* seems to be a workable protoform.

If this explanation of **ḱred-s* as dependent on **men-s* 'mind' is correct, then this presupposes that there was a verbal root **men-* in the meaning 'think', but Tocharian and Anatolian only have clear evidence for **men-* 'remain' (TB *mäsketär* 'be', Hitt. *mimma-* 'refuse'[40]) and **men-* 'look at' (CLuv. *manā-* 'look upon', *māmmanna-* 'regard with favor', *mimma-* 'regard, favor').[41] If the original meaning was 'look at' this could have developed to both 'think' (cf. Gk. σκέπτομαι 'look, consider, think') and 'remain' (cf. OHG *wartēn* 'watch for' > NHG *warten* 'wait'). It is possible that the development from 'look at' to 'think' did not take place until after the separation of Proto-Anatolian and Proto-Tocharian. If so then the collocation **ḱreds-d^heh_1-* must a fortiori be an Inner Indo-European innovation.

38 Schindler 1979: 58 compared *h_2u̯ek-s-* (Ved. *vákṣati*) vs. *$h_2$eu̯g-* 'increase' (Lith. *augti*). See Ozoliņš 2015: 133 for a variation on this approach.

39 The explanation of the length via Lachmann's Law offered by Schrijver 1991: 134 doesn't work since, to my knowledge, Lachmann's Law is only observed when a voiced consonant is devoiced.

40 Differently Kloekhorst 2008 s.v.

41 Admittedly TB *mañu* 'desire' and TA *mnu* 'desire, consideration' come very close to 'thought'. We could regard these as independent developments from 'look at'. In Anatolian the semantic space occupied by **men-* in Inner Indo-European is filled by the segmentally similar but etymologically distinct **mel-*, on which see Serangeli 2016: 186–187.

There is another school of thought on the exact morphology of **ḱred*. Sandoz[42] suggested that the form **ḱred* was an old endingless locative and that the idiom was literally 'to put (something) in the heart for someone'. In Steer, at least, this is combined with a theory that tries to explain the Schwebeablaut. Steer suggests that the Schwebeablaut was intended to distinguish the endingless locative from the strong and weak stems. But if we are dealing with an original **ē/e* root noun the endingless locative would be expected to be **ḱērd* and if we are dealing with an *e/ø* root noun the endingless locative would be **ḱerd*. By the usual theory of morphological Schwebeablaut, the neo-full-grade replaces an old zero-grade, but neither of the expectable endingless locatives had a zero-grade. So the theory of Steer introduces an entirely new type of explanation for Schwebeablaut. This endingless locative line of analysis raises the question: put what in the heart? Tremblay suggested the original meaning 'to put something (ACC) in the heart (LOC) for someone (DAT)' i.e. 'to entrust something to someone' and with ellipsis of the accusative object this became 'to trust someone (DAT)'. But this does not seem very plausible. First what is the dative in this putative original construction doing? It appears to be a facultative expression of possession. It would presumably alternate with a genitive and hence the loss of the obligatory argument and the obligatorification of the possessive dative is surprising. Further, the constructions which Tremblay pointed to in Vedic as comparanda show that when one places something in the heart for someone, one is not entrusting it at all but simply giving it, and these constructions don't normally include datives. Even an example like RV 7.86.8ab where there appears to be a dative can just as easily be taken as two clauses:

1 *ayáṃ sú túbhyaṃ varuṇa svadhāvo*
hṛdí stóma úpaśritaś cid astu
"This praise song is for you, Varuna, who are of independent will:
let it be set within your heart." (J&B)

Note too that *śrád* was treated as an accusative direct object in Vedic since it was promoted to subject in a passive construction at RV 1.104.6d *śráddhitaṃ te mahatá indriyā́ya* "Trust has been placed in your great Indrian power." and RV 1.104.7a *śrát te asmā adhāyi* "Trust has been placed in this (power) of yours." On the other hand, in YAv. we have an object Yt. 9.26 *yā.mē daēnąm māzdaiias-*

42 Sandoz 1973. Also Kellens 1974: 208, Rix 1995: 246, Tremblay 2004: 582 and most recently Steer 2013: 79.

nīm zrasca dāṯ "who has believed for me in the Mazdayasnian religion." but this replaces a dative construction in Old Avestan, and the antiquity of the dative is guaranteed by the agreement with Latin, and the Young Avestan does not continue the putative original construction semantically. The development from 'trust' to 'entrust' is made possible by the absorption of the original object into the complex verb structure, which opens a space, so to speak, for an external object, as Hackstein has convincingly argued.[43]

4.1 *The Recentness of the Compound in Celtic and Italic*

Since the parts of the compound are still separable in Indo-Iranian, they could not have been fused already in PIE (Inner PIE). Thus there is no necessary prediction that the dental plus dental cluster formed by the juncture of the two elements will behave like a primary dental plus dental cluster. In Celtic it is clear that the juncture was not treated like the original sequence. In Italic the only thing we can say with certainty is that *crēdō* must continue an earlier **krezdō*. Note CGL 5.54.12 *caesditum* : *creditum* where *caeditum* is a late spelling for *cesditum* as Lindsay prints. Perhaps *cesditum* stands for **kresditom* or is phonologically regular from **kersdatom* < **kres-datom*.

**krezdō*, in turn, must somehow continue **kredzdō*, which somehow continues **kredzdʰō*. Since we don't know what would happen to **kredzdō*, it's conceivable that the development was to *crēdō*.[44] In fact *tst* at a recent morpheme boundary has lost the first *t* (*astō* 'stand by' < **at-stō*) and *VCzD* becomes *V:D* (*trādere* 'hand over' < **trans-dere*). However, the *hasta* 'spear' < **gʰazdʰā* rule (cf. Go. *gazds* 'goad'), which devoices medial **zdʰ* (or prevents it from revoicing), might apply here leading to †*crestō*. Thus either that rule did not apply when the **z* was preceded by a stop or, more likely, the *d* was restored because of the morpheme boundary. The compound identity of *crēdō* must have been apparent well into the phonological history of Latin and, in fact, *crēdō* continues to function like a compound *-dere* verb with a paradigm exactly like *trādere*. Note too the forms *creduis, creduit, creduam, creduas, creduat* (all in Plautus), which show the analogical influence of the irregular subjunctive paradigm of *dō, dare* 'to give'. Italic and Celtic not only inherited the cognates of the Indo-Iranian forms but kept them as separable parts well into their individual prehistories.

---

43 Hackstein 2012: 90–93. Somewhat different is RV 8.75.2c. *śrád víśvā vā́ryā kr̥dhi* "Make our trust (in the sacrifice) into all things worth desiring." (J&B) where *víśvā vā́ryā* is a secondary predication.

44 Similarly Hill 2003: 250.

4.2 *Semantic History*

The Vendryes approach which focuses on the religious sphere—and perhaps our own religious associations with belief and faith—has somewhat obscured an essential aspect of the semantics of **ḱred *d^heh_1-*. If we examine the Latin side first we see that *crēdere* is not a particularly religious word. One can find instances of *crēdere* plus something in the divine sphere but these do not have a formulaic or institutional feel to them. For example there is nothing like the Vedic exhortation to trust in a god (RV 2.12.5d *śrád asmai dhatta* "Believe in him!") or a declaration of trust (RV 10.147.1a *śrát te dadhāmi*). In fact, the idiom *crēdere deōs* does not occur before Seneca.[45] Thus it is quite unlike the standard picture of Ved. *śrád dhā-* which Benveniste 1969: 174 describes as follows: "Cette croyance n' est jamais en un chose; c' est une croyance personnelle, l' attitude de l' homme vis-à-vis d' un dieu; non pas même une relation d' homme à homme, mais d' homme à dieu." In fact, the one institutional use of *crēdō* is in the realm of credit and loans, of things, people, or money entrusted to someone with an expectation that they should or must be returned. In Plautus' *Asinaria* the slave character Libanus sings a hymn to Perfidy (*Perfidiae laudes gratiasque habemus merito magnas* "I give great thanks and praise, well earned, to Treachery" 545) and his co-slave Leonidas mockingly tallies up his evil deed in high-flown style (*quae domi duellique male fecisti* "what evils you committed at home and abroad" 559). Libanus admits the truth of his charges and responds with his own epic list of Leonidas' crimes (perhaps in a mock legal style 566–572):

2 *Fateor profecto ut praedicas, Leonida, esse uera:*
Verum edepol ne etiam tua quoque malefacta iterari multa
Et uero possunt: ubi sciens fideli infidus fueris,
Vbi prensus in furto sies manufesto et uerberatus,
Vbi periuraris, ubi sacro manus sis admolitus,
Vbi eris damno ⟨*et*⟩ *molestiae et dedecori saepe fueris,*
Vbi creditum quod sit tibi datum esse pernegaris,
"I admit it's true what you say, Leonidas,
But your many misdeeds can also be listed:
when you knowingly broke trust with someone who trusted you,
when you were caught thieving red-handed and beaten,
when you perjured, when you raised your hands to the sacred,
when you were a cause trouble and shame for masters,
when you denied that what had been entrusted to you had been given."

---

45 See Ramelli 2000.

Here "denying that what was entrusted had been entrusted" ranks as a major offense. In the *Cistellaria* the slave Halisca, whose actions have led Phanostrata to be reunited with her daughter, comments that (*Cis.* 760–761):

3 *HA. Aequomst* ⟨*reponi*⟩*per fidem quod creditumst,*
Ne bene merenti sit malo benignitas.
"It's right that what has been entrusted be returned so that a kind act not turn out badly for a person who deserves well."

At *Curculio* 494–496 the title character doubts whether he should trust the word of the pimp Cappadox about emancipating Planesium if she is proved to be freeborn.

4 *Egon ab lenone quicquam*
Mancipio accipiam, quibus sui nil est nisi una lingua,
Qui abiurant, siquid creditumst?
"I should take anything formally from a pimp?! who have nothing of their own but their tongue, who swear falsely if anything is entrusted to them?"

Here we find this same focus on the criminality of denying what is entrusted to you.

The same pimp Cappadox soliloquizes about the business of loans (*Curc.* 679–681). This is a difficult passage, which has been variously interpreted and emended, but here is a way I think it could be interpreted:

5 *Argentariis male credi qui aiunt, nugas praedicant*
nec bene nec male credi dico. id adeo ego hodie expertus sum
(Lambinus: *nec bene nec male* for *nam et bene et male*)
Non male creditur qui numquam reddunt, sed prorsum perit.
"People who say it's bad to trust in bankers are talking nonsense.
For I say there is no bad or good trusting. And I experienced that today.
It's not badly entrusted to people who never repay you. It's just gone."

The essence of 680–681 seems to be that the relationship of entrusting cannot have degrees. You can't even call it bad entrusting when people aren't going to repay you. It's just throwing money away. We can extract a few key features of the credit relationship: Violating it is a serious offense. Failing to return what has been entrusted may have bad consequences for the person who fails to return. A credit relationship is not gradable. It is either is or isn't. The obligatory nature of loan repayment is explicitly stressed in the later discussion of Seneca

(*De beneficiis* 4.12) where he defines a "benefit" as a *creditum insolubile* but then goes on to distinguish a *beneficium* from an actual loan *cum dico 'creditum', intellegitur 'tamquam creditum.' … adicio 'insolubile', cum creditum nullum non solui aut possit aut debeat.* "When I say *creditum* 'loan' I mean "as if a loan" and I add *insolubile* "which cannot be repaid" because every real loan can or should be repaid." Legal works also emphasize this obligatory aspect. The meaning 'entrust' must be quite old, since it is only this meaning that allows the close secondary association with *dō, dare* 'give' noted above.

As Meillet pointed out in 1922, the verbal noun of *crēdō* is *fidēs*. (*Aul.* 614 *tuae fide concredidi aurum* "I entrusted the gold to your trust." addressed to the goddess, *Fides*). Meillet even suggested, plausibly I think, that *fidēs* owed its shape to the one-time existence of **krēdēs* < **k̑red-dʰeh₁s*. Fraenkel 1916 showed that in Old Latin *fidēs* does not normally mean 'faith' or 'belief' but 'trustworthiness', 'trust' or 'tutelage' "worauf man sich verlassen kann, Garantie im weitesten Sinne." To be sure, this view cannot be maintained quite as rigidly as Fraenkel argued, but it does get at an important aspect of the word's early use. In another famous article, Heinze 1929 argued for a double meaning 'a trust relationship', i.e. both trust which one puts in another and trustworthiness. In Heinze's summation (p. 165): "Der Römer fühlt sich in seinem geschäftlichen, gesellschaftlichen, öffentlichen Leben durch seine *fides* in mannigfaltigster Weise seinen Mitbürgern gegenüber sittlich gebunden, andererseits durch ihre *fides*, ja auch die seiner Götter gesichert."

Here are some notable idioms: *in fidem populi Romani uenire* "to come into a *fides*-relationship with the Roman people". "To be in the client relationship" was *in fide alicuius esse* (CIL 1^2.583) and the *tessera hospitalis* supposedly from Fundi, a bronze fish, (CIL 1^2.611, ILLRP 1068, early 2nd cent. BCE) says IN EIVS FIDEM OM⟨NES NOS TRADIMUS ET⟩ COVENVMIS "we all agree and hand ourselves over into his *fides*". *Fidēs*, which perhaps replaces earlier **krēdēs*, is a key term describing trust, between borrower and lender, between conqueror and conquered, and between guest and host.

Thus, if Benveniste is correct in his description of Indic *śraddhā́*, there is a notable disconnect between the Indo-Iranian and Italic meanings, and the best one could do to save the strong Vendryes hypothesis would be to say that the term was laicized on the Italic side only to become a religious term again with the advent of Christianity.[46]

But Benveniste is wrong—or more fairly, he is describing the usage of the RV alone. There is a clear nonritual, nonreligious use for *śraddhā́*. Thieme 1938,

46 So Meillet 1922.

Heesterman 1993, and in most detail, Jamison 1996 have pointed out that *śraddhā́* "expresses the trust or agreement between strangers in a hospitality relationship".[47]

In RV 10.39.5cd, the Aśvins are being asked to inspire social trust in a stranger:

6 *tā́ vāṃ nú návyāv ávase karāmahe 'yáṃ nāsatyā śrád arír yáthā dádhat*
"Now we shall make you new (for you) to help us, o Nāsatyas, so that this stranger will place his trust (in us?)." (J&B)

Chāndogya Upaniṣad 4.1.1:[48]

7 *jānaśrutir ha pautrāyaṇaḥ śraddhādevo* [corrected from *śraddhādeyo*] *bahudāyī bahupākya āsa sa ha sarvata āvasathān māpayāṃ cakre sarvata eva me 'nnam atsyantīti*
"Jānaśruti Pautrāyaṇa was (one) having *Śraddhā* as his deity, giving much, having cooked much (food). He had lodging places built everywhere (thinking) 'Everywhere (people) will eat my food'."

MBh. 5.36.33:

8 *śraddhayā parayā rājann upanītāni satkṛtim*
pravṛttāni mahāprājña dharmiṇāṃ puṇyakarmaṇām
"According to the highest *śraddhā*, o king, (these) are presented as producing hospitality by those who possess *dharma* and meritorious actions, o very wise one."

When a new king takes office, he sends the counterkings (*pratirājanaḥ*) gifts through the agency of the *satyadūtāḥ* 'messengers of truth'. They report the words of the king *abhyáṣikṣi rā́jābhūm* "I have been anointed. I have become king." By accepting these gifts they become his allies (*mitra-* BŚS 12.19) "they place their faith in him who has been inaugurated" *śrád dhāsmai suṣuvāṇā́ya dadhati* (MS 4.4.9).[49]

4.3 *Another Important Aspect of Ved.* **śraddhā́**

The standard work on this word family is Hans-Werbin Köhler's 1948 thesis first published in 1973. This work posits a meaning development from *Ver-*

47 Jamison 1996: 178.
48 Examples and translations from Jamison 1996.
49 See Heesterman 1957, 1993.

trauen 'trust' to *Treue* 'faith' to *Hingabe* 'devotion' to *Opferfreudigkeit* or *Spendfreudigkeit* 'joy in sacrifice or giving'. But a lesser known work, a response to Köhler by Paul Hacker (1963), uncovers a key aspect of the use of this word. Implicit in *śraddhā́* is a desire for obtaining something in return. To take one example that is especially instructive: RV. 7.32 is an Indra hymn by Vasiṣṭha. The hymn is loosely constructed but, as Jamison and Brereton's introduction notes, the unifying theme is "Indra's generous giving and our grateful receiving to an extent unusual even in an Indra hymn. Moreover, it is not only Indra's giving that we seek: it is repeatedly emphasized that Indra helps and gives to mortals who themselves give, that is, the patrons of the sacrifice." Stanza 14 reads:

9 *kás tám indra tvā́vasum ā́ mártyo dadharṣati*
śraddhā́ ít te maghavan pā́rye diví vājī́ vā́jaṃ siṣāsati
"What mortal will dare against him who has you as his possession, Indra? It is with trust in you, bounteous one, that on the decisive day the one vying for the prize seeks to win the prize."

or 'trusting in you' if *śraddhā́* is for *śraddhā́ḥ*, a nom. sg. adjective. According to Hacker *śraddhā́* is "ein stark wunschhaltiges, begehrendes Vertrauen oder Hoffen." In RV 10.151, a hymn dedicated to a divinized *Śraddhā́* and attributed to *Śraddhā́ Kāmāyanī* "Trust, descendant of desire" we read in stanza 4:

10 *śraddhā́ṃ devā́ yájamānā vāyúgopā úpāsate*
śraddhā́ṃ hṛdayyàyā́kūtyā śraddháyā vindate vásu
"Trust do the gods revere, sacrificing for themselves with Vāyu as their herdsman—trust, with a purpose that comes from their heart. By trust one gains possession of the good." (J&B)

which succinctly summarizes the nexus of trust and expectation of wish fulfillment and even localizes the desire in the heart. The point of trusting is not just blind faith but entering into a relationship in which one expects to give and get good. From this meaning the later sense 'desire' prominent in Classical Sanskrit is a natural development.[50]

In the Old Irish period the picture is dominated by the Christian-oriented glosses where *creitid* and its derivatives occur abundantly in the modern Christian sense of belief.[51] But the *Annals of Ulster* report that a certain Brian Ua

---

50 Benveniste makes much the same point (1973: 137): "the god who has received the *śrad* returned it to the faithful in the form of support in victory."

51 See Guyvonvarc'h 1973 for a dossier of examples.

Briain expelled the former king of Thomond, Diarmait Ua Briain, and was acknowledged by the nobles (AU 2.474.26): *Maithi Tuath Muman do creidium do* "The nobles of Thomond to put their faith in him" with the old verbal noun of *creitid*. The situation of acknowledging a new king by acknowledging the trust relationship is reminiscent of the *rājasūya-*. In the *Cogad Gaedel re Gallaib* (186.28) a panegyric for Murchad, son of Brian Boru, calls him *in-t Ectoir intamlaigtech ... ar credium* "The likeness of Hector for *creitem*". Since Hector was a pagan, and by all accounts Murchad was not notably religious, but the last man in Ireland who killed a hundred men in a day, the DIL is correct in taking *creitem* here in the meaning 'credibility', 'good standing'.[52]

On closer examination, it is not so clear that this *Paradebeispiel* of the Vendryes phenomenon holds up in quite the way Vendryes imagined. We do not find consistent religious use of the term in the earliest Western branch. And yet we do find strikingly parallel functions in Latin, Vedic, and later Sanskrit. **k̑reds *dʰeh₁-* was undoubtedly a very important idiom in the stage of PIE represented by East-West agreements, but it was not primarily a religious term. The credit act was one of putting yourself or your property in the hands or power of another with the expectation that the other individual would give good in return. This credit act was predominantly between individuals, often with a power differential (patron ~ client), and thus naturally could be extended to the relationship between men and gods, as we see with so many other terms.

5 Further Issues

What about lexical isoglosses between the Western languages and the two first outliers? In fact, there are two lexical matches between Anatolian with or without Tocharian and Italic which have an institutional character: (1) Anatolian–Tocharian–Italic: Lat. *urbem condere* 'to found a city' ~ Hitt. *warpa dai-* 'enclose', TA *warpi* 'garden', TB *werwiye* 'enclosure';[53] (2) Anatolian–Italic: Lat. *arguō* 'assert, prove' ~ Hitt. *arkuwai-* 'plead a case'.[54] On the other hand, there appear to be no exclusive Tocharian–Italo-Celtic lexical matches.[55]

52 What we call "street cred".

53 Driessen 2001, Brachet 2014.

54 Melchert 1998.

55 Pisani 1941: 159 compared TB *sākre* 'happy', TA *sākar* with Lat. *sacer*, to which MW *hagyr* 'ugly', and Gaul. PN *Sacrobena* are probably related. But the Tocharian forms may be an Iranian loanword. Pre-Khotanese **sagra-* (Khot. *sīra-* 'content, happy, satisfied', MPers. *sgr*, etc.) is actually a better semantic match. See Tremblay 2005: 441.

A quick survey of a sample of the Anatolian (really mainly Hittite) and Tocharian religio-legal lexicon reveals two very distinctive and independent profiles:

Meaning	**Anatolian**	**Tocharian B**	**Tocharian A**
law, right	*ḫandatar*	*pele, pelaikne*	*pal, märkam-pal*
custom, rite	*šāklāi-*		
treaty, obligation	*išḫiul*		
judge		*prekṣanta*[56]	
to judge	*ḫanna-*	*keś tā-*[57]	
	ḫanneššar ḫanna-		
witness	*kutruwan-*	*reme*	*ram*
to confess	*za + kanešš-*	*wināsk*—(mid.)	*käntsās-*
innocent	*parkui-* lit. 'pure'	*snai-nāki*[58]	
guilt		*peri* lit. 'debt'	*pare*
guilty	*paprant-* lit. 'impure'	*tränkossu*[59]	
to punish	*zankilai-*	*en-*	*en-*
god	*šiu-*	*ñakte*	*ñkät*
to libate	*išpand-*	*ku-*	*ku-*
to believe	*ḫā-*		
belief		*śraddhauññe*[60]	
believing		*takarṣke, perāk*[61]	*perāk*
to trust	*ḫā-*	*spantai yām-*	*puk-*
		päkw-	
to worship	*za + i̯ya-*	*wināsk-*	*winās-*
reverence	*naḫšaratt-*	*yarke*	*yärk*
heaven	*nepiš-*	*eprer*	*eprer* < TB
to sacrifice/a sacrifice	*išpand-*	*telki*	*talke*
magic	*alwanzatar*	*yātalñe*, lit. 'power'	

56 Lit. 'questioner'.
57 Lit. 'to account'.
58 ← *nāks-* 'reprove'.
59 ← *traṅko* 'sin'.
60 Obviously from Skt. *śraddha-*.
61 From Buddhist Sogdian *pyr'k* 'believing'.

In general the physiognomy is a poor match for both Italo-Celtic and Indo-Iranian.[62]

Finally, it is instructive to contrast Kretschmer's lightly curated list of Latino-BSl. matches, which is strikingly downscale: Lat. *faba* 'bean', Ru. *bob*, OPr. *babo*; Lat. *cāseus* 'cheese', OCS *kvasŭ* 'fermented milk'; Lat. *secūris* 'axe', OCS *sekyra*; Lat. *fornus* 'oven', RCS *grŭno* 'cauldron'; Lat. *dōlium* 'jar', OCS *dĭly* 'cask'; Lat. *rēte* 'net', Lith. *rẽtis* 'net, sieve'; Lat. *ansa* 'handle' Lit. *ąsà*; Lat. *uarus* 'stye', Lith. *vìras* 'pustule in pork'; Lat. *blatta* 'cockroach', Latv. *blakts* 'bug'; Lat. *combrētum* 'comfrey', Lith. *švendrai* 'cattails'; Lat. *simpulum* 'ladle', Lith. *semiù* 'I scoop'; Lat. *merda* 'shit', Lith. *smirdéti*, OCS *smrĭděti* 'to stink', Lat. *dormīre* 'to sleep', Ru. *dremat'* 'doze'; Lat. *glūtīre* 'to swallow', Ru. *glot* 'gulp, mouthful'; Lat. *aurum* 'gold', Lith. *áuksas*, OPr. *ausis;* Lat. *mentīrī* 'to lie', OPr. *mentimai* 'we lie.' There is not a single item that by any stretch can be assigned to the religio-legal sphere.

References

Adams, J.N. 2007. *The regional diversification of Latin 200 BC–AD 600*. Cambridge: Cambridge University Press.

Benveniste, Émile. 1969. *Le vocabulaire des institutions indo-européennes*. Vol. 1. *Économie, parenté, société*. Paris: Minuit. Translated by Elizabeth Palmer as *Indo-European language and society*. Coral Gables, FL: University of Miami Press, 1973.

Brachet, J.-P. 2014. Lat. *urbem condere*: de la pratique au rituel. In Charles Guittard & Michel Mazoyer (eds.), *La fondation dans les langues indo-européennes: religion, droit et linguistique*, 25–37. Paris: L'Harmattan.

Buchi, Éva, & Wolfgang Schweickard (eds.). 2014. *Dictionnaire étymologique roman (DÉRom): génèse, méthodes et résultats*. Berlin: Walter de Gruyter.

CGL = Gustav Loewe & Georg Goetz (eds.). 1894. *Corpus Glossariorum Latinorum*. Vol. 5. Leipzig: Teubner.

Chang, Will et al. 2015. Ancestry-constrained phylogenetic analysis supports the Indo-European steppe hypothesis. *Language* 91. 194–244.

CHD = Hans Gustav Güterbock, Harry A. Hoffner & Theo P.J. van den Hout (eds.). 1980–. *The Hittite dictionary of the Oriental Institute of the University of Chicago*. Chicago: The Oriental Institute.

Cheung, Johnny. 2007. *Etymological dictionary of the Iranian verb*. Leiden: Brill.

62 Weiss 2018b.

Damgaard, Peter de Barros, Rui Martiniano, Jack Kamm, J. Víctor Moreno-Mayar, Guus Kroonen, Michaël Peyrot, Gojko Barjamovic et al. 2018. The first horse herders and the impact of Early Bronze Age steppe expansions into Asia. *Science*. doi:10.1126/science.aar7711

Darmesteter, James. 1878. Notes sur l'Avesta. *çrad-dhâ, credo;—zaraz-dâ. Mémoires de la société de linguistique* 3. 52–55. = James Darmesteter. 1883. *çrad-dhâ, credo;—zaraz-dâ. Études iraniennes*. Vol. 2, 119–122. Paris: F. Vieweg.

Driessen, Michiel. 2001. On the etymology of Lat. *urbs*. *Journal of Indo-European Studies* 29. 41–68.

Dumézil, Georges. 1958. *L'idéologie tripartie des Indo-Européens*. Bruxelles: Latomus.

Dworkin, Steven. 2013. A history of the Spanish lexicon: A linguistic perspective. New York: Oxford University Press.

eDIL = *Electronic dictionary of the Irish language*. www.dil.ie/

Eichner, Heiner. 1982. Zur hethitischen Etymologie (1. *ištark-* und *ištarnink-*; 2. *ark-*; 3. *šešd-*). In Erich Neu (ed.), *Investigationes philologicae et comparativae. Gedenkschrift für Heinz Kronasser*, 16–28. Wiesbaden: Harrasowitz.

Ernout, Alfred. 1911. Skr. *çraddhā*, lat. *credo*, irl. *cretim*. In *Mélanges d'indianisme, offerts par ses élèves a M. Sylvain Lévi, le 29 janvier 1911, à l'occasion des vingt-cinq ans écolulés depuis son entrée à l'École pratique des hautes études*, 85–89. Paris: E. Leroux.

Forssman, Bernhard. 2014. Vedisch *jri* und lateinisch *gliscere*. *Münchener Studien zur Sprachwissenschaft* 68. 7–30.

Fraenkel, Eduard. 1916. Zur Geschichte des Wortes *fides*. *Rheinisches Museum* 71. 187–199.

GPC = *Geiriadur Prifysgol Cymru / A dictionary of the Welsh language*. welsh-dictionary.ac.uk/gpc/gpc.html

Guyvonvarc'h, Christian-J. 1973. Notes d'étymologie et de lexicographie gauloises et celtiques. 161. Irlandais *cretem* 'foi'; gallois *credu*; cornique *cresy*; Breton *krediñ* 'croire'; irlandais *crábud*, gallois *crefydd* 'foi, dévotion'; irlandais *cretar*, gallois *creir*, Breton *kreir(iou)* 'reliques'. *Ogam* 22(4). 241–256.

Hacker, Paul. 1963. *śraddhā. Wiener Zeitschrift für die Kunde Süd- und Ostasiens* 7. 151–189.

Hackstein, Olav. 2012. When words coalesce: chunking and morphophonemic extension. In H. Craig Melchert (ed.), *The Indo-European verb*, 87–104. Wiesbaden: Reichert.

Heesterman, J.C. 1957. *The ancient Indian royal consecration: the Rājasūya described according to the Yajus texts and annotated*. 's-Gravenhage: Mouton.

Heesterman, J.C. 1993. *The broken world of sacrifice. An essay in ancient Indian ritual*. Chicago: University of Chicago Press.

Heinze, Richard. 1929. Fides. *Hermes* 64. 25–58.

Hill, Eugen. 2003. *Untersuchungen zum inneren Sandhi des Indogermanischen: der Zu-*

sammenstoß von Dentalplosiven im Indoiranischen, Germanischen, Italischen und Keltischen. Bremen: Hempen.

Jacques, Guillaume. 2017. Sanskrit *hṛd-* 'coeur'. *Wekwos* 3. 85–90.

Jamison, Stephanie. 1996. *Sacrificed wife/sacrificer's wife. Women, ritual, and hospitality in ancient India*. New York: Oxford University Press.

J&B = Stephanie W. Jamison & Joel P. Brereton. 2014. *The Rigveda: the earliest religious poetry of India*. New York: Oxford University Press.

Kaczyńska, Elwira. 2013. The Indo-European origin of Latin *lex*. *Habis* 44. 7–14.

Kellens, Jean. 1974. *Les noms-racines de l'Avesta*. Wiesbaden: Reichert.

Kloekhorst, Alwin. 2008. *Etymological dictionary of the Hittite inherited lexicon*. Leiden: Brill.

Köhler, Hans-Werbin. 1973. *Śrad-dhā in der vedischen und altbuddhistischen Literatur*. Wiesbaden: F. Steiner.

Koncha, S.V. 2015. К вопросу об арио-итало-кельтских лексических изоглоссах. In N.N. Nižneva (ed.), *Мир языков: ракурс и перспектива: материалы VI Международной научно-практической конференции, Минск, 22 апреля 2015 г.* Vol. 1. Minsk: БГУ.

elib.bsu.by/handle/123456789/120684

Kretschmer, Paul. 1896. *Einleitung in die Geschichte der griechischen Sprache*. Göttingen: Vandenhoeck und Ruprecht.

Meillet, Antoine. 1894. De quelques difficultés de la théorie des gutturales indo-européennes. *Mémoires de la société de linguistique* 8. 277–304.

Meillet, Antoine. 1913. À propos de Avestique *zrazdā-*. *Mémoires de la société de linguistique* 18. 60–64.

Meillet, Antoine. 1922. Latin *credo* et *fides*. *Mémoires de la société de linguistique* 22. 215–218.

Melchert, H. Craig. 1998. Hittite *arku-* 'chant, intone' vs. *arkuwāi-* 'make a plea'. *Journal of Cuneiform Studies* 50. 45–51.

NIL = Dagmar S. Wodtko, Britta Irslinger & Carolin Schneider (eds.). 2008. *Nomina im indogermanischen Lexikon*. Heidelberg: Winter.

Nober, Peter. 1958. *adrazdā* (Esdras 7, 23). *Biblische Zeitschrift*, N.F. 2. 134–138.

Olivelle, Patrick. 2006. Heart in the Upaniṣads. *Rivista di studi sudasiatici* 1. 51–67.

Orel, Vladimir. 1995. Indo-European notes. *Indogermanische Forschungen* 100. 116–128.

Osthoff, Hermann. 1899. Allerhand Zauber etymologisch behandelt. *Beiträge zur Kunde der indogermanischen Sprachen* 24. 109–173, 177–213.

Ozoliņš, Kaspars. 2015. *Revisiting Proto-Indo-European Schwebeablaut*. Ph.D. dissertation, UCLA.

Pisani, Vittore. 1941. Appunti di tocarico, Glottica Parerga I. *Reale Istituto Lombardo di Scienze e Lettere, Rendiconti, Classe di Lettere* 75. 157–171.

Polomé, Edgar C. 1988. Indo-Aryan lexical correspondences with Celtic and Italic. In

Jörn Albrecht, Jens Lüdtke & Harald Thun (eds.), *Energeia und Ergon: Sprachliche Variation, Sprachgeschichte, Sprachtypologie: Studia in honorem Eugenio Coseriu*. Vol. 1, 213–222. Tübingen: Narr.

Ramelli, Ilaria. 2000. Alcune osservazioni su *credere*. *Maia* 2000 52. 67–83.

Renou, Louis. 1961. *Études védiques et paninéennes*. Vol. 8. Paris: E. de Broccard.

Rix, Helmut. 1995. Griechisch *ἐπίσταμαι*. Morphologie und Etymologie. In Heinrich Hettrich et al. (eds.), *Verba et structurae. Festschrift für Klaus Strunk*, 237–247. Innsbruck: Institut für Sprachwissenschaft der Universität Innsbruck.

Rohlfs, Gerhard. 1931. Gallo-italienische Sprachinseln in der Basilicata. *Zeitschrift für Romanische Philologie* 51. 249–279.

Sandoz, Claude. 1973. La correspondance lat. *crēdō* : skr. *śraddhā-* et le nom indoeuropéen du "coeur". *Universität Bern, Institut für Sprachwissenschaft, Arbeitspapiere* 10. 1–8.

Schaffner, Stefan. 2010. Der lateinische Priestertitel *flāmen*. *Graeco-Latina Brunensia* 15. 87–105.

Schmidt, Johannes. 1872. *Die Verwantschaftsverhältnisse der indogermanischen Sprachen*. Weimar: Böhlau.

Schindler, Jochem. 1979. Review of Jean Kellens, *Les noms-racines de l'Avesta*. *Die Sprache* 25. 57–60.

Schrijver, Peter. 1995. *Studies in British Celtic historical phonology*. Amsterdam: Rodopi.

Schulze-Thulin, Britta. 2001. *Studien zu den Urindogermanischen o-stufigen Kausativa, Iterativa und Nasalpräsentien im Kymrischen*. Innsbruck: Institut für Sprachen und Literaturen der Universität Innsbruck.

Sellmer, Sven. 2004. The heart in the R̥g-Veda. In Stanisław Schayer et al. (eds.), *Essays in Indian philosophy, religion and literature*, 71–83. Delhi: Motilal Banarsidass.

Serangeli, Matilde. 2016. PIE **mel-:* Some Anatolian and Greek thoughts—Gr. *μέλω*, Hitt. *mala-*^{ḫḫi}*/malāi-*^{mi}, CLuv. *mali(ya)-*. In David Goldstein, Stephanie Jamison & Brent Vine (eds.), *Proceedings of the 27th Annual UCLA Indo-European Conference*, 183–197. Bremen: Hempen.

Specht, Franz. 1939. Sprachliches zur Urheimat der Indogermanen. *Zeitschrift für vergleichende Sprachforschung* 66. 1–74.

Steer, Thomas. 2013. Uridg. **d*^{h}*(e)ĝ*^{h}*ōm* 'Erde' und **ĝ*^{h}*(e)i̯ōm* 'Winter'. Eine kurze Revision der Stammbildung. *Indogermanische Forschungen* 118. 55–92.

Stifter, David. 2012. Eine VIP zwischen Pannonien und Tirol. In Peter Anreiter et al. (eds.), *Archaeological, cultural and linguistic heritage. Festschrift for Erzsébet Jerem in honour of her 70th birthday*, 539–549. Budapest: Archaeolingua.

Szemerényi, Oswald. 1970. The Indo-European name of the 'heart'. In V. Rūķe-Draviņa (ed.), *Donum Balticum: To Professor Christian S. Stang on the occasion of his seventieth birthday, 15 March 1970*, 515–533. Stockholm: Almqvist and Wiksell.

Tavernier, J. 2007. *Iranica in the Achaemenid period*. Leuven: Peeters.

Thieme, Paul. 1938. *Der Fremdling im Ṛgveda.* Leipzig: Deutsche Morgenländische Gesellschaft.

Tremblay, Xavier. 2004. Die Ablautstufe des Lokativs der akrostatischen Nomina. Apophonica III. In Adam Hyllested, Anders R. Jørgensen, Jenny H. Larsson & Thomas Olander (eds.), *Per aspera ad asteriscos. Studia Indogermanica in honorem Jens Elmegård Rasmussen sexagenarii Idibus Martiis anno MMIV*, 573–589. Innsbruck: Institut für Sprachwissenschaft der Universität Innsbruck.

Tremblay, Xavier. 2005. Irano-Tocharica et Tocharo-Iranica. *Bulletin of the School of Oriental and African Studies* 68. 421–449.

de Vaan, Michiel. 2008. *Etymological dictionary of Latin and the other Italic languages.* Leiden: Brill.

Vendryes, Joseph. 1918. Les correspondances de vocabulaire entre l'indo-iranien et l'italo-celtique. *Mémoires de la société de linguistique* 20. 265–285.

Weiss, Michael. 2015. The rite stuff: Lat. *rīte, rītus*, TB *rittetär*, TA *ritwatär*, and Av. *raēϑβa-*. *Tocharian and Indo-European Studies* 16. 181–198.

Weiss, Michael. 2017a. Review article of Éva Buchi & Wolfgang Schweickard (eds.) 2014. *Kratylos* 62. 127–153.

Weiss, Michael. 2017b. King. Some observations on an east–west archaism. In Bjarne Simmelkjær Sandgaard Hansen et al. (eds.), *Usque ad radices: Indo-European studies in honour of Birgit Anette Olsen*, 793–800. Copenhagen: Museum Tusculanum.

Weiss, Michael. 2018a. On the prehistory of Latin *iūs*. In M. De Martino (ed.), *The comparative mythology today: Müller, Frazer, Dumézil. Perspectives from the past to the future. Atti del Primo Convegno del Comitato Scientifico di Speaking Souls-Animæ Loquentes, Academia Belgica in Roma, 12 ottobre 2017*. Lugano, 1–14. Rome: Agora.

Weiss, Michael. 2018b. Tocharian and the West. In Olav Hackstein and Andreas Opfermann (eds.), *Priscis libentius et liberius novis. Indogermanische und sprachwissenschaftliche Studien, FS Gerhard Meiser*, 373–382. Hamburg: Barr.

Index of Subjects